Reading the Boss

Reading the Boss

Interdisciplinary Approaches to the Works of Bruce Springsteen

Edited by
Roxanne Harde
and Irwin Streight

LEXINGTON BOOKS
A division of
ROWMAN & LITTLEFIELD PUBLISHERS, INC.
Lanham • Boulder • New York • Toronto • Plymouth, UK

Lyrics by Bob Dylan, copyright © 1966 by Dwarf Music; renewed 1994
by Dwarf Music. All rights reserved. International copyright secured.
Reprinted by permission.

Published by Lexington Books
A division of Rowman & Littlefield Publishers, Inc.
A wholly owned subsidiary of The Rowman & Littlefield Publishing Group, Inc.
4501 Forbes Boulevard, Suite 200, Lanham, Maryland 20706
www.lexingtonbooks.com

Estover Road, Plymouth PL6 7PY, United Kingdom

Copyright © 2010 by Lexington Books

British Library Cataloguing in Publication Information Available

Library of Congress Cataloging-in-Publication Data

Reading the boss : interdisciplinary approaches to the works of Bruce Springsteen /
edited by Roxanne Harde and Irwin Streight.
    p. cm.
  Includes bibliographical references and index.
  ISBN 978-0-7391-4535-7 (cloth : alk. paper) — ISBN 978-0-7391-4536-4 (pbk. :
alk. paper)
  1. Springsteen, Bruce—Criticism and interpretation. 2. Music and philosophy. I.
Harde, Roxanne. II. Streight, Irwin Howard, 1959-
  ML420.S77R43 2010
  782.42166092—dc22   2010018719

Printed in the United States of America

To my wife Susan and our children—
Jairus, Aaron, Jesse, Sage,
and Flannery Evangeline—
for waiting patiently when I fell behind.

Irwin

To Wayne,
whose love has never let me down,
and to Erin,
our living proof.

Roxanne

Contents

Section 3:   Reading Gender

Section 4:   Reading Philosophy and Religion

Acknowledgments

While writing is often a solitary endeavor, assembling a collection is not. We each put in our share of hours writing and editing, but we had many people—family members, friends, colleagues, and editors—literally and figuratively at our side. Without them, this book would never have been completed.

Together we want to extend our gratitude to:

Bruce Springsteen for granting us permission to reprint his work, and for inspiring, moving, entertaining, and teaching us.

Jon Landau Management and Grubman, Indursky & Shire, attorneys at law, particularly Mona Okada and Brittany Pollard for arranging permission for use of the lyrics.

Bruce Gentry, editor of *The Flannery O'Connor Review*, for permission to reprint material that appeared in the article, "The Ghost of Flannery O'Connor in the Songs of Bruce Springsteen" 6 (2007):11–29.

Pam Springsteen for permission to use the perfect cover photograph, and the folks at WeissArtists for patiently handling the details.

Matthew Bailey, Assistant Manager of Rights and Images at the National Portrait Gallery, London, for his prompt and amenable responses.

Erica MacDonald, Rights and Permissions Coordinator at Wenner Media, for handling details regarding use of the 5 February 2009 *Rolling Stone* cover image of the Boss.

Kirby Ruthven and Lauren Onkey for their sleuthing on the cover photo.

Lenore Lautigar, our astute editor at Lexington Books.

Our contributors for their hard work over the past two years, and for their devotion to our subject and this book.

Irwin wishes to recognize:

Jane Errington, Dean of Arts, and Jean Fugère, Dean of Graduate Studies and Research at the Royal Military College, for their generous financial support of this project.

Jim Kenny, consummate Springsteen fan, for his long-running interest in and input into this project, his helpful comments on the introduction, and for the many *Bruceucharists* we have shared at his table.

Viviane Pelletier, administrative assistant extraordinaire, for her commitment and creative solutions throughout this project, and especially for her *bonhomie*.

Steve Lukits, Head of the English Department, and Michael Hurley, inimitable colleagues and friends, for their encouragement.

Paul Wiens, Chief Librarian at Queen's University, and the staff at Stauffer Library, for providing a study place and support of my research over the years.

Suzanne Côté-Latimer, interlibrary loans clerk at Massey Library, Royal Military College, for her cheerful assistance.

Tim Drake for his insights and guidance, many consultations, and for being there from the beginning.

My colleague and coeditor, Roxanne Harde, who had the idea and gathered us all in. When the path was crooked you made the journey easy. We'll have to make another pilgrimage to the Stone Pony sometime soon.

Roxanne is grateful to:

Kim Fordham, Chair of Humanities, Augustana Faculty, University of Alberta, for generous financial support, for her wisdom and leadership, and, more, for her friendship.

The members of my Women's Writing Circle—Yvonne Becker, Kim Fordham, Anne-Marie Link, Paula Marentette, Sandra Rein, Lynda Ross, and Janet Wesselius—who make my writing better and the work more joyful.

Paula Dufresne, administrative assistant extraordinaire, for her assistance and patience.

Nancy Goebel and the inimitable staff at Augustana Library, whose efficiency and enthusiasm helped to keep me invested in this project.

My research assistants, Lindsay Hartman Yakimyshyn, Heather Van Pypen, and Erin Peters, for their talent, diligence, and enthusiasm; I wish for you all the brightest of futures.

Irwin Streight, who brings such verve, wit, and joy to even the most mundane conversations that I am compelled to turn them into book-length projects. This was fun, and I look forward to our next.

A Note on
Bruce Springsteen's Lyrics

Lyrics for Bruce Springsteen's songs from *Greetings from Asbury Park, N.J.* to *The Rising* are published, along with commentary by the Boss, in *Bruce Springsteen: Songs* (Avon, 1998; HarperEntertainment, 2003). Lyrics for the more than 260 songs in his corpus are available online from his official website brucespringsteen.net, and, of course, in liner notes from albums and booklets accompanying CDs. Even for some of Springsteen's well-known songs, however, the official published lyrics can differ—usually in minor word choices—from what one hears on the recordings. Some of these errors are corrected in the lyrics booklet that accompanies Columbia's *The Essential Bruce Springsteen* collection (2003). For the most part, contributors to this collection have relied on the lyrics as given in *Bruce Springsteen: Songs* and at brucespringsteen.net. In a few cases, the author chose to cite the lyric as heard on the studio recording when those words had a slight variance from any print form of the lyric.

Introduction

The Bard of Asbury Park

Irwin Streight and Roxanne Harde

> In the quick of the night, they reach for their moment.
>
> —Bruce Springsteen, "Jungleland"

> So quick bright things come to confusion.
>
> —Shakespeare, *A Midsummer Night's Dream*

For all of his hyperbole and chutzpah while promoting Bruce Springsteen to the legendary John Hammond and Columbia Records in the early 1970s, Springsteen's contentious first manager, Mike Appel, may have been prescient in observing that Springsteen could rank with the literary greats. On various occasions Appel put Springsteen's name together in a sentence with those of Wordsworth, Keats, and Byron, and, most notably, Shakespeare (Sawyers 35). Before we dismiss such suggestions as "vaulting ambition, which o'erleaps itself," however, it is worth giving the Shakespeare comparison, in particular, a passing thought. For one thing, it has stuck with a number of critics. Several commentators and scholars have alluded to Shakespearean elements in Springsteen's songcraft and in his vision of the human condition.[1] The moniker "The Bard of Asbury Park" that titles this introduction, with its echo of the Bard of Avon, dates from Bob Ivy's 2005 review of Jimmy Guterman's *Runaway American Dream* in the *Washington Post*. The phrase appeared as a link to a multimedia retrospective on Springsteen posted by cultural critic A. O. Scott on the *New York Times* webpage the very day this section of the introduction was being written ("Asbury Park's Bard"). And for another, Springsteen's own project to sing America is both evidently Whitmanesque in its nationalistic scope, as Brian Garman,

1

Jim Cullen, and others have argued,[2] and, if you will grant it, verging on the Shakespearean in both its humanistic substance and often theatrical lyrical form.

The comparison should not be pushed too far, of course, but it is worth entertaining. Consider for a moment the struggling young dramatist Will, whose first recorded efforts in the 1590s, *Richard III* and the three parts of *Henry VI*, draw heavily on a newly published historical record of the life and times of the British monarchy, the critically familiar *Holinshed Chronicles* (1587). Shakespeare in his first efforts wrote plays about self-defining moments in the history of the English people. The Boss, too, begins his bardic career writing songs that tell the stories of his local community, his growing up on the backstreets and boardwalks of Asbury Park, New Jersey. And as with the theatrical masterpieces of the Bard, which were written to appeal to the diverse popular audience of Elizabethan theatergoers, in his own corpus, Springsteen has composed albums with song cycles that collectively are Histories (*Greetings from Asbury Park, N.J.*, *The Wild, the Innocent & the E Street Shuffle*), dark Romances, with their ameliorating, reaffirming conclusions following story-songs of existential, political, and social confusion (*Nebraska*, *Born in the U.S.A.*, *The Ghost of Tom Joad*), and what might be construed as true Tragicomedies: collectively, the songs on *The River* include paeans to young love ("Crush on You" and "Two Hearts") and marriage ("I Wanna Marry You" and "Ramrod"), comic interludes with "Sherry Darling," "Cadillac Ranch," and "I'm a Rocker," a tale of love's regrets in the title song, and a concluding existential reflection on death in "A Wreck on the Highway," with its *carpe diem* theme. Written in the aftermath of 9/11, likewise, *The Rising*'s first two tracks begin by affirming in the face of confusion and loss that "it's alright," and hold out for "faith," "hope," and "love" to prevail in the face of the image in the closing song—a "city in ruins." *Magic*, a much underrated album, has the tragicomic arc in its lyrical progression: from "Everything . . . falling down" and a vision of "bodies hangin' in the trees," to the "long walk home," where the brave arrive to find that "the bitter fires of the devil's arcade" are burned away by the touch of love, "The beat of her heart." Springsteen writes albums not song collections, and, as the essays in this collection illuminate, the recordings of his works have large thematic arcs and dramatic narrative structures that he has consciously ordered and crafted to present his contemporary American vision of the big human themes that run through enduring works of art.

Springsteen's concern with those large Shakespearean themes of the ties of blood and friendship, commitment to country and community, the monsters of lust and jealousy, vanity and power, his exploration of the dark heart of humanity, and the hopeful pursuit of real love lift his music beyond stories of characters casing the Promised Land of America to universal matters of the heart's truth wherever it is found. Like Shakespeare, he offers astute sociopolitical critique alongside hopeful visions. And there is a range of depth and empathy and insight into the human in Springsteen's 260-plus recorded songs that merits such a grand comparison. Like that other Bard, his vision is most often turned toward the tragicomic, the authentically human. That audiences as far flung as Sweden, Finland, Spain, and Italy have embraced Springsteen's songs speaks to the universality of his themes and images. The whole world is his stage, and the players in his songs could be any people anywhere.

> Well, Shakespeare, he's in the alley
> With his pointed shoes and bells
>
> —Bob Dylan, "Stuck Inside of Mobile with the Memphis Blues Again"

Young Springsteen in the early 1970s both bore an uncanny resemblance to Bob Dylan and wrote dizzyingly expressionistic lyrics verging on the Dylanesque, a convergence of looks and songcraft that was used to full commercial effect by Columbia Record executives, who touted him as "the new Dylan" and expected big sales of his first two records. (Despite the hype and Springsteen's stock as a performer, neither of his first two albums sold well at the time of their release.) Dylan's vision in 1964 of "Shakespeare . . . in the alley" might have been self-referential, but it serves well to describe the street-smart poet revealed in Springsteen ten years down the road. Springsteen in 1974 had two albums of largely autobiographical songs behind him and was in the studio for the epic recording sessions that would produce the *Born to Run* album, his career-making creation and a work of such cultural and aesthetic significance that it is among the first one hundred recordings of American music and speech added to the National Recording Registry of the Library of Congress. Shakespeare of the boardwalk, he conjured up a cast of characters that peopled his neighborhood and hangouts in Asbury Park and sang passionately about their wild and innocent days. Sandy, Kitty, Rosalita, Crazy Janey, and Spanish Johnny, and all the "boy prophets [who] walk it handsome and hot" embody the spirit of young America as it was lived along the Jersey Shore. It is a spirit that Springsteen has followed throughout his work, giving voice and social-psychological depth to the characters who speak from and within his songs.

Springsteen in midlife, with his halo of hair, stinger goatee, and ubiquitous hooped gold earrings flanking a small gold cross he wears in his left ear (see fig. 1.1) now bears an uncanny likeness to the famous Chandos portrait of the Bard of Avon (see fig. 1.2). The similar aquiline nose, facial expression, and penetrating stare of the subject in both poses is convincingly correspondent; even the style of collar on Springsteen's bomber jacket matches Elizabethan couture. (One wonders if *Rolling Stone* photographer Albert Watson chose a deliberately parallel pose.) Whether it is fair to

Figure 1.1. Bruce Springsteen. Cover photo by Albert Watson from *Rolling Stone*, February 5, 2009. © Rolling Stone LLC 2009. All Rights Reserved. Reprinted by Permission.

Figure 1.2.   William Shakespeare. Detail from the Chandos portrait. © National Portrait Gallery, London.

say that Springsteen's scope as an artist is as well Shakespearean depends upon what part of his art you are measuring and perhaps on a willingness to accept a nonetheless meaningful hyperbole. Measure for measure, the comparison is laughable. But consider translating into "Boss time" what contemporary philosopher and critic Carlin Romano says about the Elizabethan Bard's achievement in a review of *Shakespeare the Thinker*: "That his greatness arises precisely from utter openness to the varieties of human behavior, emotion, and thought, his ability to render in concrete scenes and daring metaphors more non-reductionist nuances of the heart and mind than an army of writers." The Boss and the Bard both offer profound insight into the hungry human heart—and Springsteen, arguably, with more breadth and depth than any other current American singer-songwriter.

> That old and antique song we heard last night:
> Methought it did relieve my passion much,
> More than light airs and recollected terms
> Of these most brisk and giddy-paced times.
>
> —Shakespeare, *Twelfth Night*

Shakespeare's rather inauspicious life outside of his art is now standard critical dogma, despite efforts of critics through the ages to invent more romantic and dramatic biographical details. The Bard of Avon was a commoner, the son of a tradesman. His family, nonetheless, gained greater social respectability and some economic status as young Shakespeare found success as a playwright. He likely had only a grammar school education; he did not attend university, and by the standard of his day, say the editors of the magisterial Riverside edition of his plays, "He would not be regarded as a man of learning" (Shakespeare 3). Despite Ben Jonson's disparaging remark about his "small Latin and less Greek," Shakespeare was, nonetheless, widely read. But, continue the Riverside editors, "The book learning that Shakespeare displays here and there is far less impressive in the long run than his fund of general information. His frame of reference is so far-ranging . . . he was 'learned in human nature'" (4).

What has emerged about Shakespeare the man can equally be applied to Springsteen: that he was "an engaging, self-effacing person who, while remaining impersonal, could penetrate the minds of multitudinous personalities" (4). Shakespeare's uniqueness in the Western literary canon lies in the memorable power with which he could render the common round of individual experience. In *Henry IV, Parts One and Two*, for example, his cast of characters is drawn from virtually every level of Elizabethan society, as the scenes shift from tavern to court and soliloquies reveal authentic inner thoughts of commoners, courtiers, and kings.[3] Springsteen, like Shakespeare, possesses the gift of being able to understand and empathize with all sorts of people across the social strata, a range of human insight that is remarkable in breadth and depth. From a young single mother driven by despair to nearly drown her infant son in "Spare Parts," an ex-con struggling with his criminal impulses in "Straight Time," a racist overcoming his hatred in "Galveston Bay," to the burned-out souls that narrate songs such as "The New Timer," "The Hitter," and "The Wrestler," Springsteen has amply demonstrated that he, too, is "learned in human nature." As Dave Marsh wrote in the program for the 2009 Kennedy Center Honors, at which Springsteen was roundly feted, he possesses "a singular fearlessness about being ordinary" and "an unsurpassed ability to turn the everyday into drama and romance" ("TIVO").

In Bernard Shaw's famous coining, Springsteen is also certainly subject to a kind of *bardolatry*, an excess of adulation, which marked the responses of the literati to Shakespeare in the nineteenth century and carries on to this day, most notably in Harold Bloom's literary encomium to the Bard, *Shakespeare: The Invention of the Human* (1998). As evidenced in the host of testimonials by longtime Springsteen fans collected and analyzed in Daniel Cavicchi's *Tramps Like Us* (1998), and revealed in even a cursory scroll through the discussion threads on backstreets.com, the online fan community, Springsteen is adored and venerated beyond rock star status, as would be a spiritual master, a pop philosopher, a revolutionary, a head of state, or a saint. As *New York Times* critic Jon Pareles remarks in an article following the memorable "We Are One" concert at the Lincoln Memorial on January 18, 2009, to celebrate the inauguration of President Barak Obama, which Springsteen opened, "He has the gravitas to lead off a presidential inaugural concert and the gusto to rock the Super Bowl" ("Bruce Springsteen").

Moreover, and as the essays gathered in this collection will argue, Springsteen is a consciously literary and culturally literate songwriter, a "writing singer" and/or a "singing writer" as Robert Coles fondly describes him (45). Since the beginning of his career, Springsteen has been compared to a host of established literary figures. Appel's listing notwithstanding, in his early work as a songwriter Springsteen was seen to share themes and style with Beat writer Jack Kerouac and African American poet Langston Hughes. As a storyteller in song he has been put alongside Mark Twain and nineteenth-century naturalist writer Emile Zola, and in his stories of the downtrodden and dispossessed to novelist John Steinbeck.[4] In this volume of essays he is connected with Catholic novelist Walker Percy (Sawyers and Kobre), American short story writer Flannery O'Connor (Streight and Fury), and Renaissance giant John Milton (Fields). In *Bruce Springsteen's America: The People Listening, the Poet Singing* (2004), Coles links Springsteen to two other "New Jersey boys": iconic American poets Walt Whitman and William Carlos Williams. In their works, all three of these writers, notes Coles, are "intent on responding to a nation's people—catching alive their voices and offering them to those who read, those who listen" (18). Across geographies of place and spirit these three American bards have celebrated and adumbrated the lives of ordinary people. Most compellingly, Brian Garman's study *A Race of Singers* (2000) traces Springsteen's literary artistic lineage through that yawping bard Walt Whitman and on to Woody Guthrie, whose concerns for the welfare of the "working-class hero" and the establishment of a just and compassionate democratic society Springsteen shares.

Springsteen's songs bear witness to the dreams, struggles, disappointments, and small victories that determine our everyday lives. One of his greatest gifts as an artist is his empathetic imagination. Commenting on his chronicles of American experience in his song-stories, Springsteen remarks, "I try to meld my voice into the story I am telling. And when a moment comes in our common history, I want to be there."[5] As the current American Bard, Springsteen, sings both *"of* us while singing *to* us," as his coreligionist and admirer the late Walker Percy once remarked (quoted in Coles 8), telling us stories of our wandering selves and, sage-like, pointing the way home.

> I wanted to have my own vision and point of view and create a world of characters, which is what the writers I admired did.
>
> —Bruce Springsteen

In his commentary on his youthful intentions as a songwriter in *Songs*, Springsteen remarks on his desire to develop "a cast of characters," to "describe a neighbourhood, a way of life," and to employ "metaphor" (25) in the song-stories that make up his second album, *The Wild, the Innocent & the E Street Shuffle*. He later speaks of his struggle to find the right "tone" in his writing for the *Darkness* songs (66) and his desire on that album to create a cast of "new characters" who have grown beyond their wild innocence to become "weathered, older, but not beaten" (68). His efforts to bring a song into form, to discover its theme and center, are evidenced in the nine photo-reproduced foolscap pages of lyrics for "Prove It All Night," with Springsteen's annotations noting how the eventual song emerges after pages of exploratory writing (*Songs* 83–91). Like the writerly practice of Flannery O'Connor, whose short fiction informs the *Nebraska* album, in his early songwriting Springsteen often got his titles first, and worked the story from there. (See the photo reproduction of two foolscap sheets on page 70 in *Songs* and Springsteen's note.) The photo reproductions from Springsteen's notebooks that appear in *Songs* bear evidence of his revising hand, and are like the "poems in process" materials that often are included in anthologies of literature. Their presence in the authorized collection of his lyrics underscores, as well, that book's emphasis on the textual elements of Springsteen's songcraft.

Likewise, Springsteen refers to his long labors at crafting song lyrics in commentary on the *Joad* songs, which he says "took a good amount of research" and developed "slowly and carefully" (276). Springsteen remarks that he deliberately used minimalist, "uncomplicated" melodies in the *Joad* songs in particular so as to foreground the elements of storytelling and the revelations of character. While, as he notes, the music naturally "played an important role in the storytelling process" by helping to define how his characters expressed themselves, most important to these songs is "the precision of the storytelling," the use of "correct detail," and discovering an authentic "emotional center" for the song (274). A craftedness in the language and form of the narrative and an attentiveness to the telling detail or gesture that reveals character—these are the elements that define and describe the work of our best imaginative writers.

Like the two Catholic writers of fiction he admires, Flannery O'Connor and Walker Percy—both of whom were notoriously slow writers and avid revisers—Springsteen, too, pursues the art of songwriting exploringly and, certainly in his earlier recordings, quite often slowly. His adventures at writing, recording, and producing the *Born to Run* album are the stuff of legend in the recording industry and in the annals of Springsteeniana. In his commentary in *Songs*, Springsteen remarks that the lyrics to "Born to Run" alone took six months to write (44). Louis Masur confirms in *Runaway Dream* (2009), his detailed study of the genesis of the album, that Bruce worked steadily on the title song for months, honing the lyrics in over fifty pages of his notebook (40). Such diligence in regard to the form and content of his lyric attests to Springsteen's consummate attention to the writerly details of his songcraft.

The title of this collection of essays, *Reading the Boss*, announces the critical assumption that underlies the scholarly approaches to Springsteen's songs and songwriting in the chapters that follow: that his song lyrics are literary works of interest in their own right. While the essays in this collection treat Springsteen's works as song, performance, *and* text, much of the analysis herein is carried out through close readings of his lyrics. Springsteen's attentiveness to the language and form of his lyrics, apart from, but not excluded from, the music, lends a legitimacy to taking a literary critical approach to reading his song lyrics.

As with the lyrics of Bob Dylan and Joni Mitchell, among other contemporary singer-songwriters, Springsteen's lyrics have begun to appear in anthologies of literature used in colleges and universities throughout North America. Lyrics for "Cover Me," "Galveston Bay," "My Hometown," and "Reason to Believe," among others are offered up for study in literature courses alongside classic works of British and American poetry.[6] But, as Dylan complained about the co-opting of his lyrics by the literary academy, "Songs are more than just words" (quoted in Marshall 103). To privilege the lyrics of a rock or folk song over and apart from the music and the synergies of performance is, it must be granted, to some extent an exercise in incompleteness, as Lee Marshall argues in the recently published *Cambridge Companion to Bob Dylan* (2009). Marshall quotes Simon Frith's assertion in *Performing Rites* (1998) that "We have to treat [songs] in terms of the persuasive relationship set up between the singer and the listener. From this perspective, a song doesn't exist to convey the meaning of the words; rather the words exist to convey the meaning of the song" (quoted in Marshall 103–4).

To the extent then that Springsteen's words convey the big ideas and revelations of character that his songs intend, any analysis of his lyrics must be granted a certain *donnée* that accords with the limitations of textual analysis and its methodologies. Nonetheless, such analysis of what Frith calls "speech acts" is no different from established textual approaches to studying the plays of Shakespeare or other dramatic works or the popular ballads of antiquity that have been long standard in literary anthologies. Sonnets, elegies, dramatic monologues, free verse from Ezra Pound to the Beats are words on the page that gain their force and nuances of meaning likewise through an act of performed speech, whether read aloud or interiorly. To say as Frith does that "Songs are more like plays than poems; song words work as speech acts, bearing meaning not just semantically, but also as structures of sound that are direct signs of emotion and marks of character" (quoted in Marshall 103) is to say for the rock or folk song what must also be said for the published poem, monologue, lyric—any charactered or crafted rhythmic use of language. Not all poetry is for the ear; some is for the eye. But poetry itself is best defined as a form of singing speech, whether it tells a story or expresses an emotion.

Still, the textual critic needs to be wary of Marshall's caution not to fault by "over-emphasizing semantic meaning rather than sonic experience" when discussing a song lyric (103). The all too familiar misinterpretations of the album version of "Born in the U.S.A." are strikingly illustrative of this point: the "sonic experience" of the original recording overwhelmed the dark "semantic meaning" of the lyric and led to egregious misreadings of the song as a pro-American anthem. The song is given a more tonally appropriate, and authentic, musical presentation in the haunting, dark, acoustic version that Springsteen played on the *Joad* tour and later released on *Tracks*. The essays in this collection approach the study of Springsteen's songs from a range of disciplinary and theoretical perspectives, but with the critical mindedness that effective discussion of his song lyrics must to some degree take into account both the music and nuances of the song's performance—either on a studio recording or live.

> I set out to find an audience that would be a reflection of some imagined community that I had in my head, that lived according to the values in my music and shared a similar set of ideals.
>
> —Bruce Springsteen

Since the early 1980s, Springsteen's work has generated an enormous amount of writing. To date, the number of biographies on him seems rather excessive. The three by Dave Marsh, *Born to Run: The Bruce Springsteen Story* (1979), *Glory Days: Bruce Springsteen* (1987), and *Bruce Springsteen: Two Hearts, The Definitive Biography, 1972–2003* (2004) are among the best, although too often they lapse into glossy fan panegyrics. Three others that stand out are Marc Eliot's unauthorized biography, *Down Thunder Road: The Making of Bruce Springsteen* (1992), because it does not idealize Springsteen, and Jimmy Guterman's *Runaway American Dream: Listening to Bruce Springsteen* (2005) because it has some qualities of a critical/theoretical piece in its discussion of Springsteen's music and its evolution. Eric Alterman's *It Ain't No Sin to Be Glad You're Alive: The Promise of Bruce Springsteen* (1999) traces Springsteen's development as a musician and songwriter, offering delightful minutiae about Bruce's life interspersed with accounts of Alterman's own shenanigans as a fan. The book pays little attention to Springsteen's songs themselves and more to the personal and cultural contexts from which his music emerged. The writing is clever and detailed, and the story comprehensive up to the *Tom Joad* tour.

In her prefatory notes to *Racing in the Street: The Bruce Springsteen Reader* (2004), editor June Skinner Sawyers describes the book as a "public service," and half a decade later it continues to offer the definitive collection of reviews, editorials, and other assorted columns and short essays on the Boss. Sawyers's inclusion of a few important interviews and popular fiction that draws on Springsteen as an icon of popular culture rounds out what will remain an important resource in the emerging field of Springsteen studies. We hope that Sawyers, whose essay on Springsteen and Walker Percy follows, will update this work in new editions.

Springsteen's vision, craft, and cultural inheritance as a songwriter and lyric poet is the focus of Robert Coles's untidy but insightful sociological study, *Bruce Springsteen's America: The People Listening, a Poet Singing* (2003). The heart of Coles's book rests in the series of firsthand accounts by ordinary Americans reflecting on their interactions with Springsteen's lyrics. From the truck driver to the teacher to the lawyer, they offer their openness to being astonished or moved or made joyful by the Boss. These reflections are bracketed by equally fine chapters from Coles, who contextualizes Springsteen with other American artists who were as closely linked to their audience, to the people who understood and were inspired by them, even as they, in turn, inspired the artists who mattered so much to them. Weaving together his perspectives on the Boss alongside commentary on Walt Whitman, William Carlos Williams, Dorothea Lange, and Walker Percy, Coles looks to Springsteen's lyrics as among the best of contemporary poetry. It is no coincidence that Coles understands, as do we, that Springsteen is the bard of our time. Further in this vein, Rob Kirkpatrick's *The Words and Music of Bruce Springsteen* (2007) examines Springsteen's songwriting process, his lyrics and music, and functions like a biography of the music. These texts are important background resources for scholars, but they only rarely engage with Springsteen's work in a sustained scholarly and critical fashion.

The first two scholarly responses to Springsteen came in 1997 with *Born in the U.S.A.: Bruce Springsteen and the American Tradition* by Jim Cullen and *The Mansion on the Hill: Dylan, Young, Geffen, Springsteen and the Head-On Collision of Rock and Commerce* by Fred Goodman. In the latter, Goodman dismisses Springsteen as a mainstream commercial performer who has little impact on American society. Cullen's book, however, situates Springsteen in the broader sweep of American culture and history. The heir of Walt Whitman and Woody Guthrie, Abraham Lincoln and Martin Luther King, Jr., Cullen argues, Springsteen is an influential chronicler of our society. Even in its updated 2005 edition from Wesleyan, the text, while still important, has become dated.

If one can set aside the nearly-unreadable font in which it is typeset, Larry David Smith's *Bob Dylan, Bruce Springsteen, and American Song* (2002) offers lively and close analysis of the themes and narrative structures that run through Springsteen's oeuvre, from *Greetings* to *Tom Joad*, emphasizing the ways in which the songwriter's attention to developing character and sense of place draws on the techniques of fiction writing and film. Smith regards the Boss as a songwriter with "a coherent plan of action," and argues that his work is a consciously crafted sequence of song narratives—an "ongoing novel" in Springsteen's words—that depict the desires and dreams and personal demons of mostly working-class American baby boomers. The book is well-researched, drawing heavily on Springsteen's many interviews to extract what might be called his theory of songwriting. Smith makes a compelling argument that Springsteen's song narratives, along with the protest songs of Bob Dylan, owe their social focus and often complaining tone to the shaping influence of Woody Guthrie. Smith's narratological analysis of Springsteen's songbook up to 2002 is an important scholarly work of enduring value, though like Cullen's, it needs to be updated.

In February 2005, the Widener University School of Law in Harrisburg, Pennsylvania, hosted a symposium titled "The Lawyer as Poet Advocate: Bruce Springsteen and the American Lawyer." Later that year, the symposium proceedings were published in *Widener Law Journal* 14.3 (2005), and the issue, with its focus on social justice, stands as a valuable contribution to Springsteen studies. It is particularly interesting in its interweaving of essays about how lawyers draw on Springsteen's songs in a multiplicity of ways, with close readings of Springsteen's songs that are concerned with criminals and the justice system. Of the former, Bernard Grim, Russell Pearce, and Randy Lee offer insight into how lawyers use Springsteen's work to connect with their clients, to reaffirm their own truths about justice and the system, and to help them do what is right. Of the latter, stand out articles include Samuel Levine's essay on criminals in *Nebraska* and Samuel Bagenstos's article on Springsteen's view of negative aspects of the law.

A further collection of critical essays on Springsteen was gathered in a special issue of *Interdisciplinary Literary Studies: A Journal of Criticism and Theory* 9.1 (Fall 2007), coedited by Kenneth Womack, Mark Bernhard, and Jerry Zolten. The issue is comprised of papers presented at the Glory Days Symposium of 2005, grouped thematically (geography and place, narrative and narration, pop music and musicology, crime and dysfunction, social justice and multiculturalism), and is a useful introduction to an array of critical approaches to the Boss.

Two recent collections of essays on Springsteen go some distance in addressing the lack of theoretical readings of his work, but like Simon Frith's sociology of music, *Taking Popular Music Seriously: Selected Essays* (2007), both are narrowly focused and will appeal to only a small specialized audience. A new collection of essays edited by Randall Auxier and Doug Anderson, *Bruce Springsteen and Philosophy: Darkness on the Edge of Truth* (2008), offers readings on the philosophical nature of his work. The collection is uneven in quality and editing, and gives far too much space to the ramblings of fanhood. With the exception of a few essays, the book lacks the necessary critical engagement to make it valuable in any discipline.

Unitarian minister Jeffrey Symynkywicz explores the theological and political undertones of Springsteen's music in *The Gospel According to Bruce Springsteen: Rock and Redemption, from* Asbury Park *to* Magic (2008). Symynkywicz reads Springsteen's lyrics through a theological lens and explores their many ambiguities in the context of religion, but often reverts to composing homilies based on Springsteen's songs rather than engaged critical commentary. It is an important text, but one too narrowly focused to appeal to a wide academic audience or to many fans. Professor Louis P. Masur's *Runaway Dream:* Born to Run *and Bruce Springsteen's American Vision* (2009) offers a rich cultural studies critique of Springsteen's iconic third album. Masur discusses each of the albums songs, balancing commentary on their evolution, musical structures, lyrical content, and resonance in Springsteen's performances. His comparative thematic readings of the album's lyrics in his chapter "The Geography of *Born to Run*" are particularly insightful and underscore the integrity and vision of the album as a whole. Nonetheless, Masur critically mines only one of the rich veins in Springsteen's lyrical/musical landscape, however well and deeply.

The essays in this collection are driven by arguments based on a wide variety of theoretical and critical positions. The contributors work in the fields of American studies and popular culture, English, literary theory, environmental studies, geography, music and musicology, social theory, theology and religious studies, and gender studies. All are engaged with close readings of

Springsteen's body of work, but the variety of theoretical models and disciplinary approaches ensures a meaningful diversity.

The first section, "Reading Influence," analyzes the literariness of Springsteen's lyrics, the tropes and figures he relies upon, and the connections between his work and that of artists who inspire him. In a chapter that departs from her other celebrated work on Springsteen, "Endlessly Seeking: Bruce Springsteen and Walker Percy's Quest for Possibility among the Ordinary," June Skinner Sawyers examines Walker Percy's National Book award-winning novel *The Moviegoer* (1961) along with some of his philosophical and theoretical writings and traces their influence on Springsteen's albums, especially *The Ghost of Tom Joad*. She explores the themes of community and alienation in the more disaffected work by these men as they address moral questions about the way we live and behave toward one another. Complementing Sawyer's essay, Michael Kobre further links Springsteen to Percy in his chapter "'On Blessing Avenue': Faith, Language, and a Search for Meaning in the Works of Bruce Springsteen and Walker Percy." Taking as his touchstone Springsteen's lushly recorded and largely critically disparaged song "Queen of the Supermarket," from *Working on a Dream* (2009), Kobre discusses Springsteen's big theme of "loss and search for faith and meaning" in his songwriting as it parallels the journey of Walker Percy's character Binx Bolling in *The Moviegoer*. Kobre examines the "multi-voiced quality" in the works of each writer in light of the critical theory of Russian philosopher and semiotician Mikhail Bakhtin, and finds an ascending "spiritual vocabulary" across Springsteen's corpus, beginning with *Nebraska*'s "Reason to Believe," that parallels a similar perceptive—and linguistic—process in Percy's *Moviegoer* and other novels. The language of Springsteen's fifteenth album, like the voice in Percy's fiction, Kobre concludes, evolves/resolves into what he calls, echoing Springsteen's own words, the "sound of supplication." In the final chapter in this section, "The Flannery O'Connor of American rock," Irwin Streight considers the extent to which Springsteen's evolving narrative style of songwriting and his growing attention to developing his own characters is indebted to his reading of the short fiction of American author Flannery O'Connor. Like O'Connor, Springsteen recognizes a "meanness" (O'Connor's word *and* Springsteen's) in modern America, often manifest in some form of violence that is symptomatic of a lack of both spiritual and relational grounding. With reference to Springsteen's comments on the ways in which O'Connor has influenced his writing, Streight analyzes Springsteen's exploration of this "meanness" in his songs, particularly on his trio of *folk* albums—*Nebraska*, *The Ghost of Tom Joad*, and *Devils & Dust*—and considers in conclusion how, like O'Connor, Springsteen's art has been informed by his Catholicism.

In the second section, "Reading Place," Frank Fury considers issues of place and placelessness in Springsteen's album *Nebraska*. Drawing on the generic conventions of the short-story cycle, "'Deliver Me from Nowhere': Place and Space in Bruce Springsteen's *Nebraska*" argues that Springsteen seems not so much interested in portraying the ethos (or pathos, as it were) of any single community; rather, his dramatic monologues and confessional tales are more indicative of a universal malaise. Fury notes that if there is a single story being told in the album, it is that of the terrifying, metaphysical landscapes that foreground the emotional, moral, or socioeconomic anomie from which each of its characters suffers. The section concludes with Teresa Abbruzzese and Mike Cadó's reading of Springsteen's conjoined constructions of place and masculine identity in "Tracking Place and Identity in Bruce Springsteen's *Tracks*." Drawing on the work of geographers John A. Agnew and James S. Duncan (1989) and Noel Castree (2003), which examines the role of place in personal formation, Abbruzzese and Cadó explore dominant themes and images of real and imaginary places in Springsteen's outtakes, collected as *Tracks*. They offer a cross-disciplinary reading of Springsteen's heteronormative construction of the American working-class identity.

"Reading Gender," our third section, includes essays that use various political theories and schools to unpack the social dynamics of Springsteen's lyrics. Ken Womack draws on feminist psychological and reader-response theorists to examine Springsteen's negotiations of nostalgia and gender in his constructions of "the girl." "'Who's That Girl?': Nostalgia, Gender, and Springsteen" explores Springsteen's nostalgic yearnings through close readings of several of his female characters. Drawing on theoretical work at the intersection of psychology and musicology, particularly that of Martha Nussbaum, Womack discusses those women in Springsteen's songs who offer up the past as a seductive and promising space. In asking whose nostalgia is being experienced, the artist's or the listener's, Womack negotiates between Springsteen's aesthetic imperatives and his willingness to navigate metaphorically the "backstreets" of his fans' memories. In the next chapter, Ann Bliss traces the figure of the outsider in pursuit of the American Dream in "Growin' Up to Be a Nothing Man: Masculinity, Community, and the Outsider in Bruce Springsteen's Songs." The archetype of the outsider figure, Bliss argues, is ubiquitous in American culture and in Springsteen's songs. She explores how this figure has evolved over the course of his career, moving from consciously rejecting the conventions of the American Dream, to wanting to belong, achieving the material markers of success associated with the Dream but emotionally rejecting such materialism as fundamentally unsatisfying. In the third chapter in this section, Liza Zitelli draws from feminist cultural studies to look at male objectification of the female salvator figure in "'Like a Vision She Dances': Re-Visioning the Female Figure in the Songs of Bruce Springsteen." Springsteen's representations of women are ethereal, Zitelli argues: the women in his songs represent less individual characters and bodies than a collective embodiment of the promise and possibility for salvation. She demonstrates—through close reading of lyrics and using a postmodern gender theory framework—that Springsteen's work represents a kind of secular redemption in the symbolic union of masculine and feminine energies. Overall, Zitelli defines Springsteen's project as one that ultimately, in response to the postmodern stratification, fragmentation, and disintegration of the human spirit perpetuated by American individualist romanticism, suggests a path for salvation through a reevaluation of the consequences of governing patriarchal ideologies.

The book's final and longest section, "Reading Philosophy and Religion," brings together chapters that rely on the theories of philosophers and theologians to read Springsteen's lyrics. Stephen Hazan Arnoff argues that, like great public voices from Jonathan Edwards to Walt Whitman and Martin Luther King Jr. to Bob Dylan, Springsteen employs the biblical trope of the Promised Land—supported by themes of covenant, exile, wandering, and redemption—to critique the possibilities of America. "A Covenant Reversed: Bruce Springsteen and the Promised Land" offers close readings of his contemporary retellings of the biblical story of the Promised Land in his songs to reveal a covenant traveling in reverse—with visions progressively stark, apocalyptic, and resigned to failure—modeling how artistic fantasy and imagination can fuse grand ancient mythologies and common contemporary narratives to report the impact of a nation's failed vision on the everyday lives of its citizens. Next, Peter Fields argues that Springsteen's songs often feature an "ironic revelator" who mediates on behalf of the song's character(s), revealing a larger "inter-subjectivity" between Springsteen's speakers and the lives of his listeners. In his chapter, "Ironic Revelation in Bruce Springsteen," Fields draws on existential notions of being in Sartre and Heidegger, and on the I-and-Thou dynamics of Buber and Levinas, to show the ways in which Springsteen's narrator-revelator engages in an ontological project—pointing to a transcendent "Truth" in which both subject and speaker are ultimately conjoined.

The chapter that follows, musicologist Jack Sheinbaum's "'I'll Work for Your Love': Springsteen and the Struggle for Authenticity," explores the carefully produced authenticity of Springsteen's persona and recordings. While observing that Springsteen embodies an idealized image of masculinity and generally identifies with the working class, Sheinbaum suggests that there are levels of complexity and degrees of contradiction in the man and his music. Springsteen's personal authenticity translates into music that is perceived as regenerating the textures and simplicity of classic rock and roll while becoming, moreover, a means to create authentic community—among both his band and his listeners—more than simply a means to commercial success. By using musicological analysis, Sheinbaum notes how Springsteen breaks out of these authentic structures in some of his more iconic songs, such as "Rosalita (Come Out Tonight)" and "Thunder Road." Springsteen's persona and music is engagingly multifaceted, he concludes, thus attracting our close interest and analysis. In the final chapter, "'May Your Hope Give Us Hope': *The Rising* as a Site of Mourning," Roxanne Harde draws on Jacques Derrida's final book, *The Work of Mourning* (2001), to read the songs of Springsteen's post 9/11 album, *The Rising*. There is a telling symmetry to the ruminations on death and mourning of both these men, who are faced with and write about devastating circumstances. *The Rising* functions for its culture as a place to mourn, to rest, and to reflect on its loss, Harde argues, and the themes of suffering, time, memory, friendship, and love in its songs offer important political and social considerations.

> A nation's artists and musicians have a particular place in its social and political life.
>
> —Bruce Springsteen, *New York Times*, 5 August 2004

In his profile of Springsteen for *New York Times Magazine* in 1997, Nicholas Dawidoff remarked on the songwriter's near singular accomplishment of continuing to write powerful pop songs with commercial appeal. Now, more than a decade later, Springsteen continues to write, record, and perform with an energy and productivity unprecedented since he began his career. In the past ten years he has garnered numerous awards and honors, including a string of Grammys, most notably Best Rock Album for 2002's *The Rising*, and his 2009 Working on a Dream Tour packed stadiums across North America and Europe. His readiness to engage in populist politics has put Springsteen into the public eye and ear worldwide in ways that exceed even his astounding appearance on the covers of both *Newsweek* and *Time* in the same week following the release of *Born to Run* in 1975. As Jon Pareles notes in a *New York Times* article titled "The Rock Laureate," Springsteen has for a long time played a bardic role "as a voice of America" (26). America is still interested in Springsteen, and he has never lost interest in writing about its people, their ideals, their failures, their passions, and their dreams. Unlike many contemporary American singer-songwriters, he has not indulged in what he calls "the solipsistic approach to songwriting." Rather, like our best literary artists, Springsteen has focused his gifts of imagination and storytelling on the world outside, on lives other than his own. As he recently remarked to *Rolling Stone*'s David Fricke, "I don't want to tell you about me. I want to tell you about *you*" (44).

Flannery O'Connor once remarked in respect to her darkly tinged fiction that "People without hope do not write novels" (*Mystery* 77). Her remark is resonant as well for Springsteen the songwriter, who, as noted above, on several occasions has referred to his expansive corpus of songs as "my ongoing novel" (quoted in Larry Smith 155). Indeed, Springsteen continues to write both relevant and commercially viable songs in his sixtieth year because, despite the long-drawn darkness on the edge of Bruce, he is at heart a man filled with hope. For one thing, he still has something to say about a vision of America that he believes in, about the new possibilities of finding fulfillment, community, and purpose in the Promised Land. Newly quickened by the hoped-for changes in American government and society under the present Obama administration, Springsteen has traded in his crafted sandwich board pessimism of frustrated and failed and betrayed dreams for a new optimism. While stumping for Obama in the 2008 presidential campaign, Springsteen addressed a crowd in Philadelphia with these words:

> I've spent 35 years writing about America, its people, and the meaning of the American Promise. The promise that was handed down to us, right here in this city from our founding fathers, with one instruction: Do your best to make these things real. Opportunity, equality, social and economic justice, a fair shake for all of our citizens, the American idea as a positive influence around the world for a more just and peaceful existence. These are the things that give our lives hope, shape, and meaning. They are the ties that bind us together and give us faith in our contract with one another.[7]

His anthem that gives the title to his 2009 song collection debuted during the campaign that brought Obama to office, and offers this hopeful chorus:

> I'm working on a dream
> Though sometimes it feels so far away
> I'm working on a dream
> And I know it will be mine someday

"We are such stuff / As dreams are made on," writes Shakespeare in *The Tempest*, affirming our human aspirations and the marvellous adventure of living. As do the Bard's plays, Springsteen's songs likewise pursue the stuff of dreams and of the heart's often conflicted longings. And just as Shakespeare at the end of *A Midsummer Night's Dream* confirms through Puck's epilogue the ability of art both to represent and to speak truly to our individual and collective realities, so Springsteen's songs, as critics and fans alike have attested, comprise a kind of soundtrack for contemporary American life. Following the release of *Magic* in 2007, the Boss tells Scott Pelley of CBS's *60 Minutes*, "I'm interested in what it means to live in America. I'm interested in the kind of country we live in and leave our kids. I'm interested in trying to define what that country is. I've got the chutzpah or whatever you want to say to believe that if I write a really good song about it, it's going to make a difference" (CBS).

Jon Stewart, in his funny yet profound feting of Springsteen at the Kennedy Center Honors in December 2009, remarked on his own youthful revelation that Springsteen's art "wasn't just about the joyful parade on

stage, or the theatrics; it was about stories of lives that could be changed."
Critics, comedians, and common folk alike find in Springsteen's music and
performances and lyrics something filling and uplifting, something beyond
simply a hit song, a great show, a catchy lyric. "Bruce doesn't just sing, he
testifies," exclaimed Stewart. And what Springsteen testifies to he defines
as "the hardship and heroism of everyday life." A gifted storyteller, songwriter, and performer, and—as his friends will testify and his audiences and
chosen charities know—a generous and gifted human being as well, Bruce
Springsteen has won a place in the annals of American history. Not just as a
musician and pop star, but as a public, political, and cultural icon. And he
has been accorded that place, as Stewart reflected, in New Jersey eloquence
verging on the Churchillian, because "He empties the tank every time. He
empties that tank for his art; he empties that tank for his audience; and he
empties it for his country. And we on the receiving end of that gift," Stewart
concluded, "are ourselves rejuvenated, if not redeemed" ("Jon Stewart").

The essays in this collection bear scholarly witness to the truths about
ourselves and our society to which Springsteen testifies in his songs. It is
our hope that in the engaged scholarly explorations that follow, you will
find new insights and a deeper understanding of the songs and artistic vision of Bruce Springsteen. We invite you not only to hear the voice of the
Boss, but to read him as well.

NOTES

1. For example, Eric Branscomb writing in the *Journal of Popular Culture* glances
at Shakespeare when discussing the textures of Springsteen's language on the early
albums and his juxtaposing of seemingly incongruous metaphors, as in "Spare
Parts" and "Reason to Believe" (Summer 93, 27.1 pp. 29–42); Chris Clancey,
editor of the entertainment e-zine *ReZoom* comments that the lyrics on *Born to
Run*, "come off like Shakespeare with a Jersey accent" (http://www.rezoom.com/
entertainment/top7/169/top-7-bruce-springsteen-songs); and Unitarian minister
Jeffrey Symynkewicz opens *The Gospel According to Bruce Springsteen* (2008) with an
allusion to Shakespeare and makes Shakespearean inferences in the book's section
headings (see pp. 1, 7); Lincoln Konkle, whose presentation at the *Glory Days Symposium* in 2005 was titled "The Tragic Vision of Bruce Springsteen," argues that "In
such songs as 'Jungleland,' 'Darkness on the Edge of Town,' 'The River,' 'Nebraska,'
'Born in the U.S.A.,' 'Tunnel of Love,' and others, Springsteen creates a tragic tone
comparable to the choral odes in Greek tragedy or the soliloquies in Shakespearean tragedy." (http://app.outreach.psu.edu/springsteen/schedule/ AbstractList.asp?
TT=42#details). An earlier version of his paper had the provocative title, "Sophocles,
Shakespeare . . . Springsteen?" (e-mail correspondence with the author).

2. See Garman, *A Race of Singers: Whitman's Working Class Hero from Guthrie to
Springsteen* (2000); Greg Smith, "Whitman, Springsteen, and the American Working Class," *Midwest Quarterly* 41.3 (Spring 2000): 302–20; Coles, *Bruce Springsteen's*

America (2003): 17–18; Cullen, *Born in the U.S.A.: Bruce Springsteen and the American Tradition* (2005): 32–36.

3. This insight is indebted to Renaissance scholar Tim Drake, from his unpublished essay "Shakespeare in the Alley."

4. *Racing in the Street*, ed. June Skinner Sawyers: see respectively, Frith, p. 139; Kirkpatrick, p. 69; Cullen, p. 192; Frith, p. 136; Dawidoff, p. 264.

5. Kennedy Honors biopic, aired 29 December 2009, voiceover quotation <www .youtube.com/watch?v=3jqNXphenusat>.

6. As early as 1996, the HarperCollins textbook *Literature: Reading and Responding to Fiction, Poetry, Drama, and the Essay*, edited by Joel Wingard, includes lyrics for "Cover Me" and "4th of July, Asbury Park (Sandy)," the latter printed alongside a poem by Wallace Stevens. Also published that year, *The Bedford Introduction to Literature: Reading, Thinking, and Writing* (4th ed.), edited by Michael Meyer, includes the lyric for "Streets of Philadelphia." The lyric for "My Hometown" appears in *Literature: Reading, Reacting, Writing* (compact 3rd ed.), a college English textbook edited by Kirszner and Mandell, published by Holt, Rinehart and Winston in 1997. *Literature, Class, and Culture: An Anthology*, edited by Paul Lauter and Ann Fitzgerald, and published by Longman in 2001, includes lyrics for "Galveston Bay" and "My Hometown." W. W. Norton's popular *Seagull Reader: Poems*, 2nd ed., edited by Joseph Kelly and published in 2007, collects the canonical poems of the major British and American poets, from Sidney, Shakespeare, and Spender to Whitman, W. C. Williams, and Wallace Stevens. The lyrics of two American singer-songwriters are also included: Dylan's "The Times They Are A-Changin'" and "Tangled Up in Blue," and Springsteen's "The River" and "Born in the U.S.A." Springsteen's lyrics are anthologized along with those of Bob Dylan, Joni Mitchell, Don McLean, Michael Stipe, Kurt Cobain, and Ice T in *The Prentice Hall Anthology of American Literature*, vol. 2, edited by Dean Rader and Jonathan Silverman, published in 2009.

7. An edited text of Springsteen's speech can be found at backstreets.com.

I

READING INFLUENCE

1

Endlessly Seeking

Bruce Springsteen and Walker Percy's Quest for Possibility among the Ordinary

June Skinner Sawyers

Although at first blush, it would not seem that Bruce Springsteen and the late novelist and essayist Walker Percy[1] had much in common, appearances in this case are most definitely deceiving. Percy's work had a considerable impact on Springsteen's songwriting, especially the songs that appear on his most introspective albums, *Nebraska* and *The Ghost of Tom Joad* but on his other albums as well. Specifically, Percy's *The Moviegoer*, his highly acclaimed novel about apathy and the paralysis of ennui, as well as several of his essays, including "The Man on the Train" and "Notes for a Novel about the End of the World," expressed a way of thinking that echoes Springsteen's own thoughts. Springsteen identified with Percy's view of America. Among the themes and topics that concern both men is the notion of community, especially the imagined community of readers and listeners as seen through the darkened lens of alienation and isolation. Percy wrote disaffected fiction; Springsteen has written and continues to write disaffected songs. And both men address the moral questions about the way we live and the way we behave toward one another. The fact that they come from quite disparate socioeconomic backgrounds as well as hail from different parts of the country makes little difference. For they have more in common than what sets them apart.

"As lonely as is the craft of writing, it is the most social of vocations," Walker Percy wrote. "No matter what the writer may say, the work is always written to someone, for someone, against someone" (Percy, *Signposts* 200). One could almost say the same about the songwriting community, especially as expressed in the music and, indeed, mindset of Bruce Springsteen. Like Percy, Springsteen has always been a seeker, a searcher. Both embarked on a pilgrimage to find themselves but also to invite others into their inner circle. What's more, both express an almost obsessive interest in what it means to be alive, which is both a moral *and* religious quest.

If American novels are about everything, as Percy has claimed, then Springsteen's rich body of songs is also about everything. While his songs explore a particular time and place—late twentieth and early twenty-first century America—they are also about ideas, most compellingly, the idea of possibility. They are cautiously hopeful while firmly rooted in dire reality. Springsteen writes songs designed to affect his listeners on a deeply emotional level while oftentimes addressing social justice issues such as homelessness, poverty, and economic inequality, yet he does so without being preachy and without necessarily talking just to the converted—a sensitive line to walk. The story of an entire life is often told in the time it takes him to sing one song.

Percy's essay "The Man on the Train" is about "the wandering spirit" and revolves around a familiar Springsteen trope: the alienation of the ordinary man (*Message*). The man of the title is a commuter, detached from his fellow commuters and his surroundings. From his seat on the train, he looks out the window to see the same landscape pass him by day in, day out, without having any connection to what he is seeing—no matter how many times he has seen it. He is just passing through. Nobody knows who he is, and he knows nobody. He is in fact the literary equivalent of the tightly wound drivers in "Stolen Car" on *The River* and in "State Trooper" on *Nebraska*—or any number of lost souls and daydreamers that populate the Springsteen canon. It is not certain if these clearly alienated men can become, if you will, "unalienated." Indeed, it is highly unlikely that they will ever be able to truly connect with the larger society, and yet their stories must be told because they are one of us. They are a big part of the human fabric that Springsteen cares so deeply about: the alienated man with no place to go. They are Ralph in "Johnny 99" and the Charles Starkweather character in "Nebraska," but also the hobo in "The New Timer" and the unemployed oil worker in "Seeds" or Bill Horton in "Cautious Man" and Joe in "Downbound Train." They are the descendents of the multitudes that Walt Whitman celebrated in "Song of Myself" but also one of the isolates who sailed on Melville's *Pequod*.

Similarly, Percy's philosophical novel *The Moviegoer* is about the mundane events in the life of an ordinary man, a small-time stockbroker who loves movies and who is about to turn thirty. Written in the first person and in the present tense, it offers the Springsteenesque image of modern man alone in the proverbial crowd. Throughout his work, Percy, again like Springsteen, comments on the lives of others, observes the way things are, and anticipates the way things could be.

Binx Bolling, the unlikely hero of *The Moviegoer*, has a car but prefers to ride buses and streetcars (5). Actually he dislikes cars: "Whenever I drive a car, I have the feeling I have become invisible" (11). He also pines for his secretary, a young woman named Sharon Kincaid. He lives uneventfully in Gentilly, a middle-class suburb of New Orleans, so nondescript and bland in fact that if it were not for the banana plants and iron "curlicues" on the façade of the Walgreens drugstore, you would never know that it was part of one of the most defiantly idiosyncratic cities in America, Binx remarks. Indeed, his apartment is as "impersonal as a hotel room" (78). As in a typical chain hotel, on the wall hang Currier and Ives prints of ice skaters in New York's Central Park. And why not? Why invest in art or make the effort to decorate his place in a way that reflects his personality since he is only passing through? That's the point. Binx is so out of touch with his own feelings that he isn't able to define his own personality, never mind come up with a style that reveals who he is. He is a visitor in his own life, certainly not staying long enough to make any discernible impact. To use a Springsteen term, he is a "nothing man," as imperceptible as many of the characters who haunt Springsteen's songs. This ordinariness actually seems to please Binx. It matches his humble lifestyle. He manages a small branch office of his uncle's brokerage firm. He lives modestly too. His home is a basement apartment of a bungalow. "I am a model tenant and a model citizen and take pleasure in doing all that is expected of me," he acknowledges (6).

Binx's social life is as uneventful as his living arrangement. In the evenings he watches television or goes to the movies. (Usually his secretary accompanies him on these cinematic outings, at least in the evenings and on the weekends.) He loves all types of movies, even terrible ones. He doesn't differentiate between good or bad. "Other people, so I have read, treasure memorable moments in their lives," he narrates (7), and then recites such events as climbing the Parthenon at sunrise. What he recalls most acutely though are moments experienced vicariously on the screen: John Wayne killing three men in *Stagecoach* or Orson Welles finding a kitten in a doorway in *The Third Man.* These are the moments that thrill him.

Friendship does not come easily to Binx. In fact, for years he has had no friends. The camaraderie, the small talk that one has to cultivate in order to forge a friendship, eludes him, and seems forced and unnatural to him. Instead, he admits, "I spend my entire time working, making money, going to movies and seeking the company of women" (41). That sentence can easily describe the life of numerous characters in Springsteen's songs; indeed, even the life of Springsteen himself during the time he was writing *Nebraska* in the early 1980s, when he felt isolated from family and friends, when he turned toward music to escape from his own personal demons.

Binx is a huge movie buff, although his love affair with the cinema is largely an excuse to disengage from the world. In contrast, oftentimes Springsteen's protagonists model themselves on the characters they see on the screen: "Remember all the movies, Terry / We'd go see / Trying to learn how to walk like the heroes / We thought we had to be" ("Backstreets" from *Born to Run*) and then attempt to play the parts of those larger-than-life personas outside on the street. But movies, to Binx, are more than just a form of mindless entertainment, of escaping from the known world. They actually validate his existence. Binx refers to this feeling as "certification" (63). If he sees his own neighborhood on the big screen, for example, it makes the neighborhood, and by extension, himself, somehow visible. Rather than living Anywhere, he lives Somewhere.

Binx first becomes aware of the concepts of time and place while sitting in the dark in a movie theater watching Montgomery Clift and John Wayne engage in a fight. As he sits in the darkness, he makes a mark on his seat arm with his thumbnail, as if to say "I was here on this particular time and at this particular place. I exist." He wonders where this piece of wood will be twenty years from now, even "543 years from now?" (75).

Not surprisingly, Binx has chosen a conventional career that lacks prestige, an important consideration in his status-hungry New Orleans family. He is a stock and bond broker. His family much preferred that he had selected a more exalted field such as the law or medicine. He, too, had ambitions of a grander life but he settled for less: "[t]here is much to be said for giving up such grand ambitions and living the most ordinary life imaginable . . ." (9). Coincidentally, Springsteen's father preferred that his son do something useful with his life—become, say, a doctor or a lawyer—rather than live what his father considered a marginal existence playing in a rock and roll band.

"LET KINGDOM COME, I'M GONNA FIND MY WAY"

In Binx's thirtieth year, something inside him changes. He is aware of it, too, and it disturbs him. One morning, during his birthday year, a thought occurs to him that almost borders on the profound: the possibility of a search. What is the nature of this search? he asks, rhetorically. He answers: "The search is what anyone would undertake if he were not sunk in the everydayness of his own life" (13). He continues, "To become aware of the possibility of the search is to be onto something. Not to be onto something is to be in despair" (13). And what is it that he seeks? Is it God? Something beyond life itself? He has no real answers, but he does know that he is and shall forever remain a seeker. Many of Springsteen's characters, too, are endless seekers. One need look no further than the race car driver in "Racing in the Street" or the debt-ridden Everyman in "Atlantic City," to cite just two examples. Both are trying, in their own way, to find a larger purpose for their time spent on this earth than just racing cars or working in a dead-end job, saving enough money to make ends meet. Both are essentially asking the perennial question, What am I to do with my life?

Binx is also somewhat of an insomniac. He fears if he should fall into a deep sleep, he may miss out on something, and here he conjures up images of the bleary-eyed drivers in "State Trooper" and "Open All Night." Of course, he has no idea what that might be. "Clearly nothing," he admits (84). He gets the unsettling sensation that everyone around him is dead. There are few signs of life except, perhaps, by feeling negative emotions—hatred itself. Only the haters seem alive to him. And so he considers a minor automobile accident that he is involved in a piece of good luck because, at least for a moment, he is able to escape his suffocating malaise. Life—and its possibilities—are lost to him, "and there remains only you and the world and you no more able to be in the world than Banquo's ghost" (120).

Although Binx prefers to walk or take public transportation, he does have a car, a small red MG. He describes it as "a miserable vehicle" with only one thing going for it: it is, he believes, immune to the malaise (122). Driving down the highway in his "miserable vehicle" (preferably with a girl by his side), the malaise miraculously disappears. At one point in the story—and it is a Springsteenesque moment—he describes its effects. "The noise," he remarks, "was deafening, the wind was like a hurricane; straight ahead the grains of the concrete rushed at us like mountains" (122). Driving for Binx has the same exhilarating effect that Springsteen writes about over and over again in his songs. But, alas, even Springsteen's "suicide machines"—no matter how thrilling the journey—can only take you so far before "there's no place left to hide" ("Born to Run" from *Born to Run*).

Binx considers his "dark pilgrimage on this earth" (228) and concludes that he is in perpetual exile, the eternal outsider who never feels at home anywhere. The older he gets, the less he knows. He is, he believes, "Jewish by instinct" (89). He accepts his exile, wallows in it even, until it becomes a part of his essential being. And he discovers evidence of this self-proclaimed Jewishness. According to sociologists, Binx notes, a large percentage of solitary moviegoers are Jews. He now knows who he is: a Presbyterian loner with a Jewish mind-set in New Orleans who loves movies and little else. He goes through the motions of relationships, hoping never to get caught, to be revealed as a fraud. It reminds one of a Springsteen lyric. "And I'm driving a stolen car," Springsteen writes. "Each night I wait to get caught / But I never do." Instead, Springsteen's driver travels in fear "on a pitch-black night," terrified that the darkness will swallow him whole ("Stolen Car" from *The River*).

"IT'S EASY FOR TWO PEOPLE TO LOSE EACH OTHER"

"[F]or writers, place is a special problem because they never fitted in in the first place," observes Percy in *Signposts in a Strange Land* (5–6). Percy was the quintessential Southern gentleman writer with deep roots in his native South. Thus, like Springsteen, the concept of place looms large in Percy's work. But more than place, Percy believed that in order to write from the heart, a writer needed to know what was in his soul. He assumes that most people, consciously or unconsciously, subscribe to a theory of mankind. That is, during the course of our daily living, we have worked out or have certain assumptions about how we view life and how others view it. This assumption raises the thorny question of whether our theories—beliefs that we have held, in some cases, a lifetime—actually make sense. And if they don't, what then? What does it mean to question one's own worldview? One's reason for being? This is an existential question and one that both Percy and Springsteen obsessed over, especially the older post-*Greetings from Asbury Park, N.J.*–era Springsteen.

Theological concerns have haunted Southern literature in the same way that they have haunted Springsteen's lyrics. Whereas Percy was Southern and Catholic (albeit a converted one), Springsteen is Northern and Catholic (albeit a lapsed one). Both believe in the possibility of redemption. Springsteen gave it a name—the Promised Land—while Percy discovered it in his newfound faith. "The reason I am a Catholic," he wrote, "is that I believe that what the Catholic Church proposes is true" (*Signposts* 305). In particular, he was attracted to the Church's sacrament of penance and reconciliation (Samway 151).

Percy referred to literature and art as cognitive, its purpose being to find out, to know, and to tell: "[I]n good times and bad, [art is] a celebration of the way things are when they are right, and a diagnostic enterprise when they are wrong" (*Signposts* 207). In the essays that compose *Signposts*, he comments on the isolation, loneliness, and alienation of modern man and finds these conditions reflected in the novels, plays, and films of his day. Moral decline, he believed, was but a symptom of modernity's malaise. Instead, he felt the real pathology was "an ontological impoverishment; that is, a severe limitation or crippling of the life of twentieth-century man" (*Signposts* 214).

Percy's job as a contemporary novelist of the twentieth century was, he thought, epistemological. Of the novelist he writes, "He must know how to send messages and decipher them. The messages may come not in bottles but rather in the halting and muted dialogue between strangers, between lovers and friends. One speaks; the other tries to fathom his meaning—or indeed to determine if the message has any meaning" (*Signposts* 217). This halting and muted dialogue is on full display in Springsteen's work, too, especially, to cite just one example, the songs on *Tunnel of Love*. This introspective, love-gone-wrong album chronicles the end of relationships, when lovers do indeed become strangers and words spoken become twisted or misunderstood—when couples take "one step up and two steps back" ("One Step Up," *Tunnel of Love*).

Percy often referred to Western man's sense of homelessness and loss of community. What's more, modern man, he insists, is estranged from his own being, "from the being of other creatures in the world, from transcendent being. He has lost something—what, he does not know; he knows only that he is sick unto death with the loss of it" (*Signposts* 262). Those words were written not in the 1990s or the 1980s nor even during the 1970s or 1960s but in 1957, during the supposedly sunnier days of the so-called American century.

Percy described the 1980s as a postmodern, post-Christian age. It is post-Christian, he writes, "in the sense that people no longer understand themselves, as they understood themselves for some fifteen hundred years, as ensouled creatures under God, born to trouble, and whose salvation depends upon the entrance of God into history as Jesus Christ" (*Signposts* 309). The atrocities of the twentieth century—from the Holocaust to the brink of nuclear war—questioned the rationality of man, the goodness of man. "The present age is demented. It is possessed by a sense of dislocation, a loss of personal identity, an alternating sentimentality and rage which, in an individual patient, could be characterized as dementia" (*Signposts* 309).

Old-fashioned notions of sin and redemption, heaven and hell, appealed to Percy as they did to that other great Southern novelist, Flannery O'Connor. In such a world, Christ's goodness and Satan's evilness metaphorically combat each other, and grace and cruelty live, uncomfortably, side by side. Surely, it is no accident that these dark perspectives deeply appealed to Springsteen, the lapsed Catholic who, in his heart of hearts, preferred the old rituals that were fast disappearing when he was growing up in central New Jersey. "Judeo-Christianity is about pilgrims who have something wrong with them and are embarked on a search to find a way out. This is also what novels are about" (Percy, *Signposts* 366). And, one may add, this is what Springsteen's songs are about as well.

Springsteen, to his core, is a conservative, though not in the political sense. (He is an old-fashioned bleeding heart liberal in many ways.) Rather, he is a traditionalist. He values history, heritage, the significance of the past. He considers himself as a carrier of tradition—a link in the musical chain—rather than an innovator like Elvis Presley, the Beatles, or Bob Dylan, who changed the course of popular music. "I like the whole idea of a rock and roll lineage," he has said (Sawyers 1). This deep-rooted conservatism is reflected in his lyrics when he uses archaic words such as "pilgrim" ("Brilliant Disguise" from *Tunnel of Love*) and "rank strangers" ("Long Walk Home" from *Magic*) and in his frequent use, especially on *Nebraska*, of the deferential "sir" or his playful take on "The Battle Hymn of the Republic" ("My eyes have seen the glory of the coming of the Lord") in "Darlington County" on *Born in the U.S.A*. His is a world where the whistle of a train lingers long into the black night and couples dance beneath the stars under weeping willow trees by the river side. In his use of imagery and metaphors, he is a twentieth-century man stuck in the twenty-first century.

Although both men are Catholics, they come from different generations and, thus, approach their faith differently. Springsteen is not a consciously Catholic writer, but Catholicism—its symbols, its rituals, its language—infuses his work. Father Andrew Greeley, the iconoclastic priest, sociologist, and novelist, has gone as far as calling Springsteen "a Catholic Meistersinger" (Sawyers 155). Contrastingly, virtually all of Percy's characters are Catholic, either "bad, half-baked, lapsed, whatever," imperfect Catholics, guilty about their religious flaws ("Holiness" in *Signposts* 368). In "The Holiness of the Ordinary," Percy comments on what sets Judeo-Christianity apart from other religions, and in this essay there lies a remarkable passage that captures the essence of not only *Nebraska*-era Springsteen but also the heart of the Springsteen canon, from *Greetings from Asbury Park, N.J.* to *Working on a Dream*. "What distinguishes Judeo-Christianity in general from other world religions is its emphasis on the value of the individual person, its view of man as a creature in trouble, seeking to get out of it, and accordingly on the move," writes Percy (*Signposts* 369). He then goes on to list the "special marks" of the Catholic Church. By this, he is referring in particular to the Eucharist and how this most sacred of rituals confers "the highest significance" upon such ordinary things as bread and wine and water, and how, in the mystery of its sacrament, it is the ceremonial equivalent of "a pilgrim" (a word, remember, that Springsteen uses occasionally) whose purpose is spent searching for the elusive holy grail—in other words, modern man as seeker, as wayfaring stranger traveling through this world of woe (*Signposts* 369).

"TOMORROW THERE WILL BE SUNSHINE
AND ALL THIS DARKNESS PAST"

Like Percy, Springsteen is a regionalist, in the best and broadest sense of the word, in the same way that William Faulkner or James Joyce can be called regionalists. At one point, he too wrote about a particular place— New Jersey—but found universal themes in his stories of trapped lives and lost souls in the dusty beach towns and spooky late-night turnpikes of the Garden State. Both Percy and Springsteen describe in their own similar but different ways the alienation of man from a Judeo-Christian perspective, alienation being an enduring symptom of man's perennial estrangement from God. But what gives even the bleakest Springsteen song the light of hope is the possibility of what lies around the bend.

"The road is better than the inn," Percy writes, quoting Cervantes, referring to what Percy calls the concept of rotation, or movement; that is, the act of being mobile (*Message* 89).Whether it is a man riding in a train—Percy's example—or Springsteen's characters racing in the street, they are in the world but not entirely of it. They are transients on the distant horizon, dancing through life like the traveling companions in filmmaker Ingmar Bergman's existential masterpiece *The Seventh Seal.* In particular, Percy calls the American Western an exercise in rotation. The stranger or the man with no name enters town, gets into a series of adventures, and then moves on. John Ford's color-saturated desertscapes are journeys away from home. "Who is he, this Gary Cooper person who manages so well to betray nothing of himself whatsoever, who is he but I myself, the locus of pure possibility?" (*Message* 94).

Like Springsteen the songwriter, Percy the novelist is part poet, part storyteller, and part prophet. And like the prophet, "his news is generally bad" (*Message* 104). The characters in Percy's and Springsteen's works often are exiles and wanderers, subscribing to the prophetic-eschatological character of Christianity. If, as Percy believed, the appropriate subject of the postmodern novel is a man who has come to the end of the line, the hero of the postmodern novel is this same man who has forgotten his past and has come to the secular city. "His only problem now is to keep from blowing his brains out" (*Message* 112). Despite these dire circumstances, Percy also sees hope, or at least the possibility of it. The exile, the wanderer, the castaway, the pilgrim—whatever term one prefers—continues to search and lives in hope that a message—the message in the bottle of Percy's title—will be found.

Percy and Springsteen have another thing in common. Both have answered to no one but their individual conscience. Just as Percy wrote whatever he wanted to write, so has Springsteen, even before he earned the commercial right to do so. That is, Springsteen was the boss before he became the Boss. Writing a novel or teaching a student or composing a lyric is a magical process and can lead to unexpected connections, which "makes it all worthwhile," writes Percy (*Signposts* 355). If writing is a solitary act, then reading, Percy believed, is a social transaction in the sense that a special communication exists between writer and reader. A communion also exists, of course, between listener and songwriter; invoking the essence of mutual trust; that is, if not quite a common reader, then perhaps a common listener. Here lie the dual notions of possibility and community—two crucial elements in the work of both Walker Percy and Bruce Springsteen.

When *Magic* was released in late 2007, Springsteen tried to describe his concept of community to *Rolling Stone's* Joe Levy: "At this point, I'm in the middle of a long conversation with my audience." He calls what he does an ongoing dialogue "about what living means. You create a space together. You are involved in an act of the imagination together. . . . I can't do it by myself. I need my audience. It'll be a life-long journey by the time that I'm done. . . . So on a good night, when the band's playing real well, there's a moment when you've been a part of a collective event of imagination" (Levy 52).

The people Springsteen admires have all been searchers in their own way, quite often searchers in search of a community. They include musicians such as Hank Williams, Frank Sinatra, Elvis Presley, James Brown, Woody Guthrie, and Bob Dylan, but also political figures such as Martin Luther King Jr. and Malcolm X. Despite being quite different from one another, all were trying to bring people together, attempting to create both a tangible community and an imagined community. Springsteen has been doing this his entire adult working life—in song. In his early albums, he created the self-made community best epitomized perhaps by "Spirit in the Night" as well as painted a musical portrait of the tightly-knit community that occupied the sun-dappled, boardwalk-haunted worlds of *Greetings from Asbury Park, N.J.* and *The Wild, the Innocent & the E Street Shuffle*.

In these early works, Springsteen created a community of shared values even though the community that he sang about essentially was a transient group of friends, musicians, and passersby: "the boys from the casino" who "dance with their shirts open like Latin lovers on the shore," the greasers who get busted "for sleeping on the beach all night," "them boys in their high heels," and the factory girls "underneath the boardwalk"—all are held together by the promise of if not a better tomorrow at least another fun and idle day in the sun ("4th of July, Asbury Park (Sandy)" from *The Wild, the Innocent & the E Street Shuffle*). The music that Springsteen and his own scruffy band made helped create this illusion of community. No matter what band they were in or what type of music they played—and Springsteen often changed the direction of his music during these early years—what mattered most was that they were all in it together: one for all, and all for one, a Jersey Shore rat pack.

"WELL, SIR, I GUESS THERE'S JUST
A MEANNESS IN THIS WORLD"

But in *Nebraska*, Springsteen's commentary on life in America during the Reagan years, the protagonists are without community, strangers even to themselves. Although by 1981 he was already a multimillionaire—the success of *Born to Run, Darkness on the Edge of Town*, and *The River* virtually guaranteed that—he still did not own a house. It was a conscious decision because Springsteen felt essentially rootless and emotionally homeless. He didn't want to carry around any excess baggage, both metaphorically and literally. He had just spent a considerable period of time on *The River* tour. He returned to New Jersey and began thinking about his next record. But he dreaded returning to the sterility of the recording studio where, he observes, "I rarely got the right group of songs I was after without wasting a lot of time and expense" (Springsteen, *Songs* 135). Like Binx, he was entirely self-contained. "That way you don't get pushed around," he said. "It depends on what you need. I eat loneliness, man. I feed off it" (Marsh *Glory*, 83). Instead, Springsteen felt most at home when he was on the stage, on the road, or at the movies—again like Binx, away from the mirror of self-reflection.

Springsteen set up a four-track Teac tape machine in his bedroom at Colts Neck, New Jersey, where he recorded the songs that make up *Nebraska*, arguably his most personal and, to many critics, his best album. The cassette that he carried with him in his jeans pocket and recorded at home became the finished product. The songs themselves recall elements of his childhood, particularly the time spent in his grandmother's house when he was six (*Songs* 136).

At the same time he was recording *Nebraska*, he also was reading the short stories of Flannery O'Connor, whose dark spirituality affected him greatly, and watching several films, such as *True Confessions* and especially *Badlands*, that reflected the moral ambiguity and anarchic violence that featured so prominently in the lyrics.

Most of the songs on *Nebraska* were written and recorded quickly, sometimes requiring just three or four takes while a few songs, such as "Highway Patrolman" and "State Trooper," only took one. The entire record was completed in a matter of weeks, which was in stark contrast to his methodical approach on *Born to Run*, for which he clocked an excessive number of hours in the recording studio trying to find the right sound. The center of *Nebraska* is the title cut, Springsteen's interpretation of the Charles Starkweather–Caril Fugate murder spree of the 1950s, which left ten people dead. But other songs—"Mansion on the Hill," "Used Cars," and "My Father's House"—were based on personal experience and written from a child's point of view.

As in Walker Percy's *The Moviegoer*, the theme of *Nebraska* is a lack of community. Springsteen explores what happens to these characters, these often forlorn and lonely figures, when their entire social network disappears—no job, no family, no friends, no faith. Given the value placed on community by Springsteen, the songs on *Nebraska* may have struck some people as a departure, if not a shock, a bold bolt out of the blue. Of course, anyone who knows Springsteen's work realizes that in his world community and isolation live side by side. You cannot separate one from the other.

In "Mansion on the Hill," a child sits in the passenger seat of a parked car with his father, looking up wistfully at the fortress-like mansion on a hill. Even at this young age, the boy already realizes he is an outsider in his own town. Later in the song, he, along with his sister, hides in the corn fields, and both children listen surreptitiously from a safe distance to the sound of music and the laughter of people coming from "the mansion on the hill."

The protagonist in "State Trooper" is the ultimate loner. He drives along the New Jersey Turnpike without a driver's license or a vehicle registration, a midnight phantom who taunts the law. His only companion is the radio but even with it he gets no relief. He can't escape the sounds of the incessant chatter of "talk show stations." He loses his patience and the best he can offer is a heartfelt plea to "deliver me from nowhere." The protagonist in "Open All Night" is cut from the same cloth—the same twitchiness, the same sense of urgency. The difference is that he has a destination and a purpose—trying to get back to his sweetheart—whereas the protagonist in "State Trooper" is simply drifting with no particular place to go. Like the Charles Starkweather character and the sad sack Ralph in "Johnny 99," he is a human time bomb waiting to explode.

In a series of brief vignettes that make up "Reason to Believe," the final song on *Nebraska*, things don't go quite right for anyone: a man stands over a dead dog on the side of a highway, hoping that the animal somehow will revive itself and run off to live another day; a husband leaves his wife for no apparent reason; with its eerie echoes of Flannery O'Connor, a baby boy is baptized in the river to wash away his sins; an old man dies alone in a shotgun shack; a groom is abandoned on his wedding day. And yet "at the end of every hard-earned day," they still find a reason to believe.

More than a decade later, Springsteen released *The Ghost of Tom Joad*, a cycle of songs that continues the community theme. Their skin color may be darker and the time period different (the mid-1990s) but the characters Springsteen writes about remain lost, remote, and inaccessible. Both thematically and musically, *Tom Joad* is similar to *Nebraska*. Once again, the music is minimal—stark, austere, and acoustic—the lyrics straightforward with strong narratives. He writes about an ex-con ("Straight Time"), a bank robber ("Highway 29"), unemployed steelworkers ("Youngstown"), hoboes who ride the rails ("The New Timer"), and Mexican migrants and their often deadly experiences as they try to reach and then stay alive in the Promised Land ("Sinaloa Cowboys," "The Line," "Balboa Park," "Across the Border").

The best song on *Tom Joad* and, coincidentally, the most *Nebraska*-like, is the powerful "The New Timer." An old-timer named Frank shows a "new timer" the ropes. The younger man hoes sugar beets and picks peaches until he and Frank go their separate ways. He never sees Frank again but he soon learns that the old-timer was found shot dead, "Nothin' taken, nothin' stolen / Somebody killin' just to kill." He then has a vision of the way life could have been if he had not lost his job and left home: a small house, a woman cooking in the kitchen, a son sitting at the dinner table with his father. The new timer wonders if his son misses him and muses "Does he wonder where I am?" ("The New Timer").

Whether a hobo on the great American highway or an isolated figure walking aimlessly along the streets of New Orleans, the characters that populate the lyrics of Springsteen's songs and the pages of Percy's novels lament, in their own forlorn ways, the absence of community and yearn for a place to call their own.

"TELL ME HOW DO I BEGIN AGAIN?"

It is significant that *The Moviegoer*'s Binx is a fan of Westerns. As already mentioned, Springsteen too admires the genre and none more so than John Ford's classic *The Searchers*. For anyone unfamiliar with the plot, it stars John Wayne as Ethan Edwards, a loner and former Confederate soldier who finds it difficult to forget what happened during the Civil War and to return to civilized society. He feels uncomfortable around others and has little patience for small talk and other niceties of life. His niece, played by a young Natalie Wood, is kidnapped, and Edwards spends a good many years trying to find her. Ultimately, he does rescue her and returns her safely to her family. The last image is of Edwards walking off into the great Western landscape, alone, of course.

When Springsteen first saw *The Searchers* in the 1980s (significantly, on late-night television), it resonated with him in profound ways. Springsteen identified with the Ethan Edwards character. Like Edwards at the conclusion of the film, he could not return to "civilized" society. Edwards, like Springsteen, chose to turn his back on the community that nurtured him. In the film, he is portrayed as an utterly alienated being, a landlocked version of the isolates of Herman Melville's *Moby Dick*. He is "the searcher" of the title. But once the search is over, he has nowhere and no one to turn to.

Springsteen instinctively understood this because it reflected his own inner thoughts at the time. "I spent 20 years playing on the road with no real home life or connections except when I played at night," he told Nicholas Dawidoff. "Once I walked off the stage I didn't know how to do it, be part of it. I didn't have confidence that I could be accepted in the real world outside my work" (Sawyers 254). He feared getting too close to people. He kept his distance. If Ethan Edwards took lonely rides on his horse surrounded by the iconic landscapes of the American West, Springsteen took lonely drives through New Jersey, inevitably ending up in his hometown of Freehold, standing pensively outside his old house, and thinking about the tangled and complicated relationship he had with his father.

Springsteen's characters are, more often than not, outsiders trying to find, and sometimes fight, their way in. The characters are cut off from their own emotions. All they have left is to endure, cry out in prayer, or offer a lamentation of the soul. Ralph, the down on his luck protagonist of "Johnny 99," is a case in point. He loses his job at the local auto plant, gets drunk "from mixin' Tanqueray and wine," and shoots a night clerk. He tries to explain, not excuse, his behavior but then admits "I do believe I'd be better off dead." The songs on *Tom Joad* are even bleaker than the songs on *Nebraska*. Here there is no chance for relief, no reprieve from impending disaster. The characters are trapped in their own insular worlds and have no clue how to escape from them. Instead, Charlie in "Straight Time" just lies on his pillow and goes "driftin' off into foreign lands" while, like Ralph, the furnace worker of "Youngstown" believes that there are worse things than dying.

For all of his adult life, Springsteen has written from a dual perspective: how we live in the world and how we ought to live in the world. It is this way of looking at the world that Springsteen finds so appealing in Walker Percy's essay "The Man on the Train." Percy writes about the effect the Industrial Revolution had on the general populace, how it uprooted people who had been living in the same place for generations and how, in turn, because of economic hardship, these same people had to leave their hometowns and families behind to start all over again in order to find a new home. "I think that we're all trying to find what passes for a home, or creating a home of some sort, while we're constantly being uprooted by technology, by factories being shut down," Springsteen tells Percy's nephew, Will Percy (Sawyers 310). The essay raised questions that Springsteen had been mulling over for some time, such as "how do you create the kind of home you want to live in, how do you create the kind of society you want to live in, what part do you play in doing that?" (Sawyers 311). Springsteen, of course, does his part by telling stories about different kinds of people from different walks of life, "to establish a commonality by revealing our inner common humanity . . ." (Sawyers 312).

Admirers of both Springsteen and Percy have often wondered what they had to complain about as if writing about social justice issues was a mere form of grumbling. Percy was asked, Why write about such bleak conditions or unsavoury characters? To Springsteen the answer lies in the purpose of creativity itself. The modern artist, he believes, is the pop cultural version of the perennial canary in the mine—for society at large (Sawyers 314; Percy, *Message* 101). That is, the writer's role—the artist's role, his role—is to comment about the moral uncertainties of the modern world, to bring up uncomfortable issues so that we can if not change the world, at least reconsider the world and our role in it, to ask fundamental moral questions about the way we live and the way we treat one another. It is then up to each person, according to Springsteen, to turn art into action on an everyday level.

Music provided Springsteen with a community or series of communities. When he was writing *Nebraska*, music in fact was the *only* community he had. Springsteen has talked about real communities—the community that, say, grew around the bar bands in his adopted home town of Asbury Park—and imagined communities—the communities of ideas and values that allowed one to think of possibility. But *Nebraska* reflected his estrangement from community, and this condition weighed heavily on his soul. He knew he had to change himself. Otherwise, he feared he might end up like one of the isolates in his songs.

In a way it is ironic given his family history that Springsteen seemed so rootless during the wilderness years of *Nebraska*. As Freehold town historian Kevin Coyne asserts, there have been Dutch Springsteens in New Jersey since colonial times, indeed, as far back as circa 1664. Springsteens from Monmouth County—where he lives today—fought in the Revolutionary War as well as in the War of 1812 and the Civil War. The name itself has echoes of the earth—it literally means "springstone" or a stone from which a spring flows (370n3). In May 2008, Springsteen was inducted into the New Jersey Hall of Fame. During his speech, he commented on the importance of place and having roots in a community as well as the value that continuity brings to everyday life:

> I've always found it deeply resonant holding the hands of my kids on the same streets where my mom held my hand, swimming in the same ocean, and taking them to visit the same beaches I did as a child. It was also a place that really protected me. It's been nurturing. . . . But the thing about being in one place your whole life is that they're still around you in the water. I look towards the shore and I see my two sons and my daughter pushing their way through the waves. And on the beach there's a whole batch of new little kids running away from the crashing surf like time itself. That's what New Jersey is for me. It's a repository of my time on earth. My memory, the music I've made, my friendships, my life . . . it's all buried here. (brucespringsteen.net)

CODA: "CAN YOU HEAR ME?"

> For the place of God had become vacant, and there was a draught blowing through the world as in an empty flat before the new tenants have arrived.
>
> —Arthur Koestler (on the plight of the
> lapsed Catholic in *The Age of Longing*)

On 23 February 1989, Walker Percy wrote a letter to Bruce Springsteen when he, Percy, was fighting the prostate cancer that would eventually kill him on May 10 the following year. He wrote the letter as a peer, from one writer to another. Percy refers to it as "a fan letter—of sorts." In it, he admits that he admires Springsteen, as much for his musicianship as for "being one of the few sane guys in your field." Significantly, in the letter Percy also calls Springsteen a "postmodern musician." This is noteworthy because Percy thought of himself as a postmodern novelist, a "refugee" from the modern world (*Message* 110). Indeed, to Percy, the postmodern man is "a new breed of person in whom the potential for catastrophe—and hope—has suddenly escalated" and where there lies "unlimited possibilities for both destruction and liberation, for an absolute loneliness or a rediscovery of community and reconciliation" (*Message* 112). These ideas—the fragile union of despair and expectation—are crucial to understanding the work of both Percy, the postmodern novelist, and Springsteen, the postmodern musician, because they form the foundation of their respective careers.

In his letter, Percy expresses a particular interest in Springsteen's Catholicism and finds that through their shared religion and their mutual admiration for Flannery O'Connor that they have something quite unique in common. He seems genuinely touched that a contemporary musician, and a rock musician at that, should share his taste in literature; that they would have *anything* in common, that he has found in this New Jersey musician something of a kindred spirit. Specifically, Percy writes that he is particularly interested in Springsteen's "spiritual journey" and would like to hear more about what choices he makes in the years ahead. Of course, that was not to be.

Springsteen did eventually reply to Percy's letter, but unfortunately, to his great embarrassment, it was not until several years later. By then, Walker Percy had already succumbed to cancer. In 1998, Springsteen conducted a wide-ranging interview with Percy's nephew, Will Percy, that appeared in the spring 1998 issue of *DoubleTake* magazine, in which Springsteen talked about, among other things, the importance of Walker Percy's writing in his life and work. Springsteen composed a contrite, apologetic, and sincere four-page letter, addressing it to Percy's wife, Mary (who was known as "Bunt"). It is a letter of equals, of one man writing to the widow of another man in which Springsteen spells out what he believes has been the purpose of his life's work: "the loss and search for faith and meaning." Alas, it is also a letter that laments a lost opportunity.

> Dear Mrs. Percy,
>   This is a letter so long in coming I'm almost embarrassed to write, but I've gotten to know Will a little bit and he's encouraged me on, so here we go.
>   A few years back when I received Dr. Percy's letter, I wasn't familiar with his work. . . . It was a passionate letter about the comforts and difficulties of reconciling the inner life of a sophisticated man, a writer's life, with the Catholic faith. I recall Dr. Percy's explaining how one had brought depth of meaning to the other for him. He was . . . curious to know how I handled my issues of faith.
>   It is now one of my great regrets that we didn't get to correspond. A while after receiving Dr. Percy's letter, I picked up "The Moviegoer," its toughness and beauty have stayed with me. The loss and search for faith and meaning have been at the core of my own work most of my adult life. I'd like to think that perhaps that is what Dr. Percy heard and was what moved him to write to me. Those issues are still what motivate me to sit down, pick up my guitar and write. Today, I would have had a lot to put into that letter. (Sawyers 319–20)

How should I live my life? It is the most fundamental of moral questions. It is the question that haunted both men. And to this day, it is the underlying principle that continues to guide Springsteen along his musical and personal paths. Walker Percy, a son of the South, was a perennial searcher; he was never content with the way things were. He wrote in his fiction and in his essays about the malaise that he saw all around him. Springsteen, the quintessential Jersey boy, spent a good part of his adult life on the road, but still tried to create a community of like-minded souls wherever he went. But it is truly under a New Jersey sky where he is most at home and where the ordinariness of daily life offers the redemptive hope of possibility.

NOTE

1. Walker Percy was born on 28 May 1916, in Birmingham, Alabama. His grandfather and father committed suicide while his mother died under rather mysterious circumstances in a tragic car accident. Trained as a physician, Percy began his internship in 1942 at Bellevue Hospital in New York—ironically, the same hospital that the character in Springsteen's song "For You" (*Greetings from Asbury Park, N.J.*) takes the suicide victim. It was while an intern at Bellevue that Percy contracted tuberculosis. After a rather lengthy recuperation, he chose to give up medicine entirely to become a writer. In 1947 he converted to Catholicism. Percy died in Covington, Louisiana, from prostate cancer on 10 May 1990, at the age of seventy-three. See Patrick Samway, *Walker Percy: A Life* (Chicago: Loyola Press, 1999).

2

"On Blessing Avenue"

Faith, Language, and a Search for Meaning in the Works of Bruce Springsteen and Walker Percy

Michael Kobre

In the generally mixed response to Bruce Springsteen's 2009 release *Working on a Dream*, one point of agreement, at least among the album's detractors, was that its weakest track was "Queen of the Supermarket." "The album bottoms out," Greg Kot wrote in *The Chicago Tribune*, "in a can of pure corn." Kot continued, "'Queen of the Supermarket' was almost a parody of a Springsteen song," while Andy Whitman writing in *Paste* called the song "an absurdly overwrought wall of sound anthem." Ann Powers, who in a slightly more nuanced review for *The Los Angeles Times* described *Working on a Dream* as "boisterously scatterbrained, exhilaratingly bad," agreed that "Queen of the Supermarket" was "the album's low point," but also suggested that a more "spare and mellow" version "might have produced chills." For Powers, the version heard on the album was the equivalent of "a Broadway number."

Indeed, "Queen of the Supermarket" is a perplexing song, like almost nothing else in Springsteen's body of work. Though Springsteen had used lush, orchestrated textures before—on *Born to Run*, on parts of *The Rising* from 2002 and *Magic* from 2007, and, of course, all over the rest of *Working on a Dream*—and though he'd also previously explored the allure and perils of consumer desire in songs like "You Can Look (But You Better Not Touch)" from his 1980 album *The River* and in "57 Channels" on the 1992 release *Human Touch*, the way those elements are combined in "Queen of the Supermarket" and the song's ambiguous tone take us somewhere notably different. In "57 Channels," for instance—whether in its acoustic debut at the 1990 Christic Institute performance, the cluttered studio arrangement of *Human Touch* (Springsteen's other most beleaguered album), or the nascent hip-hop version of the *Human Touch* tour—the speaker's isolation in a media-saturated world and his rage at the false desires implanted in him are clear. There's not much ambiguity when, "in the blessed name of Elvis," the speaker in "57 Channels" blasts his TV with a Magnum. By contrast, though, what are we to make of the palpable wonder and longing in Springsteen's voice at the beginning of "Queen of the Supermarket" when he assures the listener that "aisles and aisles of dreams await you"? How are we intended to feel when his voice strains to reach a higher note as he declares his love for his inamorata at the checkout counter and then an ocean of strings swells beneath him? Is the song supposed to be ironic? Are we meant to laugh at the speaker? Or somehow, amidst all the aural tinsel of the song, strings and piano and guitars and choirs of voices, are we actually supposed to glimpse the same beauty he sees?

The answer to this question can be found, I think, in an unlikely affinity between Bruce Springsteen and the novelist Walker Percy. Percy, who was the first great novelist of the New South and a clear-eyed diagnostician of American malaise in the 1960s and 1970s, was introduced to Springsteen's music by his nephew, Will Percy (Tolson 485). In 1989, a few months before his death, Percy even wrote a fan letter to Springsteen in which, after asserting an artistic kinship between them, he asked about Springsteen's "spiritual journey." Springsteen, in turn, discovered Percy's work after the novelist's death. In a letter three years later to Percy's widow, he praised the "toughness and beauty" of Percy's classic first novel *The Moviegoer* and acknowledged in response to Percy's questions that "the loss and search for faith and meaning have been at the core of my own work for most of my adult life" (quoted in Will Percy, "Rock and Read" 42–43).

Indeed, at an almost subterranean level, concealed deep beneath the gloss of "Queen of the Supermarket," I think we hear that "loss and search for faith and meaning" in much the same way that it seethes beneath the surface of *The Moviegoer*. Published in 1961, *The Moviegoer* tells the story of Binx Bolling, the heir of a distinguished Southern family who flees from the weight of family expectations and Southern history by moving to a suburb of New Orleans and seemingly devoting himself to the pursuit of money and pleasure. At one level, it's possible to see Binx's portrayal of himself as a quintessential suburbanite as a kind of ironic imposture. His first-person narration is filled with moments when he seems to delight in calling attention to the mask he's put on. "I am a model tenant and a model citizen," he tells us, "and take pleasure in doing all that's expected of me" (6). But Binx's assertions of the peace and beauty he finds in the suburb of Gentilly are not unequivocally ironic. In a passage in which Binx admires the beauty of a parochial school across the street from his apartment, we hear the same complex mix of tones that make "Queen of the Supermarket" so baffling:

> Everything is so spick-and-span: the aluminum sashes fitted into the brick wall and gilded in the sunset, the pretty terrazzo floors and the desks molded like

wings. Suspended by wires above the door is a schematic sort of bird, the Holy Ghost I suppose. It gives me a pleasant sense of the goodness of creation to think of the brick and glass and the aluminum being extracted from common dirt—though no doubt it is less a religious sentiment than a financial one, since I own a few shares of Alcoa. How smooth and well-fitted and thrifty the aluminum feels! (10)

At first glance, there is a kind of excess to Binx's admiration of institutional architecture here that recalls the over-the-top orchestration of "Queen of the Supermarket." Binx sounds at times like a soap commercial—"Everything is so spick-and-span"—and his insistence on seeing "the goodness of creation" in the raw materials and industrial processes used to construct the school comes so close to being ludicrous that even Binx has to undercut his assertion by confessing his financial interest in Alcoa. And yet, the acuity of Binx's attention—the way he sees the aluminum "gilded in the sunset . . . the desks molded like wings"—suggests also that his appreciation of the school's beauty is not entirely misplaced.

Indeed, what seems uncomfortably skewed in both this moment in *The Moviegoer* and in "Queen of the Supermarket" is the way that elements of genuine beauty—the details Binx picks out, the tenderness in Springsteen's singing, the stately piano and guitar—are mixed up with overly inflated sentiments or a production style so grandiose that the mundane objects evoked in each work can't seem to support such excess. Consequently, that unsettling sense of excess suggests instead an ache for something *beyond* a winsome check-out clerk or a well-made building and a profitable stock portfolio. In fact, as we see over the course of *The Moviegoer*, Binx's professed admiration for the small beauties he finds in Gentilly is only a stage in a longer passage toward an acknowledgment of a yearning for a deeper, more genuine sense of "the goodness of creation." And in a similar way, the speaker's desperate need in "Queen of the Supermarket" to fulfill "the cool promise of ecstasy" in the grocery store aisles echoes against the glimpses of mortality and transcendence offered elsewhere on *Working on a Dream*. Within the larger collection of songs that compose the album, the speaker's unrequited passion, however powerfully felt, seems inadequate, incomplete—and therefore threaded with a deep, unexpressed sadness.

In *The Moviegoer* (and, in fact, throughout Percy's body of work), that uneasy mix of tones and idioms which we hear in Binx's appreciation of the school is essential to Percy's art. The defining characteristic of Binx's consciousness is the continuous tension between the various perspectives and belief-systems he encounters: the traditions of his Southern heritage, the pleasures and abundance of a consumer society, the dreams he sees magnified on the movie screen, the certainty and rigor of the scientific thought he once studied, and the mysteries of faith—particularly as those mysteries are embodied in the uncanny serenity of his dying half-brother

Lonnie. Moreover, because Binx is such an acute observer, because he's gifted with such a finely tuned ear, those different perspectives echo in the novel as distinct voices jostling against one another. Sometimes spoken aloud by a specific character—as, for instance, Binx's aunt Emily articulates the stoic values of the southern aristocracy—and sometimes heard only as faint traces in Binx's own narration—in his use of a particular phrase ("spick-and-span") or an odd inflection—these voices comprise a polyphony that sounds in the novel's prose and in Binx's consciousness.

This multivoiced quality of Binx's narrative (like a similar quality, as we'll see, in Springsteen's work) is best understood in light of the critical theory of the great Russian philosopher and critic Mikhail Bakhtin. Bakhtin's writings address a wide array of subjects, from the history of the novel to Freudian thought, but at the core of Bakhtin's literary theory is a vision of language—any national language really—stratified into a multiplicity of discourses (or "socioideological languages," as Bakhtin sometimes also called them) that reflect the varied experiences and perspectives of different generations, regions, ethnic groups, professions, and other subcultures grouped together within some tenuous national entity. As Bakhtin writes in his magisterial essay "Discourse in the Novel,"

> For any individual consciousness living in it, language is not an abstract system of normative forms but rather a concrete heteroglot conception of the world. All words have the "taste" of a profession, of a genre, a tendency, a party, a particular work, a particular person, a generation, an age group, the day and the hour. Each word tastes of the context and contexts in which it has lived its socially charged life; all words and forms are populated by intentions . . . language, for the individual consciousness, lies on the borderline between oneself and the other. The word in language is half someone else's. It becomes "one's own" only when the speaker populates it with his own intention, his own accent, when he appropriates the word, adapting it to his own semantic and expressive intention. (293)

For Bakhtin, as this passage suggests, an individual—like Binx Bolling in *The Moviegoer* or any of Percy's other protagonists—must inevitably sort through all those different discourses, embracing some ("adapting it to his own semantic and expressive intention") and rejecting others. So, for instance, by the end of *The Moviegoer*, Binx's narrative voice has largely shed all traces of an ironic consumerism or his aunt's patrician values in favor of something closer to his half-brother Lonnie's sacramental language.

In a similar fashion, something like this multi-voiced quality of Percy's fiction is also heard in Springsteen's work. At a purely sonic level, of course, Springsteen has long been the sort of artist who happily borrows from and adapts different musical traditions: rhythm and blues, country and folk, British rock, American pop, rockabilly—just to name a few. And in his lyric content too, we hear different voices: rebellious young men who speak in Dylanesque wordplay, laconic isolatos wandering through the darkness of an indifferent and sometimes hostile social order, joyous men and women intoxicated by the pleasure of physical passion or of music itself. Over approximately four decades as a songwriter, Springsteen has populated his musical world with a vast array of characters, voices, and perspectives, and the particular nature of his work, at its most ambitious and complex, depends on the way those voices echo against each other, particularly within the larger structure of an album.

Beginning at least with *The River* in 1980, the juxtaposition of these different voices is deliberately used to deepen an album's themes. So, for instance, the grand and maybe even lachrymose declarations of love offered by the speaker of "Drive All Night," the penultimate song of *The River*, are tempered by the different voice in the final song, "Wreck on the Highway" (just as the soul-oriented sound of "Drive All Night," built around Roy Bittan's piano and Clarence Clemons's sax, differs markedly from the loping, country beat of "Wreck on the Highway," which borrows its title from Roy Acuff and part of its melody from "The Green, Green Grass of Home"). When the speaker of "Wreck on the Highway" wonders about "a girlfriend or a young wife" of the "young man" he found beside the "blood and glass" of the wrecked car on the side of the road—a figure who might even have been the enraptured speaker of the previous song, rushing down the highway to "sleep tonight again" in his lover's arms—the confidence expressed in "Drive All Night" that the sheer depth of its characters' love can stave off any hurt seems more willful than realistic. And *that* recognition, which only arises out of the way those different voices echo against each other, also seems to affirm in turn—like evidence to support a thesis—the hard truths voiced in "The Price You Pay," the song that immediately precedes "Drive All Night." Ostensibly another Springsteen anthem, with soaring keyboards and a defiant speaker, "The Price You Pay" suggests that while some people can indeed make it to a kind of hard-won "promised land"— such as, perhaps, the speaker of "Wreck on the Highway," who ends that song holding his lover tight in their bed—others will be "fallen away" to the inevitable cost of human strivings. Taken together, in fact, this sequence of three songs at the end of *The River* sums up the vision of what was, at that point in Springsteen's career, his most diverse and ambitious collection of songs: a vision of a complex and almost arbitrary existence in which some fortunate souls cross over the river into a promised land while others have their dreams smashed on its banks.

In his introduction to a performance of the entire *The River* album at Madison Square Garden on 8 November 2009, Springsteen described *The River* as "a gateway to a lot of my future writing."[1] So it's no surprise to find this kind of Bakhtinian polyphony of voices on virtually all his major work from that point on. Thus, on *Nebraska*, the serial killer Charles Stark-weather's embrace of "a meanness in this world" in the title song jostles alongside another character's insistence on the responsibilities of family as the core of an ethical life in "Highway Patrolman"—"Man turns his back on his family, well he just ain't no good"—while *Born in the U.S.A.* contains both the blithely happy-go-lucky speaker trading off his buddy's "union connection" and hoping to find a good time down south in "Darlington County" and the somber father of "My Hometown" surveying the ruins of a postindustrial America. Most prominently perhaps, on *The Rising*, Spring-steen's 2002 meditation on the bloodshed of 9/11, we hear the voices of survivors, mourners, bystanders, terrorists, and the dead themselves—a collage of voices and sonic textures that resists sentimentality or polemics.

Yet within that dialogue of voices in Springsteen's work, as in the novels of Walker Percy too, another voice, heard first as a kind of ironic aside ("It gives me a pleasant sense of the goodness of creation") and then as more full-throated assertion of possibility, ultimately emerges. In "Reason to Believe" at the end of *Nebraska* in 1982, the first trace appears, but when the speaker acknowledges that "at the end of every hard earned day people find some reason to believe," he seems to speak in skeptical tones. To Dave Marsh in *Glory Days*, "Reason to Believe" "stared straight into the void . . . and found there exactly what was expected: nothing at all" (138). And yet five years later, on the 1987 release *Tunnel of Love*, the protagonist of "Cau-tious Man" sees his wife and home illuminated in "the beauty of God's fallen light," and in "Living Proof" on *Lucky Town* from 1992 a speaker who resembles Springsteen himself, on an album that's avowedly autobio-graphical, sees the birth of his son—almost in direct answer to the doubt of "Reason to Believe"—as tangible evidence of the divine. "Looking for a little bit of God's mercy," he declares, "I found living proof."

Indeed, increasingly over the last quarter-century, this spiritual voice is heard more powerfully and more frequently in Springsteen's songs. Among late works, for instance, it imbues the gospel tones of *The Rising* and is overtly manifest in "Jesus Was an Only Son" from *Devils & Dust* in 2005. Even Springsteen's commitment to social justice is voiced in the language of faith. In introducing "Across the Border" on the *Tom Joad* tour in 1996, Springsteen would regularly suggest that what seemed a political question of economic and social equity was in fact "a spiritual question."[2] "Are we all individual souls, and is there such a thing as independent salvation?" he asked in a performance in Dublin on 20 March 2006. "Can you really in the end just save yourself, or are we connected in some fashion? And do we sort of rise and fall—at least in spirit—as one?" ("Bruce's Ghost Stories"). In campaigning for Barack Obama in 2008, Springsteen again used a kind of language that united faith and politics: "Whatever grace God has decided to impart to us, it resides in our connection with one another, in honoring the life and the hopes and the dreams of the man or the woman up the street or across town. That's where we make our small claim upon heaven."[3]

Springsteen spoke openly about the source of this spiritual vocabulary in his introductions to "Jesus Was an Only Son" on the *Devils & Dust* tour in 2005. After recounting his Catholic upbringing as a child—living on a street in Freehold, New Jersey, that was bordered by a convent, a priests' rectory, and a Catholic church on the corner—Springsteen described his assimilation of the language of faith in terms that closely echoed Bakhtin's theory of how an individual experiences and assimilates the language of others. As Springsteen explained in Portland, Oregon, on 10 August 2005,

> [I]t was an interesting childhood, because it was filled with terror and mystery and poetry and power that was way beyond my understanding, but somehow you absorbed anyway. You absorbed it all. You know, the church with all its shadows and its brightness and the combination of ceremony—the constant ceremony we witnessed because we lived so close. It was an unusual upbringing.
>
> I look back into my songs, which are filled with so much religious imagery, and I guess, you know, that was the big deal. (quoted in "Catholicized")

Of course, when Springsteen recounts how he was continually exposed to the words and images of his faith in the physical and cultural landscape of his childhood he exemplifies Bakhtin's concept of language existing "on the borderline between oneself and the other." Yet even as he acknowledges how he absorbed such language, Springsteen also makes it his own. As a mature artist, he finds the "terror and mystery and poetry and power" of that language and assimilates it into the imagery of his songs and the vocabulary of his political convictions, separating it from doctrine and ritual. As Bakhtin might say, Springsteen "populates it with his own intention, his own accent . . . adapting it to his own semantic and expressive intention."

Ultimately, the way that Springsteen's spiritual voice gradually emerges in his work over decades parallels a process that is seen in *The Moviegoer* and in all of Percy's novels, in which a possibility of faith at last comes into view and consequently changes the protagonist's manner of expression and his relations to others. Over the course of *The Moviegoer*, particularly after a disastrous and mostly unsuccessful sexual encounter with his distant cousin and only confidante Kate Cutrer, Binx's various impostures—his efforts to act like the movie stars he sees on the screen, his presentation of himself as a contented suburbanite, the air of responsibility he sometimes manages to offer his aunt, even his quasi-scientific attempt to observe and record his own existential reality (what Binx calls his "search")—all collapse. In a bitter monologue afterwards, on his thirtieth birthday, he suddenly speaks in what is almost a religious voice. He refers to his life as "my own dark pilgrimage on this earth" and scourges himself for "knowing less than I ever knew before" (228). Stripped of all his well-worn masks, Binx sees a world transformed, so that the possibility and elusiveness of faith coalesce for him, moments later, in the image of a heavyset, well-dressed African American man outside a church on Ash Wednesday. Because of the man's skin color, Binx can't tell if there are ashes on his forehead, and his whole demeanor—"more respectable than respectable . . . more middle class than one could believe"—seems too worldly and stolid to genuinely embody faith (233). Yet Binx is now able to imagine that through "some dim dazzling trick of grace" even this man's most worldly actions are somehow touched also by what Binx calls "God's own importunate bonus" (235).

In trying to explain the process whereby his protagonists are able to finally perceive at least this possibility of faith, Percy in his essay "Diagnosing the Modern Malaise" cited another climactic moment in his fiction, near the end of his second novel *The Last Gentleman* from 1966, when its protagonist Will Barrett stands outside his childhood home in Mississippi where his father had taken his own life years before. As Will stands before the house remembering his father's actions, he studies the way the gnarled bark of an old oak tree has grown around an old iron hitching post nailed into the tree, and suddenly, in a kind of epiphany for Will, he's struck by the idea that his father, one of Percy's typical southern patricians, "was looking in the wrong place" for the sort of values and aesthetic experiences that would sustain him. For Will, some revelation that he can barely put into words is embodied in the "very curiousness and drollness and extraness of the iron and the bark" (319). This moment in the novel is fleeting and incomplete—Will doesn't yet fully understand what he's perceived—but as Percy explains in "Diagnosing the Modern Malaise," "in terms of traditional metaphysics, [Will] has caught a glimpse of the goodness and gratuitousness of created being" (221).

In Springsteen's work too, his characters' perceptions of the possibility of faith are experienced most fully in moments when they also "glimpse . . . the goodness and gratuitousness of created being." So, for instance, the father in "Living Proof" sees in the presence of his infant son "a little piece of the Lord's undying light," while even in a song as seemingly immersed in secular pleasures as "The Girls in Their Summer Clothes" on *Magic* the beautiful young women that the speaker admires and yearns for appear—not accidentally, I think—"on Blessing Avenue." Though "The Girls in Their Summer Clothes" is in many ways a song of earthly pleasures, its suggestion that the beauty of a summer evening is one of God's blessings evokes "the goodness and gratuity of created being"—as does, also, the lush orchestral production of the song itself.

Indeed, the realization of Springsteen's own "search for faith and meaning" is found not only in his lyric content but also in the sound of his music, particularly on later albums like *Magic* and *Working on a Dream*. In

a comment in St. Paul, Minnesota, on 10 May 2005, during the *Devils &
Dust* tour, Springsteen described the beautiful falsetto stylings of classic doo
wop singers as the sound of "supplication."[4] Springsteen used that term to
describe a surrender to earthly passion—"surrendering yourself," he said,
"giving yourself over totally"—and yet the word *supplication* is, of course,
freighted with religious connotations too, since prayer itself is one of the
most common forms of supplication. Though Springsteen's comments that
night were focused on the almost unearthly beauty of doo wop voices, it's
not hard to hear a similar kind of extravagance—another form of supplication, in effect—in the lush production of a song like "Girls in Their Summer
Clothes" with its layers of strings and voices. For all its range and power,
Springsteen's voice doesn't easily glide to the heights that classic doo-wop
singers reached, so a comparable form of supplication—what, after all, is
the speaker of "Girls in Their Summer Clothes" feeling, if not a sense of
"surrendering yourself, giving yourself over totally"?—is embodied in the
song's production. "The goodness and gratuitousness of created beauty"
that the speaker perceives in the sight of those girls "on Blessing Avenue" is
heard also in the supplicant sound of the song's pop symphony.

Ultimately, this same pop-inflected sound of supplication combines
with a lyric content that continually evokes issues of faith, transcendence,
and mortality to give *Working on a Dream* its fundamental unity. Although
Working on a Dream doesn't cohere as tightly as other albums—some of its
songs, including "Outlaw Pete" and the title track, the only songs played
with any regularity in concert, seem to fit more easily with the production
than the themes of the album—Springsteen's fifteenth collection of original songs is nevertheless a culminating moment in that "search for faith
and meaning" he'd spoken of seventeen years earlier in his letter to Walker
Percy's widow. Like the polyphony of voices and discourses that echoes in
Binx Bolling's consciousness in *The Moviegoer*, *Working on a Dream* is filled
with voices that yearn for, find, or turn away from "the goodness and gratuitousness of created being."

In many ways, in fact, the same incongruities of fate that Springsteen first
explored on *The River* are also present in *Working on a Dream*. Here, too,
some characters find joy and redemption while others, in keeping with the
vision Springsteen expressed in "The Price You Pay," are "fallen away" in
their struggles. Yet in *Working on a Dream* Springsteen's spiritual voice—
which is almost entirely absent from *The River*—frames the contrasting
fates of its characters as the workings of a complex and mysterious grace.
In "Life Itself," for instance, a dark ballad of illicit passion that is voiced by
a speaker overwhelmed by "the wine of love and destruction," the pull of
"the flowers of temptation" becomes literally a fall from grace in the song's
most devastating lines:

Why do the things that we treasure most, slip away in time
Till to the music we grow deaf, to God's beauty blind
Why do the things that connect us slowly pull us apart?
Till we fall away in our own darkness, a stranger to our own hearts

On an album haunted by mortality in songs like "Tomorrow Never Knows" and "The Last Carnival"—haunted specifically by the death of E Street Band keyboard player Danny Federici, to whom it's dedicated—some characters ultimately are touched by a kind of grace, like the speaker in "This Life," who is "blessed" by a soul-filling love in "this life and then the next," while other characters, like the howling blues voice of "Good Eye," revel in "earthly riches" or in their own willful illusions of grace, like the hapless, would-be lover of "Queen of the Supermarket."

Because, of course, that's what the speaker of "Queen of the Supermarket" really wants. Beyond whatever material or carnal desires he feels, he so desperately wants to achieve some kind of transcendence that he insists—with all the lush orchestration that the song's production can muster—that he's "lifted up" by a moment's glance at the checkout counter. And yet the sheer extravagance of the song's production and the speaker's patently ludicrous claim that "all you desire" can be found in the supermarket undermine his assertions of transcendence. We feel how much he *wants* to be "lifted up" by something even as we recognize the absurd frailty of the moment he tries to celebrate.

And this is why, in contrast to "Queen of the Supermarket," "Kingdom of Days"—arguably the album's most important song—resonates so powerfully. If the speaker of "Queen of the Supermarket" wants to believe he can be "lifted up" by a brief look from a woman he barely knows as he's paying for his groceries, then the long, loving observation of the speaker of "Kingdom of Days" offers a bracing contrast. For in "Kingdom of Days," "the goodness and gratuity of created being" is manifest in the way the speaker traces the passage of years by "the subtle change of light" on his lover's face. Though the song is rooted in an earthly love underscored by the intimations of mortality that are inscribed in "the wrinkles and grays" of the lovers' bodies, when the speaker says "I count my blessings that you're mine for always" he suggests that this enduring love is itself a sign of grace. And in contrast to the production of "Queen of the Supermarket," in which the sheer excess of the orchestration has an ironic effect, emphasizing the inflated quality of the speaker's pretensions, the way that the strings and guitars and layers of vocals rise to an ecstatic peak in the climax of "Kingdom of Days" sounds instead like a kind of genuine supplication.

At the end of Walker Percy's fifth novel, *The Second Coming*, a sequel to *The Last Gentleman* and the book that Percy called "my first unalienated novel" (*Conversations* 183), an older Will Barrett wonders about the young woman he's fallen in love with: "Is she a gift and therefore a sign of a giver?" (360). At this climactic moment in a novel that returns to and resolves many themes in Percy's fiction—the dark legacy of a suicidal father, the weight of Southern history, the fleeting and mostly artificial pleasures of late-twentieth-century consumerism—another signal characteristic of Percy's fiction is also manifest once more. As in each of his preceding novels, *The Second Coming* ends with his protagonist on the verge of an intimate relationship, a profound and life-changing dialogue; yet here, in the line quoted above, Percy makes explicit what is only implied in his previous works: that such powerful connections are themselves a form of God's grace. As he had written in an earlier philosophical essay, quoting from and then responding to Jean-Paul Sartre, "*L'enfer c'est autri*. But so is heaven" ("Symbol as Hermeneutic in Existentialism" 285).

Ultimately, this is the same heaven that some of Springsteen's characters experience, perhaps never more deeply and completely than in the earthly paradise of "Kingdom of Days." It is within such relationships, in fact, that Springsteen's own "search for faith and meaning" finds its object. In 1988, on the *Tunnel of Love* tour, Springsteen would regularly preface an acoustic version of "Born to Run" by talking about the insufficiency of escape as an end in itself. As he says in the video of the acoustic "Born to Run" on *The Complete Video Anthology/1978–2000*, "In the end, I guess, individual free-dom when it's not connected to some sort of community or friends or the world outside ends up feeling pretty meaningless." And though Springsteen in 1988 was just beginning—in songs like "Cautious Man"—to employ the sort of spiritual language that would emerge more fully in his work over the next twenty years, the vital importance of such connections has remained constant. Those deeply felt bonds with others, however difficult they may be to forge and to sustain, remain at the core of his political and moral vision and as the defining quality of whatever grace his characters might experience—as a gift perhaps and a sign of a giver, too, in Springsteen's own hard-won vision of "God's own importunate bonus."

NOTES

1. This comment was posted on the setlists page of the *Backstreets* website and can be heard on various bootleg recordings of the concert, including *Into the River We Dive* from the bootleg label Godfather Records. The significance of bootleg record-ings of live performances and unreleased tracks is a vexed question in any discus-sion of Springsteen's body of work. As a performer whose work regularly takes on new dimensions in concert and who is also notoriously selective in what he chooses to release, Springsteen is also the sort of artist whose official canon of released works offers only a partial view of his achievement. The ways that his songs are rearranged

or introduced in concert performances often lead to deeper or more revelatory experiences of Springsteen's work, experiences that are often only preserved in bootleg recordings. The best discussion of the value of bootleg recordings can be found in Robert Polito's excellent survey of Bob Dylan bootlegs—and the way those bootlegs offer an alternate vision of Dylan's achievement—in Polito's essay "Shadow Play: B-C-D and Back" in *Tin House* 3.2 (Winter 2002) and reprinted in *Studio A: The Bob Dylan Reader*. Ed. Benjamin Heidin. New York: Norton, 2004. 244–51.

2. This comment can be heard on a bootleg recording—specifically, the release *Brixton Night* from the bootleg label Crystal Cat—of a performance at Brixton Academy in London on 24 April 1996.

3. The text of Springsteen's speech for Barack Obama at a rally in Cleveland, Ohio, on 2 November 2008 was posted on the news page of the *Backstreets* website, www.backstreets.com.

4. These comments can be heard on a bootleg recording of this concert. With advances in technology, including easy ways to burn and distribute CDs and to post audience recordings of performances on the Internet, virtually any concert performance is almost immediately available to fans.

3

"The Flannery O'Connor of American Rock"

Irwin Streight

In a *Rolling Stone* interview in 1984, shortly after the release of *Born in the U.S.A.*, the album that propelled him to superstardom, Bruce Springsteen is asked about the influences on the songs for *Nebraska*, his first solo recording, and by all definitions a folk album, released in 1982. The album, he remarks, "kinda came out of the blue," but was influenced in part by seeing Terrence Malick's *Badlands*, a film about mass murderer Charles Starkweather and his girlfriend Caril Fugate, and reading a book about them. Moreover, in the intense months of writing the *Nebraska* songs, says Springsteen, "I was interested in writing kind of *smaller* than I had been, writing with just detail." And he connects a sudden transformation in his songwriting style at the time with "these stories I was reading by Flannery O'Connor," exclaiming to the interviewer, "she's just incredible" (Loder 156).

American writer Flannery O'Connor (1925–1964) was a Southerner and a Catholic who published two admired collections of short stories and two quirky novels, mostly set in her home state of Georgia. Her characters are drawn from Southern stereotypes of poor whites, sullen blacks, shiftless farmhands, steel magnolias, assorted rednecks, and, most memorably, the brand of fanatically religious hillbillies found in the Bible Belt. O'Connor's stories usually resolve with an act of violence that is meant to have a transforming effect on her usually stiff-necked or hard-headed central characters, whether or not they end up alive or dead—mostly the latter. She died at age thirty-nine of complications resulting from disseminated lupus, an immune-deficiency disease she inherited from her father, and from which she suffered for the whole of her brief writing life. Her posthumously published collected short fiction, *The Complete Stories*, won the National Book Award in 1971. Her short stories are celebrated as some of the finest examples of the

53

genre and have become standard fare in university literature courses. Music reviewers in the popular press and writers for *Rolling Stone* have noted on numerous occasions Springsteen's acknowledgment that reading O'Connor's fiction had an influence on his songwriting, particularly the songs on *Nebraska*. The influence, as Springsteen suggests, appears to be more on matters of form than on the thematic content of his songs. In a 1998 interview for *DoubleTake* magazine with Will Percy, nephew of novelist Walker Percy, Springsteen candidly recollects in detail how the reading of O'Connor's fiction influenced his craft as a songwriter. He tells Will Percy,

> I'd come out of a period of my own writing where I'd been writing big, sometimes operatic, and occasionally rhetorical things. I was interested in finding another way to write about those subjects, about people, another way to address what was going on around me and in the country—a more scaled down, more personal, more restrained way of getting some of my ideas across. So, right prior to the record *Nebraska*, I was deep into O'Connor. (38)

What Springsteen appears to have learned from O'Connor in his more "scaled down" and "restrained" narrative songs is how the materials of fiction—of character and incident—most effectively present the human and social truths that he wanted to write and sing about. Songwriting of this kind, he observes, "has a little in common with short-story writing in that it's character-driven. The characters [in my songs] are confronting the questions that everyone is trying to sort out for themselves . . . moral issues, [and] the way those issues rear their heads in the outside world" (*DoubleTake* 38). Both the mystery of our condition and the manner in which we respond to lived experience are as much the stuff of a popular song lyric as of literary fiction, Springsteen discovers.

From the outset of his songwriting, Springsteen has demonstrated a fiction writer's interest in developing characters and telling stories. He tells the *Rolling Stone* interviewer in 1984 that he has always been interested in doing "a *body* of work" rather than merely "collections of songs," and that beginning with *The Wild, the Innocent & the E Street Shuffle* he was "concerned about getting a group of characters and followin' them through their lives" (Loder 156). His albums, as he remarks about *The River*, offer a set of "song-stories" concerned with a set of characters (*Songs* 100). Indeed, in the preambles to each album's lyrics in *Songs*, Springsteen speaks less of themes and ideas and contextual social realities as impetus to his songwriting and more of his interest in developing characters. His intent as a songwriter, he says to Will Percy, has been "to establish a commonality by revealing our inner common humanity, by telling good stories about a lot of different kinds of people" (*DoubleTake* 40). His reading of Flannery O'Connor's fiction helped Springsteen to tell "good stories" in his songs—stories with an attention to small revealing details and with a depth and compression of characterization that matches the masters of the short story genre.

The Springsteen corpus presents a street-long parade of characters from a cross section of American society and from all corners of the country. As a songwriter he has imaginatively entered the skins of Jersey Shore street toughs, Mexican immigrants in Southern California, steel workers in Ohio, shrimp fishermen in the Texas Gulf, a young black boy growing up in the Bronx, middle-class, white-collar New Yorkers, drifters from the Midwest, single mothers, ex-cons, war vets, policemen, firemen, border patrolmen, a gay Philadelphia lawyer battling AIDS, a prisoner on death row. Springsteen has intentionally engaged in a project to encompass the complexity and diversity of American experience in his songs. As he tells Nicholas Dawidoff in a profile that appeared in the *New York Times Magazine* in 1997, "I had an interest in writing about the country—all of it. I was creating intimate portraits of individuals that you can draw back from and look at them in the context of the country they live in. You have to find circumstances where those characters resonate with psychological, emotional and, by implication, political issues" (259).

Springsteen's art of writing character-centered songs, rooted in place and circumstance, resonates strongly with O'Connor's theories of fiction. "Fiction," she writes, "is about everything human"; it is concerned with "all those concrete details of life that make actual our position on earth" (*Mystery* 68). Borrowing a pair of terms from Henry James, she delineates the two essential qualities that make for effective storytelling: "One is the sense of mystery and the other is the sense of manners" (*Mystery* 103). Manners we get from the social conditions in which we are born; mystery for O'Connor, who like Springsteen is a "born Catholic" (*Habit* 114), is bound up in human personality, in a sacramental vision of ourselves and others, in the moral choices we make and what determines those choices. Springsteen, like O'Connor, engages in exploring what she calls "the mystery of personality" (*Mystery* 90). He explains to Will Percy, "In most of the recent songs, I tell violent stories quietly. You're hearing characters' thoughts— what they are thinking after all the events that have shaped their situation have transpired. So I try to get that internal sound, like that feeling at night when you're in bed and staring at the ceiling, reflective in some fashion" (38). Like the writer of fiction, Springsteen taps into those gifts of imagination and spirit and language to create living characters in his songs. Invoking a truism among writers of good fiction, he remarks, "Basically, I find the characters and listen to them. That always leads to a series of questions about their behaviour: What would they do? What would they never do? You try to locate the rhythm of their speech and the nature of their expression" (*Songs* 274).

As a writer of fiction, O'Connor was most gratified by a review of her first collection of short fiction, *A Good Man Is Hard to Find* (1954), in the *New York Times* in which the esteemed critic Orville Prescott remarked of her characters, "these people live" (Prescott 23). Springsteen, too, has brought memorable characters to life in the brief space of a song lyric: Joe Roberts, the conflicted patrolman in *Nebraska*'s "Highway Patrolman" (the first character in Springsteen's lyrics with both a first and last name); Bill Horton, the "Cautious Man" in *Tunnel of Love*; Rainey Williams, the black boy from the Bronx who escapes his dysfunctional life in "Black Cowboys" on *Devils & Dust*; and most recently, the wounded narrator of "The Wrestler," the movie theme and bonus track on *Working on a Dream*. All of these characters come fully alive in Springsteen's songs because as an artist he has seen them and knows them well and has given them believable fictional form and substance. "The poet's job is to know the soul," he says to Will Percy, quoting Walt Whitman. "You strive for that, assist your audience in finding and knowing theirs. That's always at the core of what you're writing, of what drives your music" (39).

"A MEANNESS IN THIS WORLD"

O'Connor says regarding her own stories that they are "about people who are poor, who are afflicted in both mind and body, who have little—or at best a distorted—sense of spiritual purpose, and whose actions do not apparently give the reader a great assurance of the joy of life" (*Mystery* 32). Her fictional band of misfits, of displaced, deluded, and ultimately desperate "good country people" are not unlike the "characters out on the edge" (*Songs* 138) that we meet in the world of Springsteen's *Nebraska* songs. As does O'Connor in her short fiction, in the *Nebraska* songs Springsteen explores the darkness on the edge of human doings, our potential for violence and evil that may or may not have a redemptive end. The *Nebraska* characters appear unrelentingly caught in deep existential crises, facing the stark awareness that their lives are devoid of meaning, and desperate, as is the narrator of "State Trooper," to be delivered "from nowhere." In his prefatory notes to the *Nebraska* lyrics in *Songs*, Springsteen reflects on the ideas and sensibilities behind his songwriting at the time: "If there's a theme that runs through the record, it's the thin line between stability and that moment when time stops and everything goes to black, when the things that connect you to your world—your job, your family, friends, your faith, the love and grace in your heart—fail you." In a finishing comment that seems informed with one of O'Connor's central images, Springsteen declares, "I wanted the *blood* on [the recording] to feel destined and fateful" [my emphasis] (*Songs* 138–39). Moreover, the *Nebraska* songs present a cast of O'Connoresque characters, leading lives of sometimes quiet, sometimes vocal desperation, and introduce a new breed of characters into Springsteen's songs.

According to his biographer, Dave Marsh, Springsteen began reading O'Connor's short fiction at the urging of his newly acquired manager and cultural tutor, Jon Landau, and gained further insight into O'Connor's vision by viewing John Huston's film adaptation of her first novel, *Wise Blood*. Marsh reports that Springsteen was especially impressed by the "minute precision" of O'Connor's fiction, "the way O'Connor could enliven a character by sketching in just a few details." To this point in Springsteen's rise in the world of rock and roll music, he had felt that his songwriting had been "too vague, too dreamlike" (*Glory* 97). He had built his reputation as a writer of rambling song narratives such as "Spirit in the Night," "Thunder Road," and "Jungleland"—songs that Springsteen says are largely "emotionally autobiographical" if not actually so (*Songs* 69). Marsh reports that he wanted to write songs that were more detailed and concrete, away from the "clash and babble of metaphor" that often informed the song lyrics of his earlier albums (*Glory* 94). Springsteen states in the preamble to the *Nebraska* lyrics in *Songs* that he was reading O'Connor's stories "just before recording *Nebraska*." Reflecting on the transformation in his songwriting style at the time, Springsteen comments in a 1992 interview, "I wanted to have my own vision and point of view and create a world of characters, which is what the writers I admired did" (quoted in Larry Smith 152).

Critical commentary on the title song "Nebraska" invariably remarks on the influence of Terrence Malick's 1974 film *Badlands*, which gives a fictionalized account of serial killer Charles Starkweather and his girlfriend Caril Fugate, who in 1958 went on a killing spree from Lincoln, Nebraska, to eastern Wyoming, senselessly murdering ten people in eight days, including Fugate's parents and infant sister. After viewing Malick's film, Springsteen was interested enough in the details of the story to call author/broadcaster Ninette Beaver, who had written about the murderers in a biography titled *Caril* (*Glory* 97–98). His song, originally titled "Starkweather," presents a monologue by the serial killer as he faces execution by electric chair. Those familiar with O'Connor's fiction will as well find unmistakable evidence of her influence in the content of the song. In fact, the title song of the album both quotes from and echoes a theme of the title story from O'Connor's first collection—her most widely anthologized work, "A Good Man Is Hard to Find." And there are other ways in which O'Connor's fiction and vision left its mark on Springsteen's unusual first collection of *folk* songs.

Devoid of conscience and of any sense of remorse, the narrator of "Nebraska" remarks coldly, matter-of-factly of the string of murders he has committed, "I killed everything in my path." In a briefly dramatized moment of confession with a sheriff before he is executed, he remains unrepentant: "I can't say that I'm sorry for the things that we done / At least for a little while, sir, me and her we had us some fun." Springsteen's imagined monologue draws some of its details from Beaver's biography: a noted criminal psychologist who interviewed the real-life Starkweather remarked that to a paranormal degree he showed "no sign of true remorse" for his murders (Beaver 199). The listener familiar with O'Connor's story might recognize here the words of Bobby Lee, the accomplice to her escaped convict character The Misfit, who after senselessly shooting five members of a family, including an infant, remarks, "Some fun!" to which The Misfit, in the last line of the story, replies tellingly, "It's no real pleasure in life" (*Complete* 133).

Like O'Connor's The Misfit, Springsteen's killer is a man who feels himself "unfit" for human society. A jury has found him guilty and he is sentenced to death. And like O'Connor's character, he appears to be remarkably unaware of the nature of his transgressions. Moments before he shoots the garrulous grandmother in the story, the last family member alive, The Misfit remarks of his time in prison, unmindful of the offense that sent him there, "I set there and set there, trying to remember what it was I done and I ain't recalled it to this day" (*Complete* 130). Failing to find any meaningful reason for being or believing, he states his credo with a snarl, "No pleasure but meanness" (*Complete* 132). Springsteen's Starkweather character likewise remarks unwittingly about his impulse to murder, "They wanted to know why I did what I did / Well, sir, I guess there's just a meanness in this world."

A tag word from O'Connor's story, *meanness* here comes to denote for Springsteen—as well as for O'Connor's The Misfit—a response to a world that has lost meaning. O'Connor's understanding of the source of this *meanness* appears to have attracted Springsteen to her stories and influenced his own exploration of this theme in his songwriting. In the interview with Will Percy, Springsteen locates the strain of meanness in his characters in his reading of O'Connor prior to writing the songs for *Nebraska*. He explains to Will Percy,

> There was something in those stories of hers that I felt captured a certain part of the American character that I was interested in writing about. They were a big, big revelation. She got to the heart of some part of meanness that she never spelled out, because if she spelled it out you wouldn't be getting it. It was always at the core of every one of her stories—the way she left that hole there, that hole that's inside of everybody. There was some dark thing—a component of spirituality—that I sensed in her stories, and that set me off exploring characters of my own. (37)

A meanness born out of a sense of meaninglessness informs the haunting sixth song on the *Nebraska* recording, "State Trooper," whose narrator appears either to have committed some heinous deed or is about to, and is driving late at night along the New Jersey Turnpike. In the song's refrain, he pleads with an invisible state trooper, "Please don't stop me." In this song as well, Springsteen appears to quote O'Connor. This is the bleakest, most menacing song on the album, and bears overtones from a memorable scene in O'Connor's first novel, *Wise Blood.* Here is Springsteen's lyric:

> New Jersey Turnpike, ridin' on a wet night
> 'Neath the refinery's glow out where the great black rivers flow
> License, registration, I ain't got none
> But I got a clear conscience 'bout the things that I done
> Mister state trooper, please don't stop me.

The narrator's imagined reply, "I ain't got none" to a request to see his license and registration from a yet-to-be encountered state trooper, echoes the response of O'Connor's Christ-haunted street preacher protagonist Hazel Motes to the highway patrolman who stops him in chapter 13 of *Wise Blood.* Asked "Where's your license?" Hazel eventually responds, "Well I ain't got one" (208). Like Hazel at this point in O'Connor's novel, who has just killed a man by mercilessly running him down with his car, Springsteen's character is on a desperate drive, his own mind, to quote a telling adjective in the song's third stanza, getting "hazy" as he tries to make sense of the many voices coming at him as he twists the dial of the car radio through the early morning "talk show stations." The song concludes with this lone, ranging narrator's desperate last prayer, "Hi ho silver-o deliver me from nowhere." Here again an image of Hazel Motes is perhaps invoked: "Was you going anywheres?" O'Connor's patrolman asks an anxious Hazel, after having pushed his "rat-colored" car over an embankment. "No," Hazel replies (*Wise* 208).

As in O'Connor's fiction, there is an undercurrent of violence in many of Springsteen's song narratives. He remarks in the *DoubleTake* interview with Will Percy that his songs "tell violent stories quietly" (38). This is especially so in the songs on his trio of folk-inspired recordings: *Nebraska, The Ghost of Tom Joad,* and *Devils & Dust.* These three recordings form a distinctive subset within Springsteen's corpus, and, it might be argued, present his most authentic voice and vision as a songwriter. Like O'Connor's The Misfit, Springsteen's violent characters act out of a meanness born of meaninglessness. They have lost hope, and deny any possibilities of transcendence—of personal, social, or existential condition. In their quietly violent stories, O'Connor and Springsteen attest to a common understanding of evil as it is played out in the lives of individuals who, as O'Connor expressed, are driven to the extremes of their own natures, and ultimately to acts of violence (*Mystery* 113).

For O'Connor, violence is usually a means of alerting or converting her characters to the big "R" Reality of her Catholic worldview. In reflections on the art of story writing collected as "On Her Own Work" in *Mystery and Manners*, she remarks, "I have found that violence is strangely capable of returning my characters to reality and preparing them to accept their moment of grace" (112). Similarly, Springsteen remarks that the violent circumstances and impulses of his characters allow for a degree of intimacy and insight that "[takes] you inside yourself and then back out into the world" (*DoubleTake* 38). As with O'Connor's stories, the quiet strain of violence in Springsteen's songs probes at the reality of the evils that manifest themselves in desperate human hearts and in the territory of contemporary America.

Set against the economic recession in America in the early 1980s, the *Nebraska* songs, to some degree, acknowledge that dire socioeconomic realities underlie the impulse toward acts of violence. Both the speakers of "Atlantic City" and "Johnny 99" are out of work and remark similarly, "I got debts that no honest man can (could) pay." The unnamed narrator of "Atlantic City," who appears to have agreed to a contract as a hired killer, explains, "I been lookin' for a job but it's hard to find," and in his concluding remark, tells his lover and would-be accomplice, "I'm tired of comin' out on the losin' end / So honey last night I met this guy and I'm gonna do a little favor for him." Similarly, out of work after an auto plant closes down, and in despair, Ralph in "Johnny 99" gets raging drunk one evening and shoots a hotel night clerk. In his statement before the judge he initially defends himself as a desperate man, deeply in debt: "The bank was holding my mortgage and they was takin' my house away" he pleads. But, he confesses, "it was more 'n all this that put that gun in my hand."

Springsteen's probing of the heart of darkness in modern American society is concerned with the "more" that motivates acts of violence. Like O'Connor, he presents the impulse to do evil—in signature acts of violence—as something more than simply a socialized behavior or, in O'Connor's words, "this or that psychological tendency" (*Habit* 360). As Jim Cullen observes, Springsteen's *Nebraska* songs are largely concerned with "the problem—the nature—of evil." Cullen concludes, "Springsteen posits evil as a force that defies demographic specificity or rational explanation" (*Born* 173). Indeed, in Springsteen's song stories, a character's impulse to do evil is often a mystery to him. An unmotivated urge scratches at his consciousness, and he tries in some way to explain his dark desires. (Springsteen's violent characters are always male; not so for O'Connor, whose stories feature a number of women who commit acts of violence. In two of these stories, these violent acts lead to the death of another character.[1])

The litany of violence, reported and implied, in Springsteen's songs matches the variety of violent acts in O'Connor's two story collections, where, along with the cold-blooded murder of the grandmother and family on the way to Florida in "A Good Man Is Hard to Find," her characters meet with violent ends inventive enough to satisfy Quentin Tarantino. The violence in O'Connor's fiction is less quiet at times than that in Springsteen's songs—she describes violent acts; Springsteen's narrators mostly report them—but both writers intend that the violence in their work be unquieting to a similar end. For Springsteen, like O'Connor, violence is not an end in itself but a means toward some form of revelation: about the depth of "meanness" the human spirit is capable of; about the desperate conditions of individuals who, to quote Springsteen, feel "alienated from their friends and their community and their government and their jobs," and ultimately, from a sense of their own purpose. In a *Rolling Stone* interview shortly after the release of *Nebraska*, Springsteen remarks of his characters as emblematic of a kind of malaise in America: "I think you can get to a point where nihilism, if that's the right word, is overwhelming, and the basic laws that society has set up—either religious or social laws—become meaningless. Things become really dark. You lose those constraints, and then anything goes" (Loder 156). In the *Nebraska* songs, Springsteen explores the mystery of evil as incarnated in characters driven to commit acts of violence. Like the fiction writer, Springsteen is intent in these songs on drawing the listener into the hearts and minds of his characters: "I wanted to let the listener hear the characters think," he remarks in notes to his published song lyrics, "to get inside their heads, so you could hear and feel their thoughts, their choices" (*Songs* 138).

Whereas songs on *The River* and *Born in the U.S.A.* present characters who look for deliverance from their sense of isolation and despair by jumping into a fast car or into the arms of a woman, Springsteen angles at another possible resolution to a search for meaning in the closing song of the *Nebraska* album. Perhaps invoking one of the inspirations for the song, Marsh comments that the images in "Reason to Believe" "are as bizarre as anything in *Wise Blood*" (*Glory* 137). Marsh reads this and the rest of the songs on the recording as offering revelations of utmost despair, as Springsteen staring "straight into the void" of human meaning and purpose and finding "nothing at all" (*Glory* 138). But there is another more positive and equally compelling reading of the album's arcing themes and images. Redemption strains to be known in every song, even in Starkweather's uncertain explanation for his propensity to do evil. As well, the narrator of "Atlantic City" may be seen to hold out hope for redeeming a life gone wrong through reincarnation. That "mansion on the hill" in the old-time gospel parlance of O'Connor's Bible Belt characters symbolically suggests a child's hope of heaven, with its perpetual light and "music playin', people laughin' all the time." The child narrator of "Used Cars" vows to redeem the ignobility of his socioeconomics. And, of course, redemption rules the heart of patrolman Joe Roberts, who takes his foot off the accelerator of the law and graces his brother, allowing him to escape the consequences of his crime.

Everyone in these songs, however despairing, is looking for deliverance of some sort. "Reason to Believe" offers in answer to the unanswerable "Lord won't you tell us" the mystery of faith that both O'Connor and Springsteen hold on to and hold out in their works. This final song in the *Nebraska* cycle seeks to resolve the litanies of meanness, desperation, hopelessness, and longing recounted in the preceding stories, and to resolve them in a decidedly O'Connoresque fashion.

Each verse of "Reason to Believe" presents a scene of expectation. And the expected event or action has a decidedly theological, even eschatological turn. Here is the third verse, which presents the O'Connoresque image of a child baptized in a river:

> Take a baby to the river, Kyle William they called him
> Wash the baby in the water, take away little Kyle's sin
> In a whitewash shotgun shack an old man passes away
> Take the body to the graveyard and over him they pray
> Lord won't you tell us, tell us what does it mean
> At the end of every hard-earned day you can find some reason to believe

In verse one the narrator regards a man poking a dead dog lying in a highway ditch, seemingly expectant that it will come back to life. The abandoned woman in verse two waits at the end of a dirt road for her prodigal lover, young Johnny, "to come back." Catholic mysteries of sin, baptism, and the life ever after are all invoked in the third verse. The song concludes with a picture of a groom standing waiting for his bride, even after all the congregation is gone—the classic image in Christian eschatology for the expectation of Christ's return to claim *His* bride, the Church. Tellingly, Springsteen at one point considered titling the album *Reason to Believe*, which would certainly have put a more hopeful, less despairing edge on this collection of songs (*Glory* 138).

Springsteen surely pays homage to O'Connor in a song that shares a title with her most widely read story. His ballad "A Good Man Is Hard to Find (Pittsburg)" was recorded four months after the *Nebraska* collection but remained unknown until it appeared on *Tracks* (1999), a collection of previously unreleased songs. Springsteen's "A Good Man Is Hard to Find" tells the story of a love-shorn woman who has lost her soldier husband in the Vietnam War. Though the details of the story do not accord with O'Connor's life, the image of a lone woman who "sits by the light of her Christmas tree / With the radio softly on / Thinkin' how a good man is hard to find" is strikingly resonant for those familiar with O'Connor's rather isolated life and aware of the popular song by Bessie Smith from which she took her story's title. Springsteen's song joins with O'Connor's story and perhaps with O'Connor herself in the second verse, in which he says of his character, "She's gonna have to tell about the meanness in this world

/ And how a good man is so hard to find." The visionary art of O'Connor and Springsteen bears similar witness to the violence and spiritual torment that mark the lives of those who give themselves over to this "meanness."

"INCARNATIONAL ART"

Springsteen's talents for what O'Connor calls the "incarnational art" (*Mystery* 68) of storytelling find their apotheosis in the songs he wrote for *The Ghost of Tom Joad* (1995) and in the subsequent tour as a solo performer. This second collection of folk songs offers, like *Nebraska*, a set of character studies of individuals whose lives are marked by violent incidents and impulses. As with the *Nebraska* songs, these recordings have minimal instrumentation and few overdubs: seven of the eleven songs feature only the Boss playing his acoustic guitar with whisperings of synthesizer. Like the *Nebraska* songs, the raw, stripped-down tracks are as Springsteen himself first recorded them, without a backing band in mind or in a final mix. The "uncomplicated" melodies, the "simplicity and plainness, the austere rhythms" of the songs, he states, help to foreground the consciousness of the characters whose stories he tells (*Songs* 274). As the tour following the release of the album would enforce, Springsteen was aiming at something new in both his writing and delivery of a song, more "precision" in his storytelling and to create characters who would come to life for the listener. His challenge was that of the story writer or novelist: to get his characters right—to make them believable, credible, and complete in the brief song scene in which they appear. "The correct detail can speak volumes about who your character is," he writes, "while the wrong one can shred the credibility of your story." But, he adds, "all the telling detail in the world doesn't matter if the song lacks an emotional center. That's something you have to pull out of yourself from the commonality you feel with the man or woman you're writing about. By pulling these elements together as well as you can, you shed light on their lives and respect their experiences" (*Songs* 274).

As a Jersey Shore boy writing about lives in Southern California, Ohio, and the Texas Gulf, Springsteen is aware that he lacks the dirt on his boots and under his nails to know the people and places as his own, regardless of his youthful travels to visit his parents, who relocated—without Bruce—to Stockton, California, in 1969 when he was nineteen. He admits that for each social setting it "took a good amount of research to get the details of the region correct" (*Songs* 276). As the album title suggests, the songs are inspired in part by John Steinbeck's classic novel, *The Grapes of Wrath* (1939): for Springsteen, a compelling first impression of the story came from watching John Ford's film adaptation, and later from reading the novel itself. Uncharacteristically, on the back page of the lyrics booklet that accompanies the *Joad* CD, the song-writer-as-researcher acknowledges two books on the Mexican migrant experience and two editorials in the *Los Angeles Times* that informed his vision and lyric content. Like a writer of a work of historical fiction, Springsteen informs his listeners that he has done his research in order to get the details of the region and its people correct. Marsh notes, for example, that before performing "Youngstown" Springsteen would often elaborate to the audience on the book that inspired the song, *Journey to Nowhere*, written by Dale Maharidge with photographs by Michael Williamson. While Springsteen takes pains to ensure that the historical and sociological details of his songs are accurate and current, nonetheless the *Joad* songs are contemporary retellings of "the old stories of race and exclusion" as played out in the present-day lives of Mexican migrants, poor whites, and factory workers, and reiterate familiar themes throughout his corpus. Songs such as "Sinaloa Cowboys," "The Line," "Balboa Park," and "Across the Border" remarks Springsteen, "[trace] the lineage of my earlier characters to the Mexican migrant experience in the New West" (*Songs* 276). The *Tom Joad* songs are remarkable for the way in which Springsteen climbs inside the skin of his character narrators, his efforts to give the song over. His artistic challenge as a writer was to create song narratives in which, as he says, "your voice disappears into the voices of those you've chosen to write about" (*Songs* 274).

More than ten years after recording the *Nebraska* songs, Springsteen picks up the O'Connoresque themes he explored on his first acoustic album: the mystery of "meanness" in the human heart, and the violence and alienation that results. And like *Nebraska*, this song cycle ultimately, and deliberately, offers a concluding glimmer that "a tenuous peace and hope may exist" (*Songs* 276). Apart from the title song, in the *Tom Joad* recordings Springsteen as storyteller again lets his violence-driven characters speak for themselves, his own voice, as he intends, disappearing into their voices in a series of what are mostly musical dramatic monologues. The ex-prisoner Charlie in "Straight Time," who has found a job at a meatpacking plant, and has been walking the "clean and narrow" for eight years, still can "feel the itch" to commit a violent crime. Though Charlie has a nowhere job, he has a smiling wife and young children who bring him happiness and an appearance of outward stability. He is making a life, but reflects, "Seems you can't get any more than half free." In the song's refrain he forewarns the listener, "Got a cold mind to go tripping 'cross that thin line / I'm sick of doin' straight time." The song's last stanza offers a vignette of Charlie in his basement sawing off the barrel of a gun, obviously to conceal it for use in an armed assault of some kind. In the last lines of the lyric he returns after apparently committing a violent crime. He is stained with the sin of his deed: "Can't get the smell from my hands," he says as he contemplates a fugitive future.

"Straight Time" is followed on the *Joad* recording by the more graphi-
cally violent "Highway 29," another story of the mystery of evil in the human heart: how a shoe store clerk becomes a murderous bank robber after
a night of illicit sex with a seductive customer. "Highway 29" is a simple
ballad with a seesaw melody, played gently on an acoustic guitar as a song
of lament. The action and emotion in the lyrics are undercut by the lack
of any dynamics in Springsteen's matter-of-fact delivery of the song. Here,
the narrator of the song reflects on his violent crime and probes his inner
compulsions:

> It was a small-town bank, it was a mess
> Well I had a gun, you know the rest
> Money on the floorboards, shirt was covered in blood
> And she was cryin', her and me we headed south
> On Highway 29
> . . . .
> I told myself it was something in her
> But as we drove I knew it was something in me
> Something that'd been comin' for a long, long time
> And something that was here with me now
> On Highway 29.

That repeated and inexplicable "something" in Springsteen's unnamed
character is an impulse to do evil. This same impulse, a murderous meanness, in O'Connor's character The Misfit is a response to a life that is "off
balance" because it lacks the stabilizing hope of salvation from sin, offered
by faith in the Christ of the Christian gospel. Springsteen's characters,
though, do not appear to come to an awareness of their need for grace, as
do most of O'Connor's characters, however imperceptively. Nonetheless,
they respond similarly to often violent epiphanies. Like young Tarwater, the
reluctant prophet character in O'Connor's novel *The Violent Bear It Away*,
after transgressing against his great uncle's burial wishes, O. E. Parker after
his epiphany with the tattooed carnival artiste in her short story "Parker's
Back," or Mr. Shiftlet as he abandons the "angel of Gawd" and speeds
ahead of a thundercloud on his way to Mobile in "The Life You Save May
Be Your Own," Springsteen's characters mostly choose to escape after the
violent shock that has altered their consciousness. Charlie ("Straight Time")
imagines "driftin' off into foreign lands," the fugitive pair in "Highway 29"
are trying to outrun the law by fleeing to the Sierra Madres in Mexico, and
the ex-military man Carl in "The Line" leaves his job with the border patrol
to drift through the migrant towns of Southern California in search of a
Mexican woman he has helped flee across the border.

The litany of violence and destruction in the *Tom Joad* songs culminates
in the story told by the narrator of "The New Timer" about the meaning-

less murder of Frank, an old hobo found "shot dead outside of Stockton / His body lyin' on a muddy hill / Nothin' taken, nothin' stolen," the victim of "Somebody killin' just to kill." This is a desolate song, resolving on the idea that violence begets violence in a desperate cycle. No grace or mercy is possible for the narrator, who desires only "one good rifle / And the name of who I ought to kill." But Springsteen cannot leave his record here. As in the hope-filled "Reason to Believe" that closes out the despair-ridden song narratives in *Nebraska*, Springsteen records that he felt compelled as a writer to transcend the themes of "death and personal destruction" as he resolved the *Joad* song cycle (*Songs* 276). He does not angle at a theologically redemptive use of violence, as does O'Connor in her fiction; rather, in contrast, he concludes with the idea that redemption is attainable only when violence is resisted.

Before he began work on "Galveston Bay," Springsteen had already written the track that precedes it on the recording, "Across the Border." The narrator of this song is a Mexican male about to make an illegal border crossing with his lover in order to escape "the pain and sadness" of their lives and make a new life together in the promised land of America, with its idealized "pastures of gold and green." The song, says Springsteen, "is like a prayer or dream" about finding a place where "love will be rewarded" and "faith restored" and where "peace and hope may exist" (*Songs* 276). It is also a prologue of sorts to the final song in the *Joad* cycle.[2]

"Galveston Bay" presents two parallel stories, beginning with Le Bin Son, once a South Vietnamese soldier who fought beside the Americans in the Vietnam War. After the war, he comes to settle in "the promised land" along the Texas Gulf, and with his cousin eventually buys a shrimp boat and works the waters of Galveston Bay. Texan Billy Sutter fought in the same war and was wounded and shipped home. He, too, works the fishing grounds in the Gulf of Mexico, with a sense of entitlement, "In a boat that'd been his father's." As more refugees from Southeast Asia move into the communities along the coast, "the old stories of race and exclusion" begin to play out. There is "talk / Of America for Americans" and a clandestine attempt to "burn the Vietnamese boats into the sea," which ends with two Texans shot dead as Le justifiably defends himself.

Springsteen comments that the first version of "Galveston Bay" had a decidedly violent ending, which ultimately felt "false." He felt the need instead to offer "some small window of light" at the close of the *Tom Joad* song cycle, some possibility of redemption, of transcendence, through an act of the will (*Songs* 276). Billy Sutter, as Springsteen notes in his commentary in *Songs*, "is a character who is driven to do the wrong thing, but does not. He instinctively refuses to add to the violence in the world around him." Ready to commit murder out of revenge and hatred, to stick a knife into Le Bin Son, at the last moment, "with great difficulty, and against his own grain. . . . He finds the strength and grace to save himself and the part of the world he touches" and puts the weapon away (277).

"For the serious writer," says O'Connor, "violence is never an end in itself." And she adds in the next sentence, "It is the extreme situation that best reveals who we are essentially" (*Mystery* 113). Like O'Connor, Springsteen is interested in exploring artistically the responses of characters who are brought to extremes. In most cases, for both writers, their characters are either subject to or turn toward acts of violence. But, as O'Connor writes, in the best stories, those with eyes to see can often discern "the almost imperceptible intrusions of grace" (*Mystery* 112). In staying the hand of Billy Sutter in "Galveston Bay," Springsteen shows us such a moment.

Springsteen did not embark on a tour following the release of *Nebraska*. He was already at work on *Born in the U.S.A.*, having recorded versions of the title song and "Downbound Train" on the same homemade cassette that contained the *Nebraska* songs. With the *Tom Joad* songs, however, he chose to venture into new territory as a performer: to tour as a solo act. Dave Marsh, Springsteen's long-laboring biographer, observes that following the release of the *Nebraska* songs, Bruce would often perform two or three solo spots in a concert, or with one or two of the band members, but never more than two solo songs at a time, since he was sure to lose the attention of large stadium audiences. Despite the fact that he won his first recording contract as a solo act, performing alone was not his strong suit, Marsh observes. He describes an untypical Springsteen in a typical concert on the *Joad* tour in his coffee-table book, *Bruce Springsteen On Tour: 1968–2005* (2006): "The *Joad* shows opened on a virtually bare stage, Bruce alone before the microphone, holding an (amplified) acoustic guitar and wearing a harmonica in its holder around his neck. . . . This wasn't the prisoner of rock and roll. This was somebody else" (217). That somebody else was Springsteen the storyteller; this was indeed, as Marsh aptly describes, "song as story, bare to its bones" (*Tour* 217). Aware that the *Joad* songs would not attract the large core of rockers in his community of listeners, Springsteen nonetheless felt that these songs represented the best of his songwriting art to this point and also spoke of "the things [he] tried to stand for and be about as a songwriter" (*Songs* 277). And he wanted these songs to be heard and appreciated. On this tour, the Boss became the boss of his audience as well, instructing his listeners on one occasion with this patter:

> This is where I give my little speech, you know, trying to get the audience to be quiet. I don't think it is necessary, but just in case, I just wanna say singing and clapping along tonight will be viewed as a psychotic event by the people sitting around you. And it is a community event, so if somebody around you's making too much noise, please feel free to band together and politely and constructively ask them to shut the fuck up." (*Tour* 217)

Why did it matter so much to Springsteen that the audience sit in rapt silence during his one-man acoustic performances of the *Tom Joad* songs? Marsh, who evidently prefers to see Bruce the rocker, assesses his motivations for the *Joad* shows as an effort to affirm the significance of his music and of himself as a songwriter. He remarks, "The *Joad* tour was a singular rock star's way of trying . . . to make sure his music still mattered and that his self remained an honest version of the one he'd set out to create" (*Tour* 223). Contrarily, it might be argued that Springsteen's motivations were primarily artistic. He wanted to stretch his story-telling art, to discover more deeply its affective power, its ability to effect a change of heart and mind in his listeners. As O'Connor would say, he was interested in exploring mystery through manners—in music. "Music is important in formulating characters. . . . You set a certain rhythm of the man you're singing about," Marsh quotes Springsteen in regard to the *Joad* songs. This new emphasis on creating vivid characters in his songs, Springsteen adds, "is more like screen writing or short-story writing" (*Tour* 220). And so one might best conclude that the *Joad* tour brought to the fore Springsteen the writer of short stories—the mature songwriter had become like the writers he admired, creating a world of characters and with a vision of his own.

"INTERNAL LANDSCAPE"

As a storyteller, Springsteen shares with O'Connor a vision informed by his Catholic faith and upbringing. Springsteen's Catholic upbringing, including the many abuses he suffered in parochial school and in a brief stint as an altar boy, has been the subject of some of the stories he tells from the stage, and is described at length in Marsh's early biography, *Glory Days* (1981). While his faith is not specifically foregrounded in his songs, nonetheless, like O'Connor, Springsteen's way of seeing is pervasively filtered through the lens of Catholic doctrine and belief. As Jim Cullen observes in *Born in the U.S.A.: Bruce Springsteen and the American Tradition* (2005), "At the core of Springsteen's Catholicism is an 'analogical imagination' . . . a distinctively Catholic way of understanding the world" (161). Cullen remarks that Springsteen's Catholicism is "never far from the surface" of his songs (*Born* 165), and though he is certainly "no one's idea of a saint" (*Born* 189), no other contemporary popular American songwriter has a corpus so grounded in a religious sensibility or so pervaded with the language of the Christian faith. Springsteen freely describes the human condition and individual human realities in language that conveys the traditional doctrines and dogmas of the Church. He sings about religious realities of temptation, guilt, forgiveness, mystery, baptism, regeneration, the struggle of belief, his songwriting lexicon replete with a host of religious terms, most prevalently (and perhaps

Catholically), the words *faith* and *prayer* (*Songs* 9–329). A consciousness of wrongdoing and redemption, of the intrusion of divine mercy and grace, a holding on to and holding out for faith—these themes can be found in Springsteen's music from his early "It's Hard to Be a Saint in the City" (1973) to the gospel anthems on *The Rising* (2002) and the more explicit expressions of his Catholic faith on *Devils & Dust* (2005) and sacramental vision on *Working on a Dream* (2009).

As a born Catholic, Springsteen shares with O'Connor a set of theological assumptions about human nature, about what O'Connor refers to in one of her essays as "the general mystery of incompleteness," by which she means our separation from God (*Mystery* 167). As George Yamin demonstrates persuasively in his 1990 essay "The Theology of Bruce Springsteen," Springsteen's "message . . . is primarily a theological one." And his song narratives are often concerned with recasting, and to some extent reinterpreting, "the Judeo-Christian story of salvation history" (6). Springsteen's lyrics are often infused with biblical language and allusions and often subtle but occasionally explicit expressions of Christian doctrine. He is not afraid to use the word *sin*, for example, which appears more than half a dozen times in his lyrics, and most frequently denotes the theological notion of *original sin* rather than the decidedly venial sins that many of his characters are given to. Significantly, the word is often used in concert with the act of, or reference to, baptism. Baby Kyle William is baptized in a river in the third stanza of *Nebraska*'s closing song "Reason to Believe" in order to "take away little Kyle's sin." The doctrine of original sin is the explicit subject of the biblically grounded "Adam Raised a Cain" from *Darkness on the Edge of Town*, which begins with a scene of a young boy's baptism as his father looks on, and repeats the doctrine: "You're born into this life paying / For the sins of somebody else's past. . . . You inherit the sins, you inherit the flames." In "My Father's House," a song with biographical as well as anagogical overtones that precedes "Reason to Believe," the narrator laments the "unatoned" sins that have separated a father and son. Springsteen's theologically charged song narratives recall O'Connor's credo that "Where there is no belief in the soul, there is little drama," and her complementary assertion that the best stories are based "on the bedrock of original sin, whether the writer thinks in theological terms or not" (*Mystery* 167).

Catholic novelist and sociologist Father Andrew Greeley is one of the first commentators to note the Catholic overtones in Springsteen's songs, particularly in reference to his 1987 album *Tunnel of Love*. In a review article in *America* in February 1988, titled "The Catholic Imagination of Bruce Springsteen," Greeley refers to Springsteen as "a Catholic Meistersinger" (110) and insists that because he was raised a Catholic and attended Catholic school, Springsteen's "work is profoundly Catholic . . . because his creative imagination is permeated by Catholic symbolism he absorbed, almost necessarily, from the Sacraments" (111). Greeley explores the Catholic sacramentalism that informs the album's title song, "Tunnel of Love," and other songs, including "Two Faces," "Spare Parts," and the concluding track "Valentine's Day." Springsteen's symbolic use of images of rebirth and renewal charges his songs with a Catholic piety, insists Greeley, through which, to invoke a line from the album's closing song, "God's light [comes] shinin' on through." Without his necessarily being aware of it, Greeley argues, Springsteen is a kind of "liturgist" for the Catholic faith (111). And he concludes that "without a Catholic perspective," one would have great difficulty understanding these songs (114). O'Connor makes similar remarks about her own Catholic imagination in a letter to John Lynch, a priest and friend: "I write the way I do because and only because I am a Catholic. I feel that if I were not a Catholic, I would have no reason to write, no reason to see, no reason ever to feel horrified or even to enjoy anything." She concludes definitively, "I have been formed by the Church" (*Habit* 114–15).

Springsteen appears to confirm Greeley's view and to echo O'Connor's assertions in comments he makes in a *New York Times* interview following the release of *Devils & Dust* in 2005. Asked to account for the prevalent "Christian imagery and concepts" in these songs, Springsteen wryly replies with a trinity of reasons: "Catholic school, Catholic school, Catholic school" (Pareles, "Bruce Almighty" 24). In the *Times* article, Springsteen, then in his late fifties, acknowledges that his Catholic upbringing and faith was something that he "pushed off for a long time," but that he has been "thinking about it a lot lately." He observes, "I realized as time passed that my music is filled with Catholic imagery. It's not a negative thing. There was a powerful world of potent imagery that became alive and vital and vibrant, and was both frightening and held out the promises of ecstasies and paradise. There was this incredible internal landscape that [the Catholic faith] created in you. As I got older, I got a lot less defensive about it" (24). As *New York Times* reviewer Jon Pareles notes, "Thoughts of redemption, moral choices and invocations of God have been part of Springsteen's songs throughout his career, but they have grown stronger and more explicitly Christian on his 21st-century albums" ("Bruce Almighty" 24).

The collection of songs on *Devils & Dust* represents both a return and a departure for Springsteen. Following on his highly successful response to 9/11 in *The Rising*, which led to a reuniting of the E Street Band and a slew of typically energetic and emotion-filled stadium concerts, Springsteen returns to his Guthrie-style folk ballads: straight-forward storytelling with a guitar and some minor accompaniment in the mix. Songs on this collection present a cast of diverse characters—sons, and mothers, and separated lovers—who recount their stories of loss and longing and hoped for reunion. Many of the songs on this album were written and recorded in 1995 while Springsteen was composing songs for *The Ghost of Tom Joad* (Pareles, "Bruce Almighty" 24).

Devils & Dust departs from Springsteen's earlier work in the degree to which the songs reflect a Catholic spirituality. As he has grown and matured and fathered children, his songs are increasingly more grounded on the informing "internal landscape" of his Catholic upbringing, as he calls it. "I like to write about people whose souls are in danger, who are at risk," Springsteen tells the *Times* interviewer, echoing a decidedly Catholic dogma (Pareles, "Bruce Almighty"1). But redemptive acts and expectations resound in these songs as well. With overtones of St. Paul, Jeffrey Symynkywicz observes in his fittingly titled *The Gospel According to Bruce Springsteen* (2008) that "at the heart of the good news according to Bruce Springsteen is the affirmation that no principality or power—no forces seen or unseen, no terror-mad souls or devilish plots—can ever separate us from the love that is in our souls" (xiii). While the narrator of the title song warns us that "Fear's a powerful thing," *Devils & Dust* is an album ultimately grounded in love.

The spiritual landscape of the *Devils & Dust* songs begins metaphorically—and perhaps literally—in the desert. The narrator of the first and title song, who "could be a soldier in Iraq or America itself" (Pareles, "Bruce Almighty" 24) sings convincingly, "We've got God on our side / We're just trying to survive," but asks, "What if what you do to survive / Kills the things you love [?]" As sung, to the steady strumming of an acoustic guitar, accompanied with pulsing strings, the song is a gentle jeremiad: its imagery of fields of "blood and stone" and "mud and bone" with the rising "smell" of death palpably invokes the senseless carnage of war and adds to the condemnation of fear mongering in the song's prophetic and varied refrain:

> Fear's a powerful/dangerous thing
> It can turn your heart black you can trust
> It'll take your God-filled soul
> Fill it with devils and dust

The prophetic strains on the recording find fullest expression in the piano ballad "Jesus Was an Only Son," which focuses on the moment of Christ's passion and his imagined consoling words to His mother Mary: "Mother, still your tears / For remember the soul of the universe / Willed a world and it appeared." Explicating this song before an audience for the *VH1 Storytellers* series (2005), Springsteen, sounding like an Evangelical, states that it "starts from a premise that everyone knows what it is like to be saved." As he parses the song's second line—"As he walked up Calvary Hill"—Springsteen can only remark to the audience, "Once you're a Catholic, there's no getting out. That's all there is to it" (*Storytellers*). Springsteen's Catholicism is perhaps metaphorically expressed in "Maria's Bed," where the narrator, who has "walked the valley of love and tears and mystery" and has given himself "up for dead," finds life-giving "cool clear waters" and indeed "sweet salvation" in Maria's bed. (Springsteen's women are most frequently, and perhaps figuratively, named Mary or Maria.) "Leah" expresses a similar spiritual longing, its third and final verse a kind of confessional statement:

> I got somethin' in my heart, I been waitin' to give
> I got a life I wanna start, one I been waitin' to live
> No more waitin', tonight I feel the light I say the prayer
> I open the door, I climb the stairs

Lantern in hand, the narrator has been walking a road, "filled with shadow and doubt" looking for "proof" of "a world where love's the only sound." The song's title and images invoke both the biblical story of Jacob and his long-suffering love, and the famous Holman Hunt painting of Christ, holding a lantern and knocking at a door. Indeed, the artwork on the lyric sheet that accompanies the CD shows a monochromatic picture of Springsteen half visible through a half-open door, his right eye looking directly at the reader.

Fittingly, this most Catholic collection of Springsteen's songs ends with the eschatological overtones of "Matamoros Banks," a song that figuratively describes a soul's journey across a river to the Promised Land of heaven, and literally, recounts, backward, the journey from death to life of a Mexican man who attempts to swim the Rio Grande from Matamoros to Brownsville, Texas, and is drowned. As the song opens, we see his body "rise to the light without a sound." We follow his thwarted journey back as his corpse is carried on the current for two days. The water strips him of his earthly identity, his clothes gone, the flesh of his face disfigured, as Springsteen gently sings, "'Till every trace of who you ever were is gone / And the things of the earth they make their claim / That the things of heaven may do the same." A song that fuses themes of both spiritual and earthly reunion, "Matamoros Banks" is voiced in quiet liturgical tones, its repeated concluding refrain sung longingly like an invocation to the listener: "Meet me on the Matamoros / Meet me on the Matamoros / Meet me on the Matamoros banks."

"EXISTENCE ITSELF"

O'Connor once remarked, "For the fiction writer, to believe nothing is to see nothing." And she adds that her beliefs are what give her work "its chief characteristics" (*Habit* 147–48). While Springsteen does not share O'Connor's morality, nor to the same extent her Christian commitment, like O'Connor his artistic vision and spiritual perception have been inescapably shaped by his Catholic upbringing and beliefs. And like O'Connor in her fiction, Springsteen writes the kinds of songs he does because he is a Catholic. This is not to imply that he is particularly religious in his personal practices, which as he confesses to the VH1 *Storytellers* audience he is not.[3] Rather, as with O'Connor, that his artistic vision and spiritual perception have been inescapably shaped by his Catholic upbringing and beliefs. In an often-cited letter early in her writing career to a correspondent known as "A," O'Connor discusses the informing power of her Catholic faith upon her artistic vision and work. She remarks, "I won't ever be able entirely to understand my own work or even my own motivations. It is first of all a gift, but the direction it has taken has been because of the Church in me or the effect of the Church's teaching, not because of a personal perception or love of God. . . . I am not a mystic and I do not lead a holy life" (*Habit* 92). Her words could as truthfully be Springsteen's.

Like Flannery O'Connor, Springsteen is essentially a storyteller. And by his own confession, he has learned to tell a better story in his songs through an early reading of O'Connor's fiction.[4] As Nicholas Dawidoff affirms, "The best of his songs have all the tension and complexity of great short fiction" (259). The narrative-style of songwriting that is evidenced in the *Nebraska* and *The Ghost of Tom Joad* lyrics is further emphasized by the unusual typography of two of the songs in the lyrics booklet included with the *Devils & Dust* CD: the sexually explicit story in "Reno" appears as a single-typed paragraph; "Black Cowboys," the story of a boy's escape from a progressively dysfunctional mother and her drug-dealing boyfriend, is sung in largely rhyming couplets but typeset in six short paragraphs—a form that has not appeared on a Springsteen lyric sheet before. Form follows function in what is effectively a collection of song stories and character studies, the style of songwriting that Springsteen confessedly prefers over the energetic pop anthems that have built his reputation and fortune. Indeed, the Boss appears to want to transcend even the ranks of a mere folk singer: in a number of interviews he has referred to his corpus of songs as "my ongoing novel" (Larry Smith 155).

Springsteen is an artist whose songs seek both to reflect and to remediate the social and spiritual malaise of America. He is a Catholic whose faith, however faltering, has informed his artistic vision. And like Flannery O'Connor in her fiction, his songs are "about everything human" and are crafted with the storywriter's attention to "all those concrete details of life that make actual the mystery of our position on earth" (*Mystery* 68). Our best storytellers help us to make better sense of our often conflicted and confused selves and give us sight of what we might discover further on down the frequently hard roads of our lives. The often mysterious and tangled plots of our days and ways are in some way made straight as we become caught up and carried along in the words and vision of the storyteller—perhaps healed,

perhaps chastened, always more fitly human than we were before. The songs
of Bruce Springsteen have this power and effect, as attested many times over
in numerous testimonials published in books and articles about Bruce and
his music (see Cavicchi, Coles, and Cullen in particular). It might be, as
Dave Marsh describes his songwriting, that "Bruce reaches for the largest
canvas of all—he wants to portray nothing less than existence itself, as seen
at a certain time, from a certain perspective" (*Hearts* 61).

It certainly is true that Springsteen's song stories speak to our experience
of life right now. He has something to say that many have ears to hear; as
he puts it, he has been "involved in a national conversation" throughout
his career as a songwriter and performer (Boucher). His serio-comic schtick
during the Reunion Tour with the E Street Band in 1999–2000 gives a sense
of the ideals and purpose that inform Springsteen's side of the conversation. Midway through the show, as Marsh records, the Boss would put on
his preacherly persona, and, parodying the holy-roller Southern evangelists
who are familiar O'Connor stock, breathlessly proclaim his reasons for
traveling the world with a rock band: "I'm here tonight to resuscitate you,
to reeducate you, to regenerate you, to reconfiscate you, to reindoctrinate
you, to rededicate you, to *reliberate* you with the power! With the promise!
The majesty! The mystery! . . . *The ministry of rock and roll!*" (*Tour* 234).
Pop priest and occasional prophet, consummate showman and rock and
roll icon, troubadour for troubling times, and skilled storyteller—Bruce
Springsteen is all of these. His abiding interest in, as his recent lyric puts
it, "this life, and then the next" surely informs the observation of fellow
musician Toby Burke, who makes a brief and telling remark in the *Uncut:
Legends* 2004 special edition on Springsteen: "He's the Flannery O'Connor
of American rock."

NOTES

A portion of this chapter originally appeared in "The Ghost of Flannery O'Connor
in the Songs of Bruce Springsteen," *The Flannery O'Connor Review* 6 (2007): 11–29.
Reprinted with permission from the *Review*'s editor, Bruce Gentry.

1. In O'Connor's short story "A View of the Woods," 9-year-old Mary Fortune
Pitts attacks her 82–year-old grandfather after he beats her with his belt, trigger-
ing a heart attack that kills him; in "Everything That Rises Must Converge," a big,
angry black woman on a bus, who feels insulted by a well-meaning but racist white
woman, Mrs. Chestny, belts her with a heavy handbag upon exiting, ultimately
causing her to hemorrhage and die; the troubled Wellesley girl in "Revelation"
throws her psychology textbook at Ruby Turpin and tries to choke her; as well, O.
E. Parker's broom-wielding wife Sarah Ruth in "Parker's Back" beats him so severely
that large welts form on his back over a freshly tattooed image of Christ.

2. The album's final track, "My Best Was Never Good Enough" can be excluded from the cycle of song narratives as a coda of sorts, a closing comment that is intended to politicize the eleven songs that precede it. Springsteen describes the song this way: "It was my parting joke and shot at the way pop culture trivializes complicated moral issues, how the nightly news 'sound bytes' and packages life to strip away the dignity of human events" (*Songs* 277).

3. Asked by a member of the *VH1* audience to discuss the extent to which his Catholic faith informs his music, Bruce gave, in part, this response: "I'm a runaway Catholic and I have pagan babies at home. . . . But, once you're in you can't get out. . . . as I began to write and live, I found that it was just always there. I don't have a problem with it. I draw from it a lot. A lot of my imagery from when I was a kid to this record [*Devils & Dust*] is religious imagery. Religious imagery is powerful. It is a language that people understand. It is a language that we have in common. Everybody has that geography inside them—a spiritual geography of some sort. . . . I'm at a place where I don't need to hold it off and I don't need to necessarily dive in. I'm at a pretty good place with it at this point. . . . I use it for my own guidelines in different ways."

4. In the Penguin anthology of writings about Springsteen, *Racing in the Street: The Bruce Springsteen Reader* (2004), editor June Skinner Sawyers provides an appendix listing "Literary Influences" on Springsteen's songwriting. The list includes titles by James Agee, William Fox Price, Ron Kovic (*Born on the Fourth of July*), Walker Percy, and Philip Roth, with one- to six-line glosses for each. Sawyers devotes fourteen lines to a paragraph describing O'Connor's works that begins, "The short stories of Flannery O'Connor made a huge impact on Springsteen" (411).

II

READING PLACE

4

"Deliver Me from Nowhere"

Place and Space in
Bruce Springsteen's *Nebraska*

Frank P. Fury

By now, this story is well-known among Bruce Springsteen enthusiasts: In late 1972, after he had finished laying down the tracks for his first album release at Columbia Records, Springsteen was asked by studio executives to choose his design for the album cover. Columbia was pushing for a New York City–themed album cover that, because of the success of such artists as James Taylor, Joni Mitchell, Van Morrison, Cat Stevens, Harry Chapin, and Carole King, would effectively market Springsteen in the then-hip mode of "singer-songwriter," a new kind of musical identity associated with "soft rock" (Marsh, *Hearts* 75–76). Springsteen, however, foresaw the arc of his career in much more "electric" terms, and, for the New Jersey–born young rocker, his place of origin was tied intimately to his musical identity. He later would tell a reporter the year after his first album was released, "The main reason I put Asbury Park on the title of the album was because [Columbia Records executives] were pushing for this big New York thing, this big town. I said, 'Wait, you guys nuts or something? I'm from Asbury Park, New Jersey. Can you dig it? New Jersey'" (quoted in Santelli 21).

Interestingly, Columbia's marketing of Springsteen as a singer-songwriter was less important to Springsteen than was their attempt to locate him geographically within a certain musical tradition by way of New York City. It was about the identification of person with place, and, to Springsteen, that identification spoke volumes. In this light, therefore, it was not surprising that Springsteen went back to his musical roots literally and metaphorically—to the Jersey Shore, specifically Asbury Park—walked into a small shop on the boardwalk and chose a postcard that would not only supply him with the graphic for the album cover but also its title: "Greetings from Asbury Park, N.J." Drawing the name of his band from an actual street name in Asbury Park—E Street—reinforced the artistic persona Springsteen was unabashedly creating for himself. Seemingly, there was no separation between his personal and his artistic identity. Springsteen's message to the recording industry in the early 1970s thus was loud and clear: He was from New Jersey and so was his music. It was a message that would reverberate in its earnestness and its consistency for years to come, as the preponderance of *place* as a recurring concern in Springsteen's career would come to manifest itself in his music time and again. Indeed, it would not be a stretch to say that place is an important critical paradigm through which to consider Springsteen's work. A simple overview of his album titles, for instance, shows a clear geographic emphasis. His second album, *The Wild, the Innocent & the E Street Shuffle*, released a mere nine months after *Greetings*, in its title alone—but also in the content of songs such as "Fourth of July, Asbury Park (Sandy)," "The E Street Shuffle," and "Rosalita (Come Out Tonight)"—furthered the hometown connection. His most commercially successful album, *Born in the U.S.A.* (1984), posited an evolution in space, scope, and ideology from the musical infancy localized in his surrogate hometown of Asbury Park. Moreover, album titles such as *Born to Run* (1975), *Darkness on the Edge of Town* (1978), *The River* (1980), *Tunnel of Love* (1987), *The Rising* (2002), and even his 1998 box set *Tracks* while not indicative of geographic place, universalize nevertheless the individual's concern with the relative space one occupies in the world. This is indeed a notion that infuses Springsteen's best work. If an album can encapsulate an overriding theme or emotion foremost in the musical soul of an artist at the time of the album's inception, then a Springsteen discography narrates repeatedly the real and metaphorical landscapes of Springsteen's musical consciousness.

In 1981, the year in which Springsteen began composing the songs for what would eventually become *Nebraska*, he had apparently become disillusioned with the promise of the romantic heroes who populated his classic tracks on the previous albums. Specifically, on *Greetings from Asbury Park, N.J.*, *The Wild, the Innocent & the E Street Shuffle*, and *Born to Run*, Springsteen had already become well-practiced in his eventual near literary mastery of the song narrative, the dominant mode of the songs on these albums. While the subject matter of these narratives was the stuff of teenage drama, what stands out most vividly from these early tracks are both the characters—Crazy Janey and Wild Billy, Spanish Johnny, Little Dynamite and Little Gun, Magic Rat, Bad Scooter, the idealistic, unnamed narrators of "Thunder Road" and "Born to Run"—and the places—New York City, the Asbury Park boardwalk, Flamingo Lane, Easy Street, Tenth Avenue, and "the dark side of Route 88." The characters from Springsteen's first three albums tramp their way through his back streets, back alleys, open highways, deserted beaches, boardwalks, and front porches, all of which seem to promise escape or sanctuary. Though young and restless, these characters nevertheless fit their backdrops; they move through their settings as if they were eternally homeless, yet enjoyed being so. It was the sheer exuberance of these ne'er-do-wells that captured the public's imagination and partly propelled Springsteen's meteoric rise to fame. No matter the situations in which the characters of these albums found themselves, they could not be kept down.

By 1981, however, the romantic characters and places had disappeared, existing in the nostalgia of the die-hard Springsteen fans and in the three-and-a-half-hour sets of his already-legendary live stage performances. By 1981, gone even were the lost yet unapologetic and hard-as-nails narrators of the songs of *Darkness on the Edge of Town*, the ethos of which can be summed up in the lines of the title track: "Tonight I'll be on that hill 'cause I can't stop," he sings, "I'll be on that hill with everything I got / Lives on the line where dreams are found and lost / I'll be there on time and I'll pay the cost." Here we see the narrator of Springsteen's "Darkness on the Edge of Town" making a case for the salve that *rootedness* can be to the injured soul; the social anomie of modern existence, in other words, might be a little bit easier to manage if one can at least stake a claim to some small sense of place, even if it is as seemingly insubstantial as a hill. "King of the Hill" this narrator is not, yet no heroic quality is compromised by the possibility that he may be knocked off that hill. For at this point in Springsteen's career, it is the risk the narrator took in positioning himself there that matters.

Both *Darkness on the Edge of Town* and *The River*, then, evince a more realistic and matured Springsteen, for whom defeat is likely and therefore acceptable, but for whom bowing down to that defeat is not. Ironically, The Who's Pete Townshend had remarked upon the release of *Darkness on the Edge of Town* that "When Bruce Springsteen sings on his new album, that's not 'fun'—that's fucking triumph, man" (quoted in Marsh, *Hearts* 193–94). Thematically, each album speaks to the "price" (a popular word in each of the albums) that the individual has to pay in order to keep a sense of self and a sense of rootedness in a world that seems designed to strip both away. The battle is still present in tracks such as "Badlands," "The Promised Land," and "Prove It All Night" from *Darkness* and "The Price You Pay," "The River," and "Jackson Cage" from *The River*. But it is no longer a battle for romantic idealization or self-fulfillment. Rather, it is a battle simply for self-preservation amidst harsh and unforgiving settings. Indeed, the places in the tracks of these albums—"Streets of Fire," "Wreck on the Highway," "Factory," and "Cadillac Ranch," for instance—are much more ominous than those even in *Born to Run*. The young romance of the earlier albums is turned on its head in "The River," in which a young man has his promise of life thwarted at the river where he had impregnated his girlfriend Mary. Thus, Springsteen before *Nebraska* had always had a strong musical conception of the importance of place and environment in an individual's life. Indeed, in 1981, on the heels of *The River's* release, Springsteen uttered these words: "I think that all the great records and great songs say, 'Hey, take this and find your place in the world. Do something with it, do anything with it. Find some place to make your stand, no matter how big or small it is.' That's a pretty wonderful thing for a record to do" (quoted in Cullen, *Born* 102). Released the following year, the *Nebraska* album would challenge his somewhat facile conclusion.

By late 1981, after an approximately eleven-month tour that included stops throughout western Europe, Springsteen was at work on an album that he must have perceived from the start would not benefit from any attempts the members of his E Street Band could make to amplify it, either literally or figuratively. It was to be a unique work—a haunting solo effort and one that would present Springsteen in a new light for many of his fans. Of all Springsteen's albums to that point, and indeed since, *Nebraska* is Springsteen's most sustained and complex treatment of place in a career that shows a preoccupation—if not an obsession—with the individual vis-à-vis his or her surroundings. The romantic teenage protagonists of the first three albums and the defiant heroes of *Darkness* and *The River* would give way to a much more complex array of characters in *Nebraska*: unpitying state troopers, near-homicidal night riders, ethically conflicted highway patrolmen, nihilistic serial killers, hard-on-their-luck farmers, destitute families, small-time criminals, bewildered children, and jilted, abandoned lovers. Springsteen portrays these figures in stark terms, more in relief against the backdrop of their surroundings rather than in communion with them. The title of the album and its first track imply a spiritual wasteland, an emptiness that pervades the chilling acoustics of the songs and Springsteen's poetics. So, too, does the cover photo, which, along with *Greetings*, is one of the few in his career not to feature a shot of Springsteen himself. The album itself posits a strong narrativity of place, and, in fact, it is the notion of place that unites the single episodes of the album conceptually. For Bruce Springsteen there are few tropes that are as important an organizational principle in his music as that of "place." In no other recording can one find a clearer demonstration of Springsteen marrying place to artistic vision than in *Nebraska*.

The narrative structure of the songs of *Nebraska* is important to Springsteen's treatment of place throughout the album. For all but one of its ten tracks, *Nebraska* uses a first-person monologue as its narrative mode.[1] Springsteen seems intent upon fashioning this most stripped-down and bare of his works intimately. The dramatic monologues of the album thus do not merely enhance that atmosphere but rather constitute it—combined, that is, with the acoustical accompaniment.[2] The link to place, then, is that we as listeners receive place as subjective entity, modulated through the consciousness of each of the singer-narrators. Thus, we are able to envision the almost preternatural gloom of the highway through the desperate rider-narrator of "State Trooper"; we sit with "Highway Patrolman" Joe Roberts on the side of the highway as we, along with Joe, watch the car his good-for-nothing brother is driving career toward Canada. Springsteen enacts his narrative situations through the characters' voices—first-person point of view, to use the literary term. In a way not seen in other of his albums, with perhaps the exceptions of the brooding *The River* and the introspective *Tunnel of Love*, Springsteen shows the preeminence of narrative voice in determining the emotional experience of the listener.

Judging from Springsteen's use of the dramatic monologue as the dominant narrative style of the songs on *Nebraska*, he clearly sees personal storytelling as contributive not only to an implicit intimacy between speaker and listener but also to a shared sense of community. This potential for community, however, remains distant, faded, and confined to the background merely as a foil to the individual troubles of each narrator. "Highway Patrolman," for example, begins with the narrator identifying himself to the listener, "My name is Joe Roberts, I work for the state," and then making clear the bond of familiarity in order to relate to his listener: "I'm a sergeant out of Perrineville, barracks number eight / I always done an honest job, as honest as I could / I got a brother named Frankie, and Frankie ain't no good." The desired familiarity is important, because though many of Joe Roberts's implied listeners may not be police officers, many of them may have a family member with whom they have an abrasive relationship. It just happens that Roberts's occupation—which clearly he takes pride in, judging from those opening lines—demands a moral rectitude defined by state stricture that threatens to tear at the bonds of brotherhood: "Well if it was any other man, I'd put him straight away / But when it's your brother sometimes you look the other way." An immoral and criminal brother, however, cannot stay for long in the ethical world of Joe Roberts, and thus it is fitting that Springsteen has Roberts chase his brother to the Canadian border only to let him escape to the presumably safe harbor of another country. Springsteen's own country is, indeed, the United States of the early 1980s, but more accurately it resides metaphorically in the nameless and countless small-town communities that dwell in the core of his music. Joe Roberts may be a "sergeant out of Perrineville," but he also may be a sergeant out of any other town and barracks anywhere across the country. Place thus matters at least partly for Springsteen inasmuch as it reflects the values and shared bonds of a people; in "Highway Patrolman" those bonds are strained to the breaking point before Joe Roberts chooses family allegiance over the law.

The effectiveness and unity of *Nebraska*'s structure follow from not only Springsteen's mastery of the dramatic monologue in song, but also his treatment of place as a unifying trope throughout the songs. In *Nebraska*, he demonstrates that he has inherited the tradition of the local color writers of American literary history. Local color writers—as a number of late nineteenth-century American authors in New England and in the South came to be known—were concerned with this task: how to present to the skeptical reader, who hailed from a different part of the country, the manners, customs, dialect, and behavior of a people in a specific social and geographic environment. Sarah Orne Jewett was often called a local color writer, as was Mary E. Wilkins Freeman, George Washington Cable, Kate Chopin, and numerous other notable American authors. For these authors—and indeed for numerous other American authors through the years—the regions and landscapes they inhabited provided both the inspiration and the subject matter for their work. Though not native to Nebraska, Springsteen instead used his experiences growing up in his working-class hometown of Freehold, New Jersey, as his own inspiration and subject matter for not only *Nebraska* but indeed much of his work. Just as the local color writers had done nearly a century before, Springsteen appropriated the *local*—the familiar landscapes of New Jersey—and transformed and transcended the local in the universal concerns of the album *Nebraska*.

If Springsteen's work in *Nebraska* can be compared to any American author's, it seems to share more of an emotional and moral kinship with Flannery O'Connor's than it does with any other. Though the term *local color writer* was long out of vogue by the time O'Connor rose to fiction-writing prominence in the middle part of the twentieth century, she is known for her uncompromising portrayals of the Southern folk among whom she was raised. Springsteen has acknowledged O'Connor as an inspiration of sorts, and there is good reason to take Springsteen at his word, especially vis-à-vis O'Connor's short story "A Good Man Is Hard to Find."[3] A direct connection between that story, which was first published in 1955, and the title track of *Nebraska* proceeds from the last lines of "Nebraska." Springsteen's subject for this song is Charles Starkweather, the notorious serial killer from the late 1950s, who, according to Springsteen's rendition, when asked why he did what he did, responds: "Sir, I guess there's just a meanness in this world." The reference quite likely is to O'Connor's "A Good Man Is Hard to Find." O'Connor's story also features a serial killer: The Misfit, who terrorizes an unsuspecting family. When provoked by one of his cohorts after he philosophizes over the dead body of an elderly woman he had just shot, The Misfit declares: "Shut up Bobby Lee. It's no real pleasure in life" (51). The Misfit-Starkweather parallel bespeaks a similarity between O'Connor's stories and Springsteen's *Nebraska*. Like O'Connor's stories, which often proved inscrutable to many of her readers because of their refusal to offer facile conclusions and easy answers to questions of faith, Springsteen's *Nebraska* songs grate on the listener who would pursue an emotional connection through the music. Though as listeners we experience the taxing circumstances along with the narrators of the songs on *Nebraska*, the album does not allow for communion with them.

Whereas O'Connor's hapless characters are more often than not doomed by the uncertainty of their religious conviction, Springsteen's narrative personae remain haunted by feelings of emotional and psychological isolation. The opening lines of "Used Cars," for instance, express the young narrator's feelings of alienation, ironically in the close quarters of the used car his father is test driving:

> My little sister's in the front seat with an ice cream cone
> My ma's in the back seat sittin' all alone
> As my pa steers her slow out of the lot
> For a test drive down Michigan Avenue
> Now my ma she fingers her wedding band
> And watches the salesman stare at my old man's hands
> He's tellin' us all 'bout the break he'd give us if he could but he just can't
> Well if I could I swear I know just what I'd do

Though the song is set in the young narrator's hometown, he never appears to feel at home in his surroundings; rather than comfort or accommodate, his home suffocates him. The used car symbolizes both the narrator's desire to flee the dreariness of those surroundings—he lives still on the "same dirty streets where [he] was born"—and at the same time his own understanding of the car as a shameful indicator of his family's economic standing. The ambivalence here is stunning given the preeminence of cars throughout Springsteen's oeuvre, particularly in songs such as "Born to Run" and "Racing in the Street," which emphasize the liberating potential of the car. If the car can no longer offer deliverance from the individual's problems, then the result is a metaphorical imprisonment. The young narrator of "Used Cars" is not imprisoned physically but in ways that perplex him and effect his isolation from those around him. The narrator's feelings of isolation are not mitigated by his family's inclusion in his shame; that his mother, father, and sister parade down Michigan Avenue in their "brand new used car" only appears to heighten the boy's indignity.

The narrators of *Nebraska* are isolated in ways that the characters of *Darkness* and *The River* never are; while the persons from these earlier albums often contend against their surroundings, those in *Nebraska* endure *dislocation from* their surroundings more than they do *antagonism within* their surroundings. Springsteen blurs the lines of distinction, not allowing his characters to be seen in any clearly delineated light against the backdrop of landscape or place. The cast of characters in *Nebraska* seems to suffer from a postmodern middle-ground position in relation to place: there is neither harmony with one's surroundings nor disharmony. Cultural geographer Yi-Fu Tuan uses the term "indifferent" to describe the world's relationship to humankind, with place and culture as humankind's "constructive responses" to such alienating indifference (40). Tuan goes on to say that efforts to surmount the indifference of Nature toward human struggles "constitute the crucial meaning of human struggle with fate, and that the measure of success in this struggle lies in the creation of human culture in all its myriad forms, both everyday and exceptional" (41). In *Nebraska*, there is merely "being" vis-à-vis landscape, and the only meaning that exists in such a state proceeds from the subjectivity of the individuals themselves. The monologue style Springsteen employs as the narrative perspective in the songs, therefore, is essential for rendering such subjectivity.

Despite his reliance upon bewildered consciousnesses for the narrative transmission of disquieting events and circumstances, Springsteen nevertheless is careful not to let his songs enter the realm of farcical nightmare; the depictions of his down-and-outers and their pathologies never quite broach the Kafkaesque. They remain, instead, frightening because of their *realness*, their *ordinariness*, as Howard Hampton notes:

> Springsteen doesn't view *Nebraska* as a world apart, inhabited by little more than stiff-necked marionettes, monstrosities, and crash-test dummies whose heads are stuffed with true-romance and true-crime pulp: he strikes a fine balance between mundane reality and what Pauline Kael called "the glamour of delinquency," the '50s first inchoate wave of alienation given iconic status by Dean and Marlon Brando. (335)

Like a playwright using the physical dimensions of his stage to demonstrate visually his characters symbolically constricted by a confined space, Springsteen utilizes a minimalist musical style that renders a circumscribed or at other times baffling individual existence for his characters. Ralph, a.k.a. Johnny 99, for instance, is no Joseph K.;[4] Ralph's loss of home and job were only the immediate causes of what led him to kill a night clerk, and he is well aware of his predicament: "The bank was holdin' my mortgage and they was takin' my house away / Now I ain't sayin' that makes me an innocent man / But it was more 'n' all this that put that gun in my hand." Ralph's bafflement instead resides in the stultifying limitations of the fictional setting in which Springsteen has placed him; he is the lone major character of the album who is not privileged with the monologue narrative form, with Springsteen quite likely intending that the third-person narrative perspective reflect Ralph's loss of agency. Moreover, in the span of just two stanzas, Ralph is arrested, tried, and sentenced to "prison for ninety-eight and a year," a startling economy of narrative space; such economy certainly bespeaks the suffocating socioeconomic forces acting upon Ralph's life.

While the *Nebraska* characters struggle to locate themselves in a permanence of place or a fixed, auspicious reality, listeners can appreciate the degree to which Springsteen distances his characters from the social mainstream. The characters of these songs often exist liminally, on the edge of a greater expanse of space that seems to offer neither safe harbor nor inclusiveness. In *Songs* (1998), which he published nearly twenty years after the release of *Nebraska*, Springsteen himself admits that he cast his *Nebraska* characters in just this liminal position: "These new songs were narrative, restrained, linear, and musically minimal. Yet their depiction of characters out on the edge contextualized them as rock and roll" (138). The connection here is fascinating: the qualification for not only a style of music but also for a cultural identity—rock and roll—is here linked, in Springsteen's estimation, to a state of being "out on the edge." For Springsteen, it seems, rock and roll is less a musical genre or lifestyle than it is a state of existence. To be "out on the edge" for Springsteen is to live without a safety net, dangling over a precipice the fall from which threatens to rob the individual of all he or she holds dear. The quotation reveals the respect that Springsteen holds for the liminal figures on the album; it takes guts—a rock and roll bravado, if you will—to admit one has hit rock bottom and not apologize for it. The liminality of his characters is indeed what he sings about and is that which qualifies them as appropriate subject matter for a rock singer of his stature. In a way that Dylan had done some seventeen years earlier, Springsteen in *Nebraska* challenges the facile assumptions regarding musical boundaries and genres.[5]

Examples on the album of either physical or emotional liminality are prevalent. "Mansion on the Hill," for example, dramatizes socioeconomic disparity vis-à-vis physical marginalization:

> There's a place out on the edge of town, sir
> Risin' above the factories and the fields
> Now ever since I was a child I can remember
> That mansion on the hill.

Springsteen cleverly reverses the physical dynamics of liminality: it is the titular mansion that exists "on the *edge* of town," while the young narrator and his sister observe it from afar. The Gatsbyesque mansion—"In the summer all the lights would shine / There'd be music playin', people laughin' all the time"—remains inaccessible and exclusive to the narrator, ostensibly because of its distance and its height, but more so due to the socioeconomic inequities that have marginalized *him*. His figurative marginalization is depicted spatially in the song: Springsteen variously casts him with his sister sitting isolated in cornfields listening to children playing and then parked with his father "on a back road along the highway side."

Springsteen intertwines additional references to liminality with images of stasis. Though presumably relating a story of filial intimacy and thus physical closeness, "My Father's House" instead positions the titular symbol of paternal authority at a distance. His estranged father has left only a remnant of a now-broken father-son relationship represented in the solitary home; "My father's house shines hard and bright," he sings, "It stands like a beacon calling me in the night / Calling and calling so cold and alone / Shining 'cross this dark highway where our sins lie unatoned." By the song's end, the narrator is as static as that house; he is separated not only by "this dark highway" but seemingly by metaphysical forces as well. Similarly, the multiple, brief vignettes that compose "Reason to Believe" depict people who stand alone and wait. The man who encounters a dead dog lying on a highway waits interminably—so long in fact that it prompts the narrator to muse, "like if he stood there long enough that dog'd get up and run." Mary Lou "waits down at the end of that dirt road" for her lover to come back, and the jilted bridegroom "stands alone and watches the river rush on so effortlessly." These three characters from "Reason to Believe" speak to Springsteen's recurrent image throughout the album of the individual suffering from a mysterious and numbing paralysis. The irony of the song title is prefigured in the reason*less*ness for those who sit and wait, a stasis not suggestive of any wrongdoing, but of a universal condition unfathomable to the individuals in the song, including its observing narrator.

By contrast, Springsteen shows us that neither is constant movement through place and space an antidote to human bewilderment. The night-rider of "State Trooper," as a prime example, begins his confessional tale in stark terms with a description of the desolation surrounding him: the New Jersey Turnpike, "'Neath the refinery's glow, out where the great black rivers flow / License, registration, I ain't got none / But I got a clear conscience 'bout the things that I done." Why the narrator is traveling the Turnpike in the "wee wee hours" Springsteen never tell us; what we are shown, however, is the desperation the narrator feels due to his own dislocation from any sense of community, family, or place: "Hey somebody out there, listen to my last prayer / Hi ho silver-o deliver me from nowhere." The slow, brooding quality of the tune, along with the preternatural shrieks Springsteen unleashes at the song's end, enhance the song's atmospheric spookiness. A fascinating parallel is evident when we compare this song to the much more raucous, upbeat "Open All Night," which also features a nightrider who also happens to be traveling down the New Jersey Turnpike in the "wee wee hours," and which also features the line, "deliver me from nowhere."

Regardless of the style of the musical accompaniment, Springsteen seems quite concerned throughout *Nebraska* with the plight of the individual dislodged, disjointed, and displaced from his surroundings. To be "nowhere" for Springsteen—both in a geographic and in a spiritual sense—is the most terrifying state of all. All in all, the album as a whole seems to oscillate in a complex rhythm of stasis and movement that underscores simultaneously the inadequacies of place and placelessness alluded to in the songs.

It is therefore perfectly fitting that the album bears the title *Nebraska*, for the title refers simultaneously to an actual geographic place and to an indistinct space that provides the backdrop for actions of human depravity. The album as a whole seems much to rest on the internal tension between what is objectively identifiable in terms of (geographic) place and what is subjectively perceptible in terms of (universal) space. Springsteen's poetics of place in the album aligns with contemporary notions of what is termed "cultural geography." According to many theorists in the field, while "place" alludes more to location, which is inclusive of and bounds lived human activity, "space" is more a social construct, dependent upon the perception of the observer and the ideologies implicit in the time and place of that observer. Absolute space, in other words, cannot exist. Phil Hubbard points out that most current theories concerning cultural geography and the production of space employ a poststructuralist critical discourse, evincing a deep concern with language's participation in such production:

> Rejecting universal definitions of "place" or "space," such notions stress that both are real-and-imagined assemblages constituted via language. As such, the boundaries of place and space are deemed contingent, their seeming solidity, authenticity, or permanence a (temporary) achievement of cultural systems of signification that are open to multiple interpretations and readings. (46)

Just as the desolate landscapes of Nebraska, Wyoming, and New Jersey provide the open space for the characters of *Nebraska* to search for place, so too do Springsteen's words provide an open space for multiplicities of interpretation and reaction based on the disturbing situations recounted in the songs.

"Highway Patrolman" in particular presents an interesting case study of the central relationship between place and space that suffuses the *Nebraska* songs. Here the narrator Roberts identifies himself as a "sergeant out of Perrineville." "Perrineville" proves a curious choice by Springsteen for the barracks' location. There is a Perrineville in New Jersey, yet details Springsteen includes in the song make it clear that the song does not take place in New Jersey: at the song's end, Roberts chases his brother's car—"a Buick with Ohio plates"—"till a sign said 'Canadian border five miles from here.'" The song logically cannot take place in Ohio, however, since Canada is not accessible from Ohio via car. That leaves Michigan as the most logical choice for the state in which the song is set, particularly in light of references to "the Michigan line" and "Michigan County." And yet there is no such place as Perrineville, Michigan, nor is there a Michigan County in Michigan. Could this be simply an oversight on Springsteen's part? The meticulousness with which he renders the particulars—both lyrically and musically—in his songs would suggest otherwise. Perhaps the lack of an actual geographic location for the setting of the song is intentional, designed to effect an uncanny placelessness that would deepen the moral malaise Roberts tries so desperately to avoid. The geographic border to which Roberts succumbs and allows his deviant brother to escape can thus be seen more accurately as a dividing line not in terms of nation, but rather in terms of ethical choice. Roberts, by virtue of his choice, has worked out his own space of morality, and it is clearly confined to his home, where his family is rooted and where his identity as a keeper of the peace is formed.

In this light, then, the album as a whole, taking its cue from the first (title) track, is in many ways about the individual production of space—that is, Springsteen's characters' (often futile) efforts to entrench themselves in an identifiable place. In terms of stability and emotional security, the dichotomy between the two terms is an interesting one, for as Hubbard asserts, "place is often equated with security and enclosure, whereas space is associated with freedom and mobility" (43). Indeed, in *Songs* Springsteen writes of the "theme that runs through the record": "it's the thin line between stability and that moment when time stops and everything goes to black, when the things that connect you to your world—your job, your family, friends, your faith, the love and grace in your heart—fail you" (1998, 138). Springsteen thus acknowledges the centrality of dislocation to the meaning of the songs' lyrics. One of the great themes of the album is the narrators' quests for rootedness—a seeking of "security and enclosure" via *place* while at the same time needing the "freedom and mobility" afforded by *space*. The place of Nebraska—with the presumption of its open landscapes and vast expanses offering the possibility of freedom and mobility—is rather, for the album and its characters, an arbitrary geographic destination. It suggests more powerfully the possibility of *space* (freedom, mobility), which, ironically, is a goal none of the characters seems able to achieve fully or productively.

"Nebraska," the album's first and title track, prefigures the album's repeated representations of characters' desultory wanderings through space. The song recounts the chilling tale of the serial murders of a psychotic individual named Charles Starkweather. In 1958, Starkweather was convicted of the murder of "ten innocent people" in acts committed while on the run from Nebraska to Wyoming and over a nine-day span. Along with his fourteen-year-old girlfriend Caril Fugate, Starkweather earned almost immediate celebrity and has become the subject for numerous books and films over the years, his fame predicated on a mass-media frenzy that itself fed off Starkweather's self-styled, James Deanesque image. To say that Starkweather self-styled anything may, however, be giving him too much credit. By most accounts, Starkweather was "all but illiterate, and he killed as he did in part because he was superstitious as only a half-wit can be" (Marsh, *Two* 337). Dave Marsh further claims that Starkweather "certainly never harbored hope of any judgment anywhere so neutral or mystical as the 'great void.' Nor was he that matter-of-fact about the murders. He claimed that he killed in self-defense, and he made sure he dragged his girlfriend down with him" (*Hearts* 337). Despite the disparity between the real-life killer and Springsteen's rendering of him, Starkweather nonetheless is the model inhabitant of the *Nebraska* landscape in that he most typifies the above quotation from *Songs*: the character who lives "out on the edge" and thus becomes the stuff of rock and roll legend, indeed even personifies rock and roll itself.

Springsteen appears equally concerned with depicting his characters' obsessive pursuits of places that perhaps do not exist. The narrators of the *Nebraska* songs seem embroiled in a compulsive search for place that, in effect, poses a direct challenge to the aforementioned quotation from Springsteen that "all the great songs say, 'Hey, take this and find your place in the world. . . . Find some place to make your stand, no matter how big or small it is.'" Such is not the case in *Nebraska*. The songs' narrators seem less individuals with agency or direction than drifters lost amid a spiritual wasteland that does not seem to resemble any sense of place that they know—"New Jersey in the morning like a lunar landscape," as the narrator of "Open All Night" suggests. The wish for deliverance from such stultifying existence is crystallized in a line uttered in "Used Cars" that comes off as almost laughably impracticable: "I wish he'd just hit the gas and let out a cry / And tell 'em all they can kiss our asses good-bye."

"Atlantic City" picks up where "Nebraska" leaves off in Springsteen's investigation of the individual quest for place. In its reference to an infamous locale in American cultural mythology, the song evokes the expected associations of individual greed and destructively irresponsible behavior. A place "where the sand's turnin' to gold" is an enticement that few human beings would find hard to ignore; for the desperate narrator of "Atlantic City," all it takes is for him to draw "what he had from the Central Trust" and buy himself and his girlfriend "two tickets on that Coast City bus." Yet again, consistent with the quixotic search for space in *Nebraska*, Springsteen's investigation of this theme is filtered through the consciousness of his narrator, a man who must resort to performing jobs for undesirable sorts:

> Now I been lookin' for a job but it's hard to find
> Down here it's just winners and losers and don't get caught on the wrong side of that line
> Well I'm tired of comin' out on the losin' end
> So honey last night I met this guy and I'm gonna do a little favor for him.

Not getting "caught on the wrong side of that line," as the narrator warns, recalls Springsteen's comment quoted above that the theme that runs through the songs is "the thin line between stability and that moment when time stops and everything goes to black." His continued references to a "line" that separates two opposed notions support the contention that he projected his artistic vision of this album spatially. His moral schematics, though often presented complexly, are instead blurred by the difficult decisions individuals often have to make in life. For the narrator of "Atlantic City," his decision has already been made vis-à-vis place and morality: "Put your makeup on, fix your hair up pretty / And meet me tonight in Atlantic City."

In a 1996 interview, Springsteen said, "If my work was about anything, it was about the search for identity, for personal recognition, for acceptance, for communion, and for a big country. I've always felt that's why people come to my shows, because they *feel* that big country in their hearts" (Weider 46). Springsteen locates that big country ironically in Nebraska, "Nebraska," and *Nebraska*. Nebraska the state is merely representative; the Starkweather killings need not have taken place there, they simply happened to have occurred there. Any place in this nation could have provided the backdrop for a case study of the destructive potential of the manic, fame-seeking individual. In terms of the album itself, the same notion applies: the situations described in the songs are not germane necessarily to their geographic contexts—Atlantic City just as easily could have been Las Vegas, for instance. What matters to Springsteen is the manner in which the individual functions vis-à-vis whatever backdrop Springsteen has erected for him or her. Pictured in *Nebraska*'s album cover, which shows nothing more than a desolate, open highway from the perspective of a driver looking out a snow-encrusted windshield, the "country" that Springsteen speaks of is somehow inaccessible, at least to the dramatis personae of arguably his bleakest album.

Springsteen in *Nebraska* deftly renders a dichotomy marked by landscape. Geographic landscape—presumably real, tangible, and objective—gives way in this album to "human landscape," the environment of "space" subjectively experienced by the narrators of the album. The songs of *Nebraska* often specify actual geographic locations: Lincoln, Nebraska; the badlands of Wyoming; Atlantic City, New Jersey; Mahwah, New Jersey; the New Jersey Turnpike; and Perrineville are all referenced, for instance. This is not to say, however, that the actual places themselves carry any import within the specific geographic contexts mentioned—with perhaps the exception of Atlantic City, which signifies historically and socially not only for New Jerseyans but for Americans in general. As previously stated, the events in "Nebraska" could have taken place anywhere, but the mental image and association of an open landscape that the state itself conjures is seemingly the effect Springsteen was striving for. The desolation of the backdrop, in other words, gives more emotional register to the words of a man who admits there was no special reason for why he and his girlfriend went on a killing spree, but that "At least for a little while, sir, me and her we had us some fun."

For Springsteen, *Nebraska* becomes the site at which belonging and stability are contested—where place is distinguished from space, and landscape is unidentifiable. There are no names of any actual, geographic locations in "Mansion on the Hill," "Used Cars," "My Father's House," and "Reason to Believe," and the message Springsteen delivers through these particular songs and the album as a whole is clear: these are the representative citizens of an America struggling in the wake of denied promises and destroyed dreams. In the title track of his previous album, Springsteen had sung, "Is a dream a lie if it don't come true / Or is it something worse?" *Nebraska* seems unmistakably to provide an answer to this query, for the lost souls Springsteen sings about in this album are denied even the doomed but heroic battle for self-identity that pervades *Darkness on the Edge of Town* and *The River*. For Springsteen, the *state* of Nebraska is less a United "State" and more a state of being. And if the words of Charles Starkweather by way of Bruce Springsteen are any indication, that state is *nowhere*: "They declared me unfit to live, said into that great void my soul'd be hurled / They wanted to know why I did what I did / Well, sir, I guess there's just a meanness in this world."

NOTES

1. Springsteen utilizes the traditional third-person narrative perspective for "Johnny 99." One may argue that "Reason to Believe" also uses the third-person to string together its multiple mini-narratives; if one acknowledges, however, the opening phrase of the song—"Seen a man standin' over a dead dog"—as a frame device (the narrative persona *witnesses* all of these episodes by virtue of the opening word "seen") then this song too can be classified as a monologue.

2. "Open All Night" is the only track on the album that features electric guitar.

3. Springsteen wrote a song in the late 1970s with the title "A Good Man Is Hard to Find (Pittsburgh)"; the song remained unknown to anyone other than a Springsteen enthusiast or bootlegger until its official release in the *Tracks* box set in 1998.

4. Joseph K. is the protagonist of Franz Kafka's *The Trial*. K. is arrested for a crime that is never revealed to either the reader or K. himself.

5. Dylan's first rock album, *Bringing It All Back Home* (1965) and his stunning electric performance at the 1965 Newport Folk Festival were met with general dismay and outrage by Dylan's folk following.

5

Tracking Place and Identity in Bruce Springsteen's *Tracks*

Mike Cadó and Teresa V. Abbruzzese

INTRODUCTION

With a career that now spans almost four decades, Bruce Springsteen is recognized as one of the most influential popular music artists to have emerged in the late twentieth century. Known especially for his evocative lyrics and the uninhibited energy of his live shows, Springsteen has carved out a particular niche in the history of rock and roll. A superb songwriter with a vision shaped by traditions of American folk music, storytelling, and narrative poetry, Springsteen offers a distinctive fusion of the sounds and rhythms of the rock idiom with images—cars, factories, guitars, and carnivals—that are by now iconic in the American urban postindustrial landscape.

Springsteen is most prominently associated with places, both real and imagined, specific to the American rustbelt region. The importance of this particular geographical connection is highlighted in the recent Rock and Roll Hall of Fame exhibit titled "From Asbury Park to the Promised Land: The Life and Music of Bruce Springsteen." However, his appeal extends far beyond the locational limits of the rustbelt: Springsteen is revered not only throughout the United States but across North America and elsewhere around the globe. While the fact that he has recently become a key figure on the U.S. national political scene has no doubt enhanced his following, part of the reason for his widespread popularity, as we will argue here, lies in his particular handling and embodiment of place and identity. Settings, narratives, and characters that on one level are geographically specific also have a broader, more universal appeal. His treatment of relationships between husbands and wives, boyfriends and girlfriends, and employers and employees, as well as his explorations of adolescent rebellion, personal struggle, entrapment, and dreams of escape speak to a wide cross section of global humanity.

The purpose of this chapter is to examine Bruce Springsteen's representations of place and identity in the four-CD collection released in 1998 and titled, simply, *Tracks*.[1] We have chosen to examine *Tracks* for two main reasons. First, such an approach allows us to bring in unexplored songs—or as Springsteen calls them in the liner notes, "the ones that got away"—into the many and richly cross-disciplinary conversations that exist about this artist and his work. Secondly, a focus on *Tracks* helps shed a retrospective light on the man behind the public stage persona, "the Boss."

Tracks is a collection of outtakes, rare B-side singles, and previously unreleased selections. Of the sixty-six songs included in the collection, fifty had never been previously released, nine are B-side singles of popular Springsteen classics (although some of these were re-recorded for single release), and seven are alternate takes of songs Springsteen included on his studio albums. Thus, *Tracks* presents some challenges in that it is difficult to tease out neatly a particular place or an overall underlying theme for the work—something that can be done effortlessly with all other Springsteen albums. After listening to the box set several times, and analyzing the lyrics for each song, it became evident to us that the majority of the songs that appear on *Tracks* are romanticized stories of love, struggle, and escape. They are also a little lighter in thematic content than some of Springsteen's more recognized works. This does not mean that these compositions are not sufficiently Springsteenish, or that they lack the usual narratives and musical structures that we (his audience) are accustomed to hearing, however. These songs still embody all the elements of classic Springsteen material. By attending to lyrics, visuals, instrumentation, vocal timbre, and delivery in the *Tracks* songs we hope to reveal key sites of identity in Springsteen's song narratives, as well as to better understand his particular construction—both literal and figurative—of place.

The chapter is divided into three main sections. The first of these introduces the theoretical underpinnings of our analysis, pointing out the relationship of the above conceptual considerations to both the construction and representation of place and identity, as well as to the question of how meanings are produced and embodied through musical performance. In the second section, we offer an overview of the body of work presented on *Tracks*. Finally, in section three, we discuss the various physical and metaphorical expressions of place that are embedded in Springsteen's narratives of escape and struggle. In so doing, we reveal how the construction of identity is contingent upon these expressions.

"LOOKIN' FOR A PLACE TO LAND": THEORETICAL CONSIDERATIONS

The concept of place, as it relates to various types of identity, has been the subject of numerous scholarly discussions. While there are competing definitions across a range of different disciplines, human geographers often provide three conceptualizations of place: as location, locale, and sense of place. These three dimensions of place consist of *location* as a geographical coordinate shaped by historical, social, economic, and political processes; *locale* as a setting for daily social interactions; and *sense of place* as an emotional interpretation of place, which in turn shapes both individual and collective identities. All three connotations are related to the ways in which space is organized into places that are either physical locations or ideological or imagined constructions. Thus, place can define space through, for example, particular geographical coordinates, political boundaries, cultural representations, subjective meanings, and collective memory. Throughout Springsteen's oeuvre, place is not just a mere backdrop. He articulates place on various levels from local, to urban, to national, to global. In his songs, the representation of place (as physical location) tends to be heavily localized and connected to cultural and individual experiences.

For our purposes here, meanings of place as both a physical location and as an imagined or subjective space provide the conceptual apparatus with which we investigate the different places and identities presented on *Tracks*. However, by choosing specific places as settings for his narratives (for example, the Bronx in "Thundercrack" and New Mexico in "Santa Ana"), Springsteen provides a concrete historical, political, social, and economic context. Focusing on specific places lends depth to the meanings of his songs, which in turn, deterritorializes and thus universalizes their literal and geographic localness. Meanings attached to place are produced within broader processes of cultural creation. Examining place in Springsteen's songs allows us to better understand how sense of place and the embodiment of place in identity formation are meaningful to both the experience of the characters in his narratives and to the experience of his wider listening audience. Springsteen as a songwriter and performer is always in the process of imagining places (real or fictitious) so that he can situate the everyday life of his characters *somewhere*. Some of these imagined places are physical locations, such as unknown towns, city streets, roads, and highways (for example, Cason Street from "Linda Let Me Be The One"). But Springsteen also creates place through common imagery and metaphors, such as "dark streets," "bad world," "the promised land," and "hard land." Notably, he depicts "loving arms" as a place of security, while "home" is represented as a cage or prison. Analyzing the construction of place in Springsteen's music is an important means of understanding how this artist's local knowledge and experiences shape his stories. In turn, the story-making process influences dominant structures of meaning that are intertwined with conceptions of place, and that are then interpreted and re-interpreted at the collective level through his audience.

In addition to his lyrics and the images they bring to mind, Springsteen's *sound*—culturally situated within a particular music scene of the American mid-Atlantic and referred to as the Jersey Shore sound—contributes to the creation of place (Caffrey). As popular music scholar Andy Bennett has explained, attributing particular musical styles to specific urban locations creates music scenes that symbolically become key sites for the transmission and articulation of place (7).

The Jersey Shore music scene—often associated with Springsteen, Jon Bon Jovi, Southside Johnny and the Asbury Jukes—tends to focus on the daily lives of working-class Americans in industrial towns and cities. Its sound fuses an early 1960s rock aesthetic with a rhythm and blues flavor, one related more closely with Muscle Shoals (a particular style of blues referring to gritty, organic, and raw performances captured on tape) rather than the polished production ideals connected with Motown. The carnival elements of the shoreline boardwalk (also pictured in the cover art on *Tracks*) are both subliminally and overtly implied in the music of the Jersey Shore scene through sounds that mimic the pipe organ and calliope of the circus. These sounds, heard in such selections as "Bishop Danced," "Zero and Blind Terry," "Thundercrack," and "Rendezvous," are created via accordion, glockenspiel, and Danny Federici's particular use of the high flute stop on the organ.

The sonic features of this particular music scene have also been shaped significantly by the sociocultural makeup of New Jersey—a traditional immigrant-receiving area—through the infusion and influence of Italian folk music. Italian folk influences are heard in Federici's accordion contributions to the E Street Band as well as in Springsteen's countless stories of his Italian-Irish background. According to Springsteen, living in a transnational household influenced his personal connections to both the physical location that was his hometown place as well as to his sense of place in the world. As he recounts,

> I came from . . . an interesting family. My mother is only second-generation Italian. My grandmother lived to be 102 and never spoke any English. When I went into her room, I went to Italy. Everything: the Madonnas, the shawls. She lived in the country since she was in her twenties and never learned any English. So there was Italian culture, and then the Irish folks were just old-school people. (Levy 54)

Although Springsteen's local identity consisted of being a "Newarky" from the Jersey Shore, he also has (although self-admittedly ambiguous) U.S. national, and transnational (Italian and Irish) attachments to place.[2]

In his various *Rolling Stone* interviews from 1975 to the present, Springsteen does not necessarily highlight his relationship to the Jersey Shore music scene overtly. However, over the years he consistently repeats how the boardwalk of Asbury Park and the pavement of New York City were his turf, and he acknowledges that anecdotes and people surrounding his everyday life were included in his songs. As Springsteen articulated in a *Rolling Stone* interview with Joe Levy, "For me, I started with what I had. I walked down to the boardwalk about a hundred yards from here, and I looked into a little knickknack shop. There was a rack of postcards, and I pulled one out that said GREETINGS FROM ASBURY PARK. I said, "That's my album cover. This is my place" (54). It seems that the Jersey Shore music scene was an integral aspect of Springsteen's early career, as he was living, creating, performing, and producing within this scene. The scene not only influenced his sound, but it was also the location of his fan base. For instance, when *Greetings from Asbury Park, N.J.* was released in 1973, it sold only 25,000 copies, mostly to fans from the Jersey Shore (Szatmary 271).

Although Springsteen continues for a time to be a representative figure of the Jersey Shore scene, his first record deal with Columbia in 1971 reconfigured his relationship with this locality by instantaneously connecting him to a national and global music industry that turned his personal experiences into mythic representations of white working-class America. However, there are enduring elements in Springsteen's music that keep him rooted in the Jersey Shore scene, such as the thematic focus on the everyday struggles of working-class Americans, the use of carnival imagery and sounds, the roughness and erratic toughness in his characters, and in his vocal delivery.

Intersections of place, identity, and music are not only rendered through localized music scenes, however. Rather, we argue that much of Springsteen's persona and broader emotional connection to working-class Americans stems from what poststructuralist theorist Roland Barthes refers to as "The Grain of the Voice." Here, it is the performative aspect of the sung lyrics, and not necessarily the narrative itself, that creates and conveys meaning and emotion. A focus on performativity does not dismiss the importance of the lyrical content where everyday language can be manipulated to imply clever double entendres, cultural references, and sometimes an intertextual conversation—the idea that lyrics could be informed by interpretations of other texts. Instead, Barthes proposes that the emotional essence of meaning is captured through vocal phrasing, articulation, and timbre, what he refers to as "the body in the voice as it sings" (118). This idea is illustrated and extended to include other aspects of performance in Richard Middleton's analysis of performances by Pat Boone and Elvis Presley in which significance beyond the meaning of the lyrical content was produced through Presley's orgasmic releases, or what Barthes refers to as *jouissance* (Storey 107). In a further expansion of Barthes's theorizations on vocal "grain," Leppert and Lipsitz focus on Hank Williams's ability to communicate various themes by embodying the meaning of his narratives through his physical appearance, stage presence, and vocal delivery (263).

Following this particular case study in which the significance of the body in articulating meaning is highlighted, we can also borrow Barthes's central ideas on vocal timbre and delivery to demonstrate in particular how vocal grain is a key aspect of Springsteen's interpretive abilities. Whether he is expressing youthful innocence, rebellious conviction, or an introspective narrative, Springsteen manages to articulate a wide emotional spectrum through the manipulation of his voice. These expressive nuances are quite pronounced in *Tracks*. As a collection that comprises thirty years of material, *Tracks* contains many of the different bodies, narratives, and emotions that have been produced through the voice of this artist.

"THE ONES THAT GOT AWAY": *TRACKS* (1998)

The selections appearing on *Tracks* span a period from March 1972 to August 1998. They were consciously excluded by Springsteen from albums he released over the years because, in his view, they did not quite fit the thematic content of the particular album being made at the time, or they just did not seem worthy enough to make the cut. He explains his decision in the liner notes: "What we were doing in there was making a lot of music, a lot more music than I could use at any one time. As a result, my albums became a series of choices—what to include, what to leave out? I based my decisions on my creative point of view at the moment—the subject I was trying to focus on, something musical or emotional I was trying to express" (*Tracks*). According to Springsteen's biographers, record producers, and Springsteen himself, his recording sessions always yielded much more material than could ever be included on the album releases. During a 1984 *Rolling Stone* interview, when he was at the height of his popularity, Springsteen hinted at releasing these excluded songs: "I always tell myself some day I'm gonna put an album out with all this stuff on it that didn't fit in. I think there's good material there that should come out. Maybe at some point, I'll do that" (quoted in Marsh, *Hearts* 466). Although many of the songs Springsteen was referring to here were staples in his live performances, it was not until the release of *Tracks*, fourteen years later, that they were made available to the public for the first time. While the majority of the selections on *Tracks* were not included on the studio album releases because of their thematic content, it can also be argued that many of the songs were simply musically inferior or redundant in context with the other recordings made for any given album session. For example, "Trouble in Paradise," recorded during the *Human Touch* sessions, is similar in musical structure, tempo, and overall mood to "I Wish I Were Blind," one of the tracks that made the album cut. Likewise, "Iceman" includes a piano ostinato figure that is similar to that found in "Something in the Night." In addition, both selections are performed at the same tempo. Although both "Iceman" and "Something in the Night" are from the *Darkness on the Edge of Town* sessions, only the latter was included on the studio release. Therefore, it can be suggested that Springsteen and his producers made a decision to exclude these particular tracks not only because of thematic content, but to ensure a diverse set of tracks important to the overall integrity and musical variety of the studio album. Thus, through an examination of the disparate songs released on *Tracks* we also gain insight into Springsteen's creative process and his careful attention to conveying the themes that inspired him at particular stages throughout his career.

Tracks was released on November 10, 1998, almost seven months after the death of Springsteen's father. As Springsteen tells his fans in many of his live concert monologues and interviews, his father was an influential figure in his life. Although father and son relationships are a major theme in much of Springsteen's work, they are not significantly represented or explored in the compositions on *Tracks*. However, given that this collection has been marketed as a retrospective work spanning Springsteen's entire career up to the date of release, it may be that the passing of his father prompted its creation. It would have been a way for Springsteen to reflect on his past and to contemplate not only his father's death but also his own mortality.

The title of the collection, *Tracks*, warrants discussion here as it carries several meanings, both literal and metaphorical. Although the selections on any musical recording are often referred to as *tracks* (a term dating as far back as the earliest phonograph records), the word has evolved as a technical term to describe not only a product but also a process. As recording technology developed, musicians were able to record in various stages and isolate particular sonic events that could eventually be manipulated before the final product was released. The process, known as multi-tracking, depends on the available tracks that can be physically stored on the recording medium. Even though recording processes have undergone many changes, especially with the advent of digital recording, the industry has retained the term *tracks* despite its technical obsolescence. In present day vernacular, *tracks* most often indicate the musical selections found on a compact disc. In this way, the word *tracks* is parallel in usage to the term *cut* as used to describe the songs on vinyl recordings a generation earlier.

There are several literal meanings connected with the word *tracks* that can be etymologically traced to further inform our discussion. For instance, one of the earliest meanings of the noun *tracks* is "a mark left by the passage of something." Early nineteenth-century usage includes reference to a mode of travel: "lines of rails for drawing trains" (*Concise Oxford*). Thus the word *tracks*, whether the referent be real or imagined, conjures up images of a footprint, a trail, or an imprint left behind that can be followed either to trace where one has previously been, or to pursue in order to get to where one wishes to be. The verb form of the word—*to track*—comes to mind here, of course, as one follows or tracks prints in order to find something. But there is also the implied meaning of "to track down" or "capture" (Etymonline). These multiple meanings should not be overlooked, particularly when considering an artist such as Springsteen, whose constant acknowledgment of the past and continuous search for new modes of expression have proven to be the driving force of his career.

In addition, the word *tracks* also has metaphoric connotations that have evolved through meanings stemming from the construction of a given physical space. For example, tracks, and more specifically, railroad tracks, have often been associated with boundary lines that delimit a territory, both geographically as well as socioculturally. The expression *the other side of the tracks* conveys this sense of territory, usually in a negative way. On *Tracks*, Springsteen utilizes this metaphor in "Thundercrack," a song that makes reference to an ex-girlfriend and his desire to rekindle a past relationship: "Thundercrack, baby's back / This time she'll tell me how she really feels / Bring me down to her lightning shack." In the subsequent verse, Springsteen alludes to a particular savvy associated with the other side of the tracks in describing the charm and magnetism of his love interest:

> She's straight from the Bronx
> Hung off the line
> She slips, she slides, she slops, she bops, she bumps, she grinds
> Even them dance hall hacks
> From the west side of the tracks
> Move in close to catch her timin'

Here, Springsteen depicts a woman so extraordinary that even those "hacks" from the west side find her intriguing.

Finally, for Springsteen, *tracks* also symbolize a specific means of escape—*making tracks*—from the everyday struggles encountered by the protagonists in his stories. The idea of making tracks is a notion highlighted in several songs included in the collection. These include "Rockaway the Days," in which the troubled Billy seeks solace by tracking back home to Maryland, and "Don't Look Back," a depiction of two trailblazers ready to face their challenges head-on:

We're making night tracks through the blazing rain
Blowin' pistons, workin' the fast lane
Red line burnin', pocket's full of cash
Angel writes her name in lipstick on my dash
There's nothing to lose
It's a bad break but baby we're backed
Tonight we'll blow off the doors and honey we won't look back

Both examples illustrate Springsteen's metaphoric use of all that is denoted in the word *tracks*: of retracing steps and returning back to the familiar, and of forging ahead and carving out a new path full of possibilities and hope.

Since *Tracks* can be viewed as a retrospective work, looking back at the work of an influential artist over two decades, one can assume that the visual images presented in the artwork accompanying the collection also reflect the particular themes his music has grappled with since the early 1970s. Given that the images in this collection are integral in expressing some of the main themes in his music, we can assume that Springsteen contributed to the selection of photos and the artistic layout of this collection. One of Springsteen's significant artistic influences includes Robert Frank, particularly his book of photographs entitled *The Americans* (1959). As Springsteen explains to Will Percy, "I was twenty-four when I first saw the book—I think a friend had given me a copy—and the tone of the pictures, how he gave us a look at different kinds of people, got to me in some way. I've always wished I could write songs the way he takes pictures. I think I've got half a dozen copies of that book stashed around the house, and I pull one out once in a while to get a fresh look at the photographs" (quoted in Sawyers 307). According to Elizabeth Kunreuther, curator for the Center for Documentary Studies at Duke University, "Photography before Frank was pristine: carefully focused, carefully lit. Frank would intentionally lose focus, his work was shadowy and grainy, full of unconventional cropping and angles. He broke the rules in order to be true to his vision of America he saw in his travels across the country in 1955 and 1956" (quoted in Kirkpatrick, *Magic* 93). Frank's influence is considerably evident in the tone that pervades *Tracks*. Specifically, images of a side-view mirror, carousel, discarded hubcaps, a mixing board, and an inverted American flag similarly represent the American landscape that Frank depicts in *The Americans*. As we elaborate below, Springsteen complements the thematic material presented in the songs with the visual imagery of a disappearing white working-class America.

TRACKING PLACE THROUGH PHYSICAL COORDINATES

It is well known that Springsteen was, as one of his album titles proclaims, "Born in the U.S.A." Specifically, he was born and raised in Freehold, New Jersey, in a blue-collar household. This personal history perhaps at least partially answers the question of why his lyrics and sound conjure up so many images and places that depict a struggling working-class America, and, additionally, why they portray individuals trying to escape the working-class struggle.

In many of the narratives on *Tracks*, the construction of different places, times, and historical moments is integral to the framing of Springsteen's stories as well as to the establishment of the geographical and socio-economic parameters that shape his characters' lives. For instance, the stories of Eddie and Linda ("Linda Let Me Be the One"), Frankie ("Frankie"), Catherine LeFevre ("Car Wash"), Johnson Leneir ("Shut Out the Light"), and Billy and Mary ("Rockaway the Days") clearly exemplify how Springsteen's protagonists face different forms of personal struggle and attempt to escape it, either physically by running away or metaphorically through their dreams. For example, the stories of Linda and Frankie, both symbols of hope for a disillusioned narrator struggling in a postindustrial town, Catherine LeFevre, struggling with an unfulfilling job with dreams of "a million-dollar break," Johnson Leneir, the returning war veteran who feels isolation and desperation as a Johnny-come-lately in his own home, and the suicidal Billy who cannot cope with everyday struggles—all illustrate the various manifestations of escape and struggle that Springsteen grapples with in his work.

The song "This Hard Land" highlights place both as a physical location and as an imagined space. The description of place as a geographical location is conveyed through the journeys of two sets of characters. First, there is a brother and a sister on the move, together leaving Germantown and "blowin' around from town to town" looking for a place to root themselves "Back into the dirt of this hard land." Second, there is the narrator and Frank (both of them cowboys) heading south toward the Rio Grande "lookin' for lost cattle / Our hooves twistin' and churnin' up the sand." The specific geography in which these characters are located gives them a physical place from which to run and, in turn, a place to run to.

Another song employing a place-as-physical-location strategy is "Where the Bands Are." Springsteen specifically makes reference to Union Street, a common street name in towns along the Jersey Shore, and uses the image of the downtown (both physically and metaphorically) as a place that promises a sense of freedom not afforded in the everyday routine of his working-class experience:

> I hear the guitars ringin' out
> Ringin' out down Union Street
> I hear the lead singer shoutin' out, girl
> I wanna be a slave to the beat
> Yeah, tonight I wanna break my chains
> Somebody break my heart
> Somebody shake my brains

Downtown there's something that I wanna hear
There's a sound, little girl, keeps ringing in my ear

Here, the rather hard-driving pulse of the musical arrangement reflects the urban setting Springsteen depicts. His forceful vocal delivery reveals an almost harsh sense of frustration. The feeling is especially highlighted in the chorus, which is solely comprised of repetition of the line "I wanna be where the bands are." This sentiment is reaffirmed through the response of the background vocalists who seem to reinforce the potential social collectivity associated with the city. There is also a saxophone solo section in this piece, the excitement and vibrancy of which persuades the group to participate (suggesting camaraderie between the band and the audience) by clapping or feeling "the beat of the crowd," and shouting in exuberance. The inclusion of a solo by a raunchy and raucous saxophone, an instrument commonly associated with rhythm and blues, also succeeds in reaffirming the place of the city, as does the over-driven guitar solo.

These readings of "This Hard Land" and "Where the Bands Are" point out how important the role of place-making is in contextualizing narratives, furnishing Springsteen's songs with a context rooted in different locations. The two songs sonically reveal how Springsteen's persona can straddle multiple identities, ranging from the rural cowboy to the urban proletariat, both of which are connected to distinct geographical places but tied to broader cultural concerns.

TRACKING PLACE THROUGH THE IMAGINATION

As a songwriter, Springsteen seems to grapple uneasily with themes of escape and struggle in connection to imagining place. He often appears to be of two minds about whether it is appropriate or mature to have his characters escape from their plight for their own individual freedom and/or gain, or to have them remain at home, in place, and, by extension, in community. According to Christopher Phillips, editor of *Backstreets* magazine, Springsteen once explained in an interview that as a storyteller he builds a place for his characters to live in so that he can then create the conditions that shape their struggles. But it is these struggles, in turn, that give his characters the need to escape. In contrast, twenty years ago during his 1988 Tunnel of Love Express Tour, he introduced "Born to Run" by stating that the idea of a "guy and girl" running away is romantic, but that at some point he realized that he had to figure out someplace for these characters to run *to* in order for their lives to have meaning (Garman, *Race* 196). This dilemma continues to be at the forefront of Springsteen's lyrics. On one hand, there are characters who, although they desire to escape, are stuck in their own tracks; they stay in place and they stay connected to community. On the other hand, there are those who need to escape but have no place to go.

The road and/or highway—two common images in Springsteen's work—often work as metaphors for journeying, life, and, most importantly, escape. The escape vehicle of choice is typically the automobile, as articulated in "Roulette": "I took my wife and kids and left my home unguarded / We packed what we could into the car / No one here knows how it started." The automobile reference is also made in a photograph on the inside cover of the collection that shows a side-view car mirror. Reflected in the mirror is a long stretch of highway cutting through a barren landscape under a big sky.[3] This image complements and joins together many of the themes of Springsteen's songs, but with its open-road view and retrospective gaze, it connects especially well with the theme of escapism in the song "Don't Look Back": "There's nothing to lose, it's a heartbreak / The deck's stacked / So put your foot to the floor and darling don't look back." In this romanticized narrative, Springsteen encourages his female companion to leave the past behind and keep moving forward with him toward the future. There is, he feels, nothing left in their desolate small town that would warrant either of them staying. "Don't Look Back" also seems to harken somewhat to the Orpheus and Eurydice myth: one should not look back over their shoulder in life for fear of seeing what they have left behind turn to stone.

Romantic notions of escape are also revealed in the song "Two for the Road." The narrator of this song desires companionship on his journeys. As he emphatically states, "It takes one for the running but two for the road." The idea of a traveling companion is also communicated in the car mirror photo just described. It is the passenger side mirror that is being looked back through in this photo; thus, due to the particular angle and perspective represented, we can assume the driver most likely has company. It is also worthy of note that the photo is shot in black and white, so it does not precisely register a specific time of day. However, the dim lighting and grayish background suggest dusk, a common time element in Springsteen's writing. Dusk is a time when his characters seem to thrive and muster up the personal courage necessary to face their everyday struggles. For instance in "Seaside Bar Song," the narrator urges his girlfriend to escape with him into the night: "I'm gonna live a life of love and tonight you're the one / The highway is alive tonight so baby do not be frightened." Finally, off in the distance, reflected in the passenger mirror, is an image of a transport truck trailing the car. While the car is a representation of Springsteen's desire to escape, the truck seems to indicate that the desire is marred by a past that does not or will not disappear, or that he remains connected to through his blue-collar roots.

This tension between escape and struggle is conveyed symbolically through a second photograph presented on the inside cover of the box set: a riderless carousel. The carousel is located on what appears to be a board-walk set against the backdrop of a postindustrial wasteland where buildings stand abandoned. In addition, the image includes a fallen stepladder and a cast-off plaid jacket, presumably belonging to the fairground operator. These objects have been left beside the deserted merry-go-round, suggesting that the operator lost his job and/or that the traveling fairground as a popu-lar form of public leisure is no longer thriving in a postindustrial locality.

However, the carousel, and more generally the wider carnival context it suggests, also conjures up strong but mixed feelings of nostalgia, happiness, and the innocence associated with childhood. The carnivalesque reference triggers ideas of escapism and an ability to suspend time. And it may also be intended to suggest the well-known understanding of carnival as a complex inversion of the power relationships of everyday life and as a diversion (if only momentary) from that life.

The setting of the carnival can be seen as a locale in Springsteen's music. His use of the imagery associated with carnival-type places varies depend-ing on the thematic material of the particular song in question. Sometimes the carnival is a fun place to "hang out with the guys," but sometimes it is "dark and dangerous," as Gareth Palmer points out in "Springsteen and Authentic Masculinity":

> The middle-class flâneur visits the carnival to experience forbidden pleasures as it represents a licensed area for experiment. But in Springsteen's world it has only a tawdry glamour. The workers demythologise what they do while the hero sees only metaphors in the creaking motions of the Big Dipper and the Tunnel of Love. The carnival is a dark and dangerous place not because it is threatening or mysterious but because it foreshadows the grim world of mar-riage and disappointment to follow. (107)

It is worth noting that despite the strong carnival imagery in the collection's packaging, the only actual direct mention of a circus or carnival theme on *Tracks* is in "Mary Queen of Arkansas," a song originally released on Spring-steen's debut album *Greetings from Asbury Park, N.J.* In this early composi-tion, both narrative and imagery are somewhat ambiguous. Depicted are the struggles of a love-sick character. These are intertwined with vivid scenes of the circus as a place of either entrapment and/or as a means of escape, depending on how one interprets the word "border" in the following line: "Well the big top is for dreamers, we can take the circus all the way to the bor-der." However, Springsteen does accentuate the idea of role inversion that is often associated with carnival and the circus: "You're not man enough for me to hate or woman enough for kissing." This lyric suggests gender ambiguity such that the central character, Mary, the Queen of Arkansas, could be seen as a "drag queen" (Kirkpatrick, *Magic* 16; Palmer 105).

In many ways, the circular motion associated with the carousel image symbolizes the cyclical nature of some of Springsteen's narratives: there is constant motion of the storyline without the characters ever actually moving. This narrative device sets up a form of stasis that suggests the helplessness sometimes experienced by Springsteen's protagonists, working-class Americans mired in everyday struggles. These cyclic patterns of embarking on a journey but always returning home, of life as a set of repetitions without change, and the overall futility of the life experience are explored in several compositions on *Tracks*, including "Trouble in Paradise" and, the perhaps ironically titled, "Happy." "Trouble in Paradise," an easy-listening, middle-of-the-road song, presents a scenario of a domestic relationship. Life has somehow passed the couple by as they endure a daily monotony. The musical arrangement of their poignant story, sung by a wistful-sounding, introspective Springsteen, is dominated by marimba-like keyboard sounds that suggest a fairground calliope:

> You did the dusting, I did the sweeping
> You did the driving oh and I did the sleeping a little too long
> On a picnic 'neath the sky so blue
> We didn't see the rain and heartache coming through
> When it's all an old black and white movie
> And you're sure you've seen the ending twice
> Here comes trouble in paradise

For the disenchanted narrator, home as it is portrayed here represents a place of entrapment. The characters are caught in a pleasant but ultimately unrewarding cycle, and they cannot seem to break away. Their marriage is like a continuously revolving merry-go-round: enjoyable enough, but never going anywhere. This sentiment is reflected in the reference to a movie that they've seen twice before. It is also echoed in the following lines: "You said everything was fine / I'm sorry, baby, I didn't see the signs / Oh so beautifully you read your lines." Finally, the closing lines of "Trouble in Paradise" present the mature Springsteen, an individual less optimistic about the likelihood of escape, and one whose growing cynicism resonates with the weary phrase, "We do the sleeping with one eye open."

Similarly, Springsteen expresses the futility of being caught up in recurring, negative cycles and the ardent desire to escape from them in the melancholy track "Happy": "Born in this world, darling, with few days and trouble never far behind / Man and woman circle each other in a cage / A cage that's been handed down the line / Lost and running 'neath a million dead stars / Tonight let's shed our skins and slip these bars." Here, burdened by the legacy of the human condition, Springsteen strives to break free, exuberant in prose but not in musical expression. The music always returns to the complacent refrain that concludes each verse.

Similarly, the musically minimalist "Iceman," written and recorded during the *Darkness on the Edge of Town* sessions, portrays the unwillingness of a frustrated narrator to accept change, a change he feels ultimately leads to the destruction of the human spirit:

> Well it don't take no nerve when you got nothing to guard
> I got tombstones in my eyes and I'm running real hard
> My baby was a lover and the world just blew her away
> Once they tried to steal my heart, beat it right outta my head
> But baby they didn't know that I was born dead
> I am the iceman, fighting for the right to live

Rather than remain stationary, the "iceman" chooses to escape in "his dirty old Ford" to a place Springsteen describes as "the devil's door," a metaphor for any place other than where he already is. This religious imagery of the devil is reinforced by the entrance of the backing vocals during this section. The wordless choir suggests a spiritual epiphany and, as a sung vocal drone, it reinforces a sense of communal affirmation. "Iceman" never actually realizes this epiphany either lyrically or musically, however. He continues his search as expressed in the closing lines of the song:

> I say better than the glory roads of heaven, better off riding
> Hellbound in the dirt, better than the bright lines of the freeway
> Better than the shadows of your daddy's church
> Better than the waiting, baby better off is the search.

Although the instrumental texture in this song occasionally shifts with the entry of the backing vocals and the sound of the hi-hats struck lightly, the sense of unfulfilled desires is ultimately accentuated by the fact that on the recording the band never does come into full swing.

Interestingly, our examination of *Tracks* reveals that Springsteen occasionally recycles lyrics and phrases. However, his particular vocal grain shapes the intended meanings of the words differently in each case. For example, the line "I wanna go out tonight, I wanna find out what I got," occurs in "Iceman" as well as in "Badlands"—one of Springsteen's power anthems included on the album *Darkness on the Edge of Town*. Although these two songs were recorded during the same sessions, the vocal stylization of this particular line differs in each of the songs. Whereas in "Badlands" the energetic vocal delivery of the line signifies rebellious optimism and youthful curiosity, in "Iceman" it is presented in a rather monotone and drawn-out style, thus suggesting defeat, weariness, and an inability to escape the routine of everyday life.

"Cynthia" presents an upbeat foray into the juxtaposition between the monotony of the everyday working-class American man in an industrial town and the ability of a prostitute to transport him to a temporary fantasy world:

> Cynthia, when you come walkin' by you're an inspiring sight
> Cynthia, you don't smile or say hi but baby that's alright
> 'Cause I don't need to hold you or taste your kiss
> I just like knowin', Cynthia, you exist
> In a world like this
> Cynthia, when you pass it seems like this whole town drops
> Cynthia, or maybe it's just me, baby, and these fools stuck here
> punchin' this clock
> Well you give us a reason to stop just for a while
> Stop, stand and baby salute your style

Although the narrator realizes Cynthia will not fulfill his dreams of love, he does acknowledge how she succeeds in creating a world filled with ecstasy, something he does not ordinarily experience in his day-to-day existence.

The dreariness of a postindustrial landscape is represented through another image included in the collection's packaging that is evocative of Springsteen's sometimes pessimistic outlook. The discarded hubcaps that appear in this photograph are primarily from American automobiles (Oldsmobile, Ford, and Cadillac), and they are piled together in a powerful visual statement representing the transition of the U.S. Fordist regime—a political economic framework from the 1940s to the 1960s, associated with mass production and mass consumption—to the current post-Fordist regime associated, from the 1970s forward, with deindustrialization and flexible accumulation (Krims xxiv). Several selections on *Tracks* deal with this theme directly, including "Shut Out the Light," which was written for the *Born in the U.S.A.* album. The song features the line "His pa said he was sure they'd give him his job back down at the factory," indicating how the uncertainty that characterized the Fordist to post-Fordist regime transition in the United States materialized in the everyday working-class household. The selection "Frankie" addresses the need for Springsteen's character, also a victim of post-Fordist American unemployment, to pack up and travel elsewhere in search of a new life for himself: "Well lately I've been stand-ing out in the freezing rain / Readin' them want ads out on Chelsea Road / I'm winging down the street in search of new games." It is important to note that the lyrics in these songs are not entirely bleak, however. Rather, words such as "winging" and "new," for example, create a contrasting opti-mism, thus showing once again how contradictory feelings emerge and are expressed through Springsteen's construction of landscape. We might look again at the hubcap image and note the beautiful designs and the bright, almost cheerful, shine that emanates from them. The junk heap is not as dreary as we might first think. The assortment of hubcaps can also evoke nostalgic reminiscences of a Fordist past: thus we cannot completely "Shut Out the Light."

On one of the back panels of the box set cover is a close-up of a mixing board console, also shot in black and white. This image has a close visual similarity with "Old Glory" where the console seems oddly flag-like in appearance. The knobs seem to resemble the American flag's stars, and the sliders its stripes. We have in this image a cleverly combined representation of the mechanization and technologicalization of both music, and more broadly, post-Fordist American culture in general. A reprint of this same photo is also featured in the liner notes to the collection, opposite Springsteen's written introduction, where it serves to reinforce his connection and attraction to broader American social issues in relation to deindustrialization—the closing down of factories and the automation of work.

These issues are specifically related to the struggle of the disenfranchised, and Springsteen's treatment of them situates him in a long lineage of working-class American heroes. "This Hard Land," especially, bears both musical and thematic attachments to Woody Guthrie and Bob Dylan. The song begins with a rather common folk-like harmonica riff and simple acoustic guitar accompaniment, such that the listener is immediately transported into an American folk aesthetic. However, Springsteen's unmistakable raspy vocal timbre and lyrical delivery soon places us in a rock and roll aesthetic, thus creating sonic imagery that reflects the harshness of the landscape. "This Hard Land," invoking Guthrie's "This Land Is Your Land," right down to the "Okie" Southern drawl, represents Springsteen's ability to fuse different identities. He performs parts of the song as the Boss from Jersey and other parts in a persona like that of a farmer from the American South or Midwest. In so doing, he situates his listeners both historically and politically. Here, in a notable realization of Barthes's concept of "the grain," Springsteen creates multiple meanings through his personification of the different characters in "This Hard Land," a maneuver that demands we move beyond a simple literal analysis of the lyrics:

> Hey there mister can you tell me
> What happened to the seeds I've sown
> Can you give me a reason, sir, as to why they've never grown
> They've just blown around from town to town
> Back out onto these fields
> Where they fall from my hand
> Back into the dirt of this hard land
> Well me and my sister
> From Germantown yeah we did ride
> And we made our bed, sir

From the rock on the mountainside
We been blowin' around from town to town
Lookin' for a place to stand
Where the sun could break through the clouds and fall like a circle
A circle of fire down on this hard land

According to Garman's in-depth reading of the song's significance,

The narrator provides hope for the future by looking to the past, by recovering the tradition of Whitman's working-class hero to contest contemporary social relationships. Grounded firmly in nostalgic vision, "This Hard Land" bemoans the effects of commercialization and mechanization largely because, as Whitman predicted in "A Song for Occupations," they threaten both the communal and homosocial bonds that are formed in the workplace. (*Race* 255)

The final lines of "This Hard Land" metaphorically contextualize the struggles of the American working-class within a barren, desolate post-industrial landscape: "Well if you can't make it stay hard, stay hungry, stay alive if you can / And meet me in a dream of this hard land." But, once again, there is a sense of hope provided in the frontier imagery, symbolizing the possibility for escape from the routinized life of the industrial city and the potential for new opportunities.

"I'M A COOL ROCKING DADDY IN THE U.S.A": TRACING IDENTITY

Similar to the construction of place, themes of escape and struggle shape the construction of identity in Springsteen's *Tracks*. Identity is a social construction that is shaped along axes of race, gender, class, ethnicity, and sexuality. Thus people can be "multiply positioned in this world" (Katz 253). Understanding identity as a social formation, and not as biologically inherent, allows us to analyze the scalar processes associated with identity construction. Based on subjectivities, identity is a product of the way one interprets her/his body and positions herself/himself locally, nationally and/or globally, but it is also defined by differentiation. In relation to music, collective identity rooted in geographical space is articulated through a constructed sense of community that transcends place and time (Bennett 3). Springsteen's blue-collar upbringing and his personal attachment to New Jersey as his family's home have unequivocally shaped his identity. As illustrated in "The Wish" from *Tracks*, we experience a rare glimpse of Springsteen acknowledging the influence of his mother through the lines, "I remember in the morning, ma, hearing your alarm clock ring / I'd lie in bed and listen to you gettin' ready for work." This personal tribute poignantly closes with "Well tonight I'm taking requests here in the kitchen / This one's for you, ma, let me come right out and say it" as he thanks his mother for giving him his first guitar and an opportunity to pursue his dreams. Along with Springsteen's white working-class background, cultural critic Pellegrino D'Acierno emphasizes the role of ethnicity in shaping his Jersey boy image. According to D'Acierno, the roots of Springsteen's constructed identity can be situated within a broader Italian-American subculture, making him a key "figure of blue-collar rock'n'roll Catholicism" struggling to achieve the American Dream (301). As D'Acierno explains, "It is thus no accident that Springsteen's musical persona involves a recycling of Presley and Dylan through the filter of an urban Catholic—'It's Hard to Be a Saint in the City'—sensibility incubated by the New Jersey Shore scene" (301). This rootedness is pivotal in creating a sense of community among his fans at various spatial scales, from New Jersey to the rustbelt to America and beyond.

For instance, at a personal level, Springsteen is affectionately referred to as "the Boss" by his E Street bandmates. This moniker represents the power relationship that exists between this bandleader and his accompanying musicians. Springsteen is indeed the Boss in this sense, since he is ultimately responsible for overseeing the hiring of the musicians he works with. He also secures recording contracts and chooses and composes repertoire (Frith "Real" 133). However, Springsteen often inverts this position of power in both his personal and musical explorations. At a collective level, he is identified with blue-collar workers and the disenfranchised, even though his present socioeconomic status does not position him equally with many of the characters of his songs, or with many of those who regard him as "the Boss." Springsteen's moral commitment to the plight of the disenfranchised has been a consistent underlying force in his music. As a performer, he embodies his characters' stories, a gesture which in turn bestows a considerable degree of authenticity upon him. In relation to Barthes's concept of *jouissance* mentioned at the beginning of this chapter, it is through the sometimes intangible features of his performances—what some might call sheer vitality, raw energy, and expressive delivery—that Springsteen conveys working-class values. On stage, he constructs a place called "Bossland" or a specific time called "Bosstime" in order to give fans a moment of escape from their everyday lives while he works hard to produce an entertaining experience. His exuberance leads to a certain pleasure of accessibility and authenticity that audiences gravitate toward. The approach not only engages his fans, but also has generated extensive academic and popular dialogue particularly about the spiritual and transcendental aspects of his music and live performances.

Some of Springsteen's most compelling narratives on *Tracks* deal not only with the ways in which personal and collective identity formations shape many of his characters' journeys, they also serve to shape Springsteen's identity as a working-class American hero. The construction of identity is crucial in articulating the sound and overall feeling of Springsteen's albums. For example, Springsteen's earlier albums *Greetings from Asbury Park, N.J.*, *The Wild, the Innocent & the E Street Shuffle*, and *Born to Run* incorporated a musical aesthetic closely associated with the renowned Phil Spector's "wall of sound," reflecting the optimism, romanticism, and innocence of his characters. In contrast, the sonically sparser, minimalist soundscapes presented on *Darkness on the Edge of Town*, *The River*, and *Nebraska* create bleak settings in which Springsteen's characters struggle. Less studio production and a more organic approach to recording in these three latter albums emphasized the isolation, entrapment, and hopelessness that his characters embodied, as well as the more serious subject matter that Springsteen felt compelled to explore during this time. In reflecting on his 2007 album *Magic*, Springsteen describes these sound changes in his career:

> This record, I felt free to go back to the romanticism of my earliest records. I doubled my voice, I sang in a bigger voice. I'm actually looking forward to writing a little bit more in that style, to picking up some of those elements that I discarded because I wanted to make sure that the music was tough enough for the subjects I was interested in dealing with. That's what I did with *Darkness on the Edge of Town* and *Nebraska* and parts of *The River*. But now, I feel free enough to go back and reclaim those lovely elements of pop simplicity and the well-crafted three-and-a-half minute song, which I love to do. (Levy 53)

Here we gain insight into Springsteen's motivations during distinct periods in his recording career. The middle period, from 1978 to 1982, was a fertile one, as represented by the numerous selections represented on *Tracks* that were originally intended for release on albums produced during that time. This shift in recording process, as expressed by Springsteen himself above, is manifest in several outtakes on *Tracks*, most notably "Roulette," recorded in 1979. In "Roulette," Springsteen narrates the struggle of a working-class father and the helplessness he experiences while coping with difficult economic circumstances:

> I grew up here on this street
> Where nothin' moves, just a strange breeze
> In a town full of worthless memories
> There's a shadow in my backyard
> I've got a house full of things that I can't touch
> Well all those things that won't do me much good now
> I was a fireman out at Riker's, I did my job
> Mister, I've been cheated, I feel like I've been robbed
> I'm the big expendable, my life's just canceled null and void
> Well what you gonna do about your new boy

Here, the character's desperation and paranoia is reflected in Springsteen's voice and vocal phrasing. He builds a sense of anxiety and frustration that segues into the chorus, in which he comments on the randomness and vulnerability of his character's situation. Inspired by the nuclear incident at Three Mile Island in 1979, the song describes the disillusionment of the fireman with the current state of affairs. Despite his hard work and civil service, he is forced to flee with his wife and kids. According to Rob Kirkpatrick in *The Words and Music of Bruce Springsteen*, in the lyrics to this song Springsteen "began to examine the social forces behind the dangers of a Three Mile Island—and more expansively, the forces behind the economic conditions that seemed to threaten notions of the American social structure" (67). Springsteen's focus on "they" as a collective force that opposes individual well-being, in turn, reflects this more inclusive narrative stance, one that he seems to adopt later during this second phase of his career: "They say they want to help me but with the stuff they keep on sayin' / I think those guys just wanna keep on playin'." The hysterical pace of the song settles down with the inevitable demise of the character, an event which indirectly illustrates Springsteen's understanding of the structural limitations that stratify societies.

The theme of failed patriotism and disenchantment with the pursuit of the American Dream pervades much of Springsteen's music and is conveyed through a powerful photo in the box set of a backward American flag shot in black and white with glimpses of the sun attempting to shine through. As sociologist Michael Kimmel suggests, "Springsteen's lyrics painted a relentlessly bleak portrait of the downward spiral of the white working-class. Rebuffed and rejected, he sought escape or solace in sex, cars, male camaraderie, adventure, and finally, in Rock and Roll itself" (326). "Frankie" from *Tracks* illustrates this disappointment: "Well everybody's dying, this town's closing down / They're all sittin' down at the courthouse waiting for 'em to take the flag down."

This narrative of the American Dream gone bad appears throughout Springsteen's work and is a signature theme in much of his writing. Indeed, it serves as the primary focus of his major album achievements along the way, including *Born to Run*, *Born in the U.S.A.*, and *The Rising*. Like the flag mentioned above, in Springsteen's vision the dream myth of the nation takes on a nightmarish character: it unfolds in a backwards direction, it is essentially colourless, and it appears incapable of fully allowing in the light that could potentially shine on its citizens.

With the release of the *Born in the U.S.A.* album, Springsteen became increasingly identified as an American patriot whose virility embodied the intersectionality between masculinity, nationalism, and patriarchy. Springsteen's tough image and burly appearance in the 1980s represented the strength that then U.S. president Ronald Reagan connected to his constructed image of a dominant America plagued by the ever-looming threat of the Cold War. The title track of the album is not a song of celebrated patriotism, however. Rather, the song deals with failed patriotism as it focuses on a disillusioned Vietnam War veteran who questions both the U.S. role in the war, and the American values he and his brother defended. However, because of the strong punch line, "Born in the U.S.A.," and the image of the U.S. flag (without the stars) on the cover of the album as a backdrop to a working-class male body (depicted by Springsteen in a pair of jeans with a trucker cap hanging from his right back pocket), the song was misconstrued as a conservative, ideological, hard-edged proclamation of American pride. This result raises the question of multiple meanings that Springsteen's different audiences generate around his lyrics. As cultural studies scholar Lawrence Grossberg argues,

> The explanations of the success of the song "Born in the U.S.A." range from those who think it is a patriot's anthem (i.e., Reagan and the *Chicago Tribune*, which labeled him "the Rambo of Rock"), to those who think that his popularity is the result of a mishearing of Springsteen as a patriot, to those who seem to assume that all of his fans "care passionately about what his lyrics say," to more cynical views of the American myth of authenticity. (129)

Initially intended for inclusion on *Nebraska*, the original recording of "Born in the U.S.A" is included on *Tracks*. This instrumentally pared down version, lacking the rhythmic drive associated with the album version, sung in a cautious and restrained folk-style, and devoid of any pop sensibilities, could hardly have been misinterpreted as a patriotic anthem. It would have been interesting to see whether this particular version, had it been released, could have possibly changed Springsteen's image and the direction of his career. Such misconceptions of the meanings of Springsteen's lyrics and the contradictions surrounding his iconic image reveal the limitations of the cultural politics of "the Boss."

Springsteen's particular ways of seeing and interpreting socioeconomic realities through the lens of the nation, specifically the American nation in all its contradictions, has been a powerful factor in shaping his permanence as an American hero and artist. In his later career, Springsteen began to channel his voice successfully into the political sphere, particularly at the national scale. Over the years, he has had increasing involvement with leftist politics in America and he has shown ardent support for the Democratic Party. Not only have Springsteen's songs been adopted by various Democratic candidates, Springsteen himself has taken on a new role of prominence in recent presidential campaigns. In 2004, he stated support for Senator John Kerry's "Vote for Change" platform, while in 2008 he backed the election of presidential candidate Barack Obama and participated in the "We Are One" inaugural concert for the president in 2009.

CONCLUSION

Springsteen's oeuvre can be seen as a testament to both his personal life story and to the "promise of rock and roll" (Szatmary 269). Even though many of his songs have become commercial hits, Springsteen's authenticity as an artist has been consistently reinforced through his ability to suspend his superstar status in order to connect to the plight of ordinary working people. Whether it is through his simple storytelling, his jeans, his energy-driven live performances minus the theatrical frills, Springsteen's messages of hope—both lyrical and performative—carry that certain rock and roll promise of social change. As an American hero, Springsteen validates American ideals and struggles, which is why his songs are finding new relevance in the political arena today.

Tracks documents a lengthy time span in the artist's musical career and allows us—as it has allowed Springsteen himself—to track his transformation during this period. We witness at first a young rock and roller, fresh out of the Jersey Shore scene, whose concern primarily is with girls, cars, guitars, and hanging out with the guys. Over time, we encounter a more mature, socially conscious Springsteen, one preoccupied with broader socioeconomic and cultural issues in America. With a few exceptions, most of the songs on *Tracks* really did get away, since they were not released on any of his major albums. However, they are nevertheless equally imaginative and representative of Springsteen's integral themes of escape and struggle.

From an academic perspective, what can be teased out from this collection in particular is a coherent understanding of the ways Springsteen situates his characters and frames his stories, processes crucial to his construction of place and identity. His performance decisions regarding vocal phrasing, timbre, and delivery are also integral to the process, lending an edge of greater credibility to the way he embodies and personifies his characters' everyday struggles. It seems too, however, that through the process of writing and performing songs, Springsteen finds his own sense of place, leaving his identity traceable and his tracks imprinted indelibly on the rock and roll landscape.

NOTES

The authors wish to thank Anne-Marie Gallagher for her insightful comments and careful reading of several drafts of this work. A special thanks to Maria Abbruzzese; we are still enjoying the music on *Tracks* after so many years.

1. The discussion in this chapter focuses on the 1998 4–CD collection entitled *Tracks*, not to be confused with Springsteen's 1999 single disc release entitled *18 Tracks*.

2. According to Fred Schruers in his 1981 *Rolling Stone* article on Bruce Springsteen, guys like Bruce Springsteen were considered "Newarkys"—greasers who lived and played along the boardwalked Jersey Shore, drove muscle cars, and worked in garages and metal shops. Schruers is also from New Jersey.

3. The authors were not able to gain permission to reproduce the photographs featured in the liner notes to *Tracks*.

III

READING GENDER

6

"Who's That Girl?"

Nostalgia, Gender, and Springsteen

Kenneth Womack

You've heard of her before. She's the female lead in Bruce Springsteen's literary landscape. She's Sandy on the boardwalk; she's Wendy on the "streets of a runaway American dream"; she's the "barefoot girl sitting on the hood of a Dodge / Drinking warm beer in the soft summer rain." She's the immortal Mary, dancing like a vision across the porch. She's Candy, Rosalita, and Terry. She's Bobby Jean.[1] Although she comes in many guises, she's the female face at the heart of the sociocultural nostalgia that structures Springsteen's sense of pastness throughout his work. This essay discusses the nostalgic imperatives in popular music—and, more specifically, in Springsteen's songs—that allow us to enjoy a perspective toward the past as an archetypal paradise, a seductive space in which we can fulfill our collective longing for the illusory wholeness that lives in our memories and in our dreams.

There is little question that music enjoys a powerful capacity for eliciting a nostalgic response in its audience. When the conditions of the listening experience evoke nostalgic yearnings for the past, music clearly succeeds in exerting a psychological impact upon our emotional states of being. "Music seems to be profoundly connected to our emotional life," Martha C. Nussbaum observes, "indeed perhaps more urgently and deeply connected to that life than any of the other arts. It digs into our depths and expresses hidden movements of love and fear and joy that are inside us" (254). Psychologists have identified a compelling interrelationship between music and mood, arguing, for the most part, that the nature of lyrics and tonality often serves to arouse an affective and similarly directed emotional response in listeners. In their various studies of the intersections between psychology and music, Valerie N. Stratton and Annette H. Zalanowski demonstrate that the "general style of Western music has established a relationship between various components of music, such as pitch, speed, and intensity, and moods"; perhaps even more interestingly, "the presence of other mood-altering stimuli, including the client's thoughts and memories, may alter the manner in which the music is interpreted and even whether it is responded to at all" ("Effects" 126).

In short, music becomes ineluctably associated with our moods and our memories, and our aesthetic experiences with music act as the driving forces behind our cognitive responses to particular musical texts. As we learn in *Born in the U.S.A.*'s "Bobby Jean" (1984), Springsteen understands this concept implicitly. For the narrator, Bobby Jean exists as a nostalgic conduit to his past, to his youth, even to the existential fabric of his own mortality. Without Bobby Jean in this life, the narrator remains listless and disconnected, lost and distraught among the tatters of his memories: "Now we went walking in the rain, talking about the pain from the world we hid," Springsteen sings. "Now there ain't nobody nowhere nohow gonna ever understand me the way you did."[2] In this way, music enjoys a natural relationship with the feelings of nostalgia that subsequently shape—indeed, *re*-shape—the emotional texture and sentimentalized quality of our personal museums of recollection. For its listeners, music becomes inextricably bound up with our memories and our psychological states of being.

But whose nostalgia are we ultimately experiencing? Is it the artist's nostalgic yearnings through which, séance-like, we channel our memories, or does music merely serve as the catalyst for summoning forth our own deep-rooted feelings of nostalgia? In her study of music's relationship with human emotions, Nussbaum distinguishes between the role of a work's composer and the experiences of its listener during the musical event. On the one hand, a musical text inevitably reflects the "varied emotions of the composer during everyday life," especially in terms of the "emotional structures" that ultimately serve to produce the listener's aesthetic response (252). Yet on the other hand, that same aesthetic response in the listener might exist independently of the composer's emotions. From the listener's point of view, the musical text may begin to take on meanings and emotions that subsist well beyond the composer's aesthetic goals for the work in question.

In his words and music, Springsteen deftly taps into this phenomenon, metaphorically trafficking among the "backstreets" of our emotions and our memories. Featured on *Born to Run* (1975), "Backstreets" finds Springsteen's narrator hiding with lovelorn Terry among the dark alleys and secret avenues of their youth: "Laying here in the dark, you're like an angel on my chest," Springsteen sings, "Just another tramp of hearts crying tears of faithlessness." By challenging us to stare longingly into the covert spaces of our own pasts and our own memories—into our personal "backstreets"—

Springsteen draws us into the matrix, eliciting experiences and responses in his listeners' minds that he could never possibly have imagined for his composition. Musicologists describe this phenomenon in terms of an "arousal theory" of musical expressiveness that accounts for the affective response to music in which great passions become stimulated during the listening experience. For Malcolm Budd, the arousal theory involves an experience in which the musical work relates "in a certain way to an event which can be fully characterized [and valued] without reference to the nature of the work itself" (123).

While a number of musicologists and psychologists subscribe to the arousal theory—particularly in terms of its ability to represent the melismatic and emotionally charged experiences of casual listeners—Aaron Ridley argues that it neglects to "explain why we value some music [explicitly] *for* its expressiveness," a phenomenon that Ridley describes as the "heresy of separable experience" (123). Indeed, the arousal theory fails to account for the musical unity that many artists—including Springsteen—strive to assert in their work. Stratton and Zalanowski define aesthetic unity in vocal-driven music as the result of a composition in which "the lyrics dominate the affective direction, and the effort of fitting the music to the lyrics strengthens the emotion. In addition, the music itself may produce some arousal which also will be interpreted in light of the lyrics" ("Affective" 182). More importantly, the arousal theory also neglects to provide for the reflexive relationship that invariably emerges between composer and listener. As reader-response theory has so clearly demonstrated, the musical work's implied reader participates in the meaning-making process by engaging in a synergistic relationship with the work's author.[3]

In *Darkness on the Edge of Town's* "Badlands" (1978), Springsteen employs his unnamed female companion as a reflexive device for exploring the vast recesses of his own convoluted identity. In so doing, he draws his audience into engaging in a similarly uncertain enterprise—into grappling with the "badlands" of our own unexamined personae: "For the ones who had a notion, a notion deep inside / That it ain't no sin to be glad you're alive," Springsteen sings. "I wanna find one place that ain't looking through me / I wanna find one place, I wanna spit in the face of these badlands." The listener's actual emotions necessarily have a determining effect on the interpretation of the musical text in question, as do any ancillary elements that serve to affect—either directly or indirectly—the aesthetic experience. As Nussbaum points out, the listener "may be distracted, attending badly, ignorant of the work's structure, and so forth" (253). Simply put, our emotional response to music is always contingent upon a multiplicity of textual and extra-textual factors, many of which we exert surprisingly little control over during the listening experience. Perhaps this explains why music wields such a powerful psychological force in our lives: it elicits our feelings without seeking our permission, and even if we decide to subvert music's emotional effects by shutting it off, the psychological residue of the experience remains intact in our synapses, surviving, as it does, to taunt us in the silence of music's absence.

In their most sentimentalized and emotion-laden manifestations, nostalgia's musical antecedents function in much the same manner, haunting us by remote control across the staves of our memories. Vladimir Nabokov describes nostalgia—with its "heartrending oddities"—as the "insane companion" that accompanies us for the balance of our lives.[4] The alleged inauthenticity of nostalgia finds its origins in the ironic distance that, for many thinkers, exists between ourselves and the past. For Greil Marcus, nostalgia represents "a yearning for something that you probably never experienced, a sentimentalized false memory" that indulges in "emotional decadence" and serves only to provide refuge for "a crippled soul or an impoverished heart." Marcus contends that "the more deeply the well of nostalgia is plumbed, the more intense one's feelings of loss will become, and the listener will be stranded, caught between the embarrassment of mourning the loss of things that never existed and the embarrassment of finding that wounds that should have closed long ago are still open" ("Days between Stations"). Kimberly K. Smith argues that our contemporary notions of nostalgia first came into being through various nineteenth- and twentieth-century conflicts over the political significance of the past. According to Smith, nostalgia finds its origins in the historical transition from the relative stability of an agrarian society to the mounting anxiety of a largely industrial world (506).

In many ways, nostalgia's mournful response to the loss of an agrarian past in relation to an all-consuming industrial present is Springsteen's central métier. In the title track from *The River* (1980), Springsteen situates his narrator's wistful youth with his beloved Mary against a vexing, uncertain present. At the same time, the narrator braces for his new life as a construction worker—in glaring contrast with his carefree days along the pastoral river in the valley—and as the sole provider for his young wife and their newborn-to-be: "Then I got Mary pregnant and, man, that was all she wrote / And for my nineteenth birthday I got a union card and a wedding coat," Springsteen sings. "We went in town to the courthouse, and the judge put it all to rest / No wedding day smiles, no walk down the aisle / No flowers, no wedding dress." In this sense, Springsteen's overarching nostalgia emerges as a means for recontextualizing the past in terms of the present, as a form of social constructivism in which the past accrues greater meaning because of its significance and desirability in contrast with an uncertain and highly volatile contemporary moment. "To experience a memory nostalgically is not just to have certain feelings along with that memory," Smith suggests, "but to adopt a particular attitude towards it: to understand the memory and its associated feelings as the product of a psychological propensity to romanticize the past, and to value it as a vehicle for a Proustian sort of heightened sensibility or self-awareness" (509). In this way, nostalgia exists as an acculturated behavior through which we develop a perspective towards the past as a place where we might fulfill our collective longing for an "archetypal paradise" (514).[5]

Yet Marcus's and Smith's contentions about nostalgia's ostensible inauthenticity—intellectually and historically valid as they may be—make little difference, quite frankly, to mass culture's audience, a vast constituency that yearns (often unconsciously) for transcendence amidst the malaise and fragmentation of postmodern life. "When the real is no longer what it used to be," Jean Baudrillard cautions, "nostalgia assumes its full meaning" (12). While he acknowledges nostalgia's "semideluded state" and its function "as an act more of forgetting than remembrance," R. J. Warren Zanes argues that nostalgia finds its contemporary roots in our larger cultural urge to return to an unblemished past where we can revivify our notions of community and eschew the superficiality of commercialism's ceaseless engine. In contrast with our nostalgic desires for reasserting stability, the real myth, Zanes suggests, originates from "our ill-founded dreams" of a proverbial elsewhere in which our yen for consumerism replaces the emotional satisfaction that we derive from home, hearth, and humanity. As Zanes reminds us, the world of music—and rock culture in particular—"holds out the promise that such a longing might be satisfied" (62).[6] And why not? Hasn't popular music always dared us to embrace the restorative powers of love, friendship, and a universalizing belief in a redeemable past—a past in which, if our aim is really true, we can get back to where we once belonged?

In his desire to perform nostalgia throughout much of his career, Springsteen's music operates in a decidedly reciprocal fashion in which he satisfies his own needs as de facto author, as well as the needs and desires of his vast audience of listeners who also long for a sense of reconnection with the past. As Andreea Deciu Ritivoi observes, "Nostalgia is a loose concept, highly loaded with vague, poetical connotations." Ritivoi argues, moreover, for a connection between nostalgia and a theory of narrative identity in which the self operates as a "narrative project" of sorts (à la Paul Ricoeur). In this narrative project, our notions of identity presuppose "a strong sense of sameness, as well as openness to difference and change" ("Here and Now"). From his earliest moments as a recording artist through the present, Springsteen's own narrative project increasingly merges nostalgia's sentimental pangs with the bitter truth inherent in our progressively more distant and ever-shifting relationship with the past.

In many ways, the self-fulfilling prophecy inherent in this kind of wistful yearning intersects with the Levinasian concept of alterity, in which our experiences with otherness—be it human *or* historical—allow us to recognize more fully the convoluted nature of our sense of self. Hence, Springsteen's evolving need to perform nostalgia as a narratological device in his music fulfills a larger ethical desire—both for him *and* for us—to replicate sameness and to establish means of reconnecting with the past even as we make explicit attempts to break with that same past and create new inroads into an uncertain future. Yet it also underscores our vexing relationship with the past, which exerts a powerful hold upon the present, in one sense, while slowly fading from memory and metamorphosing into other perhaps more pleasing or less painful memories with each passing year. As Maurice Halbwachs reminds us, "The past is not preserved but is reconstructed on the basis of the present" (quoted in Kimberly Smith 517–18).

As the evolving vehicle for placating his nostalgic yearnings, Springsteen's women serve as the impetus for memorializing this sense of pastness through vivid, albeit highly passive lyrical images. In "4th of July, Asbury Park," winsome Sandy strolls along the boardwalk on the arms of Springsteen's speaker, who exists simultaneously in the present and the past. In the latter, he guides his less-experienced female companion on a progress under the fireworks "hailin' over Little Eden tonight" into a seamy netherworld of "stoned-out faces" and "switchblade lovers." This is a world filled with blazing contrasts—from the relative innocence of the Tilt-a-Whirl and the wizards on Pinball Way, to the Latin lovers "chasin' all them silly New York girls" and the more precarious "boys in their spiked high heels." Yet the present also features a conflicted tableau that brings the speaker's romanticized view of the Jersey Shore into stark relief, particularly when he reflects upon the wounds of his sexual past in juxtaposition with Sandy's ostensible wholesomeness. Having grown tired of the "dusty arcades, bangin' them pleasure machines," and "chasin' them factory girls," he had taken to midnight trysts with the boss's daughter—"Well, he ain't my boss no more, Sandy"—and an encounter with a seaside waitress flags after "she lost her desire for me. I spoke with her last night," the speaker confides in Sandy, and "she said she won't set herself on fire for me anymore." On the one hand, the entire song acts as a late-adolescent come-on—à la Elvis Presley's "It's Now or Never" or Lynyrd Skynyrd's "Free Bird": "Love me tonight for I may never see you again, Sandy girl." Yet on the other, the speaker desperately attempts—in the song's present-day manifestations—to stave off oblivion by eternally shining the pier lights on their past "carnival life on the water." The speaker pointedly tries to defy the loneliness of the present—and, presumably, the future—by engaging his beloved in commiseration for the loss of the past, as well as within a shared passage into an unknown and eminently more frightening future: "Sandy, the angels have lost their desire for us / This boardwalk life for me is through / You know, you ought to quit this scene, too."

Springsteen's speakers effect a similar posture throughout his corpus, particular in terms of their need for companionship in order to reconcile the backstreets of the past with the future's unknowable badlands. "Memory," Nancy Martha West observes, "depends on a personalized narrative; nostalgia transforms that narrative (including the possible stresses and uncertainties of events in progress) into fullness, innocence, simplicity" (175). In contrast with the darker images of pain and uncertainty that Springsteen later traces in the shadows of "Candy's Room," "Rosalita (Come Out Tonight)" objectifies its subject's relative sexual immaturity in relation to the speaker's knowing and more exuberant carnal experience: "Spread out now Rosie, doctor come cut loose her mama's reins / You know playin' blind man's bluff is a little baby's game." In the song, the speaker explicitly couches his carefree demeanor—"I ain't here for business, I'm only here for fun"—within the more subversive context of rampant sexual longing: "Rosalita jump a little lighter, senorita come sit by my fire / I just want to be your lover ain't no liar, Rosalita you're my stone desire." His yearning to "liberate" Rosie—indeed, to "confiscate" her—is tempered by her Old World father's determination to preserve her virtue in the face of American modernity. Yet Springsteen's speaker— already adopting the future's nostalgic stance—evinces the capacity for sentimentalizing the strife of their present-day situation: "Someday, we'll look back on this and it will all seem funny"; in nearly the same breath, though, he imagines a Western utopia, another "Little Eden," in which he and Rosie will carry out their lives: "I know a pretty little place in Southern California down San Diego way / There's a little café where they play guitars all night and day." Entreating her to listen closely—because "you can hear them in the back room strummin'"—he promises her a world of freedom and love, even though Springsteen's speaker—awash in the less-idyllic reality of the future—almost certainly knows better.

In "Born to Run," Springsteen's speaker offers a similar objectification of Wendy, whose purity affords him with reason enough to go on living in the face of an increasingly dismal present, to speed along the "highway jammed with broken heroes on a last-chance power drive." As with Sandy and Rosalita, Wendy takes on the weight of the speaker's own transgressions and guilt, providing him with a means for reconceiving the sentimentalized past and his wayward present by virtue of, well, his female companion's virtue. "I want to guard your dreams and visions," he declares. "Together, Wendy we'll live with the sadness / I'll love you with all the madness in my soul." But does this lingering sadness really belong to Wendy? Or even to Western civilization? Or is it the speaker's own angst about a perplexing future in contrast with the simpler pleasures of the boardwalk?

In "Thunder Road," Mary's immortal and seemingly permanent aura of
innocence buoys the speaker, giving him the courage to endure:

> Don't run back inside, darling you know just what I'm here for
> So you're scared and you're thinking
> That maybe we ain't that young anymore
> Show a little faith, there's magic in the night
> You ain't a beauty, but hey you're alright
> Oh and that's alright with me.

Springsteen pointedly frames Mary's skittishness in terms of a rigid Catholicism about which his speaker wryly knows better:

> You can hide 'neath your covers and study your pain
> Make crosses from your lovers, throw roses in the rain
> Waste your summer praying in vain
> For a savior to rise from these streets.

The only redemption, it seems, that the speaker can offer Mary is "beneath
this dirty hood"—the guileless freedom of the open road, where, with the
wind blowing in their hair, they'll enjoy "one last chance to make it real."
The literal Thunder Road—"lying out there like a killer in the sun"—affords
them with the manna of the future and the capacity for remaking the past.
As with many of his songs, "Thunder Road" situates its narrative in relation
to a single, last-ditch opportunity for salvation—a sense of personal renewal that the speaker can only enjoy in the company, we come to discover,
of a virtuous (or at least *semi*-virtuous) female other. In a world of dusty,
God-forsaken roads amidst the "skeleton frames of burned-out Chevrolets,"
the speaker glimpses his escape, his last great chance at living out his own
dreams and visions in the company of his beloved: "It's a town full of losers
and I'm pulling out of here to win."

With nostalgic feelings, Fred Davis remarks, "the emotional posture is
that of a yearning for return, albeit accompanied by an ambivalent recognition that such is not possible" (21). In "Jungleland," Springsteen prefigures
this "yearning for return" by setting his lovers' tragic story—for now and
forever more—"tonight in Jungleland," a sentiment that suggests that the
dark progress of the streets never ceases, that the joy of youthful flamboy-
ance, sexual discovery, and uncompromising violence never wanes even as
we recede into the future's suffocating embrace. In the midst of it all, the
"barefoot girl sitting on the hood of a Dodge" acts as the male lead's stead-
fast, albeit perpetually silent compatriot. When the Rat pulls into town, the
barefoot girl fulfills her promise of unconditional love and truth, and "together they take a stab at romance" of the last-ditch variety that abounds in
Springsteen's canon. As with the other nocturnal inhabitants of Jungleland,

the Rat and the barefoot girl are taking "one last stand" at achieving one-ness with reality—for attempting to "make it real." With encroaching con-sumerism as their only solace—living beneath "that giant Exxon sign that brings this fair city light"—the couple conducts their sensual dance to the music of high culture in step with the low noise of the streets: "There's an opera out on the Turnpike / There's a ballet being fought out in the alley." While the "hungry and the hunted explode into rock'n'roll bands," the Rat and the barefoot girl go about proving it all night. As "soul engines running through a night so tender in a bedroom locked," the Rat overcomes her "whispers of soft refusal" and wins the pennant of her virginity.[7]

Yet as the barefoot girl symbolically extinguishes her bedroom light, the Rat's "own dream guns him down" in the street violence exploding beyond Flamingo Road. The Rat's demise, Springsteen's narrator tells us, defies inscription—even intervention. It's as if the entire "death waltz / Between flesh and what's fantasy" were the unstoppable product of some kind of cosmic predestination. "The poets down here / Don't write nothing at all," Springsteen sings. "They just stand back and let it all be." And despite yet another last-ditch attempt to "reach for their moment / And try to make an honest stand," the players "wind up wounded, not even dead," forced to live out an unceasing sense of presentness in Jungleland that is both exhila-rating in its insatiable infinitude and youthful prowess, as well as mind-numbingly bewildering in its brevity and spiritual damnation.

The forlorn, soul-deafening qualities of "Jungleland" continue to reso-nate in "Candy's Room," the proverbial dark heart at the core of *Dark-ness on the Edge of Town.* As with Springsteen's earlier female characters, Candy acts as a vessel for the narrator's failings, as a vehicle for exploring the feelings of loss that he experiences as he gets older amongst the detri-tus of a rapidly encroaching present. In contrast with his earlier heroines, though, Springsteen's Candy has her own crosses to bear, her own past to conquer and usurp. "In Candy's room," Springsteen's narrator reports, "there are pictures of her heroes on the wall / But to get to Candy's room you gotta walk the darkness of Candy's hall." Her room is a shrine to a fiercely blemished past, her features a secret roadmap of a misbegotten life: "There's a sadness hidden in that pretty face," the narrator sings. The lovers' fiery embrace allows the narrator to peel back the darkness and illuminate his own sadness by opening up—indeed, revivifying—the "hidden worlds" of his youth: "When I hold Candy close," the narrator sings, "she makes these hidden worlds mine." In the end, Candy affords him with the capacity for revisiting the wild days and nights of his youth, but she does so at a great personal cost. While the narrator confesses that he would give anything to possess Candy—to spend just one night in her soul-inspiring arms—she ends up giving everything to serve as the conduit to his past.

The evolution of Springsteen's nostalgic songwriterly impulses in his post–*Darkness on the Edge of Town* years finds him shifting from a world-weary personal nostalgia to a larger, shared nostalgia that mirrors his aging audience's own desires for reconnecting with an increasingly distant and muted past. This shift in Springsteen's nostalgic tenor occurs rather precipitously with *The River*, an album in which Springsteen's characters confront the obligations and duties associated with adulthood. With "Sherry Darling," Springsteen's narrator imagines an escape from the responsibilities of his life, a harkening-back to his memories of a now-impenetrable youth: "Well, I got some beer and the highway's free / And I got you, and baby you've got me / Hey, hey, hey, what you say, Sherry Darlin'?" As with songs like "Hungry Heart," "Sherry Darling" is significant as much for its music, which makes explicit tonal reference to the good-time rock and roll inherent in the late 1950s and early 1960s. As with Candy, Springsteen's narrator involves Sherry in his quest for restorative youth, for rediscovering his past through the auspices of beer and sex. The narrator's dalliance with Sherry exists in stark contrast with the unnamed female protagonist in "Point Blank," one of *The River*'s most disturbing and mind-numbingly hopeless tracks. "Do you still say your prayers, little darlin'? / Do you go to bed at night," the narrator sings, "Prayin' that tomorrow, everything will be alright? / But tomorrow's fall in numbers, in numbers one by one / You wake up and you're dying, you don't even know what from."

The idea that we're inevitably dying from a faceless, unimaginable assailant—from time immemorial and unstoppable older age—lives at the core of Springsteen's nostalgia, an impulse that shifts increasingly from the despair of "Candy's Room" and "Point Blank" to a more hopeful longing in such works as *Human Touch*'s "Gloria's Eyes" and *Devil & Dust*'s "Maria's Bed." In such moments, Springsteen's soul-rending pain transforms into a search for possible redemption through our nostalgic excursions into the past. "I was your big man, I was your Prince Charming," Springsteen sings, but "now I'm just a fool in Gloria's eyes." Yet in contrast with his earlier female figures, Gloria holds the power for catalyzing redemption and not merely serving as a vehicle for masculine punishment or rebuke:

> Now I work hard to prove my love is true
> Now I work hard and I brought it on home to you
> At night I pray as silently you lie
> Someday my love again will rise
> Like a shining torch in Gloria's eyes.

For Springsteen, the auspices of womanhood act as a revitalizing power. As with Gloria's eyes, the soul-restoring power inherent in "Maria's Bed" affords Springsteen's narrator with the opportunity to liberate himself from the shackles of his workaday life, to find sustenance and relief from his job "on a barbed-wire highway 40 days and nights." For all of his misery on the road, Maria's bed provides him with the restfulness and understanding that the rest of his life denies. "I got run out'a luck and give myself up for dead," the narrator sings, "and I drank the cool waters from Maria's bed." Springsteen explores a strikingly similar sentiment in "Working on a Dream," the title track of his most recent studio album. As with "Maria's Bed," "Working on a Dream" asserts an innate sense of hopefulness within the narrator's female other. As with "Maria's Bed," the narrator suffers the toil of his soul-destroying employment: "Out here, the nights are long, the days are lonely," he sings. Yet when he thinks of his unnamed female counterpart, he finds the power and motivation to move forward, to attempt—in spite of life's challenging odds—to prevail: "I think of you, and I'm working on a dream." It may be a distant dream of sustenance that exists well beyond the horizon, but it's just enough, Springsteen's narrator avers, to see him through: "I'm working on a dream, / And I know it will be mine someday." In dramatic contrast with the early vessels of his nostalgia, Springsteen's latter female foils provide his narrators with far more than wormholes to reconnect with their lost or misspent youths; they afford them with something far better and eminently more lasting: the capacity for going on.

In this manner, Springsteen intuitively recognizes, as Ritivoi's narrative project reminds us, that our abiding desires for sameness are inevitably trumped by an understandable uncertainty about the future and our invariable anxiety about life's ever-shifting nature. The bitter truth inherent in the conclusion of "Jungleland"—no matter how affirming it may appear—suggests that a return to the past represents the impossible dream that nostalgia begs us to indulge. As Anthony Elliott points out, nostalgia often operates as a "means for understanding how we see ourselves today in the light of the past. From this angle, nostalgia has a certain transformative quality, permitting the recovery of lost memories, thoughts, and feelings as a medium for present artistic experience" (177). Indeed, while we cannot recoup the past through revision, we can surely interact with it via remembrance, reflection, and—in a meaningful nod to the future and our potential for interpersonal growth—revaluation. In short, although we cannot alter the past, we can reap the benefits of becoming "altered," in a Levinasian sense, in terms of our larger understanding of our memories and our nostalgic-driven emotions, even in their most sentimentalized and socially constructed aspects.

NOTES

1. The female characters appear in the following songs/albums: Sandy in "4th of July, Asbury Park (Sandy)"/*The Wild, the Innocent & the E Street Shuffle* (1973); Wendy in "Born to Run"/*Born to Run* (1975); the barefoot girl in "Jungleland"/*Born to Run* (1975); Mary in "Thunder Road"/*Born to Run* (1975); Candy in "Candy's Room"/*Darkness on the Edge of Town* (1978); Rosalita in "Rosalita (Come Out Tonight)"/*The*

Wild, the Innocent & the E Street Shuffle (1973); Terry in "Backstreets"/ *Born to Run* (1975); and Bobby Jean in "Bobby Jean"/*Born in the U.S.A.* (1984).

2. In a real sense, Springsteen's memories of Bobby Jean act as the highly personalized engine of the songwriter's nostalgia. As an ostensible metaphor for guitarist "Miami" Steve Van Zandt—who was leaving the E Street Band at the time, only to return to the fold during the 1990s—"Bobby Jean" finds Springsteen thinking wistfully, indeed sentimentally, about friendship and the heartrending prospect of saying good-bye.

3. Reader-response theory presupposes, of course, that the reading (or, by extension, listening) experience operates as a reflexive process that involves a fusion of sorts between text and reader in the production of meaning. In the world of musicology, reader-response theory's meaning-making process most closely resembles Deryck Cooke's expression-transmission theory of music. Malcolm Budd usefully summarizes Cooke's process as a reflexive event in which the composer translates "his emotions into musical sounds which are transformed into patterns in a score which, in turn, are transformed back into musical sounds which, finally, are transformed back into emotions that the sympathetic listener experiences as he hears the music" (122).

4. Our personal emotional histories are impacted by a "cognitive specificity" of sorts, Nussbaum argues, that grows and deepens as we accrue additional memories throughout our lives. Indeed, "new objects of love and anger and fear bear the traces of earlier objects," Nussbaum writes. "One's emotions toward them are frequently therefore also, in both intensity and configuration, emotions toward one's past" (175).

5. Kimberly Smith argues that the dangers of a politically engendered nostalgia extend well beyond our futile dreams for an "archetypal paradise": "If nostalgia is universal, even a return to pre-industrial society won't help. We are convinced that whatever it is we long for wasn't actually there, that we are longing for something—community, stability, the feeling of being at home—that is unattainable anywhere. Thus, not only has industrialization obliterated agrarian society, but its accompanying theory of nostalgia has destabilized our individual and collective memories of our pre-industrial past" (522–23).

6. Zanes further asserts that "there is a real connection between [rock's] cultural desire for authenticity and rock culture's fertility as a soil for traditional values, including romantic notions of artistic genius, gender norms, a nostalgic longing that is often aimed at a mythic past (a past not unrelated to the traditional family values espoused in mainstream political rhetorics), and so forth" (67). Even more significantly, Zanes argues against the intelligentsia's knee-jerk reaction to nostalgia as a balm for the masses: "I believe that denigrating nostalgic tendencies without assessing the character of those nostalgias is a mistake, primarily because nostalgia might be the most powerful political tool of our time, one worth considering as potentially oppositional rather than simply conservative" (69).

7. For the Rat, the prize of the barefoot girl's virginity will be, at most, a transitory treasure. The mysterious, transient role of Springsteen's female others throughout his career is perhaps most effectively illustrated by "Secret Garden" (*Greatest Hits,* 1995), in which the narrator's elusive beloved remains at arm's length even as their intimacy seemingly draws them ever closer. As this composition so forcefully reminds us, Springsteen's female characters are often characterized as being vast reservoirs of love and tenderness, while teetering at the same time in his narrators' minds as being fleeting, ethereal, and ultimately unobtainable: "She's got a secret garden," Springsteen sings, "Where everything you want, where everything you need / Will always stay a million miles away."

7

Growin' Up to Be a Nothing Man

Masculinity, Community, and the Outsider in Bruce Springsteen's Songs

Ann V. Bliss

Archetypal outsider figures are ubiquitous in American culture. He—and this figure is invariably male—can be found in literature, film, and music. Bruce Springsteen's songs are no exception: they are often populated by outsider figures, who have evolved over the course of Springsteen's career. Four representative songs demonstrate the evolution of the outsider across the span of Springsteen's catalogue. In "Growin' Up," the narrator is the nonconformist rebel; in "Meeting Across the River," he is tempted into some nefarious illegal action in attempting to maintain his sense of credibility; and in "Mansion on the Hill," he passively observes a seemingly unattainable way of life. However, in *The Rising*'s "Nothing Man," the figure of the outsider becomes more disturbing in that despite living a life of which the other outsider characters can only dream, he distances himself from that life. He seems to disconnect emotionally from his community, as if actively choosing not to belong, while still conforming to the conventions of his society. Despite his apparent achievement of the American Dream, the "Nothing Man" appears to occupy a much more dangerous emotional space than do the disenfranchised figures of Springsteen's earlier works.

The figure of the outsider is closely connected to another recurring theme in Springsteen's work: the desire to achieve the American Dream. Resistance to or pursuit of this hazy concept features prominently in the outsider narrative. Not easily defined, the notion of the American Dream not only changes over time, but also differs with individual desire. While the simplest form of the American Dream is associated with home ownership, Jim Cullen recognizes that it also encompasses "wealth, fame, and power." As Cullen succinctly puts it, the American Dream "can be summed up in

the following assertion: Anything is possible if you want it badly enough"
(*American* 53).

Over time, the relationship of the outsider in Springsteen's songs to the
American Dream progresses in a way that reflects the change from youthful
rebellion to a more mature disillusionment with the Dream. Initially the
outsider consciously rejects the conventions of the Dream; subsequently
wanting to embrace its tenets, he cannot move away from the societal and
economic restrictions of his life. Eventually, he achieves many of the material markers of success associated with the American Dream, but emotionally rejects such materialism as fundamentally psychologically unsatisfying.
Such disillusionment with the Dream results in emotional trauma that
reverses the paradigm of the outsider, in that he is no longer outside an
unattainable way of life, but potentially trapped within a life with which he
cannot identify and which threatens to suffocate his spirit.

WORKING-CLASS MASCULINITY

The quintessential American characteristic of individuality threaded
throughout Springsteen's lyrics is practically synonymous with masculinity. In his extensive discussion of American masculinity and manhood, E.
Anthony Rotundo argues that "individualism—expressed in the form of the
free agent, the independent citizen, the unfettered man on the make—is
vital to a free society" (292). Masculine individualism is a key concept of
the American Dream, a "largely . . . male dream," with women historically
neglected and excluded from its pursuit (Cullen, *American* 119). Not surprisingly, this historical and cultural emphasis on the individual man is the
focus of many Springsteen songs. With few exceptions, the central characters of Springsteen's songs, especially the narrators, are heterosexual white
men.[1] These characters mostly embrace the accepted conventional masculine role within their societies: they want, and usually get, the girl, and work
hard to support their families. Conforming to such conventions, though,
limits these characters societally and emotionally; as Gareth Palmer puts it,
the "tragedy" of Springsteen's male characters is their "inability to abandon
the carefully drawn markers of masculinity, which prevents escape into
the world of feeling" (101). In particular, a significant number of songs
about the individual working-class man in search of his personal American
Dream address the constriction the central character feels in conforming
to gender-specific roles; such songs consequently reinforce both masculine
and working-class stereotypes. The persistence of the working-class man in
Springsteen's work and his apparent failure to progress socioeconomically
imply that the pursuit of the Dream holds more importance than does attaining it.

The proliferation of working-class characters in so many of his songs reflects Springsteen's own background, as detailed by his many biographers. Long after Springsteen achieved all the trappings of wealth, though, his characters continue to struggle with the limitations of lower social class status. Springsteen's own public image has consistently been that of the blue-collar worker, the working-man's rocker, while simultaneously projecting a kind of hyper-masculinity (especially during the height of his popularity in the mid-1980s). To some extent, Springsteen himself (or at least that iconic Springsteen of the 1980s) embodies white masculinity; even his nickname "the Boss" connotes "mastery and authority" (Garman, *Race* 222). Michael Kimmel, though, sees this title as ironic in that Springsteen's songs are invariably about "the dead-end lives of workers," and argues that it reinforces the contradiction between the "energized, upbeat, anthemic" music and "the relentlessly bleak portrait of the downward spiral of the white working class" described in many of Springsteen's lyrics (214).

Part of the persistence of the working class in Springsteen's songs depends on the complex relationship between individualism, masculinity, and work, a relationship that eludes the outsider. According to David Morgan, "work, both in the general and specific sense, is assumed to be a major basis of identity and what it means to be a man" (quoted in Palmer 106). The elusive American Dream is inextricably entwined with the importance of work in defining masculinity; indeed, one of its most recognized tenets is the possibility of upward mobility, primarily perceived as being achieved through the rewards of hard work. Despite the apparent problems Springsteen's characters experience in making the shift from economic despair to financial stability, the songs frequently perpetuate the mythologized hope that the opportunity for such a shift exists for all. Many of Springsteen's songs address the centrality of work as an American ethos and how this ethos is threatened when the romanticized ideal of work is unavailable. Songs such as "Atlantic City" and "Johnny 99," for example, feature characters whose inability to find work leads them to criminality and violence. Conventional perceptions of American society represented in much of Springsteen's oeuvre depend on hard-working individual men whose collective work benefits society as a whole.

However, the individualistic rebel, embodied by such American icons as James Dean and Marlon Brando, is as central to male American identity as is the hard-working conformist, and ironically part of the mythos of the American man is formulated on his resistance to this model of the hard worker. Gareth Palmer considers rebellion as "crucial to masculine development" (102) and Jim Cullen recognizes that "manhood is an inevitably plural term, encompassing a variety of roles and realms in everyday life" (*Born* 122). Conventional masculinity, then, can apparently embrace these two contradictory models, a contradiction that can be resolved by considering the non-static nature of masculinity. The American man moves through boyhood and youth to a maturity often realized through fatherhood. In particular, the evolution of the father-son relationship exemplifies the trajectory of American manhood from rebellion to responsibility. Palmer sees three "typical" stages in the father-son relationship that are key to understanding masculinity: "adoration, rebellion, and *rapprochement*" (10). While allowing for individuality, these stages do not exclude the individual from participating in the greater community. Failing to follow the established trajectory and becoming either stuck in adolescence or unable to embrace individuality, the outsider seems trapped by his rebellion, even if he wants to move beyond it.

The socially accepted tenets of masculinity begin to form early in a boy's life through his participation in "boy culture," a term E. Anthony Rotundo uses to describe the aggressive and adventurous play that comes to establish accepted normative behavior for boys during the nineteenth century. American boy culture embraces qualities such as "courage . . . loyalty . . . mastery . . . and, above all, independence" and values "physical prowess, or a tendency to resist adult authority" (Cullen, *Born* 123, 124). These familiar characteristics of boyhood behavior lead naturally into the potentially risky behavior often associated with adolescence, the kind of behavior clearly seen in the young male characters of such early Springsteen songs as "Spirit in the Night" and "The E Street Shuffle." What happens, then, if these traits continue or persist beyond boyhood into adulthood?

From about their late teens to their twenties, or even thirties, according to Rotundo, boys pass from boy culture into youth culture, a time when a young man begins to think about his future while still feeling "the backward pull of boyhood" (57). Like boy culture, youth culture was first recognized during the nineteenth century and was often a time when the young man left home to travel, work, or attend college. According to Rotundo, "the greatest concern of young men facing the future was the quest for commitment to two fundamental arenas: love and work" (58). Although written about men of the nineteenth century, this statement applies equally to many of the characters inhabiting Springsteen's songs, and resolving the problems associated with these two provinces allows for movement from youthhood to maturity, and hence inclusion into the conventions of American society that remain elusive to the outsider.

Standard markers of masculinity, especially participation in work and relationships with women, present problems for the outsider figure. As we have seen, the topic of work—either its identificatory nature or its absence—features prominently in Springsteen's songs. However, the topic of women and their importance in the male characters' lives perhaps features more frequently than that of work. Palmer argues that "Springsteen's women do not exist as characters in their own right but as signifiers of domesticity and commitment against which men define their masculinity" (104). Indeed, the conflation of women with work in a character's successful transition from boyhood to manhood recurs frequently. Much of the potential for financial success or reward is associated with leaving dead-end towns, often for the coast, either east or west, as seen, for example, in "Thunder Road." The narrator presents such leaving as an adventure appropriate for boy or youth culture, with the quest for financial freedom involving escaping the limitations of the narrator's current environment. Women are often encouraged to accompany the narrator when he makes his escape. Rosalita is lured away by the narrator's potential rock star status, the record company having given him "a big advance"; the narrator of "Born to Run" wants Wendy to leave "the death trap" with him; while Mary, in "Thunder Road" is exhorted to "climb in" the car and leave the "town full of losers" with the narrator. Palmer considers independence and freedom as "the core of mythic masculinity" whereby Springsteen's characters are "tempted by the cultural bribe of a masculinity which promises to give them identity but which remains unattainable and leaves them unfulfilled" (104). Those characters who have transitioned into fatherhood, though, have fewer opportunities to escape; they are more likely to make the best of their present situation.

Springsteen's fathers—both the father of the narrator and those fathers who are the first-person narrators of a song—have passed through boy and youth culture and emerged into a maturity that seems to depend on passing their accumulated wisdom on to their sons. The impetus to escape has disappeared, having been replaced by some kind of acceptance of the narrator's father's place in his community. He, like his father before him, sits his son "up behind the wheel" of the car, telling him to "take a good look around" just as his father had done with him ("My Hometown"). Alternatively, the father reinforces the values represented by the establishment, letting the son know that the "flag flying over the courthouse / Means certain things are set in stone" ("Long Walk Home"). To reach this level of maturity, the narrator has had to successfully negotiate between the contradictory images of manhood—that of the youthful rebel and that of the pursuer of the American Dream. In doing so, he also successfully negotiates another dichotomy, that of the needs of the individual versus the needs of the community.

COMMUNITY AND THE INDIVIDUAL

The outsider cannot exist in a vacuum; defined by that which he is outside of, he can only be called an outsider if he is not an insider—part of a greater whole. Invariably in Springsteen songs, that greater whole is some kind of community. Understanding the symbiotic relationship between the individual and the community is key to fully appreciating the outsider's sense of alienation. If the trope of the outsider has been consistent in Springsteen's lyrics, then that of the community dominates. Much of Springsteen's oeuvre explores the centrality of the community in the lives of his characters, and this concept has been extensively discussed by Springsteen himself and by critics of his work.[2] The image of the community resonates metonymically in Springsteen's songs and represents both contemporary American society and the fragility of such society.

Furthermore, Springsteen's concept of community functions to support emotionally those whom Jefferson Cowie and Lauren Boehm recognize as victims of social status. Cowie and Boehm point out that "most Springsteen songs hold the possibility of redemption" and are often filled with imagery that includes "community, hope, and faith" (358–59). That sense of communality is fundamental to the individual finding his place within his society. If the community fails the individual, as it does in "Born in the U.S.A.," then, as Springsteen points out, "it's like he has nothing left to tie him into society anymore. He's isolated from the government. Isolated from his family" (quoted in Cowie and Boehm 359). According to T.V. Reed, Springsteen believes that "the pace of the modern world . . . [has] made human connection difficult to maintain and sustain" (105). Consequently, the interaction between the individual and the community becomes increasingly important, as seen in the "desire for community" in the words of "Born to Run": "*we* sweat it out on the street of a runaway American dream," not "*I* sweat it out" (Guterman 97, original emphasis). "Born to Run," then, presents a communal American Dream based on the collective working together, a concept that remains present in Springsteen's writing. A number of songs on Springsteen's 2007 album *Magic* reinforce the continued centrality of community in twenty-first-century America. Songs such as "Long Walk Home" and "Girls in Their Summer Clothes" stress the role of the collective in the emotional well-being of the individual and the individual's role in maintaining the community.

Ironically, considering that the American Dream mostly privileges the individual, for Springsteen, the community seems to succeed where the individual cannot. Many songs depict the individual unsuccessfully wrestling with capitalism, as if the working-class individual does not stand a chance of social and economic stability without the support of the community. Unable to find a job, the protagonist of "Johnny 99" resorts to drink and then murder in order to try to handle "debts no honest man could pay." However, the narrator of "Darlington County" is not obliged to manage his precarious financial situation alone and gets assistance from his friend Wayne's uncle, who has "a union connection." Apparently, in Springsteen's songs, only the working-class community, rather than the individual struggling alone, can begin to resist the controlling capitalist oppression.

Springsteen himself acknowledges the importance of community in his work and his concerts. He states, "if my work was about anything, it was about the search for identity, for personal recognition, for acceptance, for communion" (Weider 214). He remarks further, "I . . . felt that what I was doing . . . is rooted in a community—either real or imagined—and that my connection to that community was what made my writing and singing matter" (215–16). For Springsteen, these communal connections are not to be taken lightly and are essential to the message his work conveys (and the medium through which it is conveyed—the concept of community is central to his legendary concerts).

Despite his own emphasis on the centrality of community, though, much of his work emphasizes the role of the individual within a community and many of Springsteen's songs consider the consequences of individuals becoming isolated from their communities. Springsteen recognizes that the characters in his songs, particularly those in his early career, "were misfits more than outlaws" (Strauss 191). In particular, most of *Nebraska* explores the damage done to both individuals and communities if this sense of isolation persists. According to Springsteen, *Nebraska* "was about . . . American isolation: what happens to people when they're alienated from their friends and their community and their government and their job" (Garman "Ghost" 224). Many characters in the songs on this album turn to violence, as in "Johnny 99," as a means of expressing their anger and frustration with an establishment that is failing them in some way. Seemingly, these characters are the true outsiders, unable to conform to socially acceptable codes of behavior. However, Garman notes that the collective working-class struggle in itself becomes a kind of belonging, forming a community in which everyone is struggling (224). Those characters who occupy a liminal position are doubly alienated; they are stuck in a transitory phase while also being relegated to the fringes of society. They express a desire to belong without apparently understanding how to effect changes that will result in belonging. In some ways, our sense of selfhood is defined by our position within a community: we are who we are because of that position. The absence of a communal role, though, forces an individual to define himself outside the community, and the failure to benefit from the stability of that communal referent results in such an individual taking on the status of an outsider.

THE OUTSIDER

The outsider figure discussed here fails to conform on two fronts: he exists apart from his community (without rejecting it outright) and he does not follow the normative trajectory of masculine maturation. He gains his outsider identity through these twin failures, trapped in a kind of twilight boy/youth culture that makes it difficult, if not impossible, to escape the limitations of functioning outside his community. In addition, Springsteen's evolving outsider figure displays multiple masculinities while illustrating some of the problems associated with the failure to bridge the disparate aspects of masculine behavior.

Distinguishing between the individual and the outsider illuminates the peculiarly liminal position of the outsider. In particular, these two figures are differentiated by how they are treated within their communities: the individual experiences a certain level of tolerance not enjoyed by the outsider. Communities have socially acceptable ways of dealing with idiosyncratic behavior that deviates from the perceived norm, either allowing for and embracing the individual through such communally recognizable groups as the family or the union, or punishing unacceptable deviant behavior. The outsider, though, is either ostracized by the community or acts deliberately to distance himself from that community. T. V. Reed wonders "if a community must at times speak as one voice in order to generate the utmost power, is it possible still in that voicing to recognize dissent, internal otherness, or difference?" (127). For Reed, the answer to this question is mostly "no" (although he believes the possibility exists in the Chicano community). Certainly, in the four songs discussed below, the central character does not consider himself as part of the power of the collective. Even the Nothing Man chooses to distance himself from the unifying strength of the community.

Jimmy Guterman suggests that Springsteen's songs are "filled with the outsider voices that [these] songs have employed as narrator since the first song on his first album" (viii). Perhaps, though, Guterman is mistaking the individual for the outsider. That "very first song" is "Blinded by the Light," in which the narrator certainly resists authority, but he does so in the company of his peers; the song is populated by a highly individualistic group, existing within a collective of "madman drummers bummers and Indians in the summer," all of whom are referred to in the plural. Indeed, the song has perhaps more individual characters than any other Springsteen song, and while all these characters revel in their resistance to conforming, they cannot be outsiders if they are a part of a collective—even if that collective exhibits nonconformist behavior. So, if the outsider is not simply identified by maverick or nonconformist behavior, what criteria need to be considered in identifying this figure?

Outsider identity in Springsteen's work is, in part, enmeshed with working-class identity. In his discussion of the working class, David S. Sims defines working-class consciousness as an awareness that the wants and desires of the individual cannot be attained by the efforts of the individual alone (97). However, as with nonconformity, the outsider does not simply fail to recognize the limitations of the individual. He either exhibits a con-

scious decision to meet his wants and desires in an independent, potentially unorthodox, way, or he recognizes, at some level, that they cannot be
met. Springsteen himself admits the characters in his songs are "interested
in being included and they're trying to figure out what's in their way" (Will
Percy 102). Perhaps, though, Springsteen's outsider cannot not yet solve
this problem. He must first recognize what prevents inclusion in order to
overcome the problem and to begin to move toward inclusion; he must
also understand the value to the individual inherently embedded in the collective. Garman posits that "since the release of *Darkness on the Edge of Town*
(1978), Springsteen has consistently recorded material that . . . examines
the tension between individuality and community" (*Race* 196). However,
the figure of the outsider is an individual who can never be part of a community, and this unresolvable detachment is the real cause of tension.

While it is possible to maintain individuality within the community,
the outsider fails to negotiate such a position. Garman suggests that the
"homosocial and homoerotic love that has been part of the working-class
hero's politics" excludes "women and people of color from the privileges
that these men enjoy" (*Race* 224). The outsider is excluded as well, even
though he invariably fits within the working-class demographic. The outsider's resistance to toeing the conformist line means he is stuck with the
"working-class" label without the possibility of being considered a "hero."
The outsider's behavior deviates too far from the working-class norm: he
has no interest in working from nine to five, in marriage, or the dream of
home ownership. Instead, he inhabits the questionable borders of society
where he either rebels or dabbles in criminal activity. Such borders are,
according to Palmer, "significant in that they represent the limits of the
possible. If masculinity is about policing boundaries then these visits to
imprecise borders are significant, for here men go through the tests they feel
they must endure" (107).

Negotiating the conventions of American manhood becomes problematic
for the outsider as indicated by his persistent lingering on those borders.
His visits are too prolonged to be considered tests of endurance; rather they
stem from either an exaggerated rebellion or an inability to fully embrace or
participate in the pursuit of the American Dream. Yet even fully participating in expected masculine behavior is not without its drawbacks. According
to Palmer, "the empty prize of masculinity is won by following a primitive
code of loyalty which functions to limit its adherents. Men are condemned
to be active, independent, and dominating" (103). Nevertheless, persistent
adherence to boy culture works against masculine maturity, as exemplified
by the four songs examined here. When the central male characters cannot
embrace all three elements of masculinity, they risk emasculation, consequently needing to prove manhood through hypermasculine acts contain-
ing an element of danger.

Outsider acts of hypermasculinity are complicated by a corresponding failure to recognize the value of the collective. Rejection of the collective informs much of the behavior of the narrator of "Growin' Up"; his deliberate decision to shun inclusion does not depend on his knowing what gets in the way of communal participation. While the narrator of "Growin' Up" refuses to even attempt inclusion, the respective narrators of "Meeting Across the River" and "Mansion on the Hill," both of whom fall short of achieving any aspect of the American Dream, know what prevents them from enjoying the kind of inclusion Springsteen describes, but remain powerless to act on this knowledge. The narrator of "Nothing Man," however, once understood the benefits of belonging to a community, even if he failed to fully appreciate them. His exclusion seems self-imposed and is the converse of the exclusion of "Growin' Up": the Nothing Man knows what it takes to belong, but chooses not to. This choice is not youthful rebellion, though; rather he is isolated by trauma.

PROBLEMATIC REBELLION IN "GROWIN' UP" AND "MEETING ACROSS THE RIVER"

Marked by representations of resistance to conformity and subsequent rebellion, Springsteen's early work relies on these conventions to depict the trope of the outsider. Cullen points out that the characters who reside in the songs of Springsteen's first three albums "are almost always in groups, a kind of pack mentality characteristic of young males" (Cullen, *Born* 125). Highlighting male bonding within groups only reinforces the alienation of the outsider figures in "Growin' Up" and "Meeting Across the River," the earliest songs discussed here. Evincing fairly conventional acts of defiance in order to state and maintain his position as a non-conformist, a position he celebrates, the speaker of "Growin' Up" shows no desire to be part of the crowd; he wants to stroll "all alone" because this isolation preserves his individuality, leaving his "soul untouched." Persistent resistance to authority, a trait Cullen recognizes as inherent in boy culture, means this narrator cannot emerge from this developmental state; he is "never wholly detached from this adolescent world" (*Born* 124, 125). Each time the narrator is instructed to conform to societal conventions by "the crowd," he does the opposite: "when they said 'Sit down' I stood up." Despite this resistance to authority, the narrator paradoxically puts himself in an authoritative position above his own "crowd" as he "command[s] the night brigade." Although the narrator's alignment with the "night brigade" seems to confirm, rather than resist, his adherence to pack mentality, it is important to remember that the narrator is above the pack—indeed he "commands" it.

Seemingly immune to the lure of the American Dream, the narrator of "Growin' Up" prefers to break "all the rules," risking pain and rejecting the protection of the crowd. Perhaps such bravado, though, results more from necessity than desire. Douglas Robinson recognizes that the narrator of "Growin' Up" resists "the temptation to 'land,' settle down, get a job, get married, and become an upright citizen" (174). But, he points out, the song does not present an alternative to this "ideological norm. You either conform to your community or resist conforming: home is the place of repression, but it is also the only place of community" (174). In his position as commander of the "night brigade," the narrator demonstrates a penchant for authority that is at odds with someone whose identity is founded on resisting authority and on self-imposed isolation. Consequently, toward the end of the song, even though the speaker maintains "a nice little place in the stars," he admits to finally having taken "root in the earth," as if constantly resisting conforming is inherently temporary, in fact part of the transitory stage of "growin' up." Although Robinson sees the song as only "a dream of escape," acknowledging the possibility of resisting hegemonic convention differentiates this narrator from those who follow (174). Rather than representing the outsider as someone who *cannot* conform or belong, the song recognizes that escape from conforming is often desirable and is a choice made by those seeking escape.

Such a choice, requiring that the outsider remain on the periphery of his community, eludes other outsider figures in Springsteen's songs. Indeed, the position of outsider becomes almost untenable in both "Meeting Across the River" and "Mansion on the Hill," songs in which the speaker is no longer the self-conscious rebel of "Growin' Up": instead he looks for some way to join the crowd and to embrace the basic tenets of the American Dream. Maintaining the desire for individuality has given way to wanting to belong as a way of breaking out from the economic and societal limitations of the position of the outsider. Here, for those unable to escape outsider status, the act of growing up illuminates why such a position cannot be maintained. Recognizing the need to escape his socioeconomic limitations, the speaker of "Meeting Across the River" only sees one way to fulfill that desire: make money as quickly as possible, even if it means resorting to illegal and dangerous activities. The joyous piracy of "Growin' Up" has given way to disillusionment and despair; the "night brigade" has disappeared and the narrator must rely on the untried, and potentially unreliable, Eddie to lend him some money and find some means of transport. Clearly, Eddie is not of the same caliber as the pirates of the night brigade; he needs reminding to "change his shirt" and direction on appropriate behavior, having to be instructed to not say anything and "remember, just don't smile."

Cowie and Boehm suggest that the narrative of many Springsteen songs "delivers the characters to the crossroads where at least one direction might lead to a better day" (359). But there are no crossroads in "Meeting Across the River"; the decision to follow a certain path has already been taken in anticipation that it will lead the narrator out of the misery of the existence he inhabits, but this hope seems ineffably misplaced. Clearly, the narrator's action will only embroil him further in a most likely unlawful and dangerous way of life. Money earned from this unnamed activity will not buy him a better life; it will simply impress his girl and hopefully prevent her from walking out on him. Yet the futility of the situation seems lost on the speaker, even though his previous foray into illegal activity does not seem to have been particularly successful. His warning to Eddie that "if we blow this one / They ain't gonna be looking for just me this time" elides the identity of the unnamed "they," who could be either police or employees of "the man on the other side" who calls the shots. Whoever "they" are, though, they will only reinforce the speaker's outsider position. Not only is he unlikely to achieve the desired social mobility, but he could also sink further into the underclass, becoming increasingly like Eddie.

PARALYTIC PASSIVITY IN "MANSION ON THE HILL"

Apparently in an even more hopeless situation than that depicted in "Meeting Across the River," the speaker of "Mansion on the Hill" is forced simply to observe the mansion from the limitations imposed by "the factories and the fields" of Linden Town.[3] Doubly isolated, the narrator of "Mansion on the Hill" does not seem part of his own community, just as he is not part of the community he observes in the mansion. Alienation from any community is underscored here by the apparent reinforcement of the recognized masculine trajectory of the father-son relationship.

Unlike the father-son relationship depicted in "My Hometown," where the father passes on his knowledge as a kind of inheritance, in "Mansion on the Hill," the father and son fail to communicate. Driving his son "through the streets of a town so silent and still," this father instructs his son in passivity; they merely park the car and "look up at that mansion on the hill." With nothing to pass on to his son, this father cannot reinforce a sense of belonging by telling his son to "take a good look around / This is your hometown" ("My Hometown"); rather the father in "Mansion on the Hill" is as "silent and still" as the streets of the town around which he and his son ride.

The patrilineal inheritance of passivity and alienation persists into the narrator's adulthood, resulting in him watching the "cars [rush] by" while simultaneously observing the romanticized mansion, lit by the "full moon rising." While implicitly replicating the passive voyeurism of his childhood, the narrator remains alienated from both the working-class reality of the town and the unachievable potential of the mansion on the hill. Garman sees this sense of being an outsider looking in as a class marker, in that "the narrator and his family remain firmly within the boundaries of their assigned social space" (*Race* 210), but unlike a number of Springsteen's other songs that delineate social class, such as "Thunder Road" and "Atlantic City," "Mansion on the Hill" does not offer any way to escape, not even the possibility of running away. This narrator commands no one—there is no night brigade or even an Eddie—all he can do is look on with his sister from the isolation of the "tall corn fields" at the shining lights and the "people laughin' all the time." Exhibiting a passivity that approaches paralysis, he takes no action at all, illegal or otherwise.

Some critics glorify both father and son in this song to the extent that they become romanticized metaphorical figures representing the dignity of the struggles of the working class. Gareth Palmer, for example, sees the father as a heroic victim whose failure "may be down to some problems with the economy" (102). Howard Hampton describes the song as one that depicts "a vast moat of inequity [that] separates rich from poor," with the poor "stuck on the outside looking in" (337), while Geoffrey Hines sees the narrator looking at the house and its occupants as if it were "Disneyland," in contrast to the listener, for whom "the locked iron gates represent the kind of class divisions that have spoiled the American Dream" (62). However, the narrator does not seem to idealize the house in the way Hines sees; it only resembles Disneyland in that it is an unattainable fantasy. Detracting from the despair of the narrator, this kind of romanticizing makes him seem like the Little Match Girl, with his nose pressed against the windows of the wealthy. Reading the narrator in this way negates his desire to escape the limitations of the working class and fails to address the impossibility of socioeconomic mobility for this particular character; the song presents a past and a present, but no future.

Physically inaccessible, the mansion only emphasizes the disparity between the social class of the narrator and that of its occupants. Locating the mansion high above the working-class area on the outskirts of town geographically "demarcate[s] class relationships" (Garman, "Ghost" 227), a geographic and economic isolation reinforced by the "gates of hardened steel" produced by the working-class mill workers. These gates function to "segregate [workers] from the comfort and success the mansion represents," barricading them from the American Dream through the product of their labor (Garman, "Ghost" 227). The narrator's outsider status, however, not only isolates him from the mansion, as effectively locked out by the gates as are the workers who produced them, but also excludes him from the collective company of the workers themselves. Merely watching, he has no access to either mansion or mill.

This outsider's exclusion from both working and upper classes results in him inhabiting a nebulous no-man's-land, which his inherent passivity prevents him from negotiating. If, as Jim Cullen argues, the concepts of equality and social mobility are central to the American identity, what, then, is the function of the outsider in relation to these concepts? Either rebelling against societal conventions or breaking the conventions by operating outside the law, the defiant outsider helps define conventionality, even normality, by demonstrating an alternative lifestyle against which normality can be measured. The outsider who is not actively rebelling, but only passively longing to improve his economic status, confirms the position of the hegemony—that that unreachable lifestyle is indeed desirous and those who have it are to be looked up to and emulated.

TRAUMA AND INCLUSION IN "NOTHING MAN"

So far, I have suggested that outsider status depends on emotional stagnation resulting in the outsider's failure to move through conventional phases of masculinity. "Nothing Man" presents us with a markedly different outsider figure. Here is a character who is neither confined to belonging to a perpetual boy culture, nor stuck in adolescence. Instead, he possesses a maturation reflective of Springsteen himself, since, as Cullen notes, "Springsteen's experiences have been less those of a man chasing a runaway American Dream than those of one who has achieved it" (Cullen, *Born* 67). "Nothing Man," notwithstanding its unavoidable association with the after effects of September 11, depicts a man who, like Springsteen, appears to be living the dream, neither dependent on his desire to stand out from the crowd as in "Growin' Up," nor on his fragile economic status as in "Meeting Across the River" and "Mansion on the Hill." Here the speaker appears to convey a sense of belonging absent from the other pieces: he is part of the club that meets regularly at Al's Barbecue and has admiring friends who want to "buy [him] a drink and shake [his] hand."

However, the exterior normative behavior of the Nothing Man conceals the damage his job has wreaked upon his psyche. He does not display his outsider position through the way he conducts himself; rather, the Nothing Man's position is experiential and emotional. No longer a regular "Joe," he is now the local hero whose acts of heroism have been reported in his "hometown" newspaper. Dave Marsh considers this song as portraying "the disintegration of a former hero" (*Hearts* 675), but the Nothing Man's heroism is disturbingly much part of the present, and something he cannot escape, even if he wants to, as his anonymity within his community has disappeared. Unlike other Springsteen outsiders, the Nothing Man is not looking to belong but to escape, searching for the kind of invisibility experienced by the narrator of "Mansion on the Hill." While that character simply observes his working-class community, the Nothing Man's continued participation in communal activities, along with his notoriety, mean that he is almost claustrophobically embraced by his society. For Garman, Springsteen's portrayal of "the dissolution of working-class communities" means that "it is important to forge a collective working-class identity" (*Race* 226). In order to avoid the kind of working-class disintegration Garman sees happening throughout *Nebraska*, "collective bonds must be reestablished" (*Race* 211). In "Nothing Man," the community is strong, but the narrator struggles to rid himself of those communal bonds. Repeatedly reiterating his self-identity as "the nothing man," the speaker attempts to distance himself emotionally from the source of his new-found notoriety within his community and the prominent position that results from such notoriety.

Most of the songs on *The Rising* explore emotional distress arising from catastrophic events of loss. Dave Marsh suggests that the emotions in the songs on *The Rising* result from "the psychic devastation of lives that once had seemed altogether orderly, secure, and prosperous," all qualities associated with the achievement of the American Dream (*Hearts* 671). Before his act of heroism, the Nothing Man's way of life would seem to fit neatly the criteria of the Dream; now his behavior suggests that he is suffering from post-traumatic stress disorder (PTSD). Unable to remember "how [he] felt" after the traumatic event, a frequent symptom of such a condition according to trauma theorist Cathy Caruth, the Nothing Man experiences oblique, but potentially deadly, emotional distress.[4] The song's reference to "pearl and silver resting on [the] night table" is frequently interpreted as indicating the speaker's suicidal intentions, with "pearl" referring to the handle of a pistol. Marsh points out that, with one exception, "no Bruce Springsteen character... so actively chooses death... But the Nothing Man is dead at heart" (*Hearts* 676).[5]

Initially, I concurred with Marsh and other critics in considering the Nothing Man to be a dangerous figure who seems to indicate the fragility of contemporary life: that even those who appear to conform to, perhaps embody, the conventions of society are in as much peril as the risk-taking outsider. It seems that, like the speaker of "Mansion on the Hill," the Nothing Man is unable to act and only this paralysis is saving his life. However, I have come to see the Nothing Man in a more positive light. He appears to be as much an agent of change as the youthful rebel of "Growin' Up." Although from the speaker's perspective, "everybody acts like nothing's changed," for the Nothing Man, life will never be the same. Not only did he experience untold horrors in "a misty cloud of pink vapor," but his position in his community has also undergone a transformation. In actuality, everybody acts like *something's* changed. The continued meeting of the Friday night club at Al's Barbecue indicates a desire for life to remain unchanged, but the behavior of the club members toward the Nothing Man demonstrates how they recognize the changes. The speaker of "Nothing Man" cannot control the uncontrollable; he will never influence those whose actions resulted in the "pink vapor," and he cannot change the elements—"the sky is still the same unbelievable blue"—but his presence in the community represents hope: he is an emblem of survival, which is why he reads about himself in the paper and why everybody wants to shake his hand.

Even more importantly, though, he has not chosen suicide. Critics such as Marsh have interpreted the following passage as indicating the speaker's suicidal state of mind:

> You want courage
> I'll show you courage you can understand
> Pearl and silver
> Restin' on my night table
> It's just me Lord, pray I'm able

I would like to offer an alternative interpretation of this stanza. Clearly emotionally traumatized by his experiences, the speaker considers his actions neither heroic nor courageous, hence his emphasis on his nothingness. While the resolution, or working through, of grief relies in part on repetition (Scott 365), it seems that here the Nothing Man is not experiencing grief, but the intrusive nature of traumatic memory, which as Caruth points out, is the "literal return of the event against the will of the one it inhabits. . . . [T]he event returns . . . insistently" (5, 6).

Because of the recurring trauma of this experience—the Nothing Man cannot avoid repeatedly reliving the event—the courageous act is not to choose death, which would effectively halt all traumatic repetition, but to continue living. If everyday he must confront the source of the trauma while simultaneously having to accept accolades he does not believe he deserves, the Nothing Man's desire to live must be constantly eroded. I would like to propose that the ability he prays for is not the courage to use the gun on the nightstand, but, conversely, to leave it where it is. Suicide and suicidal intentions are persistently culturally unacceptable; consequently, if the Nothing Man were to take his own life, he would not be demonstrating courage his community or his lover can understand. Instead, he exhibits courage by continuing to show up every Friday night, having his drinks bought for him and his hand shaken, while concealing his outsider status from everybody.

Unlike the other Springsteen outsider figures discussed, the Nothing Man seeks help from a spiritual source, and perhaps it is his willingness to place his trust in someone or something outside himself that allows for the sense of hope lacking in the narrators of "Meeting Across the River" and "Mansion on the Hill." In his discussion of "The Rising," Bryan Garman suggests that here "individual and sacrificial acts of courage are squandered without a spiritual and political reawakening" ("Models" 81). Perhaps, then, this concept is central to understanding the Nothing Man's lack of acknowledgment of his own acts of heroism. Suggesting the Nothing Man sees himself as an imposter—someone who does not deserve the accolades—the song implies that such acts are simply a by-product of his job. Susan Jeffers argues that "the men who are thrust into heroism are not heroic in defiance of their society but in defiance of their governments and institutional bureaucracies" (quoted in Garman, *Race* 218). The hero in "Nothing Man," though, is not defiant, but just doing his job. Consequently, his appeal to a higher power is perhaps not simply a search for the courage to continue living, but also a way to come to terms with his elevated position within his community.

I began this chapter by saying that the Nothing Man occupies a dangerous emotional space, and while this statement still holds, I now see the outsider in "Nothing Man" as a mature version of the speaker of "Growin' Up," someone who has indeed grown up. I am suggesting that the speaker of "Nothing Man" has the emotional maturity to comprehend his status as outsider, as indicated by his plea for understanding, but that Springsteen allows him to transcend this societal position. The grown-up speaker chooses not to embrace the role of outsider, perhaps an affirmation that Springsteen's insistence on community has the power to heal.

In Springsteen's most recent album, 2009's *Working on a Dream*, the figure of the outsider has all but disappeared. Even Outlaw Pete, the character who comes closest to meeting the outsider criteria, marries, has a child and attempts to settle down, albeit unsuccessfully. Many of Springsteen's recent songs suggest that the healing nature of a community, combined with the maturity of the characters who inhabit these songs, result in the outsider finally being incorporated into the greater whole. These characters are no longer defined by that to which they do not belong. The trajectory of conventional masculinity has been restored, with male characters settling into relationships that endure throughout "this life and then the next."

NOTES

1. Some songs, however, do have female narrators. "Car Wash," for example is narrated from the point of view of a woman: the first lines are "My name is Catherine LeFevre / I work at the Astrowash on Sunset and Vine."

2. See Judy Wieder's interview with Springsteen and Neil Strauss's article, both anthologized in *Racing in the Street*.

3. "Mansion on the Hill" is apparently partly autobiographical; as Dave Marsh and Bryan K. Garman note, among others, the song is based on Springsteen's father's obsession with a mansion outside Freehold (Marsh, *Hearts* 371; Garman, *Race* 209).

4. Caruth says "the historical power of the trauma is not just that the experience is repeated after its forgetting, but that it is only in and through its inherent forgetting that it is first experienced at all" (8).

5. Here Marsh is referring to Charles Starkweather in "Nebraska," although Ralph in "Johnny 99" considers death preferable to a life in jail.

8

"Like a Vision She Dances"

Re-Visioning the Female Figure in the Songs of Bruce Springsteen

Liza Zitelli

In a recent conversation with a fellow Springsteen fan, I criticized the open-ing lines to the 1980 AC/DC song "You Shook Me All Night Long" as objec-tifying women in a destructive and, at the least, off-putting way. Knowing that I had just begun a project about gender in Bruce Springsteen's songs, my friend challenged me and said skeptically, "You know, Bruce could have written those same lines!" Of course, I disagreed. "Bruce," I said instinc-tively, "could *never* have written those lines." I felt this to be true deep in my guts. But with all the "babies," "little girls," "little darlings," and references to hair, makeup, stockings, dresses, and tight blue jeans in Springsteen's lyrics, I began to wonder exactly why I felt so strongly about his artistic commitment and contribution to the evolving feminist vision.

These contradictory feelings of my own, complicated further by the sort of comment my friend made about Springsteen's portrayal of women, are ex-actly what the following chapter sets out to explore and resolve. In the end, I hope to show how Springsteen's songbook critiques the patriarchal, male-dominant system as one that stifles the growth of both women and men.

FEMINISM AND SPRINGSTEEN

In this exploration, I use a feminist critical methodology, looking at ways Springsteen's songbook either complicates, challenges, or reveals some of the underpinnings of Western gender politics and patriarchal structures. A text or a work of art could either reinforce these politics and structures, through stereotype mostly, or it could resist or subvert it. This resistance is difficult to achieve in any text or work of art, of course, when it is born

151

inside the system it is trying to challenge. Even when the story is told by or focuses on a woman, the male gaze seems to pervade into the structure of story-telling itself. However, I will show that Springsteen's songs begin to challenge the gender norms of patriarchal story-telling practices by creating characters who question, or subvert in some way, the iconic patriarchal representations of both the ideal woman as well as the heroic male. These kinds of challenges separate Springsteen from the throngs of rock and roll artists who blindly re-inscribe and commodify the gender norms that exist for us today.

The critical stance on Springsteen's relationship to gender up to this point has not, unfortunately, been much different than the conventional view of Springsteen's music; superficially, the portrayal of cars, fast rides, and girls in their summer clothes seem to categorize Springsteen in league with other rock and roll artists who align women with objects to possess, drive, control, or take pleasure in.[1] Critics have often positioned Springsteen as an artist who perpetuates gender divisions. For example, Gareth Palmer suggests that women in Springsteen lyrics (especially on *The River*) "are seen as hopeless figures in need of men to protect them via marriage, thus perpetuating the male/female divide of patriarchy" (104). Using feminist theoretical perspectives, this chapter hopes to undo conventional wisdom that Springsteen's lyrics objectify women and suggests instead that his work allows us to understand the construction of gender itself as a barrier that must be crossed in order to find redemption.

There have been critical exceptions that expand our knowledge of Springsteen's portrayal of women. For example, Martha Nell Smith examines the subversive nature of Springsteen's performances, videos, and visual representations in terms of gender. She likens Bruce Springsteen's exploration of the "darkness on the edge of town" to the transgressive behaviors of a notorious American literary heroine, Hester Prynne of *The Scarlet Letter* (834). Smith stresses the anti-individualist feminist impulses behind Springsteen's urge for connectivity: "Whether readers invoke Nancy Chodorow, Carol Gilligan, or Bob Dylan, just like a woman Springsteen makes love to his audience and pleads for connection, not for the romance of each to his or her own independent existence" (834). Recognizing Springsteen's revisionist attitude towards gender conventions, Smith writes, "Springsteen exposes many assumptions and illusions underlying sex- and gender-determined divisions of our culture, and leads audiences into 'dangerous'—at least to conventional categorizations and schemes for understanding sexuality— territory," asserting that his "stage antics and speaker's performances call essentializing notions of the masculine and feminine as well as of sexuality into question" (840).[2]

Smith's viewpoint begins an important conversation about the way cultural scholars should understand Springsteen's impact on the cultural representation of gender; this chapter deepens and expands on that conversation and others like it, aiming to counter the standpoint that Springsteen in any way perpetuates the ideology of male domination.

WOMAN AS SAVIOR

One way Springsteen's body of songs works towards subverting, inverting, and complicating a male-centered ideology is by offering the traditional male subject an opportunity to come face to face with something "other" than himself—perhaps a woman, a friend, a new home, a father, a mother, a child, or even a stranger. This encounter and reconciliation with the *other* creates the possibility of achieving real humanity, and perhaps, in turn, salvation and redemption.

Springsteen's representation of salvation has been connected to masculinity, and his male subjects often serve as the protectors and salvation figures in his work. Indeed, the savior in Western consciousness is traditionally male, with Jesus Christ figuring as the literal savior, in addition to other models of salvators based on his teachings, image, or biography. These metaphorical Christ-figures appear in Western literary representations as symbols of purity, hope, innocence, sacrifice, peace, love, resurrection, and ultimate redemption of humanity.

A salvation figure conventionally is an idealized figure of perfection who sacrifices him- or herself for the redemption of others. Or, we may define a savior figure as a being whom another person or a whole culture idealizes and whose idealization and imagined perfection is relied upon by that other person or entire culture or group for redemption. Although the Christ-figures in much of this literature are often male, Springsteen's women often resemble these Christ-figures just as much or more than his men do.

Yet, most critics who have written about Springsteen and gender have categorized women in his lyrics as trophies or objects whom the male may swoop in to rescue and redeem.[3] But this interpretation fails to realize that it is the male in Springsteen's work who is in need of being rescued, and that what the male needs to be rescued from is not oppression from something outside of himself, but from oppression occurring as a result of being isolated from that which is outside himself.

Springsteen's men express their desire for something other than what they can supply themselves, confessing weakness in lines such as "I just can't face myself alone again" in "Thunder Road," or, "It's a sad man, my friend, living in his own skin and can't stand the company" from *Lucky Town's* "Better Days." These men look outward to find a pathway for redemption in something other than themselves. In creating this scenario of looking away from the self, Springsteen sketches a sad portrait of patriarchy, in which the dominating party feels the isolating effects of stratification and separation from that which it dominates.

As an attempt to rectify or reverse the isolating effects of this saddened patriarchal state, Springsteen's male characters often position the woman as savior or "salvator." In fact, the image of the savior in Bruce's work is almost always a woman and rarely a man. The man is the seeker of salvation, and a woman, the men hope and project, may hold the key to this sought-after redemption.

What are the causes, and consequences, of this concept that women might provide salvation? Springsteen's songs provide an extended exploration of our culture's notion of the ideal, salvation-providing female, embodied in the iconic character of "Mary." From the early puzzle "Mary Queen of Arkansas" and anthemic "Thunder Road," to the haunting images in works like "The Rising," Springsteen often uses this name when pairing women with themes of redemption and spiritual communion in his songs.

Mary, of course, as the Virgin mother of Christ, is Christianity's version of the ideal woman, and a prominent Western symbol for purity, motherhood, and goodness. And Mary Magdalene often represents the opposite side of womanhood—the demonized temptress in need of saving, the impure side of the Madonna/whore dichotomy. Although Springsteen plays off these connotations, his versions of "Mary" complicate and challenge them, rather than reaffirm them. Springsteen's figurations of Mary exist in songs in a wide range of scenes embodying a wide range of characters, helping to question the image of woman as symbols of either damnation or salvation. There is Mary Dove who closes the door on her trouble-maker husband Billy in "Rockaway the Days," and finds a new lover at the end of the song. There's Mary the drag queen from the Midwest, there is Mary on a porch being invited to climb into the front seat, and there is Mary who gets pregnant in high school and watches her dreams drift down the river. Mary also appears when the male character is on his way to heaven in "The Rising," and when Springsteen's characters are searching for a release from grief and loss, as in "Mary's Place."

At the least, the name *Mary* is a loaded one for Western audiences. It signifies, for the Western reader, some important underlying conversations about the constructs and concepts of gender in our culture. The name evokes questions about the patriarchal nature of our society, referencing a religious tradition whose texts portray a society in which men are dominant and women are subordinate. In Springsteen's work, his incorporation of the name fits into his larger project of questioning the identities handed down to us from our traditions, norms, and histories.

Springsteen is, above all, always searching for, and questioning, identities. A large part of our self-identity, the way we conceive of the *self* today, is linked to the ways we identify ourselves and others within gendered and sexualized groups, and how those groups are defined by relationships between a person's sexual orientation, class, economic status and opportunity, femininity, masculinity, religion, race, nationality, ethnicity, and vocation. And, one important function of Springsteen's art, I would argue, is to solidify and concretize, to explore and question, and to give voice to these personal, communal, national, and cultural identities.

Whether or not the women represented in Springsteen's songbook seem to help men achieve salvation, frequently Springsteen's songs present the male subject encountering women as *agents*, not objects—agents of movement, change, and progress, rather than solely as objects, like the machine AC/DC sings about. One such song is "Thunder Road," which typically is discussed by scholars as perpetuating the man-in-driver-seat, woman-along-for-ride stereotype. But the song is more complex than that, and gives us images and emotions that ultimately challenge those stereotypes and gender-role norms, as I hope to show. The song begins with Mary as a "vision," the object of the male gaze. It ends with an inversion of that vision; the male eyes have "ghosts" in them and look at Mary stumbling back onto the porch. With this inversion, Springsteen questions the typical romanticized notions of the male and female gender divide.

Yet, in "Thunder Road," and other songs, while Springsteen may play with images of the male gaze, the male subjects in these songs still hedge on falling into the trap of idealizing women. And that kind of idealization is another version of objectification, albeit on the other side of the spectrum. Women are either idealized as symbols of moral perfection, or they are likened to objects and thought of as possessions.

Springsteen's lyrics and music are conscious of the dangers from both ends of this spectrum: the dangers of turning women into trophies and the dangers of turning women into idealized symbols. His set of images and landscapes of American lives confirms that there is no easy road to any kind of salvation. Woman, as a possession or an idea, cannot save man, and man cannot save woman under the same conditions. Springsteen urges us to forego these typical notions of romance that exist in a patriarchal ideology. Instead, his songs aim us towards identifying with women and men as individuals, with minds, hearts, and bodies. In these instances, Springsteen's work represents the woman as a being with subjectivity, too—not just some symbol, or machine, or object to be manipulated and handled by men. Or, at least, when there is a lack of acknowledgment of female subjectivity, the audience can see that the fates of his characters are bleak.

"THUNDER ROAD" AND THE MALE GAZE

Springsteen's classic song "Thunder Road," from 1975's *Born to Run*, begins with an image of Mary: "Like a vision she dances across the porch / As the radio plays." This cinematic description situates our perspective of Mary as taken from the male gaze; the speaker is a male, in a car, watching his female vision and even ascribing a soundtrack to the scene playing out before him, "Roy Orbison singing for the lonely." Thus, Springsteen has created the conditions of a drive-in movie, with the female vision "dancing" in front of the male audience, capturing and igniting his imagination.[4]

But the image of Mary sincerely is inspiring to the speaker in particular. Her dress "sways," and the word *sway* evokes a hypnotic effect on the male spectator. She seems to "dance," instead of merely walk, across the porch, which connotes an elegance and grace that catches the speaker's eye. Finally, he compares her to a "vision," a noun that carries connotations of mysticism and inspiration. The mystic vision of Mary is then undercut by the line, "You ain't a beauty, but hey you're alright." The ideal of beauty is questioned here—the speaker is caught, held, and inspired by this vision, and yet she does not measure up to the pre-defined, cultural standards of beauty. With this line, it seems that the speaker is actually rejecting these standards, which is a good first step in exposing the cultural practices that enforce the objectification and degradation of women in society.

By invoking Roy Orbison's song "Only the Lonely," Springsteen establishes the dramatic encounter of desire on a patriarchal stage: the "lonely" male spectator wants the female spectacle to, perhaps, distract him from the reality of the self. In the line, "Don't turn me home again / I just can't face myself alone again," Springsteen uses a male character's introspection to establish the sad and unbearable twin images of "home" and "myself" as the location of an individual isolated in his lonely center. Because of the man's discontent with himself, it seems that Mary is more of a distraction from the pain of himself than she is someone he inherently desires. From a feminist critical perspective, the woman's body—that is, the vision of the woman's body, or the conceptual construction of the woman's body from the male spectator's perspective—represents the locations where the self can cross the fringes of the unconscious and the borders of the community so as to be able to imagine a more complete self.

The problem, of course, is that when we use the women's body as a symbol for anything, it diminishes the embodied experience of the actual woman. It ends up reinscribing the male gaze—as if the default cultural perspective is inherently male. Springsteen's character is not likening his woman to a car, but he does, at first, relegate her to the realm of "vision," or symbol, that represents his own release from loneliness.

Aligned with this representation of Mary on the porch are the images of night and roads that are so important in Springsteen's body of work. The classic Springsteen lyric, "Show a little faith, there's magic in the night," ascribes a fantastic quality to the darkness of night that is analogous to the inspiring vision of Mary at the beginning of the song. But this speaker wants his vision to become a reality, to see what the mystery of the night, and his spectacle of Mary, really contains. He is ready to venture into the night. The night is "busting open," and he will enter this opening in order to give up being a spectator and become a participant. The shimmering image of Mary dancing becomes real when he confronts her wholeness—her humanness: "You ain't a beauty but hey you're alright / Oh and that's alright with me." This line is one that wouldn't conventionally be the best sentiment for a seduction, as it seems, on the surface, to insult the woman, and yet women in Bruce's audience consistently appreciate it—why? The reason that women enjoy this line is that the male has abandoned his projection of Mary as a two-dimensional "vision," as on a screen, and has instead re-visioned her as a person who is *"alright,"* as in three-dimensional, complete, right, and perfect. Furthermore, the dual imagery of the road in "these two lanes will take us anywhere" evokes the image of passageway and open access from the self to the other.

Bringing us back to the idea of the female as the savior, I argue that salvation and redemption in Springsteen's work is a metaphorical expression of unity between the self and the other. In this metaphor of unity between two people in "Thunder Road," the man's communion with the night, the road, and Mary represents an alternative to the loneliness of the isolated self. The literal "Thunder Road" is "a killer in the sun," but in the mystery and darkness of the night, the road becomes a pathway to salvation of the self. The road in the daylight is a killer; the night is where transformation can take place. Springsteen calls his nighttime highway Thunder Road, which highlights the sense of energy and persuasion of the road. Thunder, the unseen counterpart to lightning, can be used "in phrases denoting great force or energy," or to mean figuratively a "threatening, terrifying, or strongly impressive utterance; a powerful eloquence" ("Thunder" *OED*). In the daylight, the rules are followed. In the night, new roles can be explored. It is only in reaching outward into the unknown, into the spaces beyond the safe borders of light, into threatening and terrifying spaces of darkness or shadows, that a self can expand, grow, and experience connection.

In exploring these connections between the self and other, Springsteen's work depicts salvation, deliverance, and redemption through the idea of promise. In "Thunder Road," the speaker invites Mary to "come take my hand / We're riding out tonight to case the promised land," establishing exactly what is at stake in their forging a connection: their salvation. They are not entering the promised land, they are "casing" it. He is not promising anything to Mary, nor is he asking for a promise in return. In fact, he says that "promises will be broken." The idea of a "promise" definitionally requires a conversation and a declaration being made between two parties, one *acting* authority declaring a future action or condition for the *acted upon* other—a dynamic which only reinforces a hierarchal relationship. The driver's invitation, then, subverts the conventional positioning of the male dominating the female, instead positing them as a united front against the organizing hierarchy itself—"the promised land." When he says, "I'm no hero that's understood / All the redemption I can offer girl / Is beneath this dirty hood," he revises the conventional hierarchy of male over female and instead asks for her to join him—to step down off her porch and "climb in"—in order to shed the fantasy of the male hero swooping in to save the damsel in distress.

Springsteen's speaker acknowledges the woman's plight in the real world—"And I know you're lonely / For words that I ain't spoken / But tonight we'll be free / All the promises'll be broken"—but instead of offering to make good on the promise, he calls for freedom from the promise—freedom, then, from the sense of authority, freedom to "make it real" and "make it good" together, liberated from the sense of separation. Paired with the phrase "tonight we'll be free," the broken promises in "Thunder Road" can be viewed not as failures but as promises that have been set free, allowing the characters to stop waiting around for what has been promised to them by something or something else. Men should not emblematize women as the deliverer of promises, and nor should women "Throw roses in the rain / Waste [their] summers praying in vain / For a savior to rise from these streets." Instead, even the twenty-four-year-old Springsteen allows this young character to realize, if only for this moment, that entertaining the idea of a promise leads to destructive and senseless waiting for a deliverance that cannot come from any one else but yourself.

Springsteen insightfully incorporates the recurring motif of *waiting* surrounding his characters' search and prayers for salvation. Judeo-Christian tradition teaches that people must wait for deliverance while still remaining faithful and have faith while still waiting for deliverance—a tradition that attempts, not always successfully, to prevent existential crisis in the cultural consciousness. One secular literary theme that responds to this existential crisis has often been the motif of *carpe diem*. The *carpe diem* poem, made famous by English Renaissance poets, explores the idea of waiting by using a sexual metaphor; in these poems, the speaker is seducing his auditor by appealing to the sense of mortality, claiming that we must *seize the day* and not only take opportunities that come our way but also work to create opportunities.

Carpe diem poems are often seen as sexual seductions cleverly and deliberately disguised as appeals to intellectual and philosophical concepts of death, mortality, and the passage of time, so that the seducer can justify his need and desire for sexual gratification. Springsteen's classic romances "Sandy," "Rosalita (Come Out Tonight)," "Born to Run," and "Thunder Road" function in the tradition of the *carpe diem* poem, evoking the sense of sexual pursuit and freedom from restraints.

But a deeper understanding of *carpe diem* comes from an understanding of a human exploration of creation: the motif of *seizing the day* points towards the idea that humans possess the distinctive ability to create possibilities for the direction of their own lives—a process that by its design of allowing humans to be *creators,* and therefore closer to God and divine enlightenment, will lead to salvation and redemption. Perhaps the anxiety for action in the present is rooted in sexual desire, but because *carpe diem* poems are about creating possibilities for sexual consummation, they further evoke ideas of creation, in that sexual acts lead ultimately to reproduction and creations and generations of families. "To generate"—the root verb of generation—is to create something out of nothing. In "Thunder Road," the characters are "scared" and "thinking that maybe we're not that young anymore," and the driver impels Mary to realizing that they have to act now, in their "one last chance," to create something.

The last verse of the song provides exposition about the destructive attempts by other men to use Mary as a saving grace:

> There's ghosts in the eyes
> Of all the boys you sent away
> They haunt this dusty beach road
> In the skeleton frames of burned-out Chevrolets
> They scream your name at night in the street
> Your graduation gown lies in rags at their feet
> And in the lonely cool before dawn
> You hear their engines roaring on
> But when you get to the porch they're gone
> On the wind, so Mary climb in
> It's a town full of losers
> And I'm pulling out of here to win.

Here, Mary is the victim of violence: her torn gown is an image of rape, but not just rape: a rape that occurs in abandoned streets in the presence of ghostly onlookers. Now, the inspiring image of Mary from the beginning of the song is flipped. Now she is broken, climbing back onto her porch, the men (or "boys") watching her walk away from them instead of towards them. The male gaze is haunted by the image it once coveted. Mary has escaped their attempts to use her for their own purposes.

In this one verse, the division between interiority and exteriority collapses into one haunting image of a broken woman, stumbling to her porch—a liminal space somewhere between public and private—abandoned by the patriarchal forces that destroy her in the process of using her. The "burned out Chevrolets" reinforce the image of a commodity run into the ground or destroyed or used up by the hungry and ne'er-satisfied consumer. These boys that "haunt the dusty beach roads" are the "losers," but Mary has lost something too, as she crawls home alone listening to the predatory consumers' "engines roaring on," leaving her alone, but off to consume something or someone else. As mentioned above, the night recurs as an important image in Springsteen's lyrics; here, the "lonely cool before dawn" allows Mary some respite from the haunt of the "boys." They scream for her at night because for Springsteen the nighttimes, like women and roads, operate as spaces inside of which individuals can experience transformation.

Springsteen critiques gender patterns that actually keep us separated instead of truly bringing us together. This analysis of "Thunder Road," for example, demonstrates that waiting for promises to be fulfilled by others only perpetuates loneliness and separation. Instead of waiting, and subscribing to what is given to him, an individual must create his life in the present. And the ride is "not free" for Mary, either. She must drop the fairytale idea of the heroic male rescuing the powerless female. They must create their own lives and not be governed by ideology. The old "promises will be broken," and "tonight [they]'ll be free." Gender constructs may in fact be destructive and divisive to the culture in some ways, by forcing individuals to conform to pre-made identities, but Springsteen's lyrics suggest that if we use these constructs not as a source for defining the self but rather as something to overcome, we can create a new life: "pulling out of here to win." The "here" in this line stands for the land of these particular set of rules, where masculinity and femininity are false religions, full of empty promises. In this land, there are illusions and lies told to serve an agenda that stratifies individuals by restrictive categories of gender and sexuality. "Pulling out" means rejecting the fantasy of these illusions, and *winning* means overcoming those restrictions.

What is great about Springsteen's contribution to social and cultural reform is that even he is constantly updating and reforming his own representations. Springsteen has discussed, in introductions to later live performances of "Thunder Road" and "Born to Run," and in various interviews, that eventually he and his characters learn that "pulling out" of a system isn't the way to transform that system. You have to transform it from within. In 1988, during his *Tunnel of Love* tour, Springsteen introduced an acoustic version of "Born to Run," saying the song was "about a guy and a girl who wanted to run and keep on running. [A]nd uh, as I got older, I realized that [. . .] I didn't want it to be . . . that I wanted to . . . learn how to make a home for myself, learn how to fit in . . . 'cause there's really nothing, there's nothing in being homeless" (quoted in Pirttijärvi). Springsteen eventually revises his vision of the "guy" pulling out with a "girl" in songs like "Born to Run" and "Thunder Road" to one of a man who wants to create a home and learn how to contribute to it from within. With this new vision comes more rounded-out versions of women in his songs. Rather than seeing women as symbols for escape and mystery, Springsteen's male characters, more and more, begin to reflect on the real lives of the women sleeping next to them. In "My Hometown," for instance, the male speaker describes himself and Kate, his wife, "[lying] in bed, talking about getting out," but this time, there is no flashy car to hop into or vision of a girl dancing and swaying in a dress. Instead, it is a responsible couple, discussing their future together, trying to find a "hometown" where they will raise their son. This image of a man lying in bed with his wife, making decisions together, is a far cry from the romance of running away in a shiny car like the couple do in "Born to Run."

KILLER GRACES, SECRET GARDENS

The songs on *Born to Run* paint a picture of romantic fantasies and promises between man and woman that seem to equate women with not only salvation but also mystery and fear. While "Thunder Road" depicts a man ready to break the rules regarding women, "She's the One" describes a man's fear of what a woman's mysterious qualities will do to his selfhood. Springsteen sings to a driving beat, like a heartbeat, wistfully creating a sense that the character is thinking about the time "back when her love could save [him] from the bitterness."

But that fantasy of being saved by her love has come to an end, apparently. Instead, the male subject seems to fear losing his individual *self* in the romantic encounter with the feminine other. Springsteen writes that the "hands on her hips" and the "smile on her lips" will "kill" him. Her eyes "shine like the midnight sun," which likens the female to something ethereal and strange, frightening and beautiful. In this song, Springsteen shows a male subject who is afraid of what the union with this woman has done to his identity. Like the vision of Mary in "Thunder Road," this woman is also "standing in the doorway like a dream," but here the man does not say, "climb in." Instead he says, "I wish she'd just leave me alone," pleading to keep himself intact and not succumb to her "killer graces." Of course, he is obviously entranced by the woman, and the desire is potent in the song. But it is Springsteen's portrait of a man who is afraid of what he desires. The "she" in "She's the One" is what is desired and feared by the man. The image of salvation we see in "Thunder Road" is flipped.

In *Darkness on the Edge of Town*, Springsteen's follow-up to *Born to Run*, the standout song for examining Springsteen's representation of femininity is "Candy's Room." Once again, the woman is associated with darkness and night —"to get to Candy's room, you gotta walk the darkness of Candy's hall"; "We go driving deep into the night / I go driving deep into the light in Candy's eyes." Here, Springsteen's parallel imagery of driving deep into the night and deep into the light in Candy's eyes aligns the mystery of darkness with the illumination of light, a paradox that implies that what is dark and mysterious may actually lead to clarity.

In addition to the recurrence of night and light imagery associated with women in Springsteen's work, "Candy's Room" also aligns the woman with secret and hard-to-access rooms and spaces, echoing the image of "secret places" that appears in the first line of "She's the One." This image of secret feminine places evokes the idea that the male subject is so estranged from the feminine aspect of humanity that he imagines a woman's body as a hidden and inaccessible space. There is a wild urgency in "Candy's Room" to become vulnerable enough to enter that space, and the fantasy of fulfillment drives the song.

Candy actually gets a voice in this song, and her advice to the male subject in this song is to be "wild," "close your eyes, let them melt, let them burn," which essentially evokes the image of letting his *self* be subject to another force. The male subject experiences intimacy with Candy's body as a violent ecstasy, suggesting that the male subject's encounter with the woman is dangerous to the subjectivity of the male, but also exhilarating for the male self: "We kiss, my heart's pumpin' to my brain / The blood rushes in my veins, fire rushes towards the sky." His heart intermingles with his brain, evoking the image of the emotional being overtaking the rational being. In psychoanalytic criticism, which feminist critics often deconstructed in order to theorize gender, emotions and the heart are commonly linked with femininity, while reason and rationality are associated with masculinity. So, Springsteen's lyric of the "heart pumping to my brain" invokes this image of the feminine energy encountering, if not overtaking, the male subject.

Feminists are wary of these kinds of representations that depict men surrendering to a kind of monstrous feminine seduction, like a siren or a Medusa-like monster who can turn men to stone by her beauty. Gender theorists have shown how these myths enforce the subordination of women. Yet Springsteen avoids villainizing Candy. Instead, she is a rounded-out character, with a voice, and a self-possessed emotional life (a "sadness hidden in her pretty face / A sadness all her own . . .") and a depth of hidden worlds, preferring passion and connection over money.

Then, his experience of letting go reinforces the male fantasy that one can attain clarity by embracing that which is the other: "'Cause in the darkness there'll be hidden worlds that shine / When I hold Candy close she makes these hidden worlds mine." These lines conveys the idea that light can come from immersion into darkness and the unknown. The lyric exposes a male fantasy that women hold some sort of magical key to the universe, and if only men can possess them, they can possess that key. Once again,

Springsteen conjures the image of a female who, as men fantasize, can offer access to some sort of deliverance.

This image of the "hidden worlds that shine," and the fantasy of the male possessing these worlds, anticipates Springsteen's beautiful, less vulnerable and urgent treatment of gender difference in "Secret Garden." The two songs are about a man desiring to access something deep and secret in a woman, fantasizing that a woman could actually fulfill all his desires if only he could get into her secret space. But in "Secret Garden," there is a more grown-up version of this desired encounter. This time, the man understands that the woman can give him a lot, and "let [him] deep inside," but there will always be "a secret garden she hides" that a man can't, and should never, own:

> She's got a secret garden
> Where everything you want
> Where everything you need
> Will always stay
> A million miles away.

"Candy's Room" and "Secret Garden" are both about feminine spaces. In both songs, the man imagines the women as possessing something he doesn't have but needs for salvation. However, the male in "Secret Garden" has come to terms with it much better than the one in "Candy's Room." He respects this space, but doesn't clamour to possess it. This acknowledgment of a woman's power transforms the pattern of male domination over women and allows for a pattern of mutual respect and love. The most important thing is that he doesn't let this acknowledgment make him feel vulnerable, which in turn drives him to dominate or own. Instead, he lets it be, lets it grow.

Even in his most recent album, Springsteen still wrestles with the emotional consequences of this great divide between men and women represented in "Candy's Room" and "Secret Garden." Again, in the face of this feeling of separation, the male subject fantasizes about fulfillment of longing that comes from a relationship with a woman: he opens "Queen of the Supermarket" with the notion that a woman promises a "wonderful world where all you desire / And everything you've longed for is at your fingertips." In the fantasy, a "cool promise of ecstasy fills the air" for the man's body that desires the woman's body at the end of the day.

In this song, Springsteen observes that the American male subject, living in his mundane world of supermarkets and checkout lines, imagines the woman as an escape from that world—a means to salvation that will "lift [him] up" and "away." The fantasy of the secret place of the other recurs here too: "Beneath her white apron her secrets remain hers." In this line, as in lines from "She's the One" and "Secret Garden," Springsteen associates the woman's body with a secret place that may or may not offer salvation and redemption for the male subject. Springsteen's characters leave us questioning whether one person, male or female, can ever save another.

"YOU ALMOST GOT ME BELIEVIN' . . ."

Though Springsteen's portrayal of gender and sexuality has definitely evolved since his first album was released in 1973, even Springsteen's earliest lyrics can be understood as challenging stereotypical representations of gender and male subjectivity. Interestingly, the first Mary in Springsteen's catalogue is one of his most enigmatic constructions of femininity in his entire body of work. The Mary in "Mary Queen of Arkansas," from Springsteen's first album *Greetings from Asbury Park, N.J.*, definitely invokes the ideas of redemption and salvation that many of Springsteen's women do, but this Mary is not exactly a two-dimensional picture of idealized womanhood or femininity. In fact, she is a mystery to most audiences. Should the name invoke Catholic images of the idealized pure woman? Might the phrase "Queen of Arkansas" refer to a specific person, or does the speaker just use it affectionately to invoke an everyday kind of woman, both regal and regional at the same time?

In any case, the speaker in this song is not interested in explaining his relationship to his audience or in describing Mary much at all for the benefit of an audience. We get no images of her long hair in a long white bow; no images of her in blue jeans or her best dress. Instead of these things, we get a song addressed to her directly. Probably one of several Springsteen circus or carnival characters (the speaker is a "lonely acrobat" by trade), this Mary's most prominent quality is that she is ambiguously gendered. Her "soft hulk" is reviving. With this description, we understand only that she is a paradox—soft signifies feminine, and hulk signals masculine. The speaker says, "You're not man enough for me to hate or woman enough for kissing," and the image of the hybrid man-woman makes her fit nicely into the world of circuses and carnivals. Circus acts—freaks, contortionists, bearded ladies, etc.—expose and exploit the performative nature of social and bodily norms by turning them upside down and performing alternative versions for their audiences. It gets transmitted, perhaps subconsciously to the audience, that gender is something constructed and performed, not from nature but from culture.

This song is being sung *to* Mary, not *about* her, which actually carves out a kind of three-dimensional space for her, because we know the man speaking is reckoning with a real human subject and relationship. Instead of seeing her image clearly from the man's point of view, we are only privy to the male character's plea for Mary to let him love her. The song is a private, desperate conversation with her; the singer is pleading with her to stay with him, to give their love a chance: "Mary queen of Arkansas, it's not too early for dreamin'." The line's syntax indicates that we as an audience have interrupted a quietly desperate argument.

There is the underlying tone of a lover's persuasive confidence feebly masking a hopeful desperation—this speaker is searching for the dream of redemption. Words like "redeeming," "reviving," "believing," and "rising" all evince images of rebirth and renewal. These images betray the plea for salvation behind the song's lyrics: "But I know a place where we can go Mary / Where I can get a good job and start all over again clean / I got contacts deep in Mexico where the servants have been seen." Here, the man is offering Mary some version of the Promised Land, presumably to escape from where they are currently. Thus begins one of Springsteen's many narratives of two people starting over somewhere else, somewhere better, together.

But the hope is obscured by the character's confusion about love, women, and Mary's persona; "Mary queen of Arkansas, your white skin is deceivin'," he sings, "You wake and wait to lie in bait and you almost got me believin' / But on your bed Mary I can see the shadow of a noose / I don't understand how you can hold me so tight and love me so damn loose." This is one of Springsteen's inquiries into the mysteries and confusions of love. How could two lovers be so close—almost one being—and yet still exist as two separate beings? Moreover, the speaker is confused not only about love but about how gender itself affects love. Again, the line "You're not man enough for me to hate or woman enough for kissing" illustrates the deep conflict an individual has with gender. He links "hate" with his own gender, and "kissing" with the opposite gender, and is left with apparently no other option between hate or intimacy. Embedded in this lack of options is a critique of the restrictive gender rules we have been trained to follow in this society. One thing is clear: gender is, from the beginning for Springsteen, a performed act, whether it is between two people or before a whole social network of people. Gender is not an inherent or essential quality—it is always constructed by performed actions and exchanges between people. And, through all of our relationships, we are always negotiating and renegotiating, sometimes painfully or longingly, the terms of this exchange.

SCRAPBOOK OF LEADING MEN

Springsteen not only exposes the performativity of gender but also reveals the social practices that enforce the gender norms we perform. In "Mary Lou," a song released on *Tracks* that shares many lyrics with the live-favorite

"Be True," Springsteen comments directly on gender, by critiquing the pop-culture fantasy version of masculinity, femininity, and love that Hollywood represents. In this indictment of Hollywood values, this Mary, according to the male character speaking, is in danger of falling into the trap of desiring the wrong thing—the fantasy of a "leading" man that a patriarchal ideology prescribes to serve its own agenda of a male-dominant culture.

The speaker notes, "Your scrapbook's filled with pictures of all your leading men," and he cautions, "Well baby don't put my picture in there with them / Don't make us some little girl's dream that can never come true / Oh baby don't do it to me, I won't do it to you." By filling up a scrapbook with glossy pictures of male heroes, the Mary he sings about is lost in the patriarchal fantasy. He urges her to not make "us"—any man—a "little girl's dream that can never come true." This man is challenging the gender roles of dominant male/submissive female. He is challenging her as a woman, not as a girl, not to buy into the Hollywood doctrine of leading men rescuing damsels in distress that ends up undermining the potential for individuality of both genders.

This song critiques the "pretty lies" of pop-culture romances, and says when you are done fantasizing, you end up hurt, crying, alone, broken-hearted, "just another lonely ticket sold" to the patriarchal machine that uses Hollywood to glamorize its male-dominant structures. And he makes it a mutual pact: "don't do it to me, I won't do it to you." It's not one-sided. Here, Springsteen shows that men suffer just as much as woman do from the structures of male-domination: "I know the hurt too much dreaming can do," the speaker says.

Mary Lou, he says, is "not like all those others girls" who are "so afraid to shake up that real world." He sees more in Mary Lou. He sees the ability to grasp hold of something real, not just hang onto dreams blindly and buy the ticket that patriarchy is selling. He wants her to strive for "a real love that can grow" rather than to fester in the hurt of chasing the unattainable illusion presented by patriarchal agendas. In this song is an incarnation of a Mary who is not the idealized innocent Madonna but a girl growing up to be a woman, while being bombarded with false gender stereotypes that only serve to hold a woman down. The speaker sees Mary Lou as someone who has the potential to break free from the empty pursuit of the Hollywood happy ending and to shake things up, to turn some gender-role norms upside down.

The song calls for a version of Mary whose status and value as a woman is not dictated by a man or by a male-dominant society, but is achieved through an agreement between two people to forego these old rules ("don't do it to me, I won't do it to you") and take action: let's not be "afraid to shake up the real world, " Springsteen's voice rasps with inspiration and earnest soulfulness, amidst strong rock and roll drumming and chiming piano, right before a searching saxophone solo by Clarence Clemons. He ends the record with a playful, "Let's go," and the song emerges as a great revision of the *carpe diem* genre: rather than the man encouraging the woman into action to satisfy his own immediate gratification, he is encouraging Mary Lou to live a full and productive life on her own terms.

THE CAGE HANDED DOWN THE LINE

At times when characters in Springsteen's work find solace in embracing or venturing out with another person, Springsteen shows a life-affirming vision of relationships, a kind of secular redemption in the symbolic union of masculine and feminine energies. Springsteen's project responds to a stratification, fragmentation, and disintegration of the postmodern subject. We are too alone, isolated and disconnected, internally and also from our community, he suggests. His work exposes this social and psychological ground-zero that we are living in, and offers a path for salvation through a reevaluation of the consequences of the modern patriarchal ideology that governs us.

This image in Springsteen's lyrics of closeness or togetherness between two people serves as a mechanism that deconstructs the male gaze, closing the distancing gap between men and women and forcing the *vision* of the woman to become an embodied reality. For example, in "Drive All Night" the image of intimacy is conveyed in the lines "Lying in the heat of the night / Like prisoners all our lives / I get shivers down my spine and all I wanna do is hold you tight." The bodies are there—the woman is not an abstraction but something real that the man is holding onto. But his men constantly struggle to make the woman more than an abstraction, even when the man achieves intimacy with the woman. As Palmer points out, the woman in "Drive All Night" is sleeping, and he suggests that the image of her sleeping in the darkness adds to her abstract quality rather than giving the woman subjectivity. Palmer explains that, in Springsteen's lyrics, "women's essential otherness is not something a man can understand, so he stands apart, at best a witness to his remoteness" (104–5). Highlighting this problem of perceived separateness between men and women, Springsteen aligns his women with night, sleep, and darkness. Indeed, it is "women's essential otherness" for his male characters to which Springsteen often draws attention in his lyrical and musical representations. In "Drive All Night," for example, the woman is a figure in the darkness, and the speaker is driving to her at night, only to "sleep tonight again in [her] arms." While the man expresses a desire for intimacy, he only goes as far as becoming intimate with the woman's body, sleeping in her arms; he does not give an account of interacting with a woman's internal subjectivity.

In addition to the man's struggle to connect with a woman's internal being, Springsteen also depicts the culture's tendency to make love itself a romantic abstraction, romanticizing love's power to provide salvation. The speaker in "Drive All Night" promises his lover that the "fallen angels" may be "waiting for us down in the street," but their "dances of the dead" and the "fire waiting on the edge of town" will not "hurt us now," because, "through the wind, the rain, and the snow, you've got my love." These representations, in combination with Springsteen's own wailing and ecstatic vocal rendering of the lyrics, show a heightened, grand version of love that ends up obscuring the subjectivities of the individual in the relationship. Love is mystical and visionary rather than embodied.

In addition to love having an abstract quality here, it also has a measure of desperation in it. The man here will do anything to try to keep his promise. In this song, the man does not simply express his desire to be the savior; rather, he is begging for it. The problem for both men and women, though, lies in the falseness of this promise to be the other one's savior. The man can't protect the woman from hurt, as he promises in "Drive All Night," any more than the vision of Mary's swaying dress can mean redemption for the man in "Thunder Road." Understanding these limitations and then moving forward is part of breaking out of the confines of gender hierarchies. Springsteen acknowledges the crisis of patriarchy for *both* genders—not simply for men. In his work, we hear many different voices and see different lived experiences of romance and marriage. Sometimes we see the ball-and-chain image, when the man feels trapped, as in "Hungry Heart," where the man with the "wife and kids" gets in his car and "never [goes] back," or when the woman is trapped, as in "Racing in the Street" and "Stolen Car."[5] Sometimes we see the image of marriage and romantic love as a stimulant for generative responsibility and a source of salvation, spiritual fulfillment, and redemption, as in "Better Days," "Leap of Faith," "If I Should Fall Behind," or "Book of Dreams." Either way, what makes Springsteen real is that he shows it all from the eyes of people living it.

Springsteen's critique of sexual politics is rooted in a sympathy for men who are frustrated when faced with lack of self-expression that comes with their place in the gender hierarchy. The men of Springsteen's world are ultimately let down by the myth of patriarchy, as Palmer says, "tempted by a cultural bribe of a masculinity which promises to give them identity but which remains unattainable and leaves them unfulfilled" (104).

An important portrait of these failures of the patriarchal system appears in "One Step Up," which describes the no-win situations males and females are put in when we ascribe to the hierarchal sexual-politics we are being offered in our society. The male speaker describes his "cold house" in which the "same old story" gets played out again and again. Younger Springsteen characters, such as those in "Born to Run" and "Thunder Road," thought they could escape in their cars with their girls. But in this song, the man says, "I went out and hopped in my old Ford / Hit the engine but she ain't turnin'." Here, Springsteen denies his character the fantasy of running away and instead laments the reality of not simply being stuck but actually going backwards, "one step up and two steps back." The images of marriage we have been given are false ones, fantasies like the "Girl in white outside a church in June" waiting for her groom; in this song, "the church bells they ain't ringing." The man in the song characterizes these sexual politics as a "dirty little war," but still dreams of reconciling: "Last night I dreamed I held you in my arms / The music was never-ending / We danced as the evening sky faded to black." These images of a man and a woman uniting, dancing under stars, are just a dream for this man, who is caught in the backwards-moving system of gender hierarchy.

Critics such as Moss, McCarthy, and Palmer have noted that the men in Springsteen's universe who are governed by the rules of gender politics, like the character in "One Step Up," have trouble crossing the boundaries of their prescribed roles. For instance, Moss argues that, in the phase of Springsteen's writing encompassed by the years 1975 through 1980, men and women play specific roles: "Women are portrayed as subordinate participants in the pursuit of the promised land. Men as orchestrators of the pilgrimage need women beside them to satisfy their own needs along the way" (171). In addition, Palmer writes, "[Springsteen's male] figures patrol borders, real and metaphorical. They capture and keep their womenfolk, and they struggle with their fathers, who are represented as embodiments of the patriarchal law. The tragedy of these figures lies in their inability to abandon the carefully drawn markers of masculinity, which prevents escape into the world of feeling" (101). Indeed, the crossing of boundaries and borders is something Springsteen's lyrics seem to obsess over, as a way for his characters to explore their own identities—to figure out who they want to be. Sometimes, these border crossings happen under the cover of darkness, as men feel their way towards an understanding of themselves and their place in the world through their encounters with women.

In Springsteen's lyrics, the male characters do reach into the darkness to find comfort in the female body. Women's bodies are more than just fleshpots—more than sex-objects or love-objects. Instead, Springsteen's male characters imagine women as substitutes for the Promised Land. For example, in "Leap of Faith" the male speaker recounts the vision of the woman's body as this space of pleasure and salvation; "Your legs were heaven, your breasts were the altar / Your body was the holy land." But, by creating the image of the female savior, by making the female body a source of redemption, the woman is still not an embodied individual with subjectivity. She is a symbol, a concept. Palmer notes that Springsteen's "[w]omen are mysterious, impenetrable and other" (103–4) and suggests that in his songs "[n]o optimistic end is possible, for both men and women are locked into blinkered positions on what is and is not their role" (103–4). But I argue that, especially in later songs, Springsteen's work separates itself from other rock catalogues that perpetuate gender hierarchy. His characters do not linger forlornly in the pessimistic realm of gender alienation. Instead, he envisions the possibility of salvation through unions like friendships, partnerships, love, and other connections between individuals. Though Springsteen does depict characters struggling within the confines of a patriarchal system that hurts both men and women, he offers hope of reconciliation between the male and the female.

Springsteen's work illuminates the symbolic burden on the female body in the patriarchal society. In songs like "Thunder Road," characters are searching for redemption, uniting with another person but rejecting the system which had falsely promised them salvation ("pulling out of here to win," "we gotta get out while we're young"). Ultimately, on later records, such as *Lucky Town, Human Touch, The Rising, Magic,* and *Working on a Dream,* Springsteen's characters return home and resolve to transform themselves from within, even if it is a struggle. These albums are filled with real but mostly hopeful images and stories of lovers, families, towns, cities, and homes that are struggling to transform from desolate to connected. Events that occur in public spaces such as streets, bars, beaches, parks, and workplaces evoke this sense of unity with another, or perhaps even the beginnings of a community, pulling characters out of private space of solitude and sterility.

Yet these older, more mature characters still fall into the trap of idealizing their women, linking them with God and heaven. In these cases, Springsteen's male characters sometimes express the belief that their happiness is based on the ability to get, and keep, a girl of their own—a girl with a face like an angel, a heart of gold, or any other numerations of idealized perfection, often with references to heavenly images. For example, in "All that Heaven Will Allow," the male character describes a cloudless sky and declares that he has can walk tall, with no real worries, all because of his girl, whose picture he keeps in a locket. You can almost imagine his jaunty stride down the street, elated, perhaps, from his recent marriage proposal, and her recent acceptance, and the life he envisions with this girl of his dreams.

The opposite is also true: sometimes these men fear that they cannot live up to their idealization of the woman. In "Cautious Man," for example, Bill Horton doubts his ability to make his wife, and himself, happy. Bill has an image of his wife as pure, innocent, and godly: "At their bedside he brushed the hair from his wife's face as the moon shone on her skin so white / Filling their room with the beauty of God's fallen light," and he worries that he is not worthy of this heavenly body.

In "Leah," which appears on *Devils & Dust*, the speaker sketches a sort of partnership in which everything seems equal between the man and the woman: he wants to "figure it all out / With Leah," and he wants to "live in the same house, beneath the same roof / Sleep in the same bed, search for the same proof / As Leah." The recording features ramshackle percussion, melodies that surprise the ear, and choral harmonies, all of which give the song a quiet spirit of hope. In this song, life with Leah is what the man is looking forward to, but he does not pin all of his hopes and dreams on her, waiting for her to deliver him from nowhere. Instead, he wants to stop waiting and to "shoulder his load." The listener gets the sense that this is an equal partnership; Leah is not a savior for the man but a partner, sleeping in the same bed, making decisions together, like Kate and her husband in "My Hometown."

Though Leah is not a savior in this song, Springsteen's use of the biblical name Leah does call up some interesting imagery in terms of gender, women, and female strength. In the Bible, Leah is not a savior figure either. Rather, she is a foundational figure. Along with Sarah, Rebecca, and Rachel, she is considered one of the four matriarchs in Judaic-Christian tradition. While Rachel couldn't, at first, bear children herself, Leah bore seven sons and one daughter to Jacob. According to biblical texts, Leah's descendants make up some of the most important figures in Western history and culture. Leah was chosen by God as the woman who would bear the descendants of Abraham to fulfill the prophesy of Israel. In Springsteen's song, there are also images of foundations: the speaker wants to build something with Leah—a house, a home, a place to land. It is not that Leah is some ethereal vision that inspires the man to build the house. She will build it and live in it with him.

Leah's biblical story also invokes questions about a man's desire for a woman who is ideally beautiful. Though blessed by God with many children, Leah is conventionally thought to have been homely looking. Sometimes referred to as the "first," "other," "hated," or "unloved" wife of Jacob, biblical Leah shared her marriage to Jacob with her more beautiful sister, Rachel. Jacob was in love with Rachel, explicitly described as beautiful in the Bible, but Leah's father tricked Jacob into marrying the less-pretty Leah first, to avoid the disgrace and impracticality of an unmarried eldest daughter. Leah's beauty, or lack thereof, however, is a contested premise by biblical scholars, feminists, and religious leaders alike. For example, religious studies scholar Paul Reardon explains that the biblical description of Leah only discusses her eyes, saying they are "rakkoth," which could be translated as weak, sickly, delicate, tender, or gentle (par. 3). He notes that some people believe Leah's eyes were tender from crying and praying to God so that she may be able to marry Jacob instead of his murderous brother Esau, to whom she was technically betrothed. The story is that God granted her tearful prayers. Because Leah's story resonates with such questions of cultural definitions of beauty as well as the role of women in the foundations of human history, the name *Leah* makes a fascinating choice for Springsteen to use in a song about a man and a woman's attempt to build a life together.

Women in Springsteen's work paradoxically inspire concepts both of the community at large and also of home. Like the almost mystical vision of Mary in "Thunder Road," Springsteen's women act as a source of inspiration for men to look beyond what they know and to connect with the rest of the world that they may not yet know. And, like Mary in "The Rising," who appears in a "garden of a thousand sighs" with "holy pictures of our children dancing in a sky filled with light," Springsteen's women also help men envision the redemption that resides within the home and family. Instead of something to run from or turn away from, home becomes a place we all must take responsibility for—a final resting ground, the end of the long road but not a dead end, a home that stands for creation, one we've generated, produced, and one we won't abandon.

The speaker in "The Rising," having just seen his vision of Mary in the garden, feels her "arms around [him]" and her "blood mix with [his own]," and then a "dream of life comes to [him]," like a "catfish dancing on the end of the line." The image of his blood mixing with Mary's is a powerful and moving image of unity between a man and a woman, suggesting that salvation may exist when we cease to conceive of ourselves as separate beings. Interestingly, one source notes that the catfish in Eastern cultures was mythologically accused of causing earthquakes, and, when caught, the catfish always proclaimed innocence, saying that earthquakes were actually caused by an imbalance of yin and yang, not by the single catfish ("A Brief Account," slide 5). Yin and yang are opposite energies often thought to manifest themselves in nature's binaries, such as day and night, and male and female. The image of the shimmering catfish, caught on a hook, reflecting light as it struggles to survive, representing this call for balance between opposites, brings the "dream of life" to the man, who realizes in his final moments that man and woman, and everything in between, can balance each other instead of one dominating the other.

Springsteen's image of unity between man and woman is never more beautifully articulated than it is in the song "Happy," released only on *Tracks*:

> Man and woman circle each other in a cage
> A cage that's been handed down the line
> Lost and running 'neath a million dead stars
> Tonight let's shed our skins and slip these bars
> Happy in each other's arms.

This is the perfect image of breaking out of restrictive patriarchal gender relations that Springsteen outlined in "One Step Up." Here, like the couple in "One Step Up," a man and a woman are in a cage, trapped in roles that were prescribed when these gender power structures were first put into place. In "Happy," the "million dead stars" signify not only that this is an old pattern, but a dead one too, and one that kills. Springsteen creates the image of the man and woman eluding this trap, shedding the skins that divide them into individual bodies and getting beyond the gender barriers that separate them. Neither the female savior nor the male hero exist here. Instead, the male and female are equal prisoners of something larger, "a cage that has been handed down the line." Neither the female nor male is rescuing the other from the cage. They must do it together, no one dominating or owing or promising anything to the other. The fairy tale images are cast aside and reimagined. The final image is of a man and woman, "Happy in each other's kiss / I'm happy in a love like this." In these uniting images of blood mixing, skins shedding, and spirits entwining, Springsteen turns gender difference on its head and creates an optimistic, even if distant and idealistic, vision of a relationship beyond hierarchy and beyond even equality. Maybe this vision is far off, and maybe unachievable, but by creating the vision Springsteen's work helps us imagine new possibilities for men and women.

NOTES

1. For examples of arguments that discuss Springsteen and gender relations in such a way see Kate McCarthy, "Deliver Me from Nowhere: Bruce Springsteen and the Myth of the American Promised Land"; Pamela Moss, "Where is the Promised Land? Class and Gender in Bruce Springsteen's Rock Lyrics"; and Gareth Palmer, "Springsteen and Authentic Masculinity." All three of these provide useful points of entry into the critical discussion of Springsteen and gender.

2. For an insightful analysis of Springsteen's revisionist gender implications of "Thunder Road" in live performance see Smith's article, pp. 841–42.

3. See McCarthy, Moss, and Palmer for examples of this point of view.

4. "Thunder Road" itself is a cinematic reference to the 1958 feature film of the same title.

5. One of the best renditions of "Stolen Car" that I have heard is Patty Griffin's cover, which appears on her *One Thousand Kisses* album. Hearing that song sung in a woman's voice, even without the gender of the pronouns switched, allows the audience to sympathize even more so with the hurt that both the man and woman are dealing with in their roles as husband and wife.

IV

READING PHILOSOPHY AND RELIGION

9

A Covenant Reversed

Bruce Springsteen and the Promised Land

Stephen Hazan Arnoff

> Fate hath tossed me into the wilderness of Memphis:
> Bid it carry me away and toss me yet again
> Until I behold the wilderness of Judah,
> And come to the side of the north, the beautiful height,
> And I gird me there with glory of the name of my God,
> And clothe me and veil me with the beauty of His holiness.
>
> —Yehudah HaLevi (36)

Yehudah HaLevi, medieval Spanish Jewish thinker and poet, never made it into the Promised Land. Bruce Springsteen, New Jersey rocker, never made it into Graceland. As Springsteen tells it (Marsh, *Born* 193–94), after a concert in Memphis on 30 April 1977, he and guitarist sidekick Miami Steve Van Zandt traveled to Elvis's home for an unannounced visit. After scaling a wall, Springsteen met a security guard unhappy to see him. "Is Elvis home?" he asked. "No, Elvis isn't home. He's in Lake Tahoe," was the response. Springsteen was asked to leave the premises. A few months later, Elvis was dead. Rejected in modern Memphis, Springsteen may have been thousands of miles and eight hundred years away from HaLevi the medieval philosopher's reimagined ancient Egyptian metropolis, yet the parallels of these two poets' conceptions of exile, wandering, and seeking a mythic home open a compelling track for understanding the contemporary adaptation of belief in the Promised Land at the heart of Springsteen's work.

The literal translation of the Hebrew word for Egypt—*Mitzraim*—is "the narrow straits." For HaLevi, the plight of the Hebrews in ancient Memphis in Egypt parallels his own struggle to survive as a Jew in Muslim Spain in the first half of the second millennia, unable to gain passage to the Land

177

of Israel, the home for which he longs. He aligns himself poetically and spiritually with the slavery of his ancestors, imbedding his own suffering in the glory of a story greater than himself. Springsteen's work follows a similar pattern, channelling his personal worries and passions into a national, mythic experience of the Promised Land of America grown too narrow—like *Mitzraim* of "the narrow straits"—to contain the quite reasonable dreams and expectations of a critical mass of its citizens.

Considered as a mythic backdrop throughout his career, the spectre of the Promised Land provides Springsteen—as it does HaLevi and countless other artists, poets, and thinkers—with a rich, creative template inspiring and meaningful on multiple levels, enabling him to participate in the continuing evolution of a biblical trope anchoring contemporary cultural expression. Reviewing Springsteen's work alongside scholarship on the values and techniques of traditional biblical commentary—in context of the Promised Land as well as more generally—Springsteen emerges as a worthy inheritor of a longstanding tradition of art and thought grounded in interpretation and renewal of biblical narratives. These include *retelling* archetypal biblical stories in changing contexts, a form common within the Hebrew Bible itself as well as in subsequent commentaries upon it; use of intertextuality, bundling commonplace or traditional language and images within commentaries in order to ensure a fluid, associative stream of meaningful content; and finally, the special impact afforded to commentary when it is experienced in the context of performance in ritual or liturgical settings.

Exile from Graceland is Springsteen's blessing, not his curse. While Elvis loses himself after attaining his own dreams within an empire paralleling ancient Egypt in scope of power and influence—working-class laborers supplanting Hebrew slaves and empty factories and storefronts and banks replacing Pharaoh's pyramids—Springsteen combines a personal, national, and liturgical-ritualistic approach to blend secular and religious and ancient and modern tropes challenging the community gathered around him to refine and reinterpret its own personal and national promises through transcendent art.

MORPHOLOGY OF A BIBLICAL ROCK SONG

The story of the Israelites in Egypt begins with Abraham, who travels to Egypt with his clan during a famine, nearly losing his wife in a case of forged identity along the way. Though the Abrahamic tribe that will become the Israelites ultimately escapes to other lands, their experience establishes the Egypt of the biblical narrative as a place of paradox: its life-saving riches threaten communal identity and meaning to the point of bondage. Joseph, Abraham's great-great grandson, is a wonder child cast off from his own family due to his brothers' jealousy over his special promise, amplifying the tropes established by Abraham both in his own journey and in what he represents for his people as a whole. Joseph rises from liminal status as house servant and prisoner to become viceroy of the massive Egyptian empire, placing him in a position to save his family—and in fact the entire known world according to the biblical account—during yet another famine. But in the generations after his death, Joseph's descendants fall out of favor with Pharaoh, becoming slaves themselves. Despite his mixed Israelite-Egyptian heritage, Moses is chosen to redeem them. After divinely mandated plagues and war, the Israelites escape to the desert for forty years of wandering, finally arriving in the Land of Israel, which has been promised to them on condition of their maintaining the rules and regulations of the covenant granted by God at Mount Sinai at the peak moment of their journey. As Deuteronomy 6:1–3 states,

> And this is the command, the statutes and the ordinances, which the Lord your God has charged you to teach you to do in the land into which you are about to cross to take hold of it. So that you will fear the Lord your God to keep all His statutes and His commands which I charge you—you and your son and your son's son, all the days of your life; and so that your days be long. And you shall hear, Israel, and you shall keep to do, that it may go well with you, and that you may greatly multiply, and the Lord God of your father has promised you, a land flowing with milk and honey.

Charged with establishing a covenant triply contingent on (1) proper conduct, (2) specific territory, and (3) the reach of generations, Moses dies before the Israelites arrive in the Promised Land. His descendants establish a kingdom there with the Temple at its center, embodying a monotheistic covenantal paradigm that—though it will continue to evolve in the millennia to follow—remains a central myth, promise, and obstacle to this day.

THE PROMISED LAND

"The Promised Land" from Springsteen's 1978 album *Darkness on the Edge of Town*—in both its title and in the story it tells—provides an obvious model for Bruce Springsteen as a biblical interpreter. The song exemplifies a pattern apparent throughout the arc of Springsteen's career in which he probes the theme of the Promised Land for archetypal tropes, anchoring a personal path towards redemption, such that the circumstances of the day-to-day life of Springsteen's heroes are explained through the lens of a timeless narrative.

The tale of the Promised Land conveys a communal myth distinctly applicable to America, intended by its founders as a contemporary rendition of the journey of the Israelites out of Egypt, the colonists from the old world of Europe claiming a renewed biblical covenant in a new land of milk and honey in the New World. In his excellent book-length study on Bruce Springsteen's career in context of transmitting and translating the American story—in particular in chapter 3, "Visions of Kings: Springsteen and the American Dream"(Cullen, *Born* 51–74)—Jim Cullen explains multiple manifestations of the American Dream within Springsteen's vision. Cullen begins his account by citing the 1630 sermon of John Winthrop, first governor of Massachusetts: "'We shall find that the God of Israel is among us, when ten of us shall be able to resist a thousand of our enemies, when he shall make us praise and glory that men shall say of succeeding plantations, 'the Lord make it like that of New England'" (*Born* 55). Cullen goes on to note that "the heart of the Puritans' American Dream was what they called their 'covenant,' an implicit pact that [God] would provide for them spiritually if they formed a community to honor him according to his precepts as they understood them" (*Born* 55). Even though faith in the fulfillment of this covenant of "life, liberty and the pursuit of happiness" is commonplace amongst Springsteen's generation of working class Baby Boomers, the heroes of his songs—"The Promised Land" being a prime example—grapple with realities during their lifetimes within which the promise of the land breaks down dramatically. Amidst these struggles, a hero like the narrator of "The Promised Land" plays a role in a drama greater than himself: he witnesses the unravelling of a web of relationships and commitments meant to hold this covenant together.

"The Promised Land" overflows with core elements of the biblical trope. Fusing a desert journey of escape from the pains of grim labor, a hazily defined redemption disrupting the continuity of generations, and a cause for living "the right way," the song reflects the image of the Exodus story through a modern looking glass. The song situates itself with references to a quest taking place in the Utah desert and asserts its goals in the chorus:

> The dogs on Main Street howl
> 'Cause they understand
> If I could take one moment into my hands
> Mister, I ain't a boy, no I'm a man
> And I believe in a promised land

While the technique of renewing biblical tropes might initially seem surprising in considering the realm of popular culture, Springsteen's use of the Promised Land as a resource driving the message, media, and reception of his work follows patterns common to the art of artists and thinkers throughout history eager to ground their work in something timeless. Three scholarly lenses provide useful reflection on how this process unfolds within both traditional biblical commentary and Bruce Springsteen's work.

BIBLICAL RETELLING

What biblical scholar and translator Robert Alter explains concerning the parallels between the narrative assumptions about the composition of the Bible and the contemporary writing of fiction applies to the work of Bruce Springsteen as well: "[T]he biblical writer could manipulate his inherited materials with sufficient freedom and sufficient firmness of authorial purpose to define motives, relations, and unfolding themes, even in a primeval history, with the kind of subtle cogency we associate with the conscious artistry of the narrative mode designated prose fiction" (Alter 32). And while the difference in circumstances between a modern-day rock lyricist and an ancient scribe are vast, when it comes to addressing the raw materials out of which biblical narratives are formed, certain basic conceptions amongst ancient and contemporary creative acts are shared. Namely, in taking on themes of deep social significance through the composition of formative texts, it is necessary for both kinds of authors to balance their compositions between the "freedom" of an independent vision and unique context with the demands of using and reusing traditional stories, themes, and motifs.

"The Promised Land" exemplifies how Springsteen takes on a core American myth—in this case "the grid of conventions upon which, and against which, the individual work operates" (Alter 47)—in the same manner that a biblical author might take on core myths such as the creation story, the receiving of the Law, or the establishment of a monarchy through multiple tellings. Both within the biblical text itself and then as part of an endless stream of commentaries utilizing the same set of core elements, individuals and clusters of thinkers shift in tone, context, and style based on their particular perspectives—a composing culture in which archetypal materials are continually adapted, challenged, translated, transmitted, and re-imagined. As an example of this pattern, and conveniently referencing a portion of the biblical trope of the Promised Land précised above, Alter notes that three times in the book of Genesis alone "a patriarch is driven by famine to a southern region where he pretends that his wife is his sister" (49). These retellings are essentially elastic, relating details of a narrative that both blends and challenges other accounts, creating a cacophony of meanings over generations for even a relatively simple narrative arc. As will be demonstrated below, Springsteen follows a similar pattern of telling and retelling a core narrative of exile and redemption not only as a reflection of the biblical myth, but as a self-commentary on his own narrative evolution and creative tension as a thinker, believer (or nonbeliever—or both), and artist dealing with its themes.[1]

Much more can be said about the ways that Robert Alter's depiction of biblical telling and retelling of root narratives is reflected in Springsteen's work, but one additional point will suffice. Alter describes the core biblical notion about the nature of human and divine roles: "[There are] two, approximately parallel, dialectical tensions . . . [one is] between the divine plan and the disorderly character of actual historical events . . . the other is a tension between God's will, His providential guidance, and human freedom, the refractory nature of man" (Alter 33). Springsteen has often been asked to describe his mission over the course of his career, and his responses consistently attempt to trace the grand scope of an idealized America where people's needs and desires often outrace their ability to achieve them—despite an illusion that all is possible. In an interview with Judy Wieder, Springsteen notes, "If my work was about anything, it was about the search for identity, for personal recognition, for acceptance, for communion, and for a big country. I've always felt that's why people come to my shows, because they feel that big country in their hearts" (quoted in Sawyers 214). Compare this quotation with another synthesis by Alter explaining how narratives are designed to navigate the complexities of the human/divine covenant throughout the Bible: "[H]istorical destiny does not just happen; you have to know how to make it happen, how to keep your eye on the distant horizon of present events" (Alter 35). Springsteen, as pop culture masters are wont to do, compresses the cogency of long-held values and beliefs into phrases and melodies both familiar and fresh. The chorus of "The Promised Land" serves as a rock and roll translation of the biblical pattern of the human struggle to meet the call of individual desire and destiny amidst the inevitable pull of forces greater than that for which any single person could account.

Belief in an ancient covenant filtered through the terms of the American Dream drives Springsteen's narrator/hero to strive for a life deeper and better despite the howling dogs on Main Street. By echoing what Alter (in the context of biblical literature) deems knowing "how to keep your eye on the distant horizon of present events," the hero of "The Promised Land" reimagines the biblical trope in order to retell a story of redemption in a contemporary landscape where the country is big enough to contain its potential—but only as long as seekers of redemption can still keep their eyes on its "distant horizon." In the evolution of biblical text and commentary, just as in Springsteen's work, a covenant is, by definition, a joint agreement between people and an entity greater than their collective. The bigness of Springsteen's "big country" is fully and mutually dependant on everyone engaged with it as well as a grand destiny worth believing in—both human and divine.

INTERTEXTUALITY

In 1990 Daniel Boyarin used postmodern literary theory to explain the nature of the rabbinic practice of midrash. Covering a cluster of texts and methods of pedagogy attributed to teachers between approximately the second and seventh centuries, the term *midrash* denotes the formulaic, self-referential, and deeply-learned clusters of commentaries on biblical literature created through the lens of the law, practice, and thought of Jewish communities in the Land of Israel and surrounding communities of the Mediterranean and Near East. While it is comprised of a complex web of hermeneutical strategies, midrash can be described in simple terms as the art of "filling in the gaps" of the Hebrew Bible—from accounting for the identity of an anonymous biblical character to completing disjointed or illogical narratives to resolving outstanding moral dilemmas. Following the teaching of various literary theorists, Boyarin's description of midrash holds that "the romantic view of literary creation as *creatio ex nihilo* . . . cannot be sustained" (Boyarin 12).

In other words, Robert Alter claims that the chain of tradition demands that authors and commentators across generations inevitably replay the same narrative scenes over and over, their subtle shifts and alterations revealing what is unique about the specific cultural matrix out of which they compose. The basic outline of a classic story is replicated from thinker to thinker—the biblical Promised Land offering a reusable trope for HaLevi's account of exile through medieval eyes, Springsteen's modern working-class story of redemption, and many more. But Boyarin takes this conception further. If the art of biblical narrative requires composition based on a fixed form, like the image of a jigsaw puzzle necessarily reworked across generations, Boyarin holds that the pieces of the puzzle at each artist's finger tips (including words, phrases, literary and cultural allusions, and other formulae) are inherited and rearranged in an exhaustive cycle of creativity: "The midrash realizes its goal by means of a hermeneutic of recombining pieces of the canonized exemplar into a new discourse" (Boyarin 38). This conception of midrash claims that great artists and thinkers on a biblical arc—and presumably along other lines of traditional content as well—master their craft because they can seamlessly hear and recreate both the traditional outline of ancient stories and the minutiae of narrative parts that animate it. Then they recalibrate all of this content in a manner that is deeply original and deeply traditional at the same time.

From the beginning of his career, Springsteen has been recycling raw material of stories, characters, images, and other narrative elements in a pattern that would be familiar to the theories of both Alter and Boyarin. Returning to "The Promised Land," Springsteen's intertextuality vis-à-vis the Exodus story is, again, fairly obvious. More than anything, asserting himself upon the

story of the Promised Land in the title of the song presents a major intertextual commitment. This introduction of a classic trope continues as the story
of the song unfolds in the first verse, the hero describing an anguished journey through the desert, trying to escape from his "daddy's garage." Because
of its obvious reference to the Exodus story in the title, "daddy's garage" becomes a modern reflection of the authoritarian bondage of Pharaoh's grasp
on the disempowered Israelites. In the era of Joseph, the Israelites had been
protected en masse by the Pharaohs—leaders serving as pseudo parents for
Joseph himself and then for a nation otherwise orphaned. But as described
in the opening of Exodus 1:8, within the course of a few generations, the
Israelite nation, once protected as family due to the intimate attention
generated by Joseph, finds itself reserved in the direction of the dark side
of intimacy, the wrath of a loved one singled out for exclusion: "Now there
rose a new king over Mitzraim [Egypt] who knew not Joseph." In a larger
metaphorical sense, the hero of "The Promised Land" faces the same bitter
choice of exposure and exclusion encountered by the Israelites. The space of
his "daddy's garage" is a place where vital things are meant to be fixed, and
the family should generate its livelihood, just as Egypt has saved a people
from famine and allowed them the safety and industry to thrive and grow.
But "daddy's garage," again like Egypt, has become a painful trap representing not only the implosion of a family business, but the devolution of entire
American working communities whose labor is no longer generative, in fact
restricting the essence of peoples' being.

The title "The Promised Land" reflects further intertextuality within its
basic contours thanks to Springsteen's apparent reference to Chuck Berry's
1964 song of nearly the same title, "Promised Land," which is a happy-go-
lucky story of a "poor boy" traveling coast to coast seeking adventure and
riches. Berry's song cites the popular spiritual "Swing Low, Sweet Chariot,"
which itself recasts a biblical trope onto the African-American landscape
of slavery and redemption. Berry's song of the American Promised Land—
both ironic and cheery as his songs often are—would not be an unusual
reference for Springsteen, who, as will be noted below, participates fully in
the endemic intertextual tradition of popular music. Songwriters liberally
reference work from their contemporaries alongside those from years and
decades past. In "The Promised Land," the result is a triple lens reflection
on a core myth—the Exodus story, African American history as described
by a traditional spiritual, and Chuck's Berry's conception of America—combined as a cluster of intertextual references anchoring Springsteen's overall
interpretation of the narrative.

Another aspect of Springsteen's use of intertextuality in "The Promised
Land"—and a method common throughout his work—reflects not only the
external tropes he interprets, but also how he reuses content he himself has
developed in his canon. Consider Springsteen's application of the concept

of the "street" in "The Promised Land." The chorus turns on the phrase "The dogs on Main Street howl," a disturbing image of a thoroughfare at the core of the image of small town life in America: the street of commerce, parades, city hall, and, in symbolic terms, consensus. In "The Promised Land," the street is empty but for the hero and a pack of dogs. These are runaway dogs looking for their masters, wild dogs, dogs chained to the fences of their owners, or dogs disturbing the neighborhood when people want to sleep. All of these images of dogs are fitting personifications of the unhappy state of the hero. The dogs and the hero share a deep need to cry out for redemption beyond what Main Street can provide. But peeking around the corner of Main Street, which often appears in bittersweet scenes mixing nostalgia, hope, and anger in his songs (as in "Long Walk Home" or "My Home Town"), Springsteen thrives on describing a set of other streets where the real action in any town lies.

His band since the early 1970s, the E Street Band, is named after a locale where, according to 1973's "The E Street Shuffle," "Sparks light . . . when the boy prophets walk it handsome and hot." In this context, Springsteen's band embodies the crossroads where prophetic truth germinates. Throughout Springsteen's career, both Main Street and the streets beyond it provide venues for some of Springsteen's richest metaphors. On *Darkness on the Edge of Town*, the album on which "The Promised Land" appears, there are also "Streets of Fire," inspiring a sense of isolation wherever they lead: "I live now only with strangers / I talk to only strangers," he sings "I walk with angels that have no place / Streets of fire." Most poignantly, in recalling the 1964 hit "Dancing in the Street" by Martha and the Vandellas, there are the dead-end, one way streets of "Racing in the Street," which literally lead nowhere:

> We take all the action we can meet
> And we cover all the northeast states
> When the strip shuts down we run 'em in the street
> From the fire roads to the interstate
> Some guys they just give up living
> And start dying little by little, piece by piece
> Some guys come home from work and wash up
> And go racin' in the street
> . . . .
> For all the shut-down strangers and hot-rod angels
> Rumbling through this promised land

Here, Springsteen employs intertextuality to rework the lyrics and melody of an earlier call for joyous rebellion with a flat, methodical march of hot-rodders with nothing to live for. They are uninspired by work, love, and even their next race. Seekers of the redemption of the Promised Land find themselves on streets "[r]umbling through this promised land," carrying a heavy load of sins and worry as part of their quest. The burden of meaning-lessness on a Main Street abandoned to the dogs—*Exile on Main Street* in the parlance of the Rolling Stones's classic album released in 1972—forces racers, dreamers, fighters, and boy prophets to cast about for any other avenue of freedom they can find. As Springsteen gathers the threads of the myth of the Promised Land and binds them to contemporary frustration on Main Street, he creates a widely referential vessel of depth and versatility. In the words of 1975's "Jungleland," "The Promised Land" models sublima-tion of anxiety and tradition through music, allowing Springsteen's heroes to survive their situations despite Main Street's broken promises:

> The street's alive as secret debts are paid
> Contacts made, they vanish unseen
> Kids flash guitars just like switch-blades
> Hustling for the record machine
> The hungry and the hunted
> Explode into rock and roll bands
> That face off against each other out in the street
> Down in Jungleland

But before turning to a wider view of Springsteen's use of the Promised Land throughout his career, it is important to explore how this sublimation of pain and longing into *texts* fusing tradition and innovation is elevated further by musical performance, producing not only masterful intertextual retellings of formative narratives, but also constructing lasting contempo-rary liturgies for millions of listeners.

PERFORMANCE

The word *text* derives from the Latin *texare*, meaning "to weave." Texts are essentially clusters of cultural material bound around a pattern—a definition easily applicable to songs, which consist of words, rhythm, and melody woven together in a pattern. Intertextuality recognizes that arts of communication such as writing and music embody a fluid process of weav-ing together content. Be it the formulaic categorization described by Albert S. Lord, the "technologies" of the spoken word embedded in all language as explained by Walter Ong, or the evidence of interpenetration of orality and textuality explicated by the theories of "oral residue" in the work of John Miles Foley, the past several decades have produced a rich literature in the field of oral performance applicable to all variety of traditional texts—from poetry and epics to a range of ritual texts and liturgy.

Two issues from the realm of oral performance theory are of particular use for approaching the work of Bruce Springsteen. First, oral performance theory enables scholars to place content in its "immanent context"—a term generated by the Foley school to describe the natural milieu where the qualities of orally mediated media fulfill their purpose best. In his work on the methodologies and meanings of preserving and interpreting traditional texts whose oral experience has been lost—Homeric epics for example—Foley holds that "to ignore the immanent context is to force situated words out of their natural significative setting—obviously a crippling and artistically violent reorientation" (Foley xi). In other words, a reader, translator, or interpreter of orally significant texts—in this case the music of Bruce Springsteen—must recognize a text's natural environment of performance. Words or music on a page or even an audio or video recording of a live event cannot capture performed content on the level experienced in an actual performance.

Second, the art of ethnopoetics, a method within the larger field of oral performance studies, grants the tools for scholars to notate elements of performances beyond lyrical or musical notation, which Foley notes as "scoring . . . translated libretti for oral realization by readers."[2] Richard Bauman calls this practice the "keying of performance" (Bauman 15), a method for capturing critical influences on the performed experience, including insinuation, joking, imitation, translation, quotation, disclaimer, and a variety of pauses and nonverbal gestures. According to Foley, this type of "keying" of texts reveals "the set of metonymic, associative meanings institutionally delivered and received through a dedicated idiom or registered either during or on authority of traditional oral performance" (Foley 209).

Though any lengthy analysis of Springsteen's work must focus on his talents as a songwriter, anyone who has followed Springsteen's career knows that he has built and maintained his appeal through spectacularly intense, lengthy, eclectic, and heartfelt concerts driven by humor, passion, physical movement, and ambition. The text may offer a narrative template for Springsteen, but his embodiment of these narratives in performance releases his creative power, and, of course, the power of the written narrative as well. Jim Cullen reflects on the power of Springsteen's performance ethic and experience: "Springsteen may well be unique in the degree to which he has sought to make playing—in the general and musical sense of the word—a form of joyful work" (Cullen, *Born* 107). Robert Coles extends this description in context of the "immanent context" in which Springsteen's songs come to their fullest expression:

> Springsteen's vigorous performance holds his viewers still, stirred, stunned even, as they follow him moving, entertaining, exclaiming, exhorting, exulting, lamenting, sometimes pleading, or worrying about so much that doesn't

work, or is plain wrong, [about] the country he obviously holds in high regard and treasures. . . . [T]he Boss's concert audiences, whose members can be seen looking up, paying close attention to this writing singer, both inward and outward looking, become for many a secular idol venerated with a certain abandonment, enjoyed with a certain hunger that is fueled by the disappointments which other onetime idols have of late prompted: political figures and churchmen whose deceits, and worse, whose betrayals of trust and affection and belief give special, contrasting significance to a particular performer's time spent with all those sitting and yearning people, some clapping, some shouting (*Bruuuce!*), some waving, some crying, some singing along, his words arriving, caught, held tight, as they are dispatched. The result is a communion of earnest, energetic expression and a crowd that is interested, grateful: a reception, a bond that takes place outside an immediate setting, and across land, even oceans. (Coles 44–45)

Coles's description of Springsteen as a performer contains elements that fuse precisely the sort of evidence scholars utilizing oral performance theory seek for categorizing the impact of performance on text, performer, and audience. As emphasized by the assertions of ethnopoetics, Springsteen's presentation of the texts of his songs is made dynamic by force of the gestures, movements, expressions, and other nonverbal functions he brings to his performance. If his goal in songwriting revolves around chronicling the status of the Promised Land in real time, tracking the reality of the American covenant for people in a "big country," Springsteen's performance both in front and much as a part of an audience relies on an elaborate set of verbal and nonverbal, poetic, and ethnopoetic skills producing a kind of ritual re-enactment of the experience of the covenant at the heart of his work.

First and foremost, his performances are embedded in the community of his band—a group of long-time travelers with the same mixed personae of familiarity and outsider status on "Main Street" engaged by Springsteen's songs. They joke, reminisce, mime, get bored, hug and kiss, dance, flip, kneel and bow, freeze, fight, and sweat before the audience like a small city straining and celebrating within the spaces of the texts of their leader's songs. That for nearly two decades Springsteen's wife Patti Scialfa has been a part of the band portends an even deeper family resonance in an already intimate experience witnessed by the audience. On stage the band pounds through Springsteen's songs, a distinctly unfashionably dressed cluster of ethnically and racially diverse characters ritualizing a covenantal drama deeply resonant with their audience on every level.

Coles rightly describes Springsteen in performance in the role of charismatic high priest, general, mayor, or prophet gathering not only the band around his mission, but, obviously, the audience as well. Springsteen's concerts represent a perfect storm of covenantal catharsis: ancient archetypes bound to popular culture and the ritual power of performance match the demands for leadership and inspiration by a temporary community of witnesses representing the nation as a whole. In introducing Springsteen at the Kennedy Center Honors, President Obama remarked, "His tours are not so much concerts but communions" (Obama). A Springsteen concert serves as a catalyst urging all of these elements to peak expression, with song texts serving as a map for the expectations, frustrations, and exhortations of the Promised Land.

Midrashic commentary delivered in a synagogue during holiday or Sabbath celebrations or a Sunday church sermon bridging contemporary and biblical themes uses essentially the same mix of elements—text, tradition, community, and ritual. But these are religious rites, identified as such by ministers, priests, rabbis, and congregants alike. Though his work is thick with religious references, Springsteen presents himself as ecumenical, pluralistic, and non-sectarian. He accepts the template of an ancient myth at the core of his work, but demands that its enactment serve all who encounter it. He makes no claim for a single dogma driving these myths, choosing the stories of a diverse array of heroes in original narratives to interpret traditionally religious themes. And more than all else, his performances—part town hall gathering, part opera, part communion ritual—demand recognition of a shared goal of experiencing "a big country."

Introducing his participation in a voter registration event sponsored by then Democratic candidate for president Barack Obama, Springsteen said, "I've spent most of my creative life measuring the distance between [the] American promise and American reality" (Vote). In blurring the lines between text and performance, witnessing and listening, religious and secular, and ancient and modern, Springsteen animates the story of America as Promised Land with pluralistic interpretation and embodiment of the meaning of the Promised Land that is difficult to match on such a large scale for such an extended period anywhere else in contemporary American culture.

BRUCE SPRINGSTEEN'S PROMISED LAND

Having posited a template for Springsteen's unique fusion of biblical retelling, intertextuality, and performance it is now possible to review his approach to the Promised Land over the span of his career. Each studio album of original material captures a set of songs, which, when heard in context of the themes of exile and redemption, demonstrates how Springsteen has matured as an artist in parallel to expressions of the American covenant changing around him.[3] While the raw material at the heart of his work remains consistent, demonstrating the sharpness of Springsteen's discipline as a lyricist, the evolution of his work reveals much not only about Springsteen's creative path, but the relative dissolution of American life during his time on the public stage—a pattern of disturbing decline in the essential promise of the Promised Land.

Greetings from Asbury Park, N.J. (1973), *The Wild, the Innocent & the E Street Shuffle* (1973), and *Born to Run* (1975) share the exuberance of escape from the captivity of narrow straits of social mores and boredom through music, romance, and the open road. The Promised Land is any place but the place where the journey begins. *Darkness on the Edge of Town* (1978), *The River* (1980), *Nebraska* (1982), and *Born in the U.S.A.* (1984) trace the minutiae of disappointment when dreams of survival or escape fail—even as flashes of rebellion remain—and the narrator who is "born to run" finds himself unable to manage the realities of the place to which the journey has led him. *Tunnel of Love* (1987), *Lucky Town* (1992), and *Human Touch* (1992) suggest different forms of escapism for encountering the challenges of the Promised Land, primarily through love. These albums capture a body of work Springsteen wryly calls his "happy songs."[4] While the challenges of establishing a fulfilling romantic and home life introduce additional layers to Springsteen's religious metaphors—particularly as his partners guide him through both the suffering and bliss of a personal redeemer—his focus on the essential elements of the Promised Land outside of his own experience is blurred, asserted particularly powerfully in his most recent cluster of recorded work: *The Ghost of Tom Joad* (1995), *The Rising* (2002), *Devils & Dust* (2005), and *Magic* (2007). In this phase, Springsteen shadows his own satisfaction in a sustaining personal redemption with an apocalyptic vision of America as a failed Promised Land—a landscape politically corrupt, emotionally drained, and physically wasted.

BORN TO RUN: ESCAPE FROM CAPTIVITY

The first set of responses to the Promised Land in Springsteen's work actually begins not so much with a goal of getting somewhere, but rather, of getting anywhere—anywhere but the place where his heroes begin. Whether it is home, school, or the smallness of their hometowns that troubles them, Springsteen's first group of seekers run away from home to somewhere better, music being the primary mode for inspiring and sustaining their escape.

In "Rosalita (Come Out Tonight)"—since the mid-1970s, consistently the high point of Springsteen's live shows—the song's hero sings to his lover, trapped in her parents' home, a state from which her boyfriend is likely not so far removed himself. He wants to "liberate" and "confiscate" her, despite the objections of the girl's father that he is a ne'er-do-well musician. But when the hero announces that "a record company, Rosie, just gave me a big advance," he is ready to break free and demands that she join him:

> I know a pretty little place in Southern California down San Diego way
> There's a little café where they play guitars all night and day
> You can hear them in the back room strummin'
> So hold tight baby 'cause don't you know daddy's comin'

In a common American trope—reworked dramatically by Springsteen during his most recent period of songwriting launched by *The Ghost of Tom Joad*—California plays a role as a sort of Promised Land within the Promised Land. It is a vaguely defined Nirvana in the West, a musical Oz where guitars rule both day and night, freeing all those who embrace this culture.

For Springsteen's heroes on the run, there is little to lose in a rush to leave the exile of a hometown, but achieving freedom is far from easy, requiring a skilful fusion of lessons learned in grim realities before a first pass at experiencing fantasies of freedom in life on the road. In "Growin' Up," the narrator has come of age an outcast, throwing up when he should have "stood up," drifting with his head in the stars when he should have been focused on the mundane world of those around him. When he finally finds his own two feet and manages to get grounded in the Promised Land—be it California, a parking lot, or elsewhere—it is only after accepting that he must blend his instinctual penchant for rebellion with something more lasting. Continuity emerges in one of Springsteen's most abiding symbols, which competes for meaning with the metaphorical force of music throughout his career. Here, he finds himself in a car, the vehicle of redemption in so many of Springsteen's songs, that is used and in need of repair, just like the world. Still, through the alchemy of a daring musical spirit, he can bring it to life:

> I took month-long vacations in the stratosphere and you know it's really hard to hold your breath.
> I swear I lost everything I ever loved or feared, I was the cosmic kid in full costume dress
> Well, my feet they finally took root in the earth but I got me a nice little place in the stars
> And I swear I found the key to the universe in the engine of an old parked car

For Springsteen, the fantasy of freedom is continually tempered by metaphors of mundane reality—a car or an imperfect lover or money primary among them. On *Born to Run*, his true breakthrough album after *Greetings from Asbury Park, N.J.* on which "Growin' Up" appears, a potential companion on the road learns just how complex this escape might be. "Thunder Road" is one of the most haunting and honest serenades in recent popular music:

> Well now I'm no hero
> That's understood
> All the redemption I can offer, girl
> Is beneath this dirty hood

> With a chance to make it good somehow
> Hey what else can we do now
> Except roll down the window
> And let the wind blow back your hair
> Well the night's busting open
> These two lanes will take us anywhere
> We got one last chance to make it real
> To trade in these wings on some wheels
> Climb in back, heaven's waiting on down the tracks

The car, the open road, and the lover all meet at the crossroads of the escape of a hero who openly presents himself as "no hero" to a girl whom he calls "no beauty" earlier in the song. But in a classic Springsteen lyrical twist, components of pop music escapism merge seamlessly with deep myth. The couple does not head to the drive-in or to a booth in the corner of a diner or a quiet cul-de-sac for their private adventure. Instead, they head for the Promised Land, as "Thunder Road" continues: "Oh oh come take my hand / We're riding out tonight to case the promised land." And if there is any doubt about the seriousness of their journey, the song concludes with a reference to "promise" again:

> From your front porch to my front seat
> The door's open but the ride it ain't free
> And I know you're lonely
> For words that I ain't spoken
> But tonight we'll be free
> All the promises'll be broken

The Promised Land may be within reach, but the freedom it promises carries prices and rewards unknown.

The musical anthem of Springsteen's first creative period is "Born to Run," a song which opens with a statement of purpose synthesizing the passion and frustration that sets most of his heroes on their search for the American covenant in the first place:

> In the day we sweat it out in the streets of a runaway American dream
> At night we ride through mansions of glory in suicide machines
> Sprung from cages out on Highway 9
> Chrome wheeled, fuel-injected and steppin' out over the line
> Baby this town rips the bones from your back
> It's a death trap, it's a suicide rap
> We gotta get out while we're young
> 'Cause tramps like us, baby we were born to run

While a couple seeks escape in "Born to Run" just like the couple in "Thunder Road," the "we" of this song represents much more dramatically a community-at-large—a band, a gang, an audience, or some other microcosm of discontented young Americans for whom the American Dream has been lost. Again, as with the narrative of "Thunder Road," it is not clear what awaits the runaways. Like Springsteen himself, the narrator knows that which the myth of the Promised Land has taught him: there is a special place waiting at the other end of the journey. He describes this place to his lover (and to his audience as a whole) in terms even less defined than Southern California in "Rosalita." There is sun, at least, but the destination's only really clear quality is that it is "where we really want to go":

> Someday girl, I don't know when, we're gonna get to that place
> Where we really want to go
> And we'll walk in the sun
> But till then tramps like us, baby we were born to run

Springsteen commences his pursuit of the Promised Land with a burning sense of destiny and purpose tempered by humble acceptance that no amount of running guarantees what he and his fellow travelers might find. Faith, passion, and lack of any other choice must be their guides.

BORN IN THE U.S.A.: THE MINUTIAE OF DISAPPOINTMENT

If the impassioned rebels of "Growin' Up" or "Born to Run" are somehow related to the struggling son of "The Promised Land," perhaps they represent the best friend who did not take the chance to leave town. Or perhaps he is in fact one of the rebels himself, returned to his hometown after traveling across the country only to discover that nothing awaits him in either place. Regardless, in this second phase of Springsteen's work, the covenental turmoil of his heroes spreads. Home and exile become one and the same, carrying an extreme sense of rootlessness. In a sort of hyper-intertextuality, Springsteen purposefully conflates place names as part of the map of America where these heroes live and roam, resulting in an essentially monolithic blend of towns, roads, and counties that add up to seeing and being nowhere at all.

Consider that "The Promised Land" begins, "On a rattlesnake speedway in the Utah desert" and then describes "Driving 'cross the Waynesboro county line." There is no Waynesboro County in Utah—though there are Waynesboros in Pennsylvania, Virginia, Georgia, and Tennessee. And the Rattlesnake Speedway proper is not in Utah either, but in Nevada. While Springsteen is not a geographer and is, of course, not accountable for accuracy of place names in his mix of hard facts and imaginative truths, his use of familiar sounding names in mixed-up order and contexts reveals a technique for crafting a vision of a grand American landscape that is *almost* real. This creative twist results in an overriding theme of rootlessness in the Promised Land. The hero of "The Promised Land" travels through this geographical fog saying, "I got the radio on and I'm just killing time."

In an earlier phase of Springsteen's career, when kids "flash guitars just like switchblades" and the open road symbolizes radical if undefined freedom, the combination of music on the radio, a car, and an open road across uncharted territory are likely cause for celebration. Here, the sounds emanating from the radio are as meaningless as the flat mass of the landscape the hero traverses, and time itself—once reflected in the urgency of late night calls for a lover to get out of town before it is too late—is not even worth keeping. As a commentator on the biblical story, Springsteen performs a radical shift on a core value of the tale. If the biblical covenant depends on a combination of rootedness in the earth (the Land of Israel serving as the Promised Land), here there is only meandering and rootlessness without purpose—an endless "Utah desert." The Israelites wander Sinai for forty years, but ultimately reach the Promised Land. Springsteen's hero keeps believing, but that does not save him from ceaseless wandering.

The River, Springsteen's follow-up to *Darkness on the Edge of Town*, extends the litany of songs of restlessness and rootlessness with dark undercurrents of pessimism. Heroes and their friends and lovers still play with life fully in spurts and still cheer for rebellion as they can, but the core narrative of this double album flows through songs like "The Price You Pay," where the risks in setting out for the Promised Land described in "Born to Run" clearly are not rewarded:

> You make up your mind, you choose the chance you take
> You ride to where the highway ends and the desert breaks
> Out on to an open road you ride until the day
> You learn to sleep at night with the price you pay
> . . . .
> Little girl down on the strand
> With that pretty little baby in your hands
> Do you remember the story of the promised land
> How he crossed the desert sands
> And could not enter the chosen land
> On the banks of the river he stayed
> To face the price you pay

Here Springsteen refers directly to one of the stark, disturbing realities of the Exodus story in the Bible: God prohibits Moses from entering the Land of Israel due to his transgressions of hubris while serving as appointed leader of the Israelites in the desert. Though Moses leads the people out of slavery, he himself dies just steps away from the nation's ultimate goal. So, too, the hero of "The Price You Pay," whose actual "price"—described generally as the same fate as Moses—is never quite defined. Whether the song refers to a young man who has traveled the open road and taken great chances or a young woman (perhaps the unwed mother of some new abandoned baby Moses) when the Promised Land is close enough to feel, its seekers remain in exile. "The Price You Pay" describes a shift from the passion and urgency of the first phase of Springsteen's heroes' pursuit of the Promised Land to a clear sense of anger, chronicled in great detail through the familiar metaphors of cars and lovers reappraised in a full stock of songs from this period. Prime examples include the lovers of "The River" and "Point Blank" from *The River* and the cars of freedom harbouring destruction on *The River*'s "Wreck on the Highway" and *Nebraska*'s "Stolen Car." In these songs, Springsteen introduces a series of witnesses to relationships wracked by misunderstanding, violence, broken promises, and lack of satisfaction.

As the signature song of the album and tour that launched Bruce Springsteen to a level of mass appeal and cultural influence achieved by few performers, the title track of *Born in the U.S.A.*, delivered in a ragged, screaming vocal throughout, directly traces the desolation of the hero of "Born to Run":

> Down in the shadow of the penitentiary
> Out by the gas fires of the refinery
> I'm ten years burning down the road
> Nowhere to run, ain't got nowhere to go
> Born in the U.S.A.
> I was born in the U.S.A.
> Born in the U.S.A.
> I'm a long gone daddy in the U.S.A.

In Springsteen's pleas to Rosalita, "daddy's comin'." In "Born to Run," Wendy agrees to join "daddy" on the open, risky road out of exile. By the time of "The Promised Land," the young hero is really no different than his presumed daddy in "daddy's garage"—stuck and confused and perhaps even dead. After a span of ten years from "Born to Run" to "Born in the U.S.A.," Springsteen offers a cutting intertextual reference to his own work, admitting that the Promised Land has spit out at least one of its inhabitants. Daddy is now a "long gone daddy," not only a wanderer, but a burnout lacking all positive choices—literally facing either the gas fires of the refinery or jail. The one "born to run" is left with *nowhere* to run in the U.S.A.

HUMAN TOUCH: HAPPY SONGS

As noted previously, in his acceptance speech at his induction into the Rock and Roll Hall of Fame in 1999, Springsteen describes his creative work following *Born in the U.S.A.* as "happy songs." But during this period, first Springsteen girds himself during a failing and ultimately dissolved first marriage, and then describes a successful second one. A song like "Leap of Faith" from 1992's *Lucky Town* exemplifies an essential hiatus from the daring narratives of "a big country." For the purposes of exploring the intimacies of his own experience of couplehood, Springsteen removes his songwriting from more epic struggles. In "Leap of Faith," religious metaphor still permeates his imagination, but in its contentment with the narrator's situation, the song forces the metaphor flat:

> Now you were the Red Sea, I was Moses
> I kissed you and slipped into a bed of roses
> The waters parted and love rushed inside
> I was Jesus' son sanctified

By literalizing the story of Moses and then Jesus in context of romantic love, Springsteen celebrates his personal redemption. Yet for most Springsteen observers, and certainly in context of his work on the Promised Land, this period represents a creative lull. When he returns to the jagged and unresolved questions of the Promised Land last channelled through songs on *Born in the U.S.A.*, he returns with a vengeance.

MAGIC: AMERICAN APOCALYPSE

In his 1995 album *The Ghost of Tom Joad*, Springsteen, like Woody Guthrie more than a half century before him, is compelled to create an extended commentary on John Steinbeck's *The Grapes of Wrath*, the 1939 novel chronicling the journey of an Oklahoma Dust Bowl family to the Promised Land of California. For a songwriter long enamored with stories of exile and redemption generally and the allure of California specifically, this narrative is an appropriate if challenging choice. *The Grapes of Wrath* is one of the most widely read American novels of the twentieth century. Choosing to rework and update its story in 1995 reflects not only a bold career choice, but a return to the sense urgency about the state of the nation driving Springsteen's best work. Just as the title of "The Promised Land" frames that entire song as a re-imagined biblical narrative, the title of *The Ghost of Tom Joad* establishes this entire album as a new set of myths wrapped around an old one. Because the story of the Joad family itself echoes the Exodus story—a clan travels a long journey from a home of corrupt servitude to powerful agencies, as well as the plagues of natural disaster, across a deserted landscape towards the Promised Land—it is a fitting narrative foundation for Springsteen's consideration of the biblical trope.

One of the most striking of an array of powerful elements in Springsteen's reflection of Steinbeck is the choice of calling Tom Joad a "ghost." A heroic if scarred figure sacrificing himself like Moses or Jesus in "Leap of Faith," Joad could easily be described more as an affirmative force. Yet here, even if he symbolizes compassion, he is dead. And according to the chorus of the song, he is lost as well:

> The highway is alive tonight
> But nobody's kiddin' nobody about where it goes
> I'm sittin' down here in the campfire light
> Searchin' for the ghost of Tom Joad

In the Promised Land of America, Springsteen's narrator seeks Tom Joad, a hero of generations who has gone missing and has broken his own promise to his mother at the end of *The Grapes of Wrath* that he will never die. Instead of Tom Joad's living spirit, the highway, just like so many thoroughfares beyond Main Street over the course of Springsteen's career, is alive. Still, its force of life reflects fear and resignation, not light. The line "nobody's kiddin' nobody about where it goes" demands that listeners recognize that just like the road in "Born in the U.S.A.," this highway leads nowhere. Even if the circumstances of the heroes of "Rosalita" or "Born to Run" require scrappy hustle and scrimping together scarce resources for their journeys, hopes remain high. Contrastingly, a sense of poverty and low expectations pervades Tom Joad's Promised Land revisited:

> Got a one-way ticket to the promised land
> You got a hole in your belly and a gun in your hand
> Sleeping on a pillow of solid rock
> Bathin' in the city aqueduct

With this living nightmare on American highways in mind, Springsteen proposes in "The Ghost of Tom Joad" the possibility that the Promised Land has lost its ability to produce something generative, having swallowed up all but a distant memory of Tom Joad, one of the imagined patron saints protecting the American covenant. Similarly, the hero of "Straight Time" from the same album cannot escape either the exile of jail or the exile of a mundane life of "straight time" working at a rendering plant. Here, a struggling hero dreams of absenting himself from his home country altogether: "Come home in the evening, can't get the smell from my hands / Lay my head down on the pillow / And go driftin' off into foreign lands."

What might be deemed *foreignness* emerges as part of Springsteen's growing commitment to recognizing the struggles of immigrants and illegal aliens embedded within and deep below the working class he has chronicled throughout his songwriting career. "Galveston Bay," again from *The Ghost of Tom Joad*, traces the intractable struggle of a Vietnamese immigrant and a hapless white Vietnam veteran. Their parallel paths of economic and social violence rooted in the war they share unfold in America, the place where Le Bin Son "brought his family to the promised land." It is the character *not* "Born in the U.S.A."—unlike his counterpart Billy Sutter, the Vietnam vet—who now understands America's promise best. So, too, in several songs in the most recent phase of Springsteen's career, that feature Mexican travelers who have illegally crossed the American border in pursuit of opportunities—often illusory and often illegal—dependant on myths of what America supposedly has to offer its inhabitants, but, in these songs at least, cannot.[5]

Springsteen describes a continuing quest to find promise in America, but his narrators encounter an environment increasingly disconnected from this goal. The wanderer of 1978's "The Promised Land" longs to escape his own sense of isolation and despair even as his radio and his map of places and time itself converge into meaninglessness. By 2007, in "Radio Nowhere," meaninglessness is a national epidemic. It is not just a single searcher at risk. In "Radio Nowhere," the hero cannot find his way home, let alone the path to redemption. Around him all is night, static, and forced solitude. And, sadly, he is far from alone in his plight:

> I was tryin' to find my way home
> But all I heard was a drone
> Bouncing off a satellite
> Crushin' the last lone American night
> This is radio nowhere, is there anybody alive out there?

From the same album, perhaps ironically entitled *Magic* despite being thick with a series of narratives seemingly devoid of the spark of life, "Last to Die" carries forward the same intertextual set of symbols prominent in Springsteen's previous work—a highway, conflated names of seemingly familiar places, and sounds from a radio:

> We took the highway till the road went black
> We'd marked Truth or Consequences on our map
> A voice drifted up from the radio
> And I thought of a voice from long ago.

Offering a clear commentary on the Iraq War, Springsteen calls the nation to task for its complacency, as a family—just like other microcosms of society such as Springsteen's band or an audience of witnesses—drives aimlessly. Unaware of the danger ahead, hapless parents watch death after death pollute the landscape of a journey, again, leading nowhere:

> Kids asleep in the backseat
> We're just counting the miles, you and me
> We don't measure the blood we've drawn anymore
> We just stack the bodies outside the door

Who'll be the last to die for a mistake
The last to die for a mistake
Whose blood will spill, whose heart will break
Who'll be the last to die, for a mistake

Examples of Springsteen's resigned, broadly pessimistic messages abound in this fourth phase of his career. His vision of America over the past decade in particular has grown dark to the point of forcing the question not only whether specific mistakes such as electing corrupt leaders, poisoning the economy with hubris and greed, or fighting unjust wars can be survived, but how long the American project of the Promised Land can continue to falter before it calcifies into a mistake without recourse for correction.

The betrayals described in Springsteen's world have become ever more intimate, violent, and inevitable. The tributaries of working-class dreams and labor, which once irrigated the Promised Land, have all but dried up. Functional, conservative neighborhoods with borders too narrow for many of Springsteen's earlier heroes to abide are now rotted through and through. Impoverished immigrants—often migrant workers, the most invisible of all Americans—seek hardscrabble survival on unforgiving soil in songs such as "Sinaloa Cowboys" and "Balboa Park." Now *thirty* years down the road, Springsteen speaks for men and women who should be in the prime of their lives yet mourn not only the loss of their youthful adventure and re-bellion, but also the disintegration of the economic and social foundation that the Promised Land was supposed to provide.

Speaking at the rally for then presidential candidate Barack Obama in Philadelphia noted earlier, Springsteen describes his quest for the Prom-ised Land, a fitting summary of the seemingly simple facts and aspirations upon which he has spun such a complex and compelling body of work. His speech presents a vibrant vision and a somber call to duty, evidence that Springsteen is still chasing much more than the already ambitious goal of making good music that matters:

I've spent 35 years writing about America, its people, and the meaning of the American Promise. That's the Promise that was handed down to us, right here in this city from our founding fathers, with one instruction: Do your best to make these things real. Opportunity, equality, social and economic justice, a fair shake for all of our citizens, the American idea, as a positive influence, around the world for a more just and peaceful existence. These are the things that give our lives hope, shape, and meaning. They are the ties that bind us together and give us faith in our contract with one another.

I've spent most of my creative life measuring the distance between that American promise and American reality. For many Americans, who are today losing their jobs, their homes, seeing their retirement funds disappear, who have no healthcare, or who have been abandoned in our inner cities, the distance between that promise and that reality has never been greater or more painful. . . . Our sacred house of dreams has been abused, it's been looted, and it's been left in a terrible state of disrepair. It needs care, it needs saving, and it needs defending against those who would sell it down the river for power or a quick buck. It needs a citizenry with strong arms, hearts, and minds. . . . But most importantly, it needs *you*. And *me*. It needs *us* to rebuild our house with the generosity that is at the heart of the American spirit. A house that is truer and big enough to contain the hopes and dreams of all of our fellow citizens. Because that is where our future lies. We will rise or we will fall as a people by our ability to accomplish this task. Now I don't know about you, but I know that I want my house back, I want my America back, and I want my country back. (*Vote*)

NOTES

1. While it is not the topic of this essay, Springsteen's Catholic upbringing obviously greatly influences his experience and use of traditional religious tropes. On Springsteen and Catholicism see Cullen, *Born in the U.S.A.*, particularly chapter 7. On more general Christian tropes see Jeffrey B. Symynkywicz, *The Gospel According to Bruce Springsteen: Rock and Redemption, from* Asbury Park *to* Magic. Cullen makes many compelling points concerning Springsteen's work, Catholic roots, and a broader phenomenon of the influence of Catholicism on the tension between transcendence and grounded obligation in many Catholic American artists from F. Scott Fitzgerald to Martin Scorsese to Madonna. Cullen writes, "[T]hey and many others have circled, often obsessively, around the tension between transcending the limits into which they were born and honoring the obligations, moral and otherwise, of their origins (*Born* 6). Viewed through this lens, the themes of a "big country" and "The Promised Land" clearly enjoy much resonance.

2. For Foley's summary of ethnopoetics, see Foley, 1–28.

3. This list excludes official releases of live albums, including *Live/1975–85*, *Chimes of Freedom* (EP), *In Concert/MTV Plugged*, *Live in New York City*, *Hammersmith Odeon London '75*, *Live in Dublin*, *Magic Tour Highlights* (EP), greatest hits collections and outtakes including *Greatest Hits*, *Blood Brothers* (EP), *Tracks*, *18 Tracks*, *The Essential Bruce Springsteen*, a collection of covers *We Shall Overcome: The Seeger Sessions*, and countless bootleg recordings of live performances available through a vast network of Springsteen fans.

4. Referring to this body of work in his acceptance speech to the Rock and Roll Hall of Fame and Museum in 1999, Springsteen says, "I would have written just happy songs—and I tried it in the early '90s and it didn't work; the public didn't like it." 15 March 1999.

5. Consider also songs such as "Balboa Park," "Sinaloa Cowboys," and "Matamoros Banks," which share similar themes.

10

Ironic Revelation
in Bruce Springsteen

Peter J. Fields

The stories implicit to the songs of Bruce Springsteen are notable for their ability to draw down apocalypse to a small, unassuming scale. The literal events the narrator or first-person protagonist describes are not in and of themselves obviously or necessarily portentous or, if they are headline-grabbing or crassly sensational, their immediate relevance to the speaker seems unclear and elusive. A given song's power—its ability to hold our attention—issues from a tension between the apparent triviality of the speaker's personal failure and the way the same speaker seizes upon that losing ground and vanishing of prospects to project a larger image that fills up the world. That vision, dark and abysmal, seems to be of infinite descent. But the suspense that grips us is that we know these characters have not been abandoned: there is another spirit at work between the lines connecting each forlorn soul to the audience. An ironic revelator unseals these confessions, unfolds their lost meaning, and champions the speakers as he speaks through their voices.

When the first-person protagonist of "The Wrestler," from *Working on a Dream*, writhes in proud agony, invoking the pathetic imagery of scarecrows and one-legged dogs, his suffering seems all the more excruciating because it has been dismissed and over-looked, that is, until a sudden urgency drives home the refrain, "(*Then you've seen me*) I come and stand at every door / (*Then you've seen me*) I always leave with less than I had before" (emphasis added). The revelator is lending his own voice, making the wrestler's cause his own, and answering an implicit question: Are we responsible for his fate? The answer is that before we laughed and looked away, we made the wrestler a caricature of our own struggle, dispossessing him of his dignity. Almost facetiously, he adds, "Tell me friend can you

201

ask for anything more." Jean-Paul Sartre, in "Existentialism is a Humanism," tries to answer a similar question: Why should we concern ourselves
with a given speaker's self-wrought dilemma? The spectrum of doubt we
might feel seems to feature, at one end, the quasi-Marxist objection that
the solitary, isolated nature of an existential problem seems to exclude
solidarity with our fellow workers—as Sartre puts it, the liberal critic
would say, "The *ego* cannot reach them through the *cogito*" (346)—and,
at the other end, there is the religious objection that the "commandments
of God" (346) seem irrelevant. To these questions, Sartre answers that
the "man who discovers himself directly in the *cogito* [the "I think" of
Descartes] also discovers all the others, and discovers them as the condition of his own existence" (361). Springsteen's work epitomizes that
individual dilemma which, according to Sartre, requires other people—"I
cannot obtain any truth whatsoever about myself, except through the me-
diation of another" (361)—in order to make a self out of nothing. In this
way, my own becoming is necessarily a form of "self-surpassing" (368)
and what I redeem from my own dilemma I redeem for everyone: "I make
this universality in choosing myself" (362). "Man," says Sartre, "is all the
time outside of himself: it is in projecting and losing himself beyond himself that he makes man to exist; and, on the other hand, it is by pursuing
transcendent aims that he himself is able to exist" (368). Springsteen's
songs reveal a larger "inter-subjectivity" (361) of one-among-others when
the failure of the speaker, worn nakedly and obviously, points to a shared
vision of larger belonging. Springsteen's lyrical canon, from *Greetings from
Asbury Park, N.J.* through *Working on a Dream*, features the songwriter's
own answer as to how the withdrawal of individual possibility into nothingness ironically expands outward, almost *ex nihilo*, to people a landscape and outline a horizon of shared human purpose.

At the same time, ironic revelation requires what we might call by-
the-numbers *dread*, especially as we find it in Martin Heidegger's "What
is Metaphysics?" When there's absolutely nothing to hold on to—an
awareness of personal futility which Heidegger calls *nichtung* ("nihila-
tion")—we have the metaphysical basis of "being" (*Da-sein*) in which
"in the act of drawing away from us everything turns towards us" (249),
looming over us in a way that "oppresses us" (249) but which also conjures a panorama of how one world displaces another: "This projection
into nothing on the basis of hidden dread is the overcoming of what-is-
in totality: transcendence" (254). In this way, as Heidegger remarks, we
have in a nutshell the paradoxical metaphysics of being, "Being in its
revelatory sense" (265).

Probably the most common of Springsteen's revelatory techniques is for
the first-person protagonist to address a second person, a vocative friend,
mother, mister, sir, Jack, Bobbie, Mary, Maria, and a small host of "you"

second persons. Presumably, any such form of address would seem to require some variation on Martin Buber's *I and Thou* configuration, a way of standing in relation to others that privileges the other as a "thou" and not an "it." This thou "fills the firmament" (59) and even the most cloistered detachment must assume "loving responsibility for the whole unexplorable course of the world" (157). Certainly, Springsteen's early song "For You" on *Greetings from Asbury Park, N.J.* represents such an attempt to encapsulate a whole range of disparate experiences under the heading of "for you." But the "you" in question resists the speaker even though he claims to have the answers: "Crawl into my ambulance, your pulse is getting weak," he sings, "Reveal yourself all now to me girl while you've got the strength to speak / 'Cause they're waiting for you at Bellevue with their oxygen masks / But I could give it all to you now if only you could ask." In contrast to the privileged vocative of Buber, the "you" here is implicitly indicted for her ignorance. She does not know her own desperate straits. The speaker addresses her directly as "honey"—"Don't give me money *honey* I don't want it back / You and your pony face" (emphasis added). But this "honey" is spoken with the tone of someone who knows the listener would never acknowledge him as her "honey" and would resent his using this term with her.

Therefore, in ironic contrast to Buber, we have in Springsteen the specter of a much different sort of I-and-Thou dynamic, one closer to that of Emmanuel Levinas, a twentieth-century critic of traditional ontology and metaphysics. Levinas puts the emphasis on a "face to face" (79) where the second person is dominated by a diehard, indefatigable, attention-seeking first person "who disturbs the being at home with oneself" (39). The voice is provocative, utilizing a kind of metaphysical "violence" (203) that displaces every competitor, obliterates every distraction, and monopolizes and galvanizes our attention. The effect is to take the microphone from us. Springsteen insists on being what Levinas would call the "Most High" (34) speaker who "invades" his audience and "imposes" (220) his message. "Truth," which Levinas considers the "sovereign exercise of freedom, becomes henceforth possible" (101). Yes, we were free before this speaker intruded into our world. But there was no truth in that freedom until he grabbed the bullet-microphone, cupped it against his harmonica, and blew out unearthly blues riffs as if our lives depended on it.

Further reinforcing this notion of a strident "most high" speaker is the prophet described in Springsteen's rendition of "O Mary Don't You Weep" on *We Shall Overcome: The Seeger Sessions*. He is the great American revelator in rolled-up shirt-sleeves, a new kind of Moses smiting the water, not with a traditional rod or staff, but with a piece of lumber, the proverbial all-purpose "two-by-four." The term sounds mundane, even silly, in a spiritual context, but it also rivets our attention and grabs our imagination. The chapter entitled "Inherited Imagination" in Jim Cullen's *Bruce Springsteen:*

Born in the U.S.A. and the American Tradition makes the point that Springsteen's speaker is driving the "dialectical" character of Protestantism back into the "unity" of the "analogical" dynamic of Catholicism: "The former is an individualistic sensibility that emphasizes the distance between God and man, while the latter is more communal, emphasizing God's presence in the world" (*Born* 168). Cullen singles out "It's Hard to be a Saint in the City" on *Greetings from Asbury Park, N.J.* as a case in point: "Springsteen's Catholic impulses are vividly on display [in this song]; an instinctive blurring of good and evil (Jesus as devil): a fusion of matter and spirit" (*Born* 174). The "most high" revelator may seem innocuous at first, even quaint. But he has our attention from the start, as in the case of the unassuming speaker in the title song of *Magic*, who wonders, nonchalantly, if we "want to come and see" his little show where he pulls a rabbit from his hat. Assuming we have heard this pitch before, we pay little heed to the subtle iteration of "This is what will be, this is what will be." But then his message becomes sinister and alarming: "I'll cut you in half / While you're smiling ear to ear." Tie him in chains, put him in a box, and throw it in the river—that cannot stop him. He will come back. Suddenly, infernal fire erupts from below us, as if commanded by the speaker, and he points to the "bodies hangin' in the trees." Instead of polite requests for our attention, he returns to that by now nerve-racking, mordant repetition of "This is what will be, this is what will be." The prophet does not care if we want to listen to him or not. We will respect him, defer to his judgment, and obey him.

In "Thunder Road" on *Born to Run*, the first-person speaker seems to remark approvingly of Mary. Her dress "waves" and the audience might logically picture an attractive woman any young man would dream of dating, but then the speaker undercuts it: "You ain't a beauty but hey you're alright." What now would we expect of such a callous, indifferent speaker? If we were momentarily caught up in the spectacle of Mary emerging on her parents' porch, we now feel let down by the speaker, who seems to lack even the most basic "I and Thou" interpersonal skills, especially if we keep in mind our intuitive feeling that the whole reason for the conversation is that Mary's support is crucial to this speaker's confidence. He is declaring his intention to leave "a town full of losers." But he lacks the nerve to do so unless she has a "little faith" in him and takes her place beside him in the passenger seat. We, the larger audience listening in on this invitation, suspect that in "Thunder Road" the speaker is precisely the sort of loser Mary's parents would most likely abhor. The only hope the young man has of her joining him is if she values her rebellion against authority figures more than she does her self-esteem.

Of course, by the same token, we can reverse the whole scenario and focus on Mary's own unlikely credentials as prophet. Her all too frequent dismissal of would-be romantic saviors makes us doubt her. Indeed, her rejection of Messianic candidates has the effect of denuding them of flesh and blood humanity, reducing them to immaterial shadows of who they used to be. They call to her but only the first-person revelator seems capable of hearing their heart-breaking cries: "They scream your name at night in the street." We can hear their incessant car engines, which at times, unlike their screams, tend to capture (ever so distantly) Mary's attention. We see her running, hope springing eternal, back to her porch, straining to see the cars she hears: "But when you get to the porch they're gone / On the wind." At this point, we are uncomfortable with Mary's reluctance to say "yes" to the speaker. We begin to wonder if she is too diffident, even cruel. Her hesitation does not speak to wisdom or maturity but to self-righteous disregard for all the young men who crave her approval.

In Catholic tradition, Mary is supposed to be an "Advocate, Helper, Benefactress, and Mediatrix" (*Catechism* 252), through whom God inaugurated a spiritual cold war, saying to the serpent, "I will put enmities between thee and the woman, and thy seed and her seed: she shall crush thy head, and thou shalt lie in wait for her heel" (Gen. 3.15). Throughout his canon, Springsteen has hailed Mary, or Maria, as the case may be, and on *Devils & Dust*, he makes plain the importance of the relationship of Mary to Christ. Christ has hidden the secret of the universe, its generative power and creative principle, in Mary, through whom he will remake the world as his kingdom:

> Well Jesus kissed his mother's hands
> Whispered, 'Mother, still your tears,
> For remember the soul of the universe
> Willed a world and it appeared.' ("Jesus Was an Only Son")

According to the *Catechism of the Catholic Church*, Mary, the "mother of the living," redeems Eve, the mother of the dying, by becoming the "new Eve" (192). Catholic apologist Scott Hahn, in his book *Hail, Holy Queen*, in the chapter tellingly entitled, "Mary's Motherhood Is Eden Revisited," explains the Church's teaching on Mary in this way: "The medieval poets summed it up neatly by pointing out that the Angel Gabriel's *Ave* (the Latin greeting) reversed the name of *Eva*. So also did it reverse the rebellious inclination Eve left to her children—to you and me—and replace it with the readiness to obey, which Mary wants to teach us" (45).

In "Thunder Road" Springsteen's rather ironic *mediatrix* is the mother of those who must leave an old world that she herself hastened to destruction, more like the original Eve than the new Eve. The prophetic speaker and we, the all-hearing audience, are super-conscious of Mary's past lovers calling supernaturally from the dead world. They still love her, long to be her suitor and romantic savior, but she has robbed them of their mortal lives, installing them in an in-between twilight existence—"in the lonely cool before dawn" as Springsteen puts it—peopling the old world not with the living but with ghosts. As Stephen Greenblatt reminds us, in his fascinating *Hamlet in Purgatory*, one of Mary's most preeminent roles in Catholic tradition has been that of benefactor, along with Christ, to the souls in purgatory. An illustration by Hans Holbein the Younger in 1521 provides a case in point, depicting both "Christ and Mary nourishing souls in Purgatory with their blood and milk" (Greenblatt 57). Christ exposes his pierced side while Mary offers her breast (fig. 7 in Greenblatt 58).

As Greenblatt explains, the drama in regard to purgatory is the sense of damnation without the fact of it, which made medieval representations of it seem interchangeable with those of hell: the "images are virtually identical" (52). Of course, for the Catholic Church, the two experiences, purgatory and hell, are hardly interchangeable. Purgatory is the "final purification of the elect, which is entirely different from the punishment of the damned" (*Catechism* 268). Greenblatt does point out that in most depictions the souls of purgatory are notable for their "upward momentum," which Greenblatt calls a "brilliant solution to the representational problem posed by Purgatory, since it gets at a crucial way of differentiating the suffering endured for eternity by souls in Hell from that endured by souls whose term of punishment is limited" (59). Many of the illustrations cited in Greenblatt show the souls emerging from purgatory in a form reminiscent of young children. The newly purged resemble freshly cleaned toddlers being raised up from their bath. Greenblatt makes special mention of the painting *Earthly Paradise: An Ascension to the Imperium* by Hieronymus Bosch, which, while it seems to feature adult figures, offers a vision of purgatorial new birth: "we see naked souls that have been cleansed of their sins lifted by angels toward a long funnel, a kind of birth canal, at whose end figures are emerging into a blinding light" (59).

As it stands, of course, in "Thunder Road," it would seem that the ironic revelator seems intent on leaving the ghosts to their own devices. But Mary draws out his spiel by not saying an immediate, obvious "yes." If she were too much like the biblical Mary, rather than the ironic, she would have directly answered as Mary did in the *Angelus*, "Be it done until me according to thy word" (*Manual of Prayers* 55). Springsteen's Mary does not directly answer "yes" and thereby keeps the speaker right where he is, going on and on about why she cannot keep holding out for a savior to show up. In this way, these two characters in "Thunder Road" emerge as ironic embodiments of their Catholic alter egos, not only Mary, the New Eve, but also the new Adam and new Christ. "In fact," as Scott Hahn explains, "the early Christians understood Mary and Jesus to be a reprise of God's first creation. Saint Paul spoke of Adam as a type of Jesus (Rom. 5.14) and of Jesus as the new Adam or the 'last Adam' (I Cor. 15.21–22, 45–49)" (32).

When we unravel the irony of Springsteen's first-person speaker and Mary, the woman looking for a romantic savior, we find we have types who will recur throughout Springsteen's canon, especially if we can see how their lost world prefigures a kind of gospel: "The early Christians considered the beginning of Genesis—with its story of creation and fall and its promise of redemption—to be so Christological in its implication that they called it the *Protoevangelium*, or First Gospel" (32). Some people may advance other songs as better candidates for "first gospel" in Springsteen, such as "Lost in the Flood" on *Greetings from Asbury Park, N.J.*, with its "storefront incarnation of Maria" and pregnant nuns "pleading immaculate conception," or, from the same album, "It's Hard to Be a Saint in the City," in which the self-proclaimed "king of the alley," the "pimp's main prophet," speaks of the devil looking like Jesus as he beckons through the steam, "Showin' me a hand I knew even the cops couldn't beat / I felt his hot breath on my neck as I dove into the heat." Both are suggestive of antediluvian old worlds, lost Edens, ironic devil-saviors, and ironic mothers of God. However, "Spirit in the Night" comes the closest to suggesting the immaterial limbo that has displaced Springsteen's original garden. Like Mary's lost lovers, these characters are "built like light / And they dance like spirits in the night."

But we really would need all three songs to capture the elements summed up in "Thunder Road," where we have not only the old world lost in the flood, the otherworldly metaphysics of spirits in the night, and a punkish king of the alley who must suffice as our New or Last Adam, but also an ironic take on that relationship between Mary and her Son. In Springsteen's song, the speaker says, "So Mary climb in / It's a town full of losers / And I'm pulling out of here to win." Everything hinges on her answer, but we never actually hear her say "yes." By this point, we may feel we have a stake in Mary's answer. We do not want to be left behind in this in-between world. The traditional prayer, *Salve, Regina*, "Hail, Holy Queen," reflects the urgency that we, as the audience, may have for Springsteen's Mary to fulfill her role and, like the Virgin Mary, say "yes" on our behalf: "To thee do we cry, poor banished children of Eve; to thee do we send up our sighs, mourning and weeping in this valley of tears. Turn, then, most gracious advocate, thine eyes of mercy towards us; and after this our exile, show unto us the blessed fruit of thy womb, Jesus" (*Manual of Prayers* 79–80). Reading against the grain of "pulling out of here to win," we need to see that the ironic revelator is being pulled into Mary's world as much as he is drawing her out of it. Her "yes" is of a mysterious sort, an implicit, longsuffering "yes" to hearing his message (from the moment she appears on her porch), but at no point is it an explicit "yes" to leaving behind this realm of exile where ghostly lovers haunt "burned out Chevrolets." In truth, she is keeping him here, preventing his leaving—a most ironic kind of obedience.

Another Springsteen technique of ironic revelation, which is time-honored in his lyrical corpus and could serve as a signpost for each stage of his
thematic growth, would be what he does with the main character's decision,
the gesture of which, while specific, seems insignificant. In "Atlantic City"
on *Nebraska*, the speaker announces all hell breaking loose after the mob
has killed the "Chicken Man," blowing up his house even as various factions
now gear up for a turf battle: "Gonna be a rumble out on the promenade
and the gamblin' commission's hangin' on by the skin of its teeth." But
where is the speaker? He is not a central figure at the heart of the crime spree,
nor is he a player in the city's response to it. No one consults with him or
seeks his input. He is of no consequence whatsoever. He is simply one more
person who has "debts no honest man can pay." But he is about to make
a choice he regards as intrinsically fateful. As we have seen before, Springsteen's speaker downplays the significance of an invitation to join him in
this decision, telling the vocative "honey" and "baby" she ought to dress up,
"Put your makeup on, fix your hair up pretty," as if they were simply going
out to a nice restaurant. In truth, we know he is about to assign himself a
place in the moral order. We are conscious of an eternal significance that is
completely out of proportion to the usual significance we attach to someone
walking into a bank and—robbing it?—no, simply walking in and asking
to close an account. He walks out with his own money, some of which he
spends on two bus tickets. But the gesture, spiritually-speaking, is tanta-
mount to picking up a downed power line. This wire is alive with the current
that surges through the universe, binding all things together. It will not kill
him, but it endows the most trivial actions with huge tragic importance. No
matter what he does after buying the bus tickets or doing that "little favor"
for someone, he will be numbered not among the righteous but among their
cosmic alter egos, the wicked. He will be categorically guilty with Faustian
implications. An awful form of transcendence suddenly projects across the
screen of his awareness and our own. His decision is petty, desperate, but
strangely selfless and universal. He is speaking of, and heralding, a larger
dimension when he posits the ironic hope that "everything" may return.
The self-condemnation could not be more poignant: his anticipated crime
would also "come back." He is embracing the finality of that fateful choice,
one that expands all around him and fills up the world. He is about to cross
into a realm where nothing stays hidden and the damned must account for
themselves.

As the title song of *The River* indicates, deep and wide are the various
streams that lead to self-damnation, including premarital sex. In "The
River," the speaker turns around to find that his life on the banks of
paradise is suddenly both behind and beyond him, a *fait accompli* that has
already installed Mary and him in the corrupt, dead world of his parents.
She became pregnant by him and "man that was all she wrote." His former

consciousness of a different life, one that allows for the luxury of longing for and savoring possibilities, is now roped off. He is not able to go back to the riverbanks except to die. Worse, he cannot stop thinking about it. Every time he feels the old longing, his mind is awash with the river that long ago ran dry but which in his imagination still flows, torturing him with an ever-renewing sense of loss. In *The Sickness unto Death*, Søren Kierkegaard makes the point that despair—the "sickness unto death"—achieves its most profound power according to our awareness of it. Indeed, the more self-aware our despair, the more it attains to an infernal majesty: "The devil's despair is the most intense despair, for the devil is sheer spirit, and therefore absolute consciousness and transparency; in the devil there is no obscurity which might serve as a mitigating excuse, his despair is therefore absolute defiance. This is the maximum of despair" (65).

In Milton's *Paradise Lost*, Adam and Eve are disappointed that death did not immediately descend on them. Instead, they must endure a painful, dread-filled self-awareness: "Let us seek Death," Eve urges, "or, he not found, supply / With our own hands his office on ourselves. / Why stand we longer shivering under fears / That show no end but death [?]" (X.1001-4). But Adam does not bow to that counsel. Likewise, Belial cautions his fellow demons not to risk annihilation by prematurely avenging themselves on heaven. They may hate their punishment in hell but it is preferable to being extinguished completely: "who would lose, / Though full of pain, this intellectual being, / Those thoughts that wander through eternity, / To perish rather, swallowed up and lost [?]" (II.146–49). The speaker in the title song of *The River* is of a similar persuasion. He is super-conscious of absolute, irrevocable change from one sort of being to another, and he won't let go of that awareness. The curse of self-awareness is lyrically reinforced by the way the last verse keeps cycling back to "down to the river," like one of M. C. Escher's staircases. No matter where the speaker goes in his head, he comes to the same place: that bank where he once lay with Mary, "Her body tan and wet down by the reservoir." The way the song rejoins its chorus is irresistible. Before I realize it, I'm singing along in a choir of the damned, offering my own voice in ironic praise of the curse "that sends me down to the river / though I know the river is dry." The speaker seems to be trying to say he is sorry. But every time he goes to repent, he obsessively replays the sin which expelled him from paradise. In Shakespeare's *Hamlet*, King Claudius, the brother-killer and regicide, tries to repent, but awareness of his crime never becomes true remorse. He knows that his "offense is rank" (III.3.36), but his "stronger guilt defeats" his otherwise "strong intent" (40) to confess.

Claudius is not far from the speaker in the title song of *Darkness on the Edge of Town*, who straddles two worlds, that of the righteous and that of the damned. Left to his own devices by a wife who seems to look down on his pastime of car racing, the speaker feels he has nothing to lose. In fact, the song seems to be an epilogue to "Racing in the Street," also on *Darkness on the Edge of Town*, where the speaker's beloved seems increasingly anxious and frustrated with the speaker's lifestyle: "When I come home the house is dark / She sighs, 'Baby did you make it all right.'" Despite the speaker's defiance in "Darkness on the Edge of Town," he seems to question his own judgment, deeply aware that what used to be fun has become an obsession that has destroyed everything of value in his life:

> Tonight I'll be on that hill 'cause I can't stop
> I'll be on that hill with everything I got
> Lives on the line where dreams are found and lost
> I'll be there on time and I'll pay the cost
> For wanting things that can only be found
> In the darkness on the edge of town.

The lyric *noir* of Springsteen arises from a crucible of self-torment, like Milton's Satan in *Paradise Lost* who, no matter where he goes, can never leave hell because he bears "Hell within him" (IV.20). For Springsteen this self-wrought damnation becomes a universal principle in "Darkness on the Edge of Town": "Some folks spend their whole lives trying to keep it / They carry it with them every step that they take / Till some day they just cut it loose," he sings, "Cut it loose or let it drag 'em down."

Conversely, in "Hungry Heart" on *The River* we hear a kind of ironic sublime, a surprisingly uplifting, glockenspiel-driven crescendo of joy amid despair, as if like the denizens of Milton's Pandemonium, Springsteen is becoming "inured," that is, "conformed" to hell in "temper and in nature" (*Paradise Lost* II.216–18). Springsteen's speaker talks about the power of *eros*, the way such desperation can destroy the thing it seeks: "We took what we had and we ripped it apart." This character seems doomed to repeat the same mistakes, perhaps due to his own variety of original sin or paradise lost: "Like a river that don't know where it's flowing / I took a wrong turn and I just kept going." He cannot stop paying the price of rejecting love and home. The sharp edge of the vocative, "Got a wife and kids in Baltimore, *Jack*" (emphasis added) sounds both final and defiant, as if he defies his fate but also knows that since he threw heaven away, he will never be allowed back. Love for him will never be permanent, only a passing fancy or momentary reprieve ending in agonizing loss. Springsteen will recur to this motif, not to mention this type of wall-of-sound reverie, in *Magic*, especially in "Girls in Their Summer Clothes." The video for the latter features a camera swooping around Springsteen on the Jersey Shore as he seems to give himself over to the simple wonder of girl-watching. But distraction of this sort is momentary in Springsteen. We might be reminded of Satan in *Paradise Lost*, momentarily dumbfounded, or "Stupidly good"

(IX.465), when he gazes upon the beauty of Eve. It will be a moment before he remembers the hell he bears in his heart.

In "Girls in Their Summer Clothes," the speaker's immediate concern is that "things have been a little tight." He dons his jacket feeling an inchoate, inarticulate turmoil, an unfocused urge to "burn this town down." But the speaker is distracted by the girls in their summer clothes who, he remarks, "pass me by." We see his attention caught this way and that as he takes in the beauty of female passersby until he is drawn towards a brightly-lit diner, one whose gleaming and whirling neon sign he finds oddly suggestive of "a cross over the lost and found." To his chagrin, he is aware that he has avoided the worst by allowing his eyes to track first this, then that woman sauntering down the boardwalk. Consequently, he never got around to acting on his worst impulses. By comparison, the speaker in "You Can Look (But You Better Not Touch)" on *The River* is less chagrined than he is angry. He feels cheated when he turns on the TV and a "pretty little girly" fills up the screen of his desire. But on *Magic* the women who pass by the narrator are latter day Graces, like those who dance in Spenser's *Faerie Queene*, "handmaids of Venus" (VI.x.15.2) who entrance the hero with a vision of erotic perfection, but who, upon his approach, "vanish all away out of his sight" (18.2). They are precisely the transcendent of our longing that by its nature presents itself beyond our grasp. "Hello beautiful thing," says Springsteen's speaker in "Girls in Their Summer Clothes," "maybe you could save my life / In just a glance." But he also knows that such glances are only momentary reprieve, unreliable refuge, and poor prospects: "down here on magic street / Love's a fool's dance / And I ain't got much sense."

In "Reno" on *Devils & Dust* we have another false refuge and one of the most perverse imaginable for an ironic Christ who needs the blessing of Mary before he goes down the *Via Dolorosa*. He is used to bowing down, seeing her from the feet up: "She had *your* ankles. I felt filled with grace" (emphasis added). He savors the stockings the prostitute has just removed and even as the word "grace" lingers in our consciousness, we hear the price list: "Two hundred dollars straight in, / Two fifty up the ass." When the prostitute raises a toast, declaring "'Here's to the best you ever had,'" he awakens, so to speak, from his reverie, and confides to the audience, "It wasn't the best I ever had, / Not even close." He laughs with the prostitute, but he has revealed his knowledge of his own status among the damned. In "Youngstown" from *The Ghost of Tom Joad*, we find the oddest, most ironic version of false refuge, that of hell itself; "When I die I don't want no part of heaven / I would not do heaven's work well," the speaker declares, "I pray the devil comes and takes me / To stand in the fiery furnaces of hell." We are reminded that Kierkegaard, in *The Sickness unto Death*, described this type of despair as that which clings to infernal status, insisting on it, fearful that death might dissolve it: "Ah, demoniac madness! He rages most of all at the thought that eternity might get it into its head to take his misery from him!" (116).

We also see this motif of self-damnation in "Brilliant Disguise" from *Tunnel of Love*, where the speaker broods on the mystery of his beloved, doubting her fidelity, directly addressing her as "baby" as he winds slowly through the shadowy corridors of what turns out to be his own confession: "Now look at me, baby / Struggling to do everything right / And then it all falls apart." In the darkness of his fear and suspicion, he is not her husband so much as he is a "lonely pilgrim" still looking for salvation from himself. Worse, if she acts on this confession and comes closer, not just looking into his eyes but forcing back his fingers, she'll see the omen, the lines in his palm the gypsy lied about, revealing his own infernal status as betrayer of their love. This membership of the damned paradoxically requires the "darkness of our love" (46) in order to be seen.

In "Two Faces" from *Tunnel of Love*, the speaker's use of the vocative "mister" signals an especially poignant self-crafted transformation and self-assigned membership among the damned: "Sometimes, *mister*, I feel sunny and wild / Lord I love to see my baby smile," he sings, "Then dark clouds come rolling by / Two faces have I" (emphasis added). It could be that the second person "mister" is a visitor like Dante with Virgil, asking the speaker his particular story of how he arrived in this ring of hell and assumed this particular form as punishment. The two-faced man confides that he once thought of himself as righteous and worthy of the Lord's favor, but then love revealed his deep-down corruption and hypocrisy. He fully expects that we are gaping at the two sides of his head, his two faces, and that we can hear one side accusing the other. He does not fear embarrassment. He assumes that we are just as guilty, just as damned. As in the famous lines 61–62 of canto 27 of Dante's *Inferno*, a scene repeated as an epigraph to T. S. Eliot's *The Love Song of J. Alfred Prufrock*, the speaker would not reveal the nature of his sin: "*S'io credessi che mia riposte fosse / a persona che mai tornasse al mondo*" ["If I thought my reply were meant for one / who ever could return into the world"] (Dante 249). For that matter, we might wonder if Candy from *Darkness on the Edge of Town* is still here in her room, still offering the perfect facsimile of intimate love, and Joe Roberts, too, from *Nebraska*, forever lifting his foot off the gas and letting his brother's taillights disappear. The revelator keeps them here, singing along with Roberts, "nothing feels better than blood on blood." Roberts may think he tells his own story but there is a narrator as well between the lines. Does he take perverse satisfaction in hearing, over and over, the confession of this otherwise straight-arrow highway patrolman? Perhaps the speaker, rather selfishly, still visits Candy's room, still convinced that deep down she must truly love him, even though he knows that she is in torment: "There's a sadness hidden in that pretty face / A sadness all her own from which no man can keep Candy safe." But if it is the revelator himself who keeps them in their rooms and, for that matter, in their cars—Roberts's patrol car, Mary's lovers in the frames of burned out Chevrolets—perhaps he can also set them free.

In "Further On (Up the Road)" from *The Rising*, we find another sort of false refuge, or doubtful reprieve, that of the byway path. Springsteen's speaker does not claim special knowledge: "If there's a light up ahead, well brother I don't know." If indeed the speaker is a "brother" to those with whom he travels, perhaps they all wear the "dead-man's suit" and "grave-yard boots." The speaker's "smilin' skull ring" signifies membership in the biggest club of all time, the sad procession of the trooping dead. He seems to have taken a separate path, but he knows he must join his brothers in the end. In *Lucky Town*'s "If I Should Fall Behind," the speaker reminds his beloved of their mutual promise to wait for each other, that if "come the twilight" they lose each other's hand, the one should wait and watch until the other returns: "I'll wait for you / And should I fall behind / Wait for me." We wonder why the separated parties would prefer to linger alone in the gloom rather than hasten to their rendezvous by the "beautiful river." The speaker seems in dread of resuming the journey, perhaps for good reason. Hades in Ovid's *Metamorphoses* is a sucking maw, and in the words of the 1567 Elizabethan translator Arthur Golding, the ghosts travel down a "thousand ways" to hell's "thousand gates" (IV.544). The Stygian capital draws all to it irrespective of their separate byways, "as the Sea the streames of all the lande / Doth swallow in his gredie gulfe, and yet is never full" (545–46). In Homer's *Odyssey*, the newly-dead rise up in a panic. They flutter and squeal like frightened bats with "brests and wings" (*Chapman's Homer* XXIV.7), beating themselves against the cavern walls and clinging to each other, rather than of their own free will descending to Hades. But ultimately "these (grumbling) rose / And flockt together" (11–12), unable to resist the downward summoning of "Hermes with his golden rod" (1). In the *Metamorphoses*, Orpheus has nearly succeeded in rescuing Eurydice from the underworld when he feels a sudden doubt, worried "lest she fol-lowed not" (Golding X.59). He knows that he is forbidden to look back at her, but he does anyway. To his horror, his glance backward loses her just as prophesied: "Immediately shee slipped backe" (61). He desperately lunges, reaching for her with both bands, "But nothing save the slippery aire (un-happy man) he caught" (63).

The real difficulty for the audience of "Further On (Up the Road)" is that Springsteen brings up the idea of resurrection: "One sunny mornin' we'll rise I know / And I'll meet you further on up the road." Who is this speaker? In regard to the dead, Hermes only goes down, but the revelator speaks of going up. We also need to ask *which* resurrection, and, for that matter, which *kingdom*? There is the original resurrection of Easter and then there is the general resurrection as yet unfulfilled and still to come, when Christ and his saints are supposed to return, descend from heaven, and establish the Messianic kingdom on earth. Many of the spirituals of the Seeger Sessions band allude to that Second Coming. But Springsteen also requires and depends on the first resurrection, which is a form of rising together that is here and now. We are hearing New Orleans gospel, the kind played behind the coffin in the streets, a resurrection whose power draws on the first, when Christ dispossessed hell as part of his own rising. *Live in Dublin* with the Sessions Band includes a telling version of the traditional song, "When the Saints Go Marching In," in which the living join the dead in one long procession, hoping for a resurrection inclusive of all. The good thief crucified next to Christ said to him "remember me when thou comest into thy kingdom" (Luke 23:42). Christ answered that "this day" the thief would be with him in "paradise" (vs. 43). The empty tomb is the sign of this kingdom, which is present tense and fully operational, here and now. This resurrection has reversed the consequences of that Fall which expelled us from paradise and which consigned the dead to Sheol, that is, the Psalmic depths of pit and miry clay.

This first resurrection and entry into the kingdom is the one which each person's baptism categorically recreates as a sacrament, the same resurrection which rescues all the dead, going back to Adam. This tradition of Christ's original victory over death is abundantly represented in the Old and Middle English corpus and is sometimes called the "Descent of Christ" or "The Harrowing of Hell." The source document for this story is the most influential of the so-called lost gospels, *The Book of Nicodemus*. The Harrowing presumes that while Christ's body was in the tomb, he broke through the gates of hell, trod down Death, and robbed the Prince of Hell of the souls imprisoned there in abject darkness, taking them away with him to paradise, where they meet the good thief who has already arrived (Chs. 16–20). These dead include the patriarchs and prophets of the Old Testament, and all those saints who were faithful but nonetheless subject to that trooping dead motif: "And taking hold of Adam by his right hand, he ascended from hell, and all the saints of God followed him" (19:12). Again, the resurrection yet to come may be eagerly anticipated, but it cannot resurrect anyone in the here and now the way the first can.

The *Catechism of the Catholic Church* cites numerous scriptures that support the Harrowing motif, based on article 5 of the Apostle's Creed, "He descended into Hell. On the third day, He rose again" (164–66), including 1 Peter 4.6: "For to this end was the gospel preached even to the dead, that they may be judged indeed as men in flesh but may live as God lives in spirit" (165). For Springsteen's purposes, the Harrowing of Hell—the resurrection of the dead as part of Christ's own resurrection—fulfills a need for that apocalypse which is "now" and presently taking place as prophesied in John 5:25: "Amen, Amen, I say to you, the hour is coming and *now is here,* when the dead shall hear the voice of the Son of God, and those who hear shall live" (*Catechism* 165, emphasis added). For the Catholic Church, the penitential believer who feels true contrition always looks backward to this resurrection, participating spiritually in the same dilemma as those dead who awaited Christ's descent, that is, those who wandered towards, went down to, or who sat shackled in darkness, "*Sheol* in Hebrew or *Hades* in Greek" (*Catechism* 164), as in the penitential verses of Psalm 142: "For the enemy hath persecuted my soul: he hath brought my life down unto the ground. He hath made me to dwell in darkness as those that have been long dead; and my spirit is vexed within me; my heart within me is troubled" (vs. 3–4; *Manual of Prayers* 254–55). Accordingly, Springsteen's elect may not know they are prospective saints. They occupy the darkness in their chains until a light shines and a voice heralds the coming of the Lord of Hosts. Many have seen, of course, an interesting sort of universalism in this "Harrowing of Hell" tradition, the dynamics of which, as Jeffrey Trumbower attests in his recent study of the subject, *Rescue for the Dead*, "imply or make explicit that Jesus' descent entails a broader offer of salvation for all the dead, both righteous and wicked" (95).

Admittedly, while Springsteen's songs are deeply anchored, at one end, in the Psalmic *profundis*, it cannot be denied that at the other end their most immediate impact is effervescent, a *frisson* driven by two irresistible dynamics: the hope of personal transformation and the hope of "kingdom come." As the ironic revelator reinforces in "Lonesome Day" on *The Rising*, "Let kingdom come, I'm gonna find my way." The problem is that "kingdom come" is foreshadowed here and now by the infernal and diabolical: "Hell's brewin', dark sun's on the rise." There is a terrible power following him but he would rather avoid it than wield it. There is even a serpent slithering forward. Nervously, the speaker talks of someone's retaliation, but we are not sure whose: "A little revenge and this too shall pass." The hope of "kingdom come" in Springsteen's work remains the most elusive when it seems to be most evident, as in "Maria's Bed" on *Devils & Dust*, a reprieve that rebuffs the promise of a holy man: "Hold on, brother," he advises the speaker, "there's a light up ahead." The speaker's answer, "Ain't nothin' like the light that shines on me in Maria's bed," may, of course, represent emphatic agreement with the prophecy; however, it could also be that the speaker is countering the prophet, deferring from the "light up ahead" in favor of the light he already has in Maria's bed: "She gives me candy stick kisses 'neath a wolf-dog moon / One sweet breath and she'll take you, *mister*, to the upper room" (emphasis added). Given the use of the vocative *mister*, we might indeed suspect that the speaker is somewhat annoyed, even defensive. There has always been something young, naïve, and punkish about these terse rejoinders in popular music. Typically, the speaker rebukes his accuser and asserts his own superior status, the most rueful version of which would be Springsteen's "mister" from "Promised Land" in *Darkness on the Edge of Town*, "*Mister*, I ain't a boy, no I'm a man / And I believe in a promised land" (emphasis added). But these declarations are really just bravado, whistling in the graveyard, just one more way of doing the opposite of the boast: confessing our membership among those left out, the disenfranchised, or worse, the trooping dead. The "mister" we are calling down or rebuking is really our brother, one of us, as in the confessional "brother" of the title song on *Tunnel of Love*: "There's a room of shadows that gets so dark, *brother* / It's easy for two people to lose each other" (emphasis added). Darkness comes early and often in Springsteen and couples are joined by a diabolical third party: "Then the lights go out and it's just the three of us / You, me and all that stuff we're so scared of." In the case of "Maria's bed," we are not sure if Maria's bed culminates the holy man's prophecy or if she represents an outlandish variety of postponement. Perhaps we have an ironic Christ who is resisting the real "upper room," knowing what lies beyond it, and delaying the *Via Dolorosa* by finding temporary refuge in sticky, childish kisses with the ultimate maternal figure, Mary, doubtless a divine "riverhead" of "blessings," but not on these terms.

As it is, the hope of supper with the Lord in the "upper room"—the ultimate venue for both heavenly membership and male-bonding—reminds us of Bryan Garman's thesis in *A Race of Singers: Whitman's Working-Class Hero from Guthrie to Springsteen*: that Springsteen's lyrical *ethos* is self-consciously taking its place in a tradition continuous with the dust bowl ballads and union songs of Woody Guthrie and the democratic vistas of Walt Whitman, much of which is part and parcel of his celebration of male friendship. Garman uses terms like "homosocial" (*Race* 224, 233, 254) and even "homoerotic" (223, 224, 225, 226, 234) not simply to account for the tour de force gesture of the "soul kiss" (224) with Clarence Clemons onstage during concerts, but also to identify one pole of the dynamic opposition that drives Springsteen's vision. On one side of the battery is the seemingly exclusive camaraderie of the E Street Band, the thundering train which hurtles from behind Springsteen the rocker, amplifying the apocalyptic message. The opposite pole of the circuit is precisely everything such a pile-driving, high-powered "upper room" brotherhood leaves out, as Garman notes concerning Springsteen's role as the most recent representative of Whitman's "race of singers," whose band of brethren also mystically includes everybody waiting outside the "upper room" and envisions a "community in which men and women, black and white, could embrace one another in the spirit of love and equality" (*Race* 226). Garman points to the video for "Tougher Than the Rest" and the inclusion of Patti Scialfa, Springsteen's future second wife, on stage during the *Tunnel of Love* tour as indications of how this *ethos* of homosocial fellowship is really a kingdom-argument that is universal in its sense of new possibility.

Perhaps we can dance on the grave of our old selves as in "Long Time Comin'" from *Devils & Dust*, whose speaker sees himself in his negligent father but is determined to break the cycle. Camping under the stars with his wife and kids, he has an inspiration: "I reach 'neath your shirt, lay my hands across your belly / And feel another one kickin' inside / I ain't gonna fuck it up this time." As Todd May points out in his study of contemporary French thinker Gilles Deleuze, late-twentieth-century philosophy has been skewed by a pessimistic interpretation—and fundamental misunderstanding—of Nietzsche's idea of eternal recurrence in *Thus Spoke Zarathustra*: "I come back eternally to this same, selfsame life" (333; quoted in May 59). As May points out, the irony of the past is that it returns in order to break with itself and to resolve its old tensions in favor of something new: "Everything returns, yes; everything recurs" (62); however, that does not mean a "continuation of rigid forms but instead an experimentation in a world of inexhaustible creative resources" (68).

In this way Springsteen's own experiments in ontology can revisit the past of American song and yet still announce "When the New World is Revealed," to quote the cover of *Backstreets* [#85], featuring Springsteen and the Seeger Sessions band at the 2006 New Orleans Jazz and Heritage Festival (Donnelly 52–58). In the same issue, Bryan Garman takes Springsteen to task for his choice of "Jesse James" and "Old Dan Tucker" on the *We Shall Overcome* album. The first song celebrates a confederate sympathizer and the second is one of the many versions of what was once a black-faced minstrel song. As Garman notes, one of the original versions of "Old Dan Tucker" was obviously racist, especially the lines "His nose so flat, his face so full / De top ob his head like a bag ob wool." ("Old Time Rock & Roll" 27). But as Todd May points out, "everything returns, yes" but not the way it was. The version Springsteen sings with such gusto, as Garman admits, has no mention of those racist lines and, of course, avoids entirely the minstrel dialect of "ob" and "de." Instead, this song culminates with Old Dan taking turns dancing with the ladies, clearly a popular figure for all his falls from grace that "kicked up holy hell." The song recurs to the past but comes back without racial denigration, this time reminiscent of that "analogical" confounding of devil and saint which makes the song much Springsteen's own. The same could be said of "Jesse James," performed with equal relish by Springsteen on *We Shall Overcome*, but with a special emphasis on the statement "He came from a solitary race." Garman wants badly to remind Springsteen of the possible taint to the word "race," but we are also reminded that the term "race of singers" informs the title of Garman's own book. More to the point, "solitary" reminds us that the reality here is not one of color but rather of inner ordeal. We cannot be sure whether the historical Jesse James was existentially authentic, so to speak, but Springsteen's subject is clearly a lonely pilgrim working on himself and holding on until "kingdom come," at least in a Catholic sense.

Andrew Greeley, in his 1988 article "The Catholic Imagination of Bruce Springsteen," largely on the strength of *Tunnel of Love*, argues that Springsteen's imagination is Catholic, meaning that Springsteen posits the "accessibility of God in the world" (112). Greeley's argument is largely intuitive, noting "Easter/baptismal symbols of light or flowing water" (113) in a number of the songs, notably "Spare Parts," but especially the closing song of *Tunnel of Love*, "Valentine's Day," where immersion implies new birth: "I woke up in the darkness scared and breathin' and born anew." Triumphantly, Greeley concludes, "If that's despair, I'm the Dalai Lama. Rather, it is Catholicism, pure and simple" (114). However, twenty years downwind from Greeley's prescient article, we can see a clearer rationale for the "Catholic imagination" of Springsteen, specifically, two key ideas that became more evident after *Tunnel of Love*. First, salvation for Catholics is not only through faith but also works, specific actions in response to, and on the basis of, love that merit divine favor: "Moved by the Holy Spirit and by charity, we can then merit for ourselves and for others the graces needed for our sanctification" (*Catechism* 487). Peter Kreeft, an authority on the Catholic catechism, reinforces this point: "the Church insists that good works are necessary too" (126). Church historian Thomas Bokenkotter, in his chapter "The Unmaking of Christendom," reminds us that Martin Luther's dissent from the Church centered on the issue of works versus faith. Luther came to see justification as something which has nothing to do with human merit: "In other words, it is not through our merits that we are saved but through the unfathomable mercy and boundless generosity of God, who justifies us in spite of our sins. Our part in the whole process is not active but passive" (211). But the title song of *Working on a Dream* nails (so to speak) the active principle of meritorious action with a hammer: "Rain pourin' down, I swing my hammer / My hands are rough from working on a dream." In "I'll Work for Your Love" on *Magic*, there is no passive faith that is reliable: "Now our city of peace has crumbled / Our book of faith's been tossed / And I'm just out here searchin' / For my own piece of the cross." Springsteen's speaker does his work for that second person: "I think of you and I'm working on a dream." Some may argue that such love is not Christian *caritas* or *agape*, but merely romantic—between two people. But they would be missing the New Eve/Last Adam gospel message.

Songs like "I'll Work for Your Love" on *Magic* build on and extrapolate from the Marian role we observed in "Thunder Road," Springsteen's *protoevangelion*. Notable is the vocative *dear* in the refrain, "I'll work for your love, dear / I'll work for your love," a departure of sorts from "mister" and the like, but still one that affects the speaker's credentials, humbling and subordinating the "most high" revelator, making him seem like just one more weary husband who must answer to his wife. The song starts rather casually. The narrator says "Pour me a drink Theresa" as if he were addressing a bartender.

But the song quickly moves in a different direction, revealing the speaker as that ironic savior who depends on the Marian-figure to commence the work of salvation. In her autobiography, Saint Thérèse of Lisieux (a possible namesake of the song's Theresa) speaks of being moved by Christ crying out on the cross, "I thirst" (128; John 19:28). She also saw herself cast in the role of the Samaritan woman of whom Christ asked, "Give me to drink" (229; John 4:7). In Springsteen's song, when Theresa obediently turns away to take down a dusty glass for the requested drink, the speaker envisions in the ridge of the woman's back a *Via Dolorosa*, the "stations of the cross." Ultimately, he will offer his own body, his own "temple of bones" at her feet, illustrating once again that "analogical" principle Cullen cites in regard to Springsteen (*Born* 168). In this case, we hear the first and second persons of this song emulate and participate in the divinity of both Christ and the Mother of God, a New Adam and a New Eve:

> The late afternoon sun fills the room
> With the mist of the garden before the fall
> I watch your hands smooth the front of your blouse
> And seven drops of blood fall
> I'll work for your love, dear.

Here in the "drops of blood" we seem to have Saint Thérèse's consumption, which began as a froth of blood at her lips (252–53), a hemorrhage that rose to her mouth not unlike what we hear in the song: "At your lips a crown of thorns." But Springsteen's "seven" count has the effect of ascribing the blood and the "work" in question right back to the speaker, our ironic savior whose suffering is foretold by the blood on Theresa's blouse that he internalizes as his own cause: "Whatever other deal's goin' down / To this one I'm sworn." Christ bled sevenfold from back, head, feet, hands, and side. Catholic tradition cites "Seven Thanksgivings for the Seven Effusions of Our Lord's Blood": that is, blood from his circumcision at eight days old, from his sweating while praying in the garden, from his back during Pilate's scourging, from his head due to the crown of thorns, from his whole body when his clothes were torn off and he carried the cross, from his hands and feet when he was nailed to the cross, and, finally, from his side when it was pierced by the lance (*Manual of Prayers* 298–301). Naturally, as Greenblatt points out, Mary joins Christ in offering succor to souls: "The image of Mary's milk flowing into the mouths of suffering souls was widely disseminated" (58), hence perhaps this is why in the song these seven drops show first on the front of Theresa's blouse. But what the speaker sees in the woman reflects the work he himself must undertake. In "My Lucky Day" from *Working on a Dream*, the "grace of your smile" is what illuminates the "dark of this exile," a rather Marian-styled allusion and ultimately ironic form of "grace" if the dream in question is the work of salvation. Thérèse's own vocation begins with a vision of "that entrancing smile of the Blessed Virgin's" (94). In both cases, that of Thérèse and Springsteen's ironic savior, the irony of their "lucky day" is that the smile of the woman inaugurates an arduous path, as reinforced by the title song of *Working on a Dream*: "Now the cards I've drawn, it's a rough hand darlin' / I straighten my back and I'm working on a dream." Thérèse remarks that Mary's smile "brought her own Son to birth in me" (107), something that occurs in the song as well. Springsteen's speaker becomes the Christ-like sufferer.

Secondly, and most importantly, the kingdom argument of Springsteen is above all universal, a call to everyone—hence the word "catholic." There is no moment of "upper room" that is exclusive to male disciples. Salvation is achieved with others or it is not achievable at all. The "Prayer of Peace" in the Canon of the Mass puts the emphasis on a corporate belonging to God: *"ne respicias peccata mea, sed fidem Ecclesiae tuae"* ["Look not on *my* sins, but upon the faith of Thy Church"] (*Manual of Prayers* 149, emphasis added). If "Thunder Road" is his first gospel, then Springsteen's book of Revelation must be "The Rising," principally for its apocalyptic sense of connection, a profound continuity that joins the living to the dead: "Spirits above and behind me / Faces gone, black eyes burnin' bright," he prays, "May their precious blood forever bind me / Lord as I stand before your fiery light." The sweaty biracialism of the "soul kiss," Springsteen leaning against one of his "brothers" at the microphone, and a hundred other such gestures from the stage are not exclusive intimacies. They offer the audience a point of entry where they can vicariously share in that "upper room" fellowship of the band and participate in a love that drives out fear (to paraphrase both 1 John 4:18 and the knuckles of Bill Horton in "Cautious Man"), a sense of connection that taps into a spiritual force capable of exorcising "devils and dust" from "God-filled" souls. This dynamic of joyful spiritual fellowship is epitomized by Springsteen's *en plein air* stumping for the Obama campaign, especially the performance of "The Rising" at Ypsilanti, Michigan, 6 October 2008, captured and shared on YouTube. We can hear a hoarse voice (perhaps the videographer himself) awkwardly joining with Springsteen in the call to the spirits of the departed. The song never seemed more urgent, more electric with prophetic power. The serpent we might recall from both Genesis and "Lonesome Day" is about to be crushed in "The Rising."

At first, of course, no movement seems possible. If we could see in the dark, we might, like Dante in the *Purgatorio*, notice the prideful weighed down by stones on their backs; or we might see, on a higher terrace but even more stymied, those guilty of avarice, bound and prostrate, moaning the Psalmic "My soul cleaves to the dust" (*Purgatorio* XIX.70–73). In "The Rising," there is the feeling of being manacled in the depths of darkness without any hope: "I can't feel nothing but this chain that binds me" and "On my back's a sixty pound stone." But we hear the revelator. He carries his own cross, his calling, but it's a vocation that comes down to us rolling on "wheels of fire." The irony of revelation is now working in favor of the lost, those who know nothing but their own status as damned and imprisoned in Sheol. Everything that went down is really going up. The hell that burned within is now revealed not as infernal power but as celestial power, opening the way to the surface. By the time the revelator intones his reverie of "glory and sadness," we know (anyone in hearing) that the "upper room" has become a conduit between the living and the dead. The revelator's inability to see in the darkness serves as a great equalizer; living or dead, all are spirits now to him, those faithful and departed like Tom Joad, but also those he may not have otherwise recognized in the light, as in the case of the speaker singing for the "Souls of the Departed" on *Lucky Town*. In his dreams, the lieutenant envisions the souls of the war-dead rising from their corpses, "Like dark geese into the Oklahoma skies." Despite the homeliness of the simile, we know that these bodies lay along the infamous "Highway of Death," where the retreating Iraqi army was devastated from the air "on the main road north from Kuwait to the southern Iraqi city of Basra" ("Ground War," BBC News) during the first Gulf War. They are part of that spiritual community coalescing around the revelator in "The Rising," living and vital, imparting strength to him and, unexpectedly, receiving power from him as well. In Springsteen's song, the shackled speaker begins as the old Adam but then stands revealed as the new and the last Adam, capable of raising the dead with this incantation: "Come on up for the rising / Come on up, lay your hands in mine / Come on up for the rising." The spiritual dynamic of "harrowing hell" makes possible the revelator's dual role, at once the voice crying from the pit and also that savior who appears among the dead to spoil hell and rob death of its victory. Likewise, the same irony applies to the prisoners themselves. Yes, the past returns, but the damned are revealed as saints.

Suddenly, the revelator invokes a vision of the garden, this time not that which the disciples visited after the "upper room" but the one which enclosed the tomb. Mary Magdalene is there as she was in the gospel when she mistook the risen Christ for the gardener and asked him if he knew where the body had been taken (John 20:11–18). Here in this garden of the risen, Mary may not realize it but the revelator sees all around her the faces and stories of countless "holy pictures," nameless children who seem to be "dancing in a sky filled with light." The revelator, in the person of his Lord, has called to the spirits, and they have revealed their faces. The kingdom argument implicit to "Souls of the Departed" in *Lucky Town* and, more ironically and allusively in "Maria's Bed" in *Devils & Dust*, is no longer merely hinted at by terms like "upper room." The dark despair that looms at the beginning of "The Rising" culminates ironically and powerfully in an ascent that excludes no one in hearing of the revelator. Those dead who hear the call, as we noted before in the *Catechism*, fulfill John 5.25: "those who hear will live" (165). The real trajectory of ironic revelation has been all along to show that in the land of the dead the King of Glory has come for his own: that the sky of "blackness and sorrow" is also ironically a sky "of fullness" and "blessed light." This ironic revelation reveals that even those whose hands slipped out of ours, those who waited by themselves in the twilight groves, are no longer there. They do not descend anymore, but they rise together at once with the revelator, in motion with him out of the infernal regions, coming together in a new world that belongs to everyone.

11

"I'll Work for Your Love"

Springsteen and the Struggle for Authenticity

John J. Sheinbaum

Much of the existing work on Bruce Springsteen focuses on a broad theme of authenticity, largely approached through Springsteen's connections to the singer-songwriter tradition. As Simon Frith puts it, authenticity is "the recurring term used in discussions of Springsteen," and the assumption of authenticity stands at the root of "why he has become so important. . . . Despite everything, [he] still gives people a way to define themselves against corporate logic, a language in which everyday hopes and fears can be expressed" (*Music* 97). Although it's clear that many popular musicians can be interpreted in light of the idea of authenticity, the reception of rock music—and what matters most in rock—over the last generation has characteristically placed Springsteen at the center (Pfeil 80). The level of esteem regularly aimed in the direction of this one particular human being, the weight of the value system he is asked and assumed to carry, is astounding. As the editors of *Rolling Stone*, the popular-culture journal of record, assert hyperbolically, "Springsteen almost single-handedly restored commitment to rock & roll lyrics, passion to rock & roll music, and visionary belief in the notion of rock & roll itself as a cultural phenomenon capable of moving mountains" (Rolling Stone, *Files* 2).

It is worth contemplating the idea of *authenticity* in rock music itself, given how central the concept is to the value system that developed around rock music in the second half of the twentieth century. A useful framework can be derived from Allan F. Moore's *Rock: The Primary Text—Developing a Musicology of Rock.* Moore outlines three basic sorts of authenticity: a "'first-person' authenticity, or *authenticity of expression,*" where "an originator (composer, performer) succeeds in conveying the impression that his/her utterance is one of integrity"; a "'second-person' authenticity, or *authenticity*

223

of experience . . . when a performance succeeds in conveying the impression to listeners that their experience of life is being validated"; and a "'third-person' authenticity, or *authenticity of execution*," which "arises when a per-former succeeds in conveying the impression of accurately representing the presence of another" (200–201). Such a model, then, through its continued reliance on the "impression" that is "conveyed" to the audience, asserts a notion of authenticity broader than one solely centered on the relation-ship between the artist and his or her art. The nature of that relationship is largely private, unknowable; instead, what *is* possible to examine are the ways an artist chooses to communicate a version of that relationship to the public, and the ways an audience may interact with those signs, musical or otherwise, offered up for contemplation. It becomes clear when explor-ing Springsteen's reception that he easily and thoroughly communicates a sense of authenticity because all three aspects of authenticity are at play in the way we think about him and his music.

It is common to approach Springsteen from the perspective of "first-person authenticity," where Springsteen-the-performer is understood as identical to, or collapsed onto, our best sense of Springsteen-the-person. We understand him, in part, as staking a claim that says "I am real, and what I do is real." As Gareth Palmer puts it, "Springsteen is constructed throughout as an ordinary Joe. All publications conspire in the need to present him as authentically all-American and 'one of us.' Such is the power of this construct that professional rock journalists . . . (usually) paid to be cynical, find themselves writing about the image as if it were interchange-able with the knowable Bruce Springsteen" (113). The oft-told "mytholo-gized biography," as Fred Pfeil calls it, serves to reinforce the assumptions of rock culture in general: "Bruce = rock-and-roll = the sound of passion, excitement, and rebellion in industrial working-class life" (82). For many fans, although recordings serve as the tangible documents of Springsteen's music, there is an inevitable distance between artist and audience; instead the live performance, with its aura of unmediated contact with the person himself on stage, constitutes the most important Springsteen experience. Dave Marsh, Springsteen's most prominent biographer, characterizes it thus: "Bruce Springsteen isn't a noun. It's a verb . . . at times the most ac-tive verb in the English language," and as such, all recordings are inevitably doomed to "fail" (*Tour* 3–4). And indeed, over his long career, the legend-ary performances have been a constant, an essential bulwark against per-ceptions of Springsteen as merely a conventional celebrity.

An important aspect of thinking about Springsteen as *real* within a rock music context is, perhaps paradoxically, an assumption that he's not a particularly good musician from a technical point of view. This has much to do with the idea that rock music is (or was) supposed to be an anti-establishment music of resistance; good rock, in this way of thinking, is a product not of school-based training, but unstudied musical naturalness. As Marsh posits, "Springsteen's musical virtues aren't derived from technical prowess. . . . In popular music, the issue isn't how many notes you hit but how expressively you can hit them" (*Tour* 17). Similarly, Deanna D. Sellnow and Timothy L. Sellnow note Springsteen's supposed lack of good singing voice or instrumental virtuosity, and instead characterize his popularity as attributable to his "down-to-earth story" and "charismatic style" (71–72). Connected to all this, of course, is a deep-seated belief that art is diametrically opposed to business; authentic rock, popular though it is, is made by real people who have not been molded into products designed to sell to a large audience. This is the generating idea, for example, behind Fred Goodman's book *The Mansion on the Hill*. For Goodman, 1960s rock "went through a dramatic transformation" such that the music was no longer show business, but instead concerned with "creating lasting art," yet as the music industry took advantage of rock's new cultural relevance, "it bred financial opportunities for artists and a certain professionalism that has proven to be at odds with a quest for authenticity" (x–xi). Most writers, then, focus on the *normal* and *moral* aspects of Springsteen-the-person. It is his ordinariness as a family man who works hard at his job that matters most, and the recounting of stories that tell how "his good (and innocent) intentions have come up against the big bad world of business" (Palmer 113–14). In the protracted period developing the follow-up to the breakthrough album *Born to Run* (1975), which eventually became *Darkness on the Edge of Town* (1978), Springsteen regularly cast aside songs that could have been hits, and this is often explained as "remain[ing] dedicated to a career shaped more by vision than by commerce" (Kirkpatrick, *Words* 54). As Jimmy Guterman puts it with regard to Springsteen in the 1980s, it's "worth believing in" an established star who would regularly drop in unannounced to New Jersey clubs to join the bar bands for a few songs (33). And as Daniel Cavicchi explains in his study of Springsteen fans, songs that aren't on the official albums, but are performed live anyway, are "clearly embraced" because of the need to understand Springsteen as separable from his commercial existence; if he plays them, they must matter to him and the band (72).

Equally important is the strong sense of "second-person authenticity" in Springsteen reception, where listeners also receive the message that "you are real, and the experiences in your lives are real." It is common to characterize Springsteen's songs as being filled with "stories about real people whose lives contain nuance and struggle, terrible damage and small acts of resistance, repair, and a longing for something more" (Bader 32). Marsh describes *Born to Run* as "a record that took the music's possibilities from the hands of craftsmen and profiteers and gave them back to the sort of people who loved rock because they lived it" (*Hearts* 142). Robert Coles has recently placed ordinary people's voices front and center in a "kind of ethnography" (45) of "attentive" listening to Springsteen (46); thus each section of the book is based around, say, a factory worker responding to the song "Factory," or a policeman ruminating on the song "American Skin (41 Shots)," and comments often echo the truck driver who feels that "some of the words he sings tie right in close to my work, my drivin' life" (80). Indeed, for Cavicchi, "it is difficult to locate the music's meaning without talking about fans' personal lives" (134–35). Using a framework derived from William James, Cavicchi finds that fans use their fandom to shape their identities in two fundamental ways, creating an "intense self-awareness" (137) by collecting Springsteen-related objects as external representations of themselves, and developing a sense of "self-continuity" (149) where the constant of Springsteen fandom over decades of life changes helps the fan feel that he or she possesses a constant, authentic self. These connections can also encompass extraordinary events: in the wake of the September 11, 2001, attacks, for example, many felt that they "needed" Springsteen (Hoffman 397), and that his album created in response, *The Rising* (2002), represents the definitive statement regarding "what it meant to witness this moment in history, to have lived through this time" (Hoffman 399).

Fans tend to "recognize themselves, or parts of themselves, in Springsteen"—not to say, in effect, "I'm just like him," but rather "he's just like me" (Cavicchi 139). And indeed, many fans even imagine Springsteen as "'ideal' or 'potential' selves in their minds as a way to guide their actions and steady their sense of who they are and want to be" (Cavicchi 140). This is dramatized quite effectively in Stephen Frears's film *High Fidelity* (2000), in which Springsteen himself makes a cameo, materializing in the bedroom of the protagonist as he lies on his back in bed, and offering advice on how to move on with his life in the wake of numerous bad relationships.[1] What is notable about fans' sense of a personal link to and validation by Springsteen is that it flies in the face of the conventional assumption that the audience is made up of mere consumers manipulated by the music industry. Instead of functioning as objects acted upon in the name of commerce, fans feel more like fully-functioning subjects investing in a personal relationship with the artist. This can take on something like religious overtones at times, and Cavicchi even characterizes some fans' "acts of devotion" as akin to "conversion stories" (51).

The audience is thus not external to the music, from this point of view, but an essential part of it, a part that completes the circuit. Bruce Springsteen releases songs and performs them, but their meanings are somewhat fluid in the hands of an actively interpreting audience. This is no corruption of some sort of fixed, intended meaning, but an important process that allows songs to do the authentic work they need to do. In a recent radio interview,[2] Springsteen acknowledged this as a purposeful aspect of his songwriting and the reception of it, specifically with regard to a question about political content in his songs:

> It's a tricky bit of business, because for me the song has to have a life both outside of its political context, and at the same time contain your politics. [Interviewer: Meaning, it has to work as a song even if you don't follow the politics?] I think for me, yeah, otherwise you're sort of stuck with a headline, or you're stuck on a soapbox. And there's times for that, but for me I want the music to have, sort of, a variety of lives, you know? And so someone could listen to "Lonesome Day" [the opening song from *The Rising*] and it can sound like a breakup song, or it can sound like 2001. (Springsteen, *"Magic* Campaign")

Also functioning within Springsteen reception is a "third-person authenticity," which plays out through connections to other musical styles and other artists who themselves are thought to possess authenticity. For example, David Brackett asserts that the "ecstatic responses" to Springsteen during the 1970s were related to critics' "yearning to return to rock's roots," and finding salvation in Springsteen's "nostalgic, or 'retro,' aesthetic," filled with copious "references to rock 'n' roll's past" (352).[3] Third-person authenticity also lies at the root of attempts to trace Springsteen's lineage back to figures such as Woody Guthrie, and more generally to the singer-songwriter tradition.[4] As Fred Goodman puts it, Guthrie represents "the best and purest part" of rock's sources: "music having nothing to do with making money and everything to do with integrity and simplicity, delivered without pretension or ulterior motive in the sole hope of uplifting any who might hear it" (xiv). Bryan K. Garman goes back even further, to Walt Whitman, and to the idea that a poet should be "a hero who expresses the essential character of his nation, serves as that nation's moral arbiter, and conveys this morality in a manner that is musical in both form and content" (*Race* 5). In the earlier twentieth century, Guthrie "constructed himself and was constructed by others as the new Whitman," and "transformed the working-class hero from a poet to a guitar-slinging traveler of the open road" (Garman, *Race* 11), and then, a generation later, "Springsteen self-consciously adapted Guthrie's music and politics to represent the collective pain, suffering, and injustice working people have historically suffered and to articulate their dreams of a less oppressive future" (Garman, *Race* 12).

In similar fashion, for the first stage of his career Springsteen was consciously marketed by Columbia Records as a "new [Bob] Dylan" in order to tap into a third-person authenticity of this sort. Larry David Smith even uses a family metaphor to characterize the interrelationships, with Guthrie positioned as a father figure and Dylan as an older brother (122). Marsh recounts that Columbia was interested in signing Springsteen specifically as a singer-songwriter because that was "the trend," even though he had been in rock bands for the better part of a decade, and had only been trying out an acoustic solo persona for a few months. While recording the debut album, Springsteen instead wanted to play with his band—he considered working with professional studio musicians "repugnant" (*Hearts* 56)—and had strong disagreements with his manager at the time, Mike Appel, who opposed the electric guitar because "this is supposed to be a folk record and *that* is a rock and roll instrument" (*Hearts* 58). Thus, the famous 1974 assertion by Jon Landau, who was soon to become Springsteen's new manager, that Springsteen represented not the past but "rock and roll future" was important for changing perceptions, for paving the way towards making Springsteen a notable performer in his own right.

Perhaps no sources have been more influential in coding Springsteen as *authentic* than the dual cases of *Rolling Stone*, which did much to build the legend, and Marsh's biographies, which have consolidated it. In *Rolling Stone*, the first mention of Springsteen came in a brief "random note" during March 1973: John Hammond, the head of talent at Columbia who had signed both Dylan and Springsteen, had suffered a heart attack after a Springsteen show, according to his doctor, "due to Hammond's enthusiasm" (Rolling Stone *Files* 28). Not a bad way to pique a potential fan's interest. In a story published the next month, Hammond is quoted asserting that Springsteen is "much further along, much more developed than Bobby [Dylan] was when he came to me" (29). The reviews of the first two studio albums each make repeated references to Dylan as well, and by the time of Greil Marcus's review of *Born to Run*, in October 1975, Springsteen has gone beyond mere influences and potential, and has finally achieved: "It is a magnificent album that pays off on every bet ever placed on him" (Rolling Stone, *Files* 48). As for Marsh, he has recently asserted that he has made peace with the common charge that he's little more than a "hagiographer" of Springsteen. Writing in the introduction to *Two Hearts*, the 2004 single-volume version of his 1979 and 1987 biographies, he knows that his subject is "honorable, immensely gifted, and inspired," and if "somebody has a problem . . . it ain't the writer" (xvii). For Marsh, Springsteen shows that "pop stardom could be used to make art of real substance and the pop star himself could be a responsible citizen" (*Hearts* 245).

Needless to say, there is an underside to all the assumptions of authenticity that have attached themselves to this one particular performer. The multitude of information generated by Springsteen and in discussing Springsteen over the decades needs interpretation, and at times the data do not neatly fit the conventional wisdom. *Born in the U.S.A.* (1984) is an album that in particular has sparked a fair amount of hand wringing, surely in part because that was the release that resulted in Springsteen achieving true superstar status. Guterman takes Springsteen to task, calling the album a "frankly commercial enterprise" (147), and "the first Springsteen record that sounds like the performer was listening to current pop radio as it was being made" (154). The hit single "Dancing in the Dark" didn't simply possess the "Sound of the New" with its synthesizer underpinning, but managed to "crash the party" (155), and a hit dance remix of the song, authorized by Springsteen himself, is said to bring him "all the way down the rabbit hole" (157). Even Marsh in *Two Hearts* characterizes the album as a self-conscious attempt at a "blockbuster" in the mode of Michael Jackson's 1982 phenomenon *Thriller* (413), and the following stadium tour a result of "making concessions for a run at the top" (474), though, in Springsteen's defense, such a striving for celebrity "always—and justifiably—made him skittish" (414), and compared to "precursors" like Elvis Presley and Jackson, he "was more aware that what he was doing was compromising" (474). As Elizabeth Bird puts it, "in trying to blow up his image of authenticity to reach mass audiences, he effectively lost control of it" (45). At a time of increasing postmodernism and expanding media attention, "kaleidoscopic images of Springsteen appeared—a Reagan conservative, a radical, a man's man, a sex symbol, a blue-collar hero, a philanthropist, a patriot, a social critic. Just take your pick" (47). And indeed, much of the media coverage of him during the later '80s became "standard celebrity stuff . . . increasingly dissonant with [his] core image" (50).

From Goodman's point of view, the disappointing reality of Springsteen functioning within—rather than in opposition to—the music industry is more than a single moment in the 1980s, but characterizes his career in general. "Appel told Springsteen he'd have to write more commercial songs if he wanted a record deal" (256), as Goodman recounts the early career, and after only a few short months his management team "marveled at his ability to reinvent himself" (257). When his first two albums didn't sell well, and Columbia was "ready to move Bruce" to another label, Springsteen "proved far more malleable" (224). "[H]e restructured the album [that would become *Born to Run*] and gave the executives what they wanted" (270). Three months were spent on the title track alone, consciously constructing it as a Phil Spector "Wall of Sound" sort of single, in strong contrast to the one week spent on the entire first album, and the two months devoted to the second. And as Goodman characterizes it, once the "smooth machine" of Columbia sensed *Born to Run* would be a hit, the album was "fed" into its "waiting maw," and "what came out the other side was a Rock Star" (281).

Indeed, closer to reality may be the notion that for a large commercial enterprise like Bruce Springsteen to feel authentic to an audience, in any of that term's potential permutations and combinations, that aura of authenticity must be carefully produced. It may ultimately be more useful to think of Springsteen as simply the hugely effective performer that he is, and the performances—both recorded and in concert—as a theater within which he can stage a persona that resonates with the audience as *authentic.* Paraphrasing the rock critic Lester Bangs, Rob Kirkpatrick asserts that Springsteen "wasn't striving for realism; he aimed to explore the romance and mythology of American cities, American car culture, and rock 'n' roll" (*Words* xi). And as music videos became an essential method for promoting popular music during the 1980s, Springsteen's were constructed to "illustrate how the medium [could be] used to preserve his authenticity," through devices such as "footage of real events," Springsteen himself playing blue-collar characters, and shots of "Bruce and the band performing" (Palmer 110). In Frith's formulation, Springsteen represents the "pop commodity [that] stands for the principle that music should not be a commodity. . . . And what matters in this postmodern era is not whether Bruce Springsteen *is* the real thing, but how he sustains the belief that there are somehow, somewhere, real things to be" (*Music* 95). None of this, of course, suggests that Springsteen is any less of an artist. But it does call into question the usual ways authenticity is thought about in the field of rock and around Springsteen.

The persona that has been constructed around—and by—Bruce Springsteen, the projection that has allowed him to represent a focal point in discussions of authenticity within popular music, is remarkably multifaceted. It grounds itself in images of masculinity and individualism, and generally identifies with the working class as heroic. What's striking about the Springsteen persona is that it seems to integrate all three aspects of authenticity discussed above. At once, listening to Springsteen communicates the message that he, the performer, is authentically masculine; that you, the audience, are authentically heroic; and the two come together through the language of rock music to create the aura of an idealized authentic experience. Each of these aspects, though, is itself dialectically complex. The Springsteen persona may help explain why he has been able to capture the imaginations of his fans and grow his audience to superstar levels over a sustained career, but also hints at problematic strands within the reception of rock authenticity.

A common trope in discussions of Springsteen centers on traditional heterosexual maleness. As Palmer puts it, "the work of Bruce Springsteen [is] a dominant force in promoting and signifying masculinity"; he "map[s] the signifiers of the Western onto contemporary blue-collar culture," and his "performance can be interpreted as that of a man striving for authentic masculinity" (101). Characters in Springsteen songs often work at jobs that entail "physical displays" such as "dockers, construction workers, [and] police," and the notion of work itself is essential as a "key site where masculine identity is formed" (Palmer 106). Indeed, in the nineteenth century the nickname "Boss," so commonly applied to Springsteen, was used to signify paid working men as opposed to slaves, and did much to equate freedom and power with masculinity (Garman, *Race* 222). Ronald Reagan infamously attempted to appropriate *Born in the U.S.A.*-era Springsteen for his reelection campaign against the artist's wishes, and what brought the political right to Springsteen was his perceived "unabashed masculinity" (Garman, *Race* 214)—his newly muscular physique resulted in him being called "the Rambo of rock and roll" (Garman, *Race* 218)—which could fit within Reagan's attempt at "remasculinizing the country's image of itself" (Garman, *Race* 216). In Garman's words, "Springsteen's sexuality, like Rambo's, was perceived as being inextricably bound with national interests" (*Race* 222–23).

At the same time, some interpret Springsteen's images of masculinity in other sorts of ways. For some, traditional maleness might lie at the center, but can be understood as performing a sort of cultural work that is ultimately problematic. From this perspective, father figures tend not to be role models, but instead are "continually defeated by the work process and can offer his family only an embittered husk at the end of the day," leaving sons in a "mythic . . . struggle to break free." At the same time, female characters are characteristically mere "decorative angels" or "signifiers of domesticity and commitment against which men define their masculinity" (Palmer 102–3). In one of Coles's first-person accounts, a sixth-grade teacher discusses her husband's attempts to convince her to become a Springsteen fan. She resists, largely because of the gender politics she hears: "We're born in the U.S.A. too, you know!" Her husband's response, meanwhile, is not to disagree, but rather to assert that such results are inevitable expressions of identity when "you've got a man singing a man's songs" (89). Some close readings, meanwhile, argue that such strong gender coding can hint in other directions entirely. Pfeil suggests that the masculinity of rock music is "almost exactly as transgressive as it is normative," partaking of the "musical-libidinal resources of Blackness" within its perceived whiteness, and of "emotional vulnerability" and "open sexuality" within its sexist "narcissistic arrogance." Within the political context of the 1960s in which rock came of age, the music's "broadly political hue" functioned as an "opposition to everything 'straight'" (75–76). Martha Nell Smith takes this one step further: while the usual story, of course, is that Springsteen is "the most heterosexual person" and a "manly icon" (848), if we choose to look for "conflicting and ambiguous sexual expressions" we can, indeed, find them, whether in his nightly kisses of saxophonist Clarence Clemons onstage, the "elaborate homoerotic dances" with guitarist Steven Van Zandt in the "Glory Days" video (834–35), or in the songs' characters who are often named androgynously, such as "Bobby Jean" or "Sandy" (838–39).

In light of all this, an iconic Springsteen song like "Born in the U.S.A." is telling. The musical style is easily read as signifying traditional masculinity, such as in Max Weinberg's pounding snare drum, and in the power and volume of Springsteen's pushed-to-the-limits vocals. But the song's structure seems not to celebrate this aggressiveness so much as treat it as limiting, even claustrophobic. Most rock songs contain at least two contrasting sections, as in the alternation between verses and choruses, but here the verse and chorus are built around the same melody, chords, and accompaniment pattern. Such a structure does not lead toward a purer sense of elemental rock-and-roll authenticity or an authenticity grounded in American folk song structures; instead, the song comes apart at the seams. As such, "Born in the U.S.A." forms a much closer musical counterpart to its negative lyrics—the final line is "nowhere to run, ain't got nowhere to go"—than is usually recognized (see table 11.1). The song begins as expected, with two verse-chorus cycles, the second one seeing the entrance of the full band. At this point, instead of a guitar solo, or some other sort of contrasting section, we head straight into a third cycle (1:21–1:52), but the space for the chorus, the eight bars following the verse, notably contains only the instrumental accompaniment; Springsteen's vocals are relegated to occasional, and wordless, laments. The lead singer is missing, and the hook of the song goes silent this time around. A fourth verse follows (1:52–2:07), and now the chorus space is excised entirely, the eight-bar verse continuing directly into a fifth verse section. Further, the fourth verse is incomplete lyrically: there are only three lines taking up six measures, leaving the last two bars, where the fourth line of lyrics is supposed to go, for the accompaniment alone. The fifth verse (2:07–2:23) moves even further in this direction, with only four bars of vocals, four bars of accompaniment, and again no chorus. Next is a sixth verse, and this time, though the vocal space is filled, the accompaniment drops out to the sparse levels of the original verse; after all these verses, no progress has been made. The song's structure undermines its presumed powerful masculine ethos.

A second important complex strain within the Springsteen persona is the perceived glorification of individualism, which embodies a heroic self-reliance. As Guterman contemplates Springsteen's long career, he sees the 1978 *Darkness on the Edge of Town* as the key album in the sequence, primarily because it was here that "Springsteen found the topic—decency in the face of defeat—that would fuel a quarter century of writing." The notion of individuals rising above their circumstances, working through them rather than feeling born to run away, was a "distinct, personal statement" for Springsteen, and the "stripped down," guitar- and drum-fueled "power" of the songs functioned as a sonic correlate to the lyrics' focus on the individual (106–7). And thus it is no surprise to learn, through Marsh, that in the wake of 9/11, which brought Springsteen back to work, he took his "role" of "local hero" as a "moral imperative" (*Tour* 254).

In this orbit, once again the mid-80s *Born in the U.S.A.* is something of a flashpoint. While Springsteen's lyrics largely continued to explore how ordinary characters grapple with difficult lives, many heard the music of the album as contradictorily upbeat, full of "foot-tapping melodies" (Garman,

Race 214) and the "contemporary feel" of 80s pop music (Mackey-Kallis and McDermott 5). The album could thus be heard "without emphasis on its message" (Mackey-Kallis and McDermott 5). At the least, there is a complex multivalence at work such that "Springsteen was able to give a sense of hope not found" on his previous record, the stark solo recording *Nebraska* (1982) (Sellnow and Sellnow 79). The wedding of individualism with this positive musical sheen surely contributed to Reagan's invocation of Springsteen as a hard-working model for America, one that, in Jim Cullen's estimation, no matter how deep or willful the misinterpretation, "functioned . . . effectively" for the political right. Even if meant to be a "leftist critique of American politics," *Born in the U.S.A.* ultimately "fits squarely within the privatized individualism that lies at the heart of right-wing ideology" ("Bruce" 3).

At a deeper level, perhaps, is the paradoxical notion that Springsteen's music, though it evokes the plight of the individual, results instead in the formation of a community. As Parke Puterbaugh puts it, with reference to the *Darkness* tour, "it was a strange phenomenon. The more Springsteen sang about alienation, the more people turned out to listen. His marathon concert rituals became a way of overcoming alienation, of forging a larger sense of community, however fleetingly, in increasingly depressing, isolated times" (Rolling Stone, *Files* 16). In the wake of the right-wing use of Springsteen, the artist himself attempted to reappropriate his message by focusing instead on "rock and roll as a vehicle for community." It was at this point that Springsteen began his now long-standing practice of promoting local charities at each show, asking for donations not only as a "refutation" of Reagan, but also to "leave something behind in the cities through which they barnstormed" (Marsh, *Hearts* 492). And in 1999, after a decade-and-a-half-long period of solo projects, Springsteen reunited the E Street Band—Springsteen's community of musicians—because, as Marsh puts it, "rock and roll is the language of individualism, but it is also the language of the human bond, the story of each struggle and the realization that all those struggles are one" (*Tour* 235).

A sonic correlate of the complex interrelationships between individual and community can be heard in the many instrumental strands coming together to form a participatory musical texture. Textures constructed like this are among the most salient characteristics of the arrangements heard on the bulk of Springsteen's recorded output, especially his albums with the E Street Band. As Guterman suggests in the context of *The Wild, the Innocent & the E Street Shuffle*, "Springsteen intended [that the album would be] the romanticized story of a community, and his band was intended to stand in for that community" (63). In a model of American civics at its best, all work together for a common purpose, but each individual's voice is still heard and is never entirely subsumed into the collective. In Frith's words, "the E Street Band makes music as a group, but a group in which we can hear every instrumentalist. Our attention is drawn, that is, not to a finished sound but to music-in-the-making. This is partly done by the refusal to make any instrument the 'lead.' . . . And partly by a specific musical busy-ness—the group is 'tight,' everyone aiming for the same rhythmic end, but 'loose,' each player makes their own decision how to get there" (*Music* 100).

All this is fully formed by the first track on the first album, "Blinded by the Light," the opener of *Greetings from Asbury Park, N.J.* (1973) (see table 11.2). Each layer of the musical texture has its own audible identity, but at the same time the lines dovetail and fit comfortably with each other to create a collective sound, neatly illustrating the complexities surrounding the construction of individualism in the band's music. And the arrangement is careful to allow separate entrances for each instrument, so as to highlight this duality between distinct individual and participation within the community. The introduction starts out with three distinct guitar sounds all playing at the same time (though all are performed, thanks to the studio, by Springsteen himself): a rhythm electric guitar line, a reinforcement of that line on acoustic guitar, and a lead electric guitar. Then on the last beat of the second measure, Garry Tallent's bass enters and slides down to land on the tonic pitch E for the following downbeat. On that downbeat Vinnie Lopez's drums begin with activity alternating on hi-hat cymbals and tom-toms, and then two bars later Clemons adds his sax licks for two more bars, completing the feeling that the full band is jamming along. Then the first verse repeats the community-joining gesture. After the six-bar intro everyone drops out (:12), leaving only a rhythm guitar strumming along and quarter notes on the hi-hat to keep the beat. For the third and fourth measure of this new introduction, the bass reenters with melodic fills. Over this texture Springsteen's vocals begin the verse for its first eight bars (:20–:37). Then for the next eight bars (:37–:52) David Sancious's organ is added, and the phrase concludes with a lead guitar lick doubled at the end by Clemons. At this point the drums give a clear accent on the last beat, and the second half of the verse begins, finally, with the full band grooving in support, each part discernible but clearly functioning within the thick texture.

While the band is a participatory collective, the figure of Bruce Springsteen himself is carefully positioned as the leader of this musical community. Often, he enacts performative guiding gestures, such as counting the band off or signaling the entrance of an important new section. This can be heard in early songs like "Wild Billy's Circus Story," from *The Wild, the Innocent*, where Springsteen's voice is heard giving a quiet "a-one, two, three, four" to set up the tempo for the tuba, acoustic guitar, and accordion introduction, and in more recent ones, like *The Rising*'s "Waitin' on a Sunny Day," where drummer Max Weinberg begins with a crisp groove on the drums, but it's Springsteen's energetic "one, two, three, four" a measure later that brings in the rest of the band.

A particularly notable example of Springsteen in this role can be heard on his signature song, the 1975 magnum opus "Born to Run," itself a song with thick musical textures that purposefully evoke the "Wall of Sound" and create a portrait of communal music making. After two cycles of the main song (1:50), Springsteen gives the band four vocal quarter note exclamations, to performatively lead the band into the contrasting middle section. Its first wave is a hard-driving Clemons solo (1:52–2:11), and this gives way to a second, dreamy vocal phase (2:11–2:38). Then the music shifts again; Springsteen leads the way with a "huh!," and an intense instrumental passage follows (2:38–2:53), which leads to the song's dramatic climax: the entire band, in unison, plays a complete downward chromatic scale from B down to the B an octave lower, and in rhythms so syncopated that our sense of the beat dissolves (2:53–2:59). The low B is now held, with no loss of volume or intensity, for what seems like an undetermined and extended amount of time (2:59–3:05). A hero is needed to pull us out of this crisis, and Springsteen comes to the rescue. He counts the band off, and brings us back to the main song for a final cycle of the main material, now with a triumphant synthesis, as the instrumental melody previously only heard alternating with the song's vocal sections is finally heard simultaneously with it.

But Springsteen's persona of leadership often masks the fact that the band is using conventional musical devices that need no leader to propel the music forward. Springsteen's counting is best understood as a theatrical, rather than a musical, gesture; he is playing the character of the bandleader at least as much as actually leading the band through the performance. This plays itself out at the climax of "Born to Run." As disorienting as it is, the full scalar descent functions to outline the note B, the traditional dominant within the home key of E from which the song came, and to which it will return. Springsteen's heroic counting the band back in is largely for show; though surface rhythmic activity stops for the held low B, the underlying timeline never does. The note actually lasts for a straightforward, easy-to-count four measures before the third verse begins. The timing of this is so strict that it's likely a metronomic click track was used in the studio, and the counting over the fourth measure a redundancy, included largely for dramatic purposes. The illusion is supremely effective, but an illusion nonetheless.

Similarly complex is Springsteen's focus on the working class. As Frith points out, while the tendency in Europe is for an artistic critique of societal power structures to result in an avant-garde, in the United States it has been possible to develop a "tradition of the artist as the common man" (*Music* 101), and thus Springsteen's success is largely attributable to the fact that his songs are "almost exclusively concerned with the working class" (*Music* 98). Class issues are also relevant from outside the confines of serious art: contemplating the Springsteen phenomenon instead from the perspective of popular music, a 1985 *Rolling Stone* article by Merle Ginsberg argues that fans are "drawn to Springsteen for precisely the opposite reason that most fans are drawn to a rock star: Instead of offering an escape from the mundane by creating a fantasy world of flash and glitz, Bruce glorifies the ordinariness of life" (Rolling Stone *Files* 188). Unlike the "entertainment establishment" of movie stars and pop singers, rockers like Springsteen stand authentically "outside" because they tend to come from "working-class backgrounds" and "lack . . . grooming" and professional polish (Marsh, *Hearts* 67–68).

As a manifestation of his identification with the ordinary person, the trope of Springsteen-as-worker is most pronounced in the frequent intimations of how hard he works on stage. In Palmer's formulation, "the performances can be read as celebrations and validations of heavy, physical unambiguously 'masculine' work." The band, meanwhile, "act[s] out the industrial fantasy of efficiency" while embodying "an idealized workplace representing a cross-section of American males," yet all the while cedes authority to "the Boss . . . at the head of this gang" (109). As Goodman puts it, "artistically, and especially in concert, he could deliver. More important, he insisted that he was not a rock star, but a man doing a job." And with reference to the E Street Band, "that shared history of scuffling around the bars of the Jersey Shore created a mythology built on a blue-collar, lunch-bucket ethic" (294). In contrast to the conventional image of the decadent rock star on tour, Clemons said the following at the conclusion of the *Born in the U.S.A.* tour: "When you go backstage at a Bruce Springsteen show, you don't see a circus. . . . Everybody has a job to do, and everybody goes about it seriously. Bruce instills the moral fiber that runs through the whole organization" (Rolling Stone *Files* 202). Indeed, even Springsteen's evolution over the decades to becoming a bigger and bigger star, and a performer in larger and larger venues, which might be interpreted as bending to commercial interests, is instead usually understood through the lens of hard work, and hard work as a moral good. With the move into arenas for the *Darkness* tour, we are told that Springsteen "spent hours every day at sound checks that involved him taking a seat in every section of the building to make sure the sound was clear" (Marsh, *On Tour* 110). And the explicit goal with the move to enormous stadiums in the midst of the *Born in the U.S.A.* tour was not only to be able to reach all the fans that wanted to see him, but "to make a stadium show that amounted to more than a spectacle" (Marsh, *Tour* 152), for "if all the audience saw was a star, the whole thing would have come tumbling down" (Guterman 164).

Working-class overtones are similarly at play in Springsteen's choices of musical style. The "joy" of Springsteen's first albums, the attempt to capture the "early vitality" of rock as "a celebration of male working-class adolescence," as Cullen calls it, was in great contrast to the "dour" styles of metal and glam rock, and to the "self-absorbed" singer songwriters then current ("Bruce" 5). And as working-class resonances came to the fore even more strongly while developing *Darkness*, there was a conscious move away from the frequent extended long songs on earlier albums that smacked of indulgent psychedelia (Goodman 299–300). New manager Jon Landau was pushing Springsteen to digest the work of authors such as John Steinbeck and Flannery O'Connor, and film directors like John Ford (Garman, *Race* 197), and these influences were instrumental in the thematic shift from the "escaping" of *Born to Run* to the "heroism [of] . . . decent, productive lives" seen on *Darkness* (Garman, *Race* 199–200).

But this mode of understanding surrounding Springsteen's music often leads, erroneously, to the assumption that Springsteen's music is simple; as Larry David Smith puts it, "his mystery is genuine, but his art is without mystery" (122). In Frith's estimation, "the textures and, more significantly, the melodic structures of Springsteen's music make self-conscious reference to rock and roll itself, to its conventional line-up, its clichéd chord changes, its time-honored way of registering joys and sadness" (*Music* 100). Meanwhile, Springsteen's lyrics are thought to function similarly; as Frith puts it, "the formal conservatism of the music reinforces the emotional conservation of the lyrics" (*Music* 99). For most writers, the assertion of simplicity is of a piece with the aura of authenticity. As Palmer puts it, it is "important to note . . . how conservative much of the music is. But this is the point. True authenticity as a rocker involves strict adherence to rock and roll's traditions. A lack of innovation here is a sign of commitment to the fan" (110). Regarding how songs tend to evolve over years of performance, Guterman's positive comments about "Badlands," as performed on the election-themed 2004 Vote for Change tour, are directly related to maximizing simplicity: "with each tour a great song gets a little bit flabbier, a little farther away from the tightly compressed original. This time out, [though,] . . . most of the fluff in the song has been excised: no false ending, no singalong, no coda after coda. Just direct expression" (14–15). Simplicity strikes us as authentic because we assume that the musical directness is not a pose or a choice, but a natural outgrowth of music made by naturally simple people; as Marsh asserts, "basic three-chord rock" lies at the heart of this music not "out of commitment to pure simplicity or simple purity, but because the basics were their limit" (*Tour* 22–23).

Yet across Springsteen's output with the E Street Band, and encompassing some of his most iconic songs, there is a notable tendency to incorporate musical passages that belie and go beyond the usual musical boundaries of straightforward rock and roll. The conventional view of Springsteen's music does not begin to do justice to the careful and detailed ways the songs are constructed, nor to the ways the music affects its listeners. I do not mean to imply that Springsteen's music is good music because it's complex, but rather that the value system of authenticity built around Springsteen does not fully capture the music-cultural strains at play within the music, its creation, and its reception.

For example, the overwhelming tendency in Springsteen's songwriting is to go beyond the simple alternation of a verse-chorus form, and to include a third section, a bridge, between the second and third cycles of the main material, and one that is meant to contrast with both of the already contrasting chief sections. As John Covach points out, such forms are "more complicated" than the baseline structures found in classic rock and roll, and this formal type is most characteristic of 1970s rock, not the earlier styles most assume lie at the heart of Springsteen's music (74). And often Springsteen does not stop at the mere fact of such a section and its overall structural implications; he creates bridges that are of provocative interest in their own right. These sections function as much more than merely filling boxes in an abstract formal scheme, and often include details that themselves aspire to structural importance. The seven-minute "Rosalita (Come Out Tonight)," from *The Wild, the Innocent & the E Street Shuffle* (1973), for example, which for most of Springsteen's career has been an anchor of his live shows, has a middle section that encompasses a number of its own sprawling passages, and itself lasts for a full two minutes (3:18–5:18 on the studio recording). According to Marsh, "Rosalita"'s "extended middle" was originally developed for practical purposes, to create a space in which Springsteen could introduce the band in concert, and to fill time when they were newly headliners (*Tour* 58), but such long musical journeys did much to make the shows "more and more theatrical" (*Tour* 59). In songs like these, as Marsh puts it, "you can hear a musician overcoming both his own limits and the restrictions of the form" (*Hearts* 95).

As "Rosalita"'s middle section begins, not unlike the climax of "Born to Run," Springsteen incorporates an area of floating musical chromaticism, where the music seems to leave the harmonic strictures of basic three-chord rock, and the listener tends to lose all sense of the home key, or any sense of key at all. After the second chorus the song moves from its F-major home to an arpeggio built around a C chord (3:18). This is reasonable enough at first; C is the fifth note of the F scale, and the chord built on the fifth note is called the dominant because it's the main place tonal music moves to create contrast. It sounds normal to our ears—and is indeed quite common—for music in many styles to move back and forth from the home tonic to its dominant. But after two measures of this, the arpeggios start to move in their own pattern, and without reference any longer to the key of F. Over and over again the music rises by half step, and we quickly lose our bearings. The C chord moves up chromatically for two measures of C sharp, and this is followed by two measures built around D, and two more on D sharp. We then move up one more half step, to E; this sonority lasts for an excruciating eight full measures, and by this point we have no idea where we are or where we're going, other than the fact that we know that something big is going to happen next. And indeed it does: the band drops out (3:42), and four times in a row an unaccompanied Clemons sax line sounds, answered by gestures of two big chords by the rest of the group, and only then does the song move on to the next phase of the middle section, which has not yet even approached its halfway point. "Rosalita"'s musical structure encompasses more complex perspectives than a simple rock-and-roll song would conventionally be presumed to have.

Even though later songs tend to be more concise, the care and musical interest put into them never abates; in Marsh's words, "the music felt more honed now, the jam-band elements losing ground to rock songs with tighter, though often still elaborate, structures" (*Tour* 62). Many songs incorporate passages where the music jumps, unprepared, into tonalities distinct from the ones that define the main sections of a song, such as "Racing in the Street" from *Darkness on the Edge of Town* (at 2:36), and "Backstreets" from *Born to Run* (at 2:44). Some are even more radical in their overall structure, using the last cycle of main material not as a sign of satisfying closure, but instead as a mere way station on the path to another destination entirely. Calling the idea of closure into question, these songs move instead to new sections of seemingly endless groove after what we already thought was the song's conclusion. The most iconic is "Thunder Road," the opening song from *Born to Run*. When the song eventually seems to reach a powerful conclusion—there's a dramatic move to an emphatic tonic chord, and Springsteen tells us he's "pulling out of here to win"—we realize instead we'll get a sense of the journey that follows. At 3:50 a new instrumental section begins, and tellingly, each phrase ends on the dominant, which brings us back to the beginning of yet another phrase. The song, at least in our imaginations, never truly ends; it eventually fades away instead, leaving us imagining the hero's car off in the distance, driving out of view. The song's structure is thus generally of a piece with the desire for escape described by the lyrics: "these two lanes will take us anywhere."

At the same time, Springsteen's focus on nostalgic musical styles inevitably brings up the specter of race. The working-class image promulgated by Springsteen tends to be specifically a *white* one; "he ain't anywhere *close* to being Black," as Pfeil puts it (88). As Springsteen became exponentially more popular, he also moved decidedly away from the jazz- and rhythm & blues-tinged sounds of the first two albums, and towards a more straightforward rock sound, but this resulted in what Guterman calls a "whitening" of Springsteen's music (99). There's a paradoxical "complete reversal" at work here, of course: whereas early rock in its own cultural context was heavily coded with signs of presumed blackness, over the last generation the centrality of hip-hop and rap in popular music has left Springsteen's sort of rock seeming to "hold the line" *against* black music, an "icon of reassurance, . . . whiteness and stability." As Marsh puts it, "I doubt if one in a million Springsteen fans hates black skin. . . . But it's also true that eyeballing the crowd at any E Street gig conveys the impression that [only] about one in every ten thousand Bruce fans is something other than Caucasian" (*Tour* 194–95).

Thus, the overall Bruce Springsteen persona is one that largely seems coherent and stable, while at the same time embracing a raft of potential contradictions. He is a worker, though a millionaire many times over; he comes across like a mid-level employee, though he is "the Boss"; he's middle-aged, but makes music that can appeal to teens; he seems approachable and seems to care about us, though he's a superstar; he's best as a live performer, but by necessity we know him mostly through recordings (Frith *Music* 95–97). Springsteen's songs might initially strike us as straightforward, but close examination shows that instead they are dialectical expressions that give voice to while simultaneously calling into question the structural expectations and cultural resonances of the authentic rock song itself. And from the perspective of reception, as Cavicchi relates, many assert Springsteen's "universality" (149), while at the same time female, or non-white, or non-working-class, or non-American fans report being treated as lesser sorts of fans "because of an inability to really relate to the music" (144). As Garman puts it, Springsteen sits squarely in a tradition of art that "imagined a more just social order," but paradoxically formulated this in a way that "often excluded women and people of color, thereby safeguarding, sometimes inadvertently, the social advantages ascribed to manhood and whiteness" (*Race* 4).

Taken as a whole, these perspectives add an important layer of nuance and texture to our current approaches to Bruce Springsteen. Simply put, Springsteen's music cannot be adequately perceived through the lenses conventionally applied to it. A pure singer-songwriter model may place him squarely in the tradition of American working-class heroes, but sidesteps his rock-and-roll background, and his longstanding collaborative music making. Notions of unproblematic stylistic unity may center on Springsteen the rocker, but inevitably marginalize the complexities and structural shifts employed throughout his songwriting. And constructions of pure rock-and-roll authenticity speak to the artist we may want Bruce Springsteen to be and the styles we expect to hear, but ultimately we're confronted with a multifaceted persona, and challenged by sublime musical passages that incorporate a multiplicity of visions. Springsteen's art, in its deceptive simplicity, is open to multifarious interpretations.

Table 11.1. Example 1: "Born in the U.S.A." (1984), phrase vs. vocal length, verse 1 through verse 6 (changes from expected patterns are italicized)

Section	Timing	Relative Texture	Phrase Length	Vocal Length
verse 1	(:18–:33)	thin	8 mm.	8 mm.
chorus	(:33–:49)	thin	8 mm.	8 mm.
verse 2	(:49–1:05)	full band	8 mm.	8 mm.
chorus	(1:05–1:21)	full band	8 mm.	8 mm.
verse 3	(1:21–1:37)	full band	8 mm.	8 mm.
chorus	(1:37–1:52)	*no vocals*	8 mm.	0 mm.
verse 4	(1:52–2:08)	full band	8 mm.	*6 mm.*
verse 5	(2:08–2:23)	full band	8 mm.	*4 mm.*
verse 6	(2:23–2:39)	*thin*	8 mm.	8 mm.

Table 11.2. Example 2: "Blinded by the Light" (1973), textural layers, introductions and verse 1 (staggered x's imply instrument that enters in midst of phrase)

a) introduction (:00–:12)

instrument	mm. 1–2	mm. 3–4	mm. 5–6
voice			
rhythm guitar	x	x	x
acoustic guitar	x	x	x
lead guitar	x	x	x
bass		x	x
drums		x	x
saxophone			x
organ			

b) second introduction and verse 1 (:12–1:22)

instrument	mm. 1–2	mm. 3–4	mm. 5–12	mm. 13–20	mm. 21–36
voice			x	x	x
rhythm guitar	x	x	x	x	x
acoustic guitar				x	x
lead guitar				x	x
bass		x	x	x	x
hi-hat only	x	x	x	x	x
drums					x
saxophone				x	x
organ				x	x

NOTES

1. The film is an adaptation of Nick Hornby's 1996 novel of the same title. At about 43:00 into the film, the character Rob says "I want to see Penny and Charlie and Sarah; all of them, y' know, just see 'em and talk to 'em. You know, like a Bruce Springsteen song." As these lines are spoken the soundtrack moves toward an electric guitar improvising around blues changes, and it turns out that is no prerecorded musician on a scoring stage, but Springsteen himself, right there in the room. Springsteen continues playing, and responds: "You call, you ask 'em how they are, you see if they've forgiven you." And the conversation continues:

Rob: Yeah, then I'd feel good. And they'd feel good.

Springsteen: Well, they'd feel good maybe, but you'd feel better.

Rob: I'd feel clean, and calm.

Springsteen: If that's what you're looking for, y' know, get ready to start again? That would be good for you.

Rob: Great, even.

Springsteen: Give that final good luck and good-bye to your all-time top 5 and just move on down the road.

Rob: Good luck, good bye. Thanks, Boss.

2. The entire excerpt is not included in the print version of the story that appears on the NPR website, but only in the full audio link of the interview. This portion of the interview begins at about 2:00 into the recording.

3. Brackett's comments are part of the introduction to a reprinting of Marsh's first published article on Springsteen (which appeared in the October 1975 issue of *Creem* magazine).

4. The term "singer-songwriter" is here defined "more broadly" than the orbit implied by the James Taylor–Carly Simon "cadre of musicians of the early 1970s." See James E. Perone's "Series Foreword" to the Praeger Singer-Songwriter Collection in the front matter to Kirkpatrick's *The Words and Music of Bruce Springsteen*.

12

"May Your Hope Give Us Hope"

The Rising as a Site of Mourning

Roxanne Harde

Those traumatized by extreme events, as well as those empathizing with them, may resist working through because of what might almost be termed a fidelity to trauma, a feeling that one must somehow keep faith with it. Part of this feeling may be the melancholic sentiment that, in working through the past in a manner that enables survival or a reengagement in life, one is betraying those who were overwhelmed and consumed by that traumatic past.

—Dominick LaCapra, *Writing History, Writing Trauma*

One should not develop a taste for mourning, and yet mourn we *must*. We *must*, but we must not like it—mourning, that is mourning *itself*, if such a thing exists: not to like or love through one's own tear but only through the other, and every tear is from the other, the friend, the living, as long as we ourselves are living, reminding us, in holding life, to hold on to it.

—Jacques Derrida, *The Work of Mourning*

Sing me a song to make death tolerable.

—William Carlos Williams, *Paterson*

The sky was falling and streaked with blood
I heard you calling me then you disappeared into the dust
Up the stairs, into the fire
Up the stairs, into the fire
I need your kiss, but love and duty called you someplace higher
Somewhere up the stairs into the fire

—Bruce Springsteen, "Into the Fire"

In a 2004 interview with *Rolling Stone* editor Jann Wenner, Bruce Springsteen returned to the now-famous story about the fan who stopped in traf-
fic to tell Springsteen, the day after the attacks of 11 September 2001, that
he was needed:

> I've had a long life with my audience. I always tell the story about the guy
> with *The Rising*: "Hey, Bruce, we need you!" he yelled at me through the car
> window. That's about the size of it. You get a few letters that say, "Hey, man,
> we need you." You bump into some people at a club and you say, "Hey, man,
> what's going on?" And they go, "Hey, we need you." Yeah, they don't really
> need me, but I'm proud if they need what I do. That's what my band is. That's
> what we were built for. (76)

Springsteen is, as usual, fairly oblique about what it is he and his band do
and are built for, but by 2001, fans around the world had come to rely on
him for musical experiences that offered them an ongoing commentary on
and critique of contemporary American society. What "we" needed after the
September attacks was someone to put into words collective and individual
pain and loss, an artist who could model the way to work through absence
and mourning, someone to sing "a song," as William Carlos Williams pleads
in my epigraph, "to make death tolerable." Springsteen and the E Street Band
were built to answer—and *The Rising* more than meets—this need. Jeffrey Symynkywicz describes the album as "heralded in the mainstream media as the
first major cultural response to the events of September 11. . . . The stories,
emotions, and impressions of September 11 seem to breathe from just about
every song" (140). However, *The Rising* is far more than simply a response to
or replay of the attack on the World Trade Center or the Pentagon. Instead,
Springsteen's songs address and work through the aftermath of emotional
devastation caused by the events of 9/11. Refusing to blur the distinction
between absence and loss, to offer pat answers or convenient closures when
none were or are possible, and to avoid the deeply painful journey that comprises working through grief, *The Rising* functions as a site of cultural memory
and mourning.

Considered alongside theoretical discourse that analyzes the opera-
tions of mourning, and responses to absence and loss caused by trauma,
the songs on *The Rising* offer far more than witness or even testimony. In
Writing History, Writing Trauma, Dominick LaCapra cautions that because
of personal loss or general empathy, people may invest trauma with value
to which they remain "dedicated or at least bound. The situation may create a more or less unconscious desire to remain within trauma," which is
both intolerable and no solution to absence or loss (23). Delineating the
difference between loss—which is personal, historical, and specific—and
absence—which is transhistorical and general, LaCapra argues that to work
through trauma means articulating affect and representation in a way that

precludes transcendence. To work through absence means recognizing first the dubious natures of ultimate solutions and closures and, second, that accompanying anxiety may not be eliminated but it can be lived with. In *The Work of Mourning*, Jacques Derrida suggests that recognizing death and working through grief is a supremely verbal act. Even as he notes the impossibility of speaking at times of mourning, Derrida considers silence "another wound, another insult" (50). Refusing to make of death, and therefore mourning, an allegory or even a metaphor, Derrida models mourning as a movement toward life, a kind of ongoing work, "In and of itself. Even when it has the power to give birth, even and especially when it plans to bring something to light" (142–43). For both LaCapra and Derrida, and for Springsteen, mourning allows an engagement with trauma that insists on a reinvestment in life. *The Rising* is "a dream of life," and the abiding movement in the album is one of ascension. In a 2002 interview with *Nightline*'s Ted Koppel, Springsteen responded to the suggestion that the album gestures toward the resurrection by noting that the images of the Catholic tradition in which he was raised "are always close and they explain a lot about—a lot about life." However, he exchanges the idea of resurrection for the more general image of ascension: "And I knew—well I was trying to describe the most powerful images of the 11th, and that I'd read in the paper, was when some of the people coming down talked about the emergency workers who were ascending." By sidestepping the specifically Christian tenet of the resurrection, and by rejecting outright the idea of transcendence—an upward movement, true, but one invested in the idea of surpassing something lesser for once and all—Springsteen offers in *The Rising* a perpetual rising toward light and life, a continuing upward movement that engenders the working through trauma articulated by LaCapra and insists on the work of mourning described by Derrida. Along the way, the Boss considers and rejects ideas about and impulses toward vengeance, and he offers instead the erotic as a means of working through loss and mourning and re/turning to life.

"EMPTY SKY, EMPTY SKY": WORKING THROUGH ABSENCE

Mourning, however, is not the first reaction to loss, to absence, to disaster. While several songs on *The Rising* grapple with the work of mourning, discussed below, other songs undertake a necessary engagement with absence. In a *Nightline* interview with Ted Koppel, Springsteen focuses on the emptiness that is central to these songs: "There was a bridge that you can see the World Trade Center from. We're actually only 10 or 15 miles from downtown New York here. It's close by water. And you cross this little bridge. And they always sat—they sat dead in the middle of it. And so towards the end of the day we got in the car and too and—you know, drove over it and they were gone." In discussing how disaster "ruins everything, all the while leaving everything intact," Maurice Blanchot suggests that disaster, an experience we generally may witness but have not usually experienced, "obliterates . . . our relation to the world as presence or as absence" (1, 120). In short, disaster, or trauma for that matter, changes everything. LaCapra also focuses on absence and emptiness after trauma; he calls it a "disruptive experience that disarticulates the self and creates holes in existence" (42). The effects of trauma, LaCapra suggests, are controlled only with difficulty, in part because working through the past might feel like a betrayal of those who were consumed by it. Facing the absence caused by trauma, as Springsteen does when he drives over the bridge, and bringing oneself into relationship with it, as he does in *The Rising*, provides a means of controlling the effects of the disaster, of working through trauma. His inclusion of "Nothing Man" on the album, a song "originally written in 1994 about a Vietnam veteran suffering from post-traumatic stress syndrome," provides one intimate staring down of trauma (Symynkywicz 143). The speaker faces his changed life, now one of profound absence, with a combined nihilism and hope as he faces the gun on his night table and prays for courage, either to end his life or to live it.

This profound hope in the face of overwhelming absence plays out in several songs on the album. As Tod Hoffman notes, artists "can contribute to monumental events. They can't tell us about why it happened or its lasting implications: they can articulate a collective awe and grief and prepare us to hope" (399). The destruction of the World Trade Center left an emptiness, a gaping absence, on the Manhattan skyline and in the cultural consciousness. When the towers fell, they took with them a sense of security that now seems, some nine years later, as unrecoverable as any attempt to build on the site seems unthinkable. The absence that remains, now named for that place situated immediately under an exploding bomb, has become, in Richard Stamelman's terms, "a memory site" (15). In a discussion of the terminology of "ground zero," Stamelman notes that the site "has literally and physically been taken over by a word whose evocation of vacuity truly represents and symbolizes it—the pit at ground zero in place of the once-looming towers" (15). By bringing himself and his audience into the presence of this absence, Springsteen enables the "working through trauma" described by LaCapra as "the effort to articulate or rearticulate affect and representation" (42). *The Rising*, then, can be understood as such re/articulation.

With many songs invoking the missing and the disappeared, emptiness and nothingness, *The Rising* works to represent the trauma of 9/11 and its effects, but nowhere more emphatically than in "Empty Sky." From its first stanza, where the speaker wakes up to air full of dust and a home full of loss—"I woke up this morning, I could barely breathe / Just an empty impression / In the bed where you used to be"—this is a song about absence. Its governing image is emptiness; fully half of its lines are repetitions of "Empty sky, empty sky / I woke up this morning to an empty sky." The second stanza articulates trauma and loss of life. Its visceral imagery reminds me of Emily Dickinson's Civil War poems, in particular her reflections on the battle of Antietam, "The name—of it—is 'Autumn' / The hue—of it—is blood," and "Whole Gulfs—of Red, and Fleets—of Red / And Crews—of solid Blood" (*Poems* 465 and 468). Where Dickinson attempts to represent a trauma she has not witnessed, to turn absence into a loss she can then come to terms with, Springsteen first attempts to exchange one effect of 9/11—the horrific amount of detritus in the air—with another, a visceral representation of the immolated dead:

> Blood on the streets
> Blood flowin' down
> I hear the blood of my blood
> Cryin' from the ground

"Empty Sky" then continues to gesture downward instead of rising upward in the third stanza. I examine the song's discussion of revenge below, but this downward focus is coupled with, or possibly forced by, the continued absence, the empty sky. The speaker moves from crafting a bow from a tree of evil and good to a desire for his lost lover, a desire that manifests as the desire for revenge, but gives way to an ever present and stark reality: "Empty sky, empty sky / I woke up this morning to the empty sky." Absence and emptiness haunt the post-9/11 landscape and psyche and preclude mourning. With "Empty Sky," Springsteen stares down absence by facing the emptiness in the skyline and at ground zero.

Following LaCapra, the difference between loss and absence might be seen, in the case of 9/11, as the difference between the specific, personal pain caused by the confirmed loss of a loved one and the general affect caused by the devastation and uncertainty resulting from the terror attacks. "Losses cannot be adequately addressed when they are enveloped in an overly generalized discourse of absence," LaCapra cautions, but converting absence into loss, "increases the likelihood of misplaced nostalgia or utopian politics in quest of a new totality or fully unified community" (45–46). This quest becomes evident in "Waitin' on a Sunny Day," a song invested in nostalgic longing for something and someone now absent. Avoiding specifics and therefore the discourse of loss, the song longs for a utopian day when the sun shines and everything is all right again. Driven by a straight-ahead pop rhythm and an optimistic chorus—Rob Kirkpatrick describes it as "a song about wanting to be happy again"—the song seems out of place on an album about trauma (*Words* 143). Still, if the chorus seems to expect happiness to return, its abiding action is one of simply waiting: "I'm waitin', waitin' on a sunny day / Gonna chase the clouds away / Waitin' on a sunny day." While the three verses yearn for a missing person, "Your smile girl, brings the mornin' light to my eyes / Lifts away the blues when I rise / I hope that you're coming to stay," all the imagery up to that final yearning centers on the absent or disappeared. From the first line's description of rain from an empty sky, "It's rainin' but there ain't a cloud in the sky / Musta been a tear from your eye," to the middle stanza's incompleteness, "half a party . . . deserted street," the song offers only flashes of hope against the unremitting certainty that "Hard times baby, well they come to us all / Sure as the tickin' of the clock on the wall / Sure as the turnin' of the night into day." A fixation on absence, which is ongoing and unreconcilable, LaCapra warns, might offer "an interminable aporia in which any process of working through the past and its historical losses is foreclosed"; however, he also points out that converting absence (an infinite site of pain) into loss (which is finite with the thing or person lost and mourned), allows a "crucial distinction between then and now wherein one is able to remember what happened to one in the past but realizes one is living in the here and now with future possibilities" (46–47). For all the sunniness of its expectations, its attempts to "chase the clouds away," the song is fixated on what is missing and can only gesture toward future possibilities, the sunny day that comes after loss and mourning.

The final song on *The Rising* offers the movement from absence to loss to mourning. "My City of Ruins" was written for a city other than New York, but as Springsteen explained at the *America: A Tribute to Heroes* telethon, "This was a song that I wrote for Asbury Park. Songs go out into the world and hopefully they end up where people need 'em. So I guess this is a gift from Asbury Park to New York City in its time of need" (quoted in Marsh, *Tour* 237). By offering this song to a suffering city, Springsteen suggests that the song offers what is needed. The song catalogs instances of suffering and absence, beginning with "a blood red circle / On the cold dark ground." From a missing congregation in an open church, to "boarded up windows / The empty streets," to a bed empty except for "tears on the pillow," this city is a site of trauma, loss, and absence. Each verse culminates in grief and the last in a pleading question:

> My soul is lost, my friend
> Tell me how do I begin again?
> My city's in ruins
> My city's in ruins

Between the second and third verses, however, Springsteen includes a bridge that he then extends into a choral event at the song's end. Repetitions of "Come on, rise up!" give way to prayers that begin with the personal and expand in an ever-increasing circle, as "I" becomes "we," concern about personal suffering becomes concern for the world, and strength in community engenders new possibilities:

> With these hands,
> With these hands,
> I pray for the faith, Lord
> We pray for your love, Lord
> We pray for the lost, Lord
> We pray for this world, Lord
> We pray for the strength, Lord

The song ends with "Come on, rise up," chanted in the way that seems certain that hope can become reality. Describing "My City" as "'The Rising' Part Two," Kirkpatrick argues that the song "occupies a spiritual space between gospel and secular soul, and with the song's prayerful crescendo . . . the call to (once again) rise up is all-encompassing" (*Words* 144). Prayer, which insists on looking outward and past one's pain, coupled with the call for a community to again "rise up," answers the speaker's plaintive "How do I begin again?" The song may begin with a city in ruins, but it ends with the beginning of rejuvenation, reconstruction, rebirth. Along the way, it plays the crucial role of witness.

In a reflection titled "Wounded New York," published six months after the attacks, Judith Greenberg considers the majority of people affected by 9/11, those who did not lose a loved one in the planes, the towers, or the Pentagon: "How do those of us whose grief is harder to specify address our encounter with violence and death?" she asks, and how do we come to "what remains missing"? (23). The reality is that even with thousands of dead and disappeared, the majority of people affected by 9/11 did not lose someone they loved or even knew. We became a world hurt by a tragedy that was not specifically, personally our own, a world wounded by a devastating emptiness. Greenberg suggests that "mourning needs to heal the wound, to build a scar, but the missing cannot be buried. As I write six months later, bodies continue to be exhumed, and many will never be recovered. It takes time to convert absence into death. Wounds remain open despite the yearning for rapid closure" (25). As part of this yearning, we became a world overwhelmed, as Greenberg points out, "by the need to witness" (27). Witnessing functions as part of working through absence in a way that recognizes the "dubious nature of ultimate solutions and the necessary anxiety that cannot be eliminated" (LaCapra 58). Witnessing, then, in LaCapra's terms, "opens up empowering possibilities . . . in the creation of a more desirable, perhaps significantly different—but not perfect or totally unified—life in the here and now" (58). In an interview with Josh Tyrangiel, Springsteen connected bearing witness and performing "with the concept of our band as a group of witnesses. . . . That's one of our functions. We're here to testify to what we have seen" (59). Greenberg writes that we are a world of witnesses at ground zero, "trying to reencounter memory in this absent landscape" (30), and Hoffman suggests that in the future, he will "listen to Springsteen and revisit what it meant to witness this moment in history" (399). Witnessing enables mourning; "Empty Sky" functions as testimony, as Springsteen bearing witness to overwhelming absence. "Waitin' on a Sunny Day" centers on the missing, but in looking ahead it works to comprehend absence, to turn the wound into a scar and move back into life. "My City in Ruins" moves past absence into the work of mourning that, LaCapra contends, "brings the possibility of engaging trauma and achieving a reinvestment in, or recathexis of, life, which allows one to begin again" (66). Beginning again, the quest of "My City," is predicated on mourning, however, not on revenge.

(INTERCALARY) "I WANT AN EYE FOR AN EYE": REJECTING VENGEANCE

A number of secondary themes run through *The Rising*, and I address them in intercalary sections, this being the first. I use the term *intercalary* as John Steinbeck used it to describe the general migration narratives dispersed among the chapters telling the story of the Joads in *The Grapes of Wrath*, a book that has inspired some of Springsteen's best work. While Steinbeck relied on the term's meaning as *something inserted*—usually a unit of time to harmonize the calendar with the solar year, to make things come out right—*intercalary* is also defined as a refrain, those portions that hold a song together and give the whole its shape. LaCapra writes that the absence caused by trauma is attended by an anxiety that "is one basis for the typical projection of blame for a putative loss onto identifiable others" (58). Absence needs to be faced and worked through, LaCapra argues, and not converted into something "that one believes could be made good, notably through the elimination or victimization of those to whom blame is imputed" (65). Springsteen's secondary themes or intercalaries—in this case, the juxtaposition of absence and the all-too-human urge for revenge and, in the next, the use of the erotic as the means to move through grief to a reinvestment in life—form a refrain that begins the work of mourning and helps to make things come out right, to lift humanity above violence and into life.

"Lonesome Day," the album's first song, begins with reference to a missing loved one and the assertion that "it's gonna be okay / If I can just get through this lonesome day." The second stanza opens with dark images culminating in a house on fire and a viper in the grass; the idea of vengeance is introduced and then quickly dismissed to be replaced with something far more life-affirming: "A little revenge and this too shall pass / This too shall pass, I'm gonna pray." The final stanza warns about the costs inherent in taking revenge:

> Better ask questions before you shoot
> Deceit and betrayal's bitter fruit
> It's hard to swallow, come time to pay
> That taste on your tongue don't easily slip away

After this caution about the taste of revenge, a dish that seems unappetizing and even dangerous whether cold or not, the song culminates in the affirmation that the "lonesome day" will be gotten through, and closes with repeated reaffirmations that "It's alright." *The Rising* thus begins with a recognition of loss, an intentional turn away from revenge and more loss, and a movement towards life.

Critical and creative responses to 9/11 share a common concern that this movement will not be the one taken, that New York and the United States will respond to trauma and loss with vengeance. In "Wounded New York," Greenberg muses, "It is not clear that we will remain a city, a nation, or a world of respectful mourners working through the trauma. We risk repeating behaviors, identifying with the aggressors, or otherwise enacting scenes we could not know" (31). In her prose-poem elegy "The Dead of September 11," Toni Morrison also yearns for a mourning that in no way includes the quest for vengeance:

> If I can pluck courage here, I would like to speak directly to the dead—the September dead. . . . But I would not say a word until I could set aside all I know or believe about nations, war, leaders, the governed and un-governable; all I suspect about armor and entrails. First I would freshen my tongue, abandon sentences crafted to know evil. . . . Speaking to the broken and the dead is too difficult for a mouth full of blood. Too holy an act for impure thoughts. (48)

Writing immediately after the 9/11 attacks, Morrison voices both the expected urges for revenge and the concern held by many Americans who worried that these acts of terrorism would feed the Bush administration's imperialistic agenda in the Middle East. Real compassion and grief cannot be accompanied by bloodlust, by "impure thoughts" that would fall precisely in line with political rhetorics of greed masked as ideology. Ann Cvetkovich writes of looking for ways to prevent the emotional responses to 9/11 "from being channeled into forms of patriotism and militarism that offer reassuring and simplified solutions. Although there have been enormous spectacles of public mourning in the wake of September 11, there has been little room for connecting grief with expressions of dissent from the actions of the U.S. government" (60). Rather than entering into political debates and campaigns, something he would not do purposefully until the United States invaded Iraq, Springsteen simply voices the human need for vengeance and then moves on. "Empty Sky," one of the starkest songs on the album, a song haunted by absence, acknowledges loss, pauses briefly over vengeance, before conjoining absence and continued life, as discussed above: "I want a kiss from your lips / I want an eye for an eye / I woke up this morning to an empty sky." Even "Further On (Up the Road)," a song with an ominously threatening speaker wearing "lucky graveyard boots" and "a smilin' skull ring," avoids any threat of violence and rests its message in song and sunny mornings: "a song to sing, keep me out of the cold." The song might nod briefly to conjoined vengeance and greed, "Where the miles are marked in blood and gold," but it moves past that two-headed monster with a steadily rocking beat toward the promise of meeting "further on up the road."

Instead of engaging for any length of time with revenge and violence, *The Rising* offers as an alternative a non-selective compassion. LaCapra calls responsiveness to the traumatic experiences of others an "empathic unsettlement," which disallows "closure in discourse and places in jeopardy harmonizing or spiritually uplifting accounts of extreme events from which we attempt to derive reassurance" (41). Arguing that the historian—or anyone, I would add—who writes about trauma should consider the trauma suffered by the perpetrator as well, LaCapra notes that the historian, "should attempt to understand and explain such behavior and experience as far as possible—even recognize the unsettling possibility of such behavior in him- or herself" (41). This historian, or anyone, becomes a witness to trauma, and Kalí Tal, in *Worlds of Hurt*, notes that "bearing witness is an aggressive act. It is born out of a refusal to bow to outside pressure to revise or to repress experience, a decision to embrace conflict rather than conformity, to endure a lifetime of anger and pain rather than to submit to the seductive pull of revision and repression. Its goal is change" (7). There are two songs on *The Rising* in which Springsteen, who has described himself and the E Street Band as witnesses, as I note above, bears witness to both sides in this conflict, to suffering in the West and in the Muslim world, and gestures towards change. Appearing in the middle of the album, "Worlds Apart" narrates the love held by an American soldier in Afghanistan for a Muslim woman: "In this dry and troubled country, your beauty remains. . . . 'Neath Allah's blessed rain, we remain worlds apart." The speaker and his lover are haunted by their reality, asking "May the living let us in, before the dead tear us apart," even as the song itself seems haunted by the vocals of Asif Ali Khan and his group of singers and musicians on the harmonium and tabla.

Springsteen made a bold move in including a group of Sufi Muslim musicians on a record about the trauma caused by Islamic extremists, but it is a move that insists on seeing at least a glimpse of both sides, something the American government refused to consider. A Sufi parable says that music is the sound made by the gates of Paradise as they open. As the facts behind the 9/11 attacks became public, we learned that the suicide-hijackers had been promised a Paradise full of virgins as their reward for carrying out plans made by others. In the penultimate song on *The Rising*, Springsteen deliberately undermines both Christian and Islamic notions of heavenly consolation. "Paradise" replaces the promise of heaven with absence as it describes first a Muslim suicide bomber taking the schoolbooks from his or her child's backpack and replacing them with a bomb. The bomber enters a "crowded marketplace" and waits "for paradise." The song then turns to a speaker who has lost a loved one in the attack on the Pentagon. Focused only on absence and loss, "I taste the void upon your lips," the speaker attempts suicide by drowning in his or her own search for paradise. Springsteen connects these speakers through the kisses they give their loved ones, the first a "breath of eternity," the second "a void," and through their attempted suicides. The first looks into faces, then holds his or her breath. The second, under water, must also have stopped breathing. The movement is one of sinking further down, but the speaker does not find paradise. Instead, he or she rises; after a bleak sinking, "I see you on the other side / I search for the peace in your eyes / But they're as empty as paradise," the speaker rejects death. "I break above the waves / I feel the sun upon my face" ends the song and reaffirms life for the second speaker. Because of their connected kisses and planned suicides, these speakers also seem connected in the return to life. The promise of heaven, everyone's heaven, is shown here to be empty and meaningless alongside a life well-lived. Perhaps the song ends with both of them in the sunlight. In any case, both embarked on horrible and horribly misguided plans, and in conjoining them, Springsteen insists that his audience have empathy for both speakers. With "Worlds Apart" and "Paradise," he suggests that differences between *us* and *them* are negligible in the extreme and movement toward vengeance will only perpetuate violence and suffering for everyone.

"MAY YOUR LOVE BRING US LOVE": WORKING THROUGH MOURNING

Thus far this discussion has addressed those songs on *The Rising* that face absence and look toward mourning, and those that reject vengeance to do the same. How then does Springsteen perform the work of mourning for people he has never met; how do we? How do any of us offer the

respectful grief we feel we must offer without lapsing into empty sentimentality, into untruthful connections? Toni Morrison writes of her own
fears about grieving for the dead of 9/11: "To speak to you, the dead of
September, I must not claim false intimacy or summon an overheated
heart glazed just in time for a camera. I must be steady and I must be
clear, knowing all the time that I have nothing to say—no words stronger
than the steel that pressed you into itself; no scripture older or more ele-
gant than the ancient atoms you have become" (49). However, Morrison
makes a gesture that connects her life to the lives lost and that enables
her to mourn: "And I have nothing to give either—except this gesture,
this thread thrown between your humanity and mine: *I want to hold you
in my arms* and as your soul got shot of its box of flesh to understand,
as you have done, the wit of eternity: its gift of unhinged release tearing
through the darkness of its knell" (49). Before giving up the victims of
9/11 to eternity, one must mourn them; in order to do that, one must
think of them as individuals, consider their lives and what was actually
lost. This is a consideration Springsteen undertook before he could write
the songs that work through mourning. Tyrangiel reports that

> Stacey Farrelly's husband Joe was a fire fighter with Manhattan Engine Co. 4 and,
> as his obituaries noted, a lifelong Springsteen fan. Recalls his widow: "At the
> beginning of October, I was home alone and, uh, heavily medicated. I picked up
> the phone, and a voice said, 'May I please speak to Stacey? This is Bruce Spring-
> steen.'" They talked for 40 minutes. "After I got off the phone with him, the
> world just felt a little smaller. I got through Joe's memorial and a good month
> and a half on that phone call." Suzanne Berger's husband Jim was memorial-
> ized in the *New York Times* under the headline "Fan of the Boss." She too got a
> call. "He said, 'I want to respect your privacy, but I just want you to know that I
> was touched, and I want to know more about your husband,'" she recalls. "He
> wanted to hear Jim's story, so I told him." (54)

Although Berger's story of the lives her husband saved or Farrelly's description of the daily love notes her husband wrote her are "obviously critical
to the creation of *The Rising*," as Tyrangiel argues, in the interview, "Springsteen freezes when the subject of the phone calls comes up. He doesn't
want publicity for ordinary kindness, and he doesn't want to be seen as
exploiting people whose suffering is well known" (54). Springsteen might
not want to discuss his communication with those who lost loved ones in
the attacks, but his contact with them brings him into the kind of connection that Morrison seeks. Hearing their stories and their pain gives him the
insight needed to power his imagination and creative force; their stories
and their pain immerse him in the compassion that drives the songs that
work through mourning. He brings the lives behind the names and the
faces in the obituaries into close enough contact that he and his audience

can enter into some understanding of just who and what we lost, and into mourning for them.

How, then, does this discourse of mourning function? The editors of Derrida's *The Work of Mourning,* a collection of eulogies written on the deaths of his friends and discussions of the eulogy as a genre, suggest that we are invited "to use these deaths and the lessons learned from them to understand the deaths of those dear to us" (8). Derrida finds that ultimately, the living can only give the dead something in us, our memory. He works not to abandon the concept of mourning, but to inhabit both the concept and the genre of mourning, and thus reinvent in a politics/poetics of mourning situated in speaking of the dead, their works, deeds, signature, essence, the best of them. One must speak of the dead, in Derrida's terms, "to combat all the forces that work to efface or conceal not just the names on the tombstones but the apostrophe of mourning" (30). This apostrophe, the address to the living, the eulogy, meets a number of needs, as Derrida asks, "What are we doing when we exchange these discourses? Over what are we keeping watch? Are we trying to negate death or retain it? Are we trying to put things in order, make amends, or settle our accounts, to finish unfinished business? . . . What in this century has come to replace the funeral oration?" (50–51):

> We could study the corpus of declaration in newspapers, on radio and television; we could analyze the recurrences, the rhetorical constraints, the political perspectives. . . . In its classical form, the funeral oration had a good side, especially when it permitted one to call out directly to the dead. . . . This is, of course, a supplementary fiction, for it is always the dead in me, always the others standing around the coffin whom I call out to. But because of its caricatured excess, the overstatement of this rhetoric at least pointed out that we ought not to remain among ourselves. The interactions of the living must be interrupted, the veil must be torn toward the other, the other dead in us though other still. (51–52)

Derrida is not writing about 9/11—he is, in fact, speaking on the occasion of Roland Barthes's death in 1980—but he could be. I, many of the scholars on whom I rely in this paper, and many others, including Springsteen, have spent a good deal of time studying the corpus of discourse about 9/11. And we have done so, in part, to call out to the dead, which is the first, if fictional, act of mourning, an act that brings us into community with other mourners and interrupts life in order to tear the veil and recognize fully what is lost. *The Rising* functions as that act and recognition; its songs give the dead a voice, in some instances, and call out to the dead, thereby giving a voice to the living, in most instances.

"Into the Fire" gives voice to the living and details what was lost. Told by a speaker who has lost his lover, one of the many emergency workers who died in the towers, the song is about loss and mourning, but it also eulogizes the woman who sacrificed herself. I want to point out that there is a pervasive tendency in criticism of this album to argue that in these songs about a lost loved one, emergency worker or not, the speaker is female and the lover male. On the one hand, Springsteen does occasionally write from the perspective of a woman, but only occasionally. And on the other hand, as Catharine MacKinnon makes clear in "State of Emergency," "The atrocities of September 11 were gender-neutral on the victim side. Women were people along with men that day, jumping from upper floors, rushing up and up and up to help, crawling down and down and down being helped, fleeing covered with fear, becoming ash" (7). "And there they are," she notes, "one at a time on the special pages of the *New York Times* every day for months, their faces smiling, before. In remembrance, they are individual, are everyone, do everything, had every prospect. Then on one crushing day, they were vaporized without regard to sex" (8). First of all, MacKinnon is as taken as is Springsteen with the rising motion of the rescue workers and the downward focus of those faced with absence. Second, like MacKinnon, Springsteen was aware that women numbered among each demographic of the dead of September 11. In 2002, *New York Magazine* reported that one-third of the dead in the towers were female, and that while the ratio of female to male emergency workers was considerably lower, female EMTs and police officers numbered among the dead. Springsteen may begin with the loss suffered by Stacey Farrelly and Suzanne Berger, but I think that for him to speak as a woman when it is not his habit would be to disrespect or disregard the many women who died, something I do not believe an artist so invested in speaking the truth would do, and I read these songs as spoken by a man mourning his loss. "Into the Fire," in MacKinnon's words, is about a woman who is individual, is everyone, did everything, and had every prospect. And it is about the man who must face the loss of her and all she was.

The second song on the album, "Into the Fire" follows the abiding movement of rising, the rising of a rescue worker as she ascends the stairs, but also the rising prayer of her lover. Facing the starkness of the disaster, "The sky was falling and streaked with blood," the song immediately counters falling with rising: "I heard you calling me, then you disappeared into dust / Up the stairs, into the fire / Up the stairs, into the fire." The pervasive repetition of these last two lines throughout the song suggests the kind of inarticulate wonder felt by many of us at the courage of the rescue workers who did their duty and climbed into an inferno. Derrida writes that in the face of death, being at a loss for words "says something, of course, about its truth, the impossible mourning that nonetheless remains at work, endlessly hollowing out the depths of our memories" (95). But if Springsteen seems to be using language to invoke speechlessness, he also allows, as does

Derrida, the dead to "speak, to turn speech over to him, his speech, and especially not to take it from him, not to take it in his place . . . to allow him to speak, to occupy his silence or to take up speech oneself only in order, if this is possible, to give it back to him" (95). The speaker of "Into the Fire" hears his lover speak, and then faces her death: "I need your kiss, but love and duty called you someplace higher / Somewhere up the stairs, into the fire." The majority of the song closely resembles a Buddhist prayer, one that honors the dead, in particular those attributes that she likely valued most in herself; in short, the prayer gives back to her what mattered:

> May your strength give us strength
> May your faith give us faith
> May your hope give us hope
> May your love bring us love

However, the prayer also engages the living in a community that faces death even as it seeks the resources to continue living. "May your love bring us love" reminds its speaker and Springsteen's vast audience that we are living and obliged to hold on to life.

The speaker's engagement with the work of mourning continues in his reflections on what he has lost. The final two stanzas purposefully blur the distinction between their love, both physical and emotional, and her sacrifice:

> You gave your love to see, in fields of red and autumn brown
> You gave your love to me and lay your young body down
> Up the stairs, into the fire
> . . . .
> It was dark, too dark to see, you held me in the light you gave
> You lay your hand on me
> Then walked into the darkness of your smoky grave
> Somewhere up the stairs, into the fire

Love is love, the song seems to say, and her love for him grounds the love that led to her death. "Into the Fire" demands that its audience both rise with the rescue worker and remain with her mourning lover. It offers not a false intimacy but a compassionate understanding about choices and loss. The speaker turns to a universal prayer offering a site for mourning and the hope for the world's reinvestment in life; he lifts the veil and embraces that soul "shot of its box of flesh," thereby allowing the dead to continue as the other, a positive and nourishing other, in us, allowing her "love to bring us love," her "hope to give us hope."

"You're Missing" turns from rising heroes and prayers to the many details of mourning as it juxtaposes presence with loss, in this case a woman and what that loss means to her family: "Shirts in the closet, shoes in the hall / Mama's in the kitchen, baby and all." The contents of daily life come up against the hard reality of this mother's death: "Everything is everything / Everything is everything / But you're missing." The song details a home suffering from loss—dishes, papers, and clothes strewn about—as it builds an urgent poignancy to make the point that "Your house is waiting, your house is waiting / For you to walk in, for you to walk in / But you're missing." The bridge emphasizes the speaker's mourning and his need to help his children understand and mourn:

> You're missing when I shut out the lights
> You're missing when I close my eyes
> You're missing when I see the sun rise
> . . . .
> Children are asking if it's alright
> Will you be in our arms tonight?

There is no rising in "You're Missing," only a detailed meditation on death and loss, phone calls from concerned friends and family, and a turn to mourning with a play on words, "Morning is morning, the evening falls I got / Too much room in my bed." The song ends with the teardrop that Derrida discusses, the tear through which the world is now suspended, "through which everything from then on, through which the world itself—and this day will come—will come to be reflected quivering, reflecting disappearance itself" (107). This is also the tear, Derrida argues, that reminds us "in holding life, to hold on to it" (110). The mourning speaker of "You're Missing" looks not up but down at the detritus of 9/11 and his own grief: "I got dust on my shoes, nothing but teardrops." Derrida writes that "death takes from us not only some particular life within the world, some moment that belongs to us, but, each time, without limit, someone through whom the world, and first of all our own world, will have opened up in both a finite and infinite—mortally infinite—way. That is the blurred and transparent testimony borne by this tear" (107). In looking down, Springsteen's speaker looks to and through what is lost and what is now closed; the song becomes a testimony, a eulogy to his dead lover, his children's dead mother. The pain of deep mourning in "You're Missing" seems reflected in this tear, offered up to listeners trying to understand and empathize with those in mourning.

The work of mourning is the labor or travail of suffering or of giving birth, Derrida suggests, which means the work of mourning can be understood as the work of one who "engenders, produces, and brings . . . to the light of day and gives something to be seen, who enables or empowers, who gives the force to know and to be able to see . . . the one who takes the pains to help us see, read, and think" (142). After the initial intense pain, there are more stages to mourning, and I turn now to two songs in which Springsteen engenders light and a return to life: "Countin' on a Miracle" and "Mary's Place." The first features an upbeat rhythm that balances a broken-hearted absence against an urgent need "to come through." Beginning with "It's a fairytale so tragic / There's no prince to break the spell," the song uses the trope of the fairytale to narrate the end of a love story, complete with royalty, wolves, magic, and a tower; it can thus be read outside the context of 9/11 as simply about a broken relationship. The song, however, elides its own metaphor as the speaker notes that while "Sleeping Beauty awakes from her dream / With her lover's kiss on her lips," for this lover, "Your kiss was taken from me / Now all I have is this." "This" is detailed in the bridge, and includes first her kiss, heart, and touch, and second the strength, hope, faith, and love that the lover is left with in "Into the Fire." While the chorus claims to be "countin' on a miracle / To come through," coming through, surviving profound loss, happens not by a miracle but by mourning, as the song reflects on both loss and life:

> Your heaven's here in my heart
> Our love's this dust beneath my feet
> Just this dust beneath my feet
> If I'm gonna live I'll lift my life to you
> Darlin' to you

"When one works at the work of mourning," Derrida writes, "one is already ... from the start, letting it work within oneself, and thus authorizing oneself to do it" (142). "Countin' on a Miracle" seems to me to be a song in which the mourning lover engages fully with the work of mourning; along with Springsteen's other mourning lovers, he seems to authorize the theme of mourning running through *The Rising*, the work that engenders and empowers, and brings life back to light.

"Once the sad reality of sacrifice is mourned," Symynkywicz notes of Springsteen's mourning songs, the "verses explode into the living gospel of lives well lived" (142). After the sacrificed lives detailed by mourning lovers in "Into the Fire," "You're Missing," and "Countin' on a Miracle," "Mary's Place" bursts into just that kind of explosion. Part of the explosion comes from the party and a gamut of other offerings intended to help the work of mourning, to offer the love or friendship that Derrida argues "would be nothing other than the passion, the endurance, and the patience of this work" (146). The song opens with imagery from various religions, "seven pictures of Buddha / The prophet's on my tongue / Eleven angels of mercy." However, these images and angels are "Sighing over that black hole in the sun," as the speaker mourns in the way Derrida describes as waging a clandestine war against death, a defiance "that follows death but also the mourning that is prepared and that we expect from the beginning to follow upon the death of those we love" (146). We expect to mourn, or be mourned by, those we love; we do not expect to lose each other in a terror attack. The song pairs death with the will to live in a number of ways:

> My heart's dark but it's risin'
> I'm pullin' all the faith I can see
> From that black hole on the horizon
> I hear your voice calling me

The speaker then turns to the first of three raucous choruses that begin by defiantly chanting "Let it rain," calling to everyone, "Meet me at Mary's place, we're gonna have a party," and asking, "How do we get this thing started?" With all the religious imagery, "Mary's place" might well be read as a synonym for heaven, but it seems more likely, given the detailed focus on embodiment and corporeal pleasure, that this party is more an earthy, earthly wake than an ascension. "This thing" is the start of a relationship or a party or both; it heralds a rocking good time with music playing loud and the furniture "out on the front porch," but in the song's movement from darkness into light, in its depiction of the death of a loved one, the thing that needs to get started is life after loss.

The second stanza places a party alongside death, like a wake: "Familiar faces around me / Laughter fills the air / Your loving grace surrounds me." In the midst of fun, loss is recognized and becomes part of a communal embrace: "Music's up loud / I dream of you in my arms / And I lose myself in the crowd." The middle chorus changes the question to ask, "how do you live broken-hearted," and the answer in the following stanza suggests that if getting a party started is the way back to living, then holding memory close is the way to mourn. As the stanza builds to the climax of a terrific party, the speaker holds a picture in a locket close to his heart. It offers a "light shining in my breast / Leading me through the dark," a memory that in turn offers the ability to return fully to life. The speaker/singer details the party in a self-reflexive manner that shows how he can flood the darkness with light, while the crowd chants "Turn it up" and fills the party with joy:

> Your favorite record's on the turntable
> I drop the needle and pray
> [Turn it up]
> Band's countin' out midnight
> [Turn it up]
> Floor's rumblin' loud
> [Turn it up]
> Singer's callin' up daylight
> [Turn it up]
> And waitin' for that shout from the crowd
> [Turn it up]

The final chorus, amid repetitions of "Turn it up" and "Let it rain," offers the resilience and defiance needed to turn from death and reengage with life.

(INTERCALARY) "YOUR KISS AND I'M ALIVE": REAFFIRMING LIFE

From the youthful promise to Rosalita that "The only lover I'm ever gonna need's your soft sweet little girl's tongue," on *The Wild, the Innocent & the E Street Shuffle* (1973), to the almost sedately seductive, "I finger the hem of your dress, my universe at rest" on *Working on a Dream* (2009), Springsteen has written the erotic, but never so explicitly as on *The Rising*. I speak of the erotic here, not crass sexuality or intercourse driven by power imbalances: the joy of "Maria's Bed" rather than the painful exchange between speaker and prostitute in "Reno," both on *Devils & Dust* (2005). I speak of the exchange between consenting adults that, as Audre Lorde argues, is a source of power and knowledge, of creative energy, and is "an assertion of the life force" (55). In "Uses of the Erotic," Lorde makes clear the power of communication and knowledge inherent in the erotic: "the sharing of joy, whether physical, emotional, psychic, or intellectual, forms a bridge between the sharers which can be the basis for understanding" (56). This erotic sharing of joy might also enable a sharing of pain, a means of understanding loss, and a way of working though mourning. In the way we want comforting, satisfying food at funerals, sharing physical joy seems a way of engaging with life in the face of death. Born of chaos and creativity, the erotic reasserts "the life force" (55). With its overarching metaphor of ascension, *The Rising* offers erotic moments of rising passion that also explode back into living.

"Let's Be Friends (Skin to Skin)" is the first of these moments. The lyrics combine a number of themes; the song might be about a postmodern "friends with benefits" proposition, a more meaningful sexual relationship, or a reconciliation of lovers. However, the second stanza turns away from the past and into a relationship of some kind with "The time has come to let the past be history / Yeah, if we could just start talkin'"; further, the song ends with friends united in a common effort, "There's a lot of walls need tearing down / Together we could take them down one by one," and thus points toward a wider reconciliation. The song begins with a fascinated would-be lover, "watchin' you a long time," who decides "The time is now maybe we could get skin to skin." The chorus repeatedly cautions "Don't know when this chance might come again / Good times got a way of coming to an end," but getting "skin to skin," as the title also desires, becomes the way to hold off the bad times that come with trauma and death. From the first chorus on, Springsteen's voice is entwined with that of his wife and

backup singer, Patti Scialfa. Through the second and third stanzas, Scialfa's
soprano winds around Springsteen's baritone, sometimes rising above and
sometimes underpinning him. Through the choruses, they exchange "Let's
be friends / Baby let's be friends" in an entwined call-and-response that
seems every bit as erotic as getting "skin to skin." With "Let's Be Friends,"
the poet who has for decades crooned "it ain't no sin to be glad you're
alive" urges his audience toward connections far more profound than those
made through fear, toward relationship and citizenship founded in shared
responsibility. As the song sets aside the past, tears down walls, and looks
to the future, it suggests that the erotic might be an important and effective
way to reengage with life after trauma and loss.

"The Fuse" provides a more explicitly erotic response to death. It is the
song William Carlos Williams calls for in *Paterson*, as he writes, "Sing me a
song to make death tolerable, a song / of a man and a woman: the riddle of
a man / and a woman" (107). Dark images of the ceremonies surrounding
death open "The Fuse," but they quickly give way to the images and movements surrounding domesticity and passion:

> Down at the court house they're ringin' the flag down
> Long black line of cars snakin' slow through town
> Red sheets snappin' on the line
> With this ring will you be mine
> The fuse is burning
> (Shut out the lights)
> The fuse is burning
> (Come on let me do you right)

The ordinariness of an autumn day gives way to a funeral procession and
a sky rife with the detritus of 9/11: "Trees on fire with the first fall's frost /
Long black line in front of Holy Cross / Blood moon risin' in a sky of black
dust." From disaster the speaker turns to ask his partner "Tell me Baby who
do you trust?" as he urges her toward the bedroom. Noting that we are
taught early to separate the erotic from other vital areas of our emotional
and physical lives, Lorde argues against these limits: "For as we begin to
recognize our deepest feelings, we begin to give up, of necessity, being
satisfied with suffering and self-negation, and with the numbness which
so often seems like their only alternative" (58). Under repetitions of "The
fuse is burning," the speaker croons the parenthetical promise, "(Shut out
the lights. . . . Come on let me do you right)," and builds erotic connections between deepest mourning and deepest love. In the face of 9/11, the
song rejects ignited jet fuel for ignited passions, and answers death with an
explosion of life.

The song's bridge begins on a note more ominous than funerals and
hearses as it gestures toward the paranoia that gripped America and the

Western world after the terror attacks: "Tires on the highway hissin' something's comin' / Feel the wires in the tree tops hummin' / Devil's on the horizon line." However, its final line, "Your kiss and I'm alive," rejects paranoia and fear and turns to living in the moment. "The erotic is not a question only of what we do," Lorde offers, "it is a question of how acutely and fully we can feel in the doing" (54). Can we mourn the dead more fully through the erotic? "The Fuse" suggests that we can:

> Quiet afternoon in the empty house
> On the edge of the bed you slip off your blouse
> The room is burning with the noon sun
> Your bittersweet taste on my tongue

Turning from trauma and death, funerals and fear, to a sunny afternoon of lovemaking while the children are at school seems a way to sort out chaos and chaotic emotional responses. In "The Fuse," the erotic affords a sacramental act where the physical and emotional connect and affirm the continuity of existence. The erotic exchange in this song seems as much a requiem as the service at the Court House or the mass at Holy Cross; it functions as the eulogy Derrida insists upon, a way to honor the dead by living fiercely.

"A DREAM OF LIFE": TURNING TO LIFE

In his eulogy for Louis Althusser, Derrida quotes at length from Althusser's commentary on Marx, comments about shared ideology and experience: "We have the same war at our gates, and a handsbreadth from us, if not in us, the same horrible blindness, the same dust in our eyes, the same earth in our mouths. We even have the same dawn and night, we skirt the same abysses . . . the same history" (quoted in Derrida 118). As Derrida well knew, the eulogy is for the living who share the experience of mourning, if no other. The events of 9/11 invoked the kind of general compassion and empathy that insisted millions of bystanders share the disaster in their imaginations, including Springsteen. "When you're putting yourself into shoes you haven't worn," he reflects, "you have to be . . . just thoughtful, is the way that I'd put it. Just thoughtful. You call on your craft, and you go searching for it, and hopefully what makes people listen is that over the years you've been serious and honest. That's where your creative authority comes from. That's how people know you're not just taking a ride" (quoted in Tyrangiel 58). "The Rising" is a deeply meditative response to death, a poem that makes loss immediate to its audience even as it looks past mourning to offer hope. It turns that image of rescue workers rising up through the smoke and debris into a rising up for hope, for justice, and for life.

The song opens with first-person perspective of 9/11:

> Can't see nothin' in front of me
> Can't see nothin' coming up behind
> I make my way through this darkness
> I can't feel nothing but this chain that binds me
> Lost track of how far I've gone
> How far I've gone, how high I've climbed
> On my back's a sixty-pound stone
> On my shoulder a half mile of line

The chorus offers an affirmation of life, calling people to come into community for an indeterminate rising, a lifting of spirits or souls, perhaps, a show of solidarity in the face of uncertainty, a rejection of more death and destruction:

> Come on up for the rising
> Come on up, lay your hands in mine
> Come on up for the rising
> Come on up for the rising tonight

In *The Words and Music of Bruce Springsteen*, Kirkpatrick reads this song as told by a rescue worker in the midst of 9/11, carrying his equipment up the stairs, seeing "spirits above and behind me / Faces gone black, eyes burnin' bright," a reading born out by Springsteen's explication of the song on VH1's *Storytellers*. However, the song seems both about a 9/11 firefighter and about more than that; in his discussion, Springsteen repeatedly uses the word "transformation" to explain these lyrics. He even describes the several repetitions of the line "Li, li, li, li, li, li, li, li, li," as part of the "unspoken subtext of rock and roll," in that "they say sing with me; they also say stand alongside me." As Kirkpatrick and other critics have noted, the religious imagery is pervasive here, but it is also a religious viewpoint heavily invested in corporeal life. The disaster may put this rescue worker in the Lord's "fiery light," he may see "Mary in the garden" with "holy pictures" of their children, but he *feels* "their precious blood" both bind him and mix with his. He wants to feel her arms around him, and his dream is not of death but of life: "A dream of life comes to me / Like a catfish dancin' on the end of my line." The song might be one of the most positive affirmations of life on the album, and is likely the reason that "The Rising" was the first song played over the loudspeakers after Barack Obama's history-making first speech as U.S. president-elect. It might also be the signal that Springsteen was going to get political. As he told Jann Wenner, "I knew after we invaded Iraq that I was going to be involved in the election. It made me angry. We started to talk about it onstage. I take my three minutes a night for what I call my public-service announcement" (74).

The bridge in "The Rising" might be his most profoundly hopeful public-service announcement. It is the type of cultural-political inquiry Joan Cocks describes that "makes its major moves back and forth between some individual train of thought or action or sensibility and the larger, collective political and cultural world" (14). As it moves from the immediate experience of the speaker to wider concerns, the bridge forces a turn away from disaster and refuses to codify trauma into a perpetual reality, as it turns to light and life, and changes the burning towers into a burning wind made of spirit:

> Sky of blackness and sorrow (a dream of life)
> Sky of love, sky of tears (a dream of life)
> Sky of glory and sadness (a dream of life)
> Sky of mercy, sky of fear (a dream of life)
> Sky of memory and shadow (a dream of life)
> Your burnin' wind fills my arms tonight
> Sky of longing and emptiness (a dream of life)
> Sky of fullness, sky of blessed life (a dream of life)

Springsteen refuses to allow 9/11 to turn into the sort of unspoken warfare that Michel Foucault argues is re-inscribed by political power "in social institutions, in economic inequalities, in language, in the bodies themselves of each and every one of us" (90). Instead, he rises past that, past a devastated landscape of absence into "a dream of life" blessed and lived fully. In an album that faces trauma and absence, rejects vengeance, and mourns with the deepest hope and loving kindness, "The Rising" transforms this death into an abiding communal prayer for life:

> Come on up for the rising
> Come on up, lay your hands in mine
> Come on up for the rising
> Come on up for the rising tonight.

Credits

The editors and publisher gratefully acknowledge permission for the use of the following material:

"This Hard Land" by Bruce Springsteen. Copyright © 1998 Bruce Springsteen (ASCAP). Reprinted by permission. International copyright secured. All rights reserved.

"This Life" by Bruce Springsteen. Copyright © 2009 Bruce Springsteen (ASCAP). Reprinted by permission. International copyright secured. All rights reserved.

"Thunder Road" by Bruce Springsteen. Copyright © 1975 Bruce Springsteen, renewed © 2003 Bruce Springsteen (ASCAP). Reprinted by permission. International copyright secured. All rights reserved.

"Thundercrack" by Bruce Springsteen. Copyright © 1998 Bruce Springsteen (ASCAP). Reprinted by permission. International copyright secured. All rights reserved.

"Trouble in Paradise" by Bruce Springsteen. Copyright © 1998 Bruce Springsteen (ASCAP). Reprinted by permission. International copyright secured. All rights reserved.

"Tunnel of Love" by Bruce Springsteen. Copyright © 1987 Bruce Springsteen (ASCAP). Reprinted by permission. International copyright secured. All rights reserved.

"Two Faces" by Bruce Springsteen. Copyright © 1987 Bruce Springsteen (ASCAP). Reprinted by permission. International copyright secured. All rights reserved.

"Two for the Road" by Bruce Springsteen. Copyright © 1998 Bruce Springsteen (ASCAP). Reprinted by permission. International copyright secured. All rights reserved.

"Used Cars" by Bruce Springsteen. Copyright © 1982 Bruce Springsteen (ASCAP). Reprinted by permission. International copyright secured. All rights reserved.

"Valentine's Day" by Bruce Springsteen. Copyright © 1987 Bruce Springsteen (ASCAP). Reprinted by permission. International copyright secured. All rights reserved.

"Waitin' on a Sunny Day" by Bruce Springsteen. Copyright © 2002 Bruce Springsteen (ASCAP). Reprinted by permission. International copyright secured. All rights reserved.

"Where the Bands Are" by Bruce Springsteen. Copyright © 1998 Bruce Springsteen (ASCAP). Reprinted by permission. International copyright secured. All rights reserved.

"Wild Billy's Circus Story" by Bruce Springsteen. Copyright © 1974 Bruce Springsteen, renewed © 2002 Bruce Springsteen (ASCAP). Reprinted by permission. International copyright secured. All rights reserved.

"Working on a Dream" by Bruce Springsteen. Copyright © 2008 Bruce Springsteen (ASCAP). Reprinted by permission. International copyright secured. All rights reserved.

"Worlds Apart" by Bruce Springsteen. Copyright © 2002 Bruce Springsteen (ASCAP). Reprinted by permission. International copyright secured. All rights reserved.

"Wreck on the Highway" by Bruce Springsteen. Copyright © 1980 Bruce Springsteen (ASCAP). Reprinted by permission. International copyright secured. All rights reserved.

"You're Missing" by Bruce Springsteen. Copyright © 2002 Bruce Springsteen (ASCAP). Reprinted by permission. International copyright secured. All rights reserved.

"Youngstown" by Bruce Springsteen. Copyright © 1995 Bruce Springsteen (ASCAP). Reprinted by permission. International copyright secured. All rights reserved.

Bibliography

AC/DC. *Back in Black*. Sony, 1980. CD.

Alter, Robert. *The Art of Biblical Narrative*. New York: Basic Books, 1981. Print.

Alterman, Eric. *It Ain't No Sin to Be Glad You're Alive: The Promise of Bruce Springsteen*. Boston: Little, Brown, 1999. Print.

"Asbury Park's Bard." *New York Times*. Web. 8 April 2010.

Auxier, Randall E. and Anderson, Doug, eds. *Bruce Springsteen and Philosophy: Darkness on the Edge of Truth*. Chicago: Open Court, 2008. Print.

Backstreets #85 22.1 (Spring 2006). Print.

Bader, Michael J. "Bruce Springsteen, Tom Joad, and the Politics of Meaning." *Tikkun* 11.2 (1996): 32–33. Print.

Badlands. Dir. Terrence Malick. Perf. Martin Sheen, Sissy Spacek, and Warren Oates. Warner Bros., 1973. Film.

Bakhtin, Mikhail. "Discourse in the Novel." *The Dialogic Imagination*. Trans. Caryl Emerson and Michael Holquist. Ed. Michael Holquist. Austin: University of Texas Press, 1981. 259–422. Print.

Barthes, Roland. *Image, Music, Text*. Trans. Stephen Heath. New York: Hill and Wang, 1977. Print.

Baudrillard, Jean. *Simulations*. Trans. Paul Foss, Paul Patton, and Philip Beitchman. New York: Semiotext(e), 1983. Print.

Bauman, Richard. *Verbal Art as Performance*. Prospect Heights, IL: Waveland, 1977. Print.

Beaver, Ninette. *Caril*. New York: Lippincott, 1974. Print.

Bennett, Andy. "Music, Space and Place." *Music, Space and Place: Popular Music and Cultural Identity*. Eds. Sheila Whiteley, Andy Bennett, and Stan Hawkins. Burlington: Ashgate, 2004. 2–8. Print.

Bible. *The Lost Books of the Bible*. Ed. William Hone. Trans. Jeremiah Jones [Apocryphal books including *The Gospel of Nicodemus*] and William Wake [Apocryphal epistles]. [Originally published in London in 1820.] New York: Random House & Crown, 1979. Print.

Bible. *Holy Bible.* New Catholic Edition. Translated from the Latin Vulgate. *The Old Testament,* Douay Version. *The New Testament,* Confraternity Edition. New York: Catholic Book Publishing, 1948. Print.

Bird, Elizabeth. "'Is That Me, Baby?' Image, Authenticity, and the Career of Bruce Springsteen." *American Studies* 35.2 (1994): 39–57. Print.

Blanchot, Maurice. *The Writing of the Disaster.* Trans. Ann Smock. Lincoln: University of Nebraska Press, 1986. Print.

Bokenkotter, Thomas. *A Concise History of the Catholic Church.* Revised and Expanded Edition. New York and London: Doubleday, 2004. Print.

Boucher, Geoff. "Bruce Springsteen, Tour 2009: Working on a Dream." *Los Angeles Times* 5 April 2009. Web. 9 April 2009.

Boyarin, Daniel. *Intertextuality and the Reading of Midrash.* Bloomington: Indiana University Press, 1990. Print.

Brackett, David. *The Pop, Rock, and Soul Reader: Histories and Debates.* New York and Oxford: Oxford University Press, 2005. Print.

"A Brief Account of the Catfish as a Cultural Symbol in Japan." *Scribd.com.* Web. 20 February 2010.

Bruce Springsteen: The Rolling Stone *Files—The Ultimate Compendium of Interviews, Articles, Facts, and Opinions from the Files of* Rolling Stone. Intro. Parke Puterbaugh. New York: Hyperion, 1996. Print.

Bruce Springsteen. VH1 Storytellers. Sony, 2005. DVD.

"Bruce's Ghost Stories." *Backstreets* 53 (Summer 1996): 16. Print.

Buber, Martin. *I and Thou.* Trans. Walter Kaufmann. New York: Scribner's, 1970. Print.

Budd, Malcolm. *Music and the Emotions: The Philosophical Theories.* London: Routledge, 1985. Print.

Burke, Toby. "Sidebar." *Uncut Legends #4: Springsteen Special Issue.* 1.4 (2004): 24. Print.

Caffrey, Dan. "Where We Live: The Jersey Shore Sound." *Consequence of Sound. Consequenceofsound.net.* 13 January 2009. Web. 21 March 2010.

Caruth, Cathy. *Unclaimed Experience: Trauma, Narrative, and History.* Baltimore: Johns Hopkins University Press, 1996. Print.

Catechism of the Catholic Church. Liguori, MO: Liguori, 1994. Print.

"Catholicized! Introducing 'Jesus Was an Only Son.'" *Backstreets* 83/84 (Winter 2005/2006): 100. Print.

Cavicchi, Daniel. *Tramps Like Us: Music and Meaning Among Springsteen Fans.* New York and Oxford: Oxford University Press, 1998. Print.

Chapman, George. *Chapman's Homer: The Odyssey.* Ed. Allardyce Nicoll. Bollingen Series XLI. Princeton: Princeton University Press, 1956. Print.

Cocks, Joan. *The Oppositional Imagination: Feminism, Critique, and Political Theory.* New York: Routledge, 1989. Print.

Coles, Robert. *Bruce Springsteen's America: The People Listening, A Poet Singing.* New York: Random House, 2003. Print.

Covach, John. "Form in Rock Music: A Primer." *Engaging Music: Essays in Music Analysis.* Ed. Deborah Stein. New York and Oxford: Oxford University Press, 2005. 65–76. Print.

Cowie, Jefferson, and Lauren Boehm. "Dead Man's Town: 'Born in the U.S.A.,' Social History, and Working Class Identity." *American Quarterly* 58.2 (June 2006): 353–78. Print.

Coyne, Kevin. "His Hometown." In Sawyers, ed., *Racing in the Street*, 366–70. Print.

Cullen, Jim. *The American Dream: A Short History of an Idea That Shaped a Nation.* New York: Oxford University Press, 2003. Print.

———. *Born in the U.S.A.: Bruce Springsteen and the American Tradition.* New York: HarperCollins, 1997. Print.

———. "Bruce Springsteen's Ambiguous Musical Politics in the Reagan Era." *Popular Music and Society* 16.2 (1992): 1–22. Print.

Cvetkovich, Ann. "Trauma Ongoing." *Trauma at Home: After 9/11.* Ed. Judith Greenberg. Lincoln: University of Nebraska Press, 2003. 60–66. Print.

D'Acierno, Pellegrino. "After the Long Good-bye: From Frank Zappa to Bruce Springsteen and Madonna." In Sawyers. 300–304. Print.

Dante Alighieri. *The Divine Comedy of Dante Alighieri.* Trans. Allen Mandelbaum. 3 vols. [Includes the original Italian.] New York: Bantam Classics, 1984. Print.

Davis, Fred. *Yearning for Yesterday: A Sociology of Nostalgia.* New York: Free, 1979. Print.

Dawidoff, Nicholas. "The Pop Populist." In Sawyers, ed., *Racing In the Street,* 246–65. Print.

Derrida, Jacques. *The Work of Mourning.* Ed. Pascale-Anne Brault and Michael Naas. Chicago: University of Chicago Press, 2001. Print.

Dickinson, Emily. *The Poems of Emily Dickinson: Variorum Edition.* Ed. R.W. Franklin. Cambridge: Belknap Press of Harvard University Press, 1998. Print.

Donnelly, Tim. "Here Comes the Sun: NOLA gets the Rainbow Sign as Springsteen Lights up Jazz Fest." *Backstreets* [# 85] 52–58. Print.

Dylan, Bob. *Blonde on Blonde.* Columbia Records, 1966. CD.

Elliott, Anthony. *The Mourning of John Lennon.* Berkeley: University of California Press, 1999. Print.

Foley, John Miles. *The Singer of Tales in Performance.* Bloomington: Indiana University Press, 1995. Print.

Foucault, Michel. *Power/Knowledge: Selected Interviews and Other Writings 1972–1977.* New York: Pantheon, 1980. Print.

Fricke, David. "Bruce's Dream." *Rolling Stone* 5 February 2009: 44. Print.

Frith, Simon. "The Real Thing—Bruce Springsteen." In Sawyers. 130–39. Print.

———. *Music for Pleasure.* New York: Routledge, 1988. Print.

Garman, Bryan K. "The Ghost of History: Bruce Springsteen, Woody Guthrie and the Hurt Song." In Sawyers. 221–30. Print.

———. "Old Time Rock & Roll." *Backstreets* [#85] 25–31. Print.

———. "Models of Charity and Spirit: Bruce Springsteen, 9/11, and the War on Terror." *Music in the Post-9/11 World.* Eds. Jonathan Ritter and J. Martin Daughtry. New York: Routledge, 2007. 71–90. Print.

———. *A Race of Singers: Whitman's Working Class Hero from Guthrie to Springsteen.* Chapel Hill and London: University of North Carolina Press, 2000. Print.

Golding, Arthur. *Ovid's Metamorphoses.* The Arthur Golding Translation of 1567. Ed. John Frederick Nims. Philadelphia: Paul Dry Books, 2000. Print.

Goodman, Fred. *The Mansion on the Hill: Dylan, Young, Geffen, Springsteen, and the Head-On Collision of Rock and Commerce.* New York: Times, 1997. Print.

The Grapes of Wrath. Dir. John Ford. Perf. Henry Fonda, Jane Darwell, and John Carradine. Twentieth Century Fox, 1940. Film.

Greeley, Andrew M. "The Catholic Imagination of Bruce Springsteen." *America: The National Catholic Weekly* 6 February 1988: 110–115. Print.

Greenberg, Judith. "Wounded New York." *Trauma at Home: After 9/11.* Ed. Judith Greenberg. Lincoln: University of Nebraska Press, 2003. 21–35. Print.

Greenblatt, Stephen. *Hamlet in Purgatory.* Princeton: Princeton University Press, 2001. Print.

Grossberg, Lawrence. "Rockin' with Reagan, or the Mainstreaming of Postmodernity." *Cultural Critique* 10 (1988): 123–49. Print.

"Ground War. February 24–28, 1991." Gulf War: 1991. *Saddam's Iraq: Key Events.* BBC News. Web. 10 January 2010.

Guterman, Jimmy. *Runaway American Dream: Listening to Bruce Springsteen.* Cambridge, MA: Da Capo Press, 2005. Print.

Hahn, Scott. *Hail, Holy Queen: The Mother of God in the Word of God.* New York and London: Doubleday, Image, 2001. Print.

HaLevi, Jehuda. *Selected Poems of Jehudah HaLevi.* Ed. Heinrich Brody. Philadelphia: The Jewish Publication Society of America, 1954. Print.

Hampton, Howard. "Nebraska." *The Rose and the Briar: Death, Love and Liberty in the American Ballad.* Ed. Sean Wilentz and Greil Marcus. New York: Norton, 2005. 329–46. Print.

Heidegger, Martin. "What Is Metaphysics?" Trans. R. F. C. Hull and Alan Crick. Kaufmann 233–79. Print.

High Fidelity. Dir. Stephen Frears. Perf. John Cusack. Dog Star Films, 2000. Film.

Hines, Geoffrey. *Born in the U.S.A.* New York: Continuum, 2005. Print.

Hoffman, Tod. "Rock and Redemption." *Queen's Quarterly* 109.3 (2002): 397–401. Print.

Hubbard, Phil. "Space/Place." *Cultural Geography: A Critical Dictionary of Key Concepts.* Ed. David Atkinson, et al. New York: I.B. Tauris, 2005. 41–48. Print.

Ivy, Bob. "The Bard of Asbury Park: Review of *Runaway American Dream* by Jimmy Guterman." *Washington Post* 17 July 2005. Washingtonpost.com. Web. 13 April 2010.

"Jon Stewart Speaks About Bruce Springsteen at the Kennedy Center Honors." *YouTube.com.* Web. 8 April 2010.

Katz, Cindi. "Social Formations: Thinking about Society, Identity, Power and Resistance." *Key Concepts in Geography.* Eds. Sarah L. Holloway, Stephen P. Rice, and Gill Valentine. London: Sage, 2003. 249–66. Print.

Kierkegaard, Søren. *The Sickness unto Death.* Trans. Walter Lowrie. Princeton: Princeton University Press, 1941. Print.

Kimmel, Michael S. *Manhood in America: A Cultural History.* 2nd. ed. New York: Oxford University Press, 2006. Print.

Kirkpatrick, Rob. *The Words and Music of Bruce Springsteen.* Westport, CT and London: Praeger, 2007. (Also published in paper as *Magic in the Night: The Words and Music of Bruce Springsteen.* New York: St. Martin's Griffin, 2009.) Print.

Koestler, Arthur. *The Age of Longing*. New York: Hutchinson, 1970. Print.

Kot, Greg. "Album Review: Springsteen's *Working on a Dream* Underwhelms." *Chicago Tribune*. Web. 22 January 2009.

Kreeft, Peter J. *Catholic Christianity: A Complete Catechism of Catholic Beliefs Based on the Catechism of the Catholic Church*. San Francisco: Ignatius Press, 2001. Print.

Krims, Adam. *Music and Urban Geography*. New York: Routledge, 2007. Print.

LaCapra, Dominick. *Writing History, Writing Trauma*. Baltimore: Johns Hopkins University Press, 2001. Print.

Lawson, Lewis A., and Victor Kramer, eds. *Conversations with Walker Percy*. Jackson: University Press of Mississippi, 1993. Print.

Leppert, Richard, and George Lipsitz. "'Everybody's Lonesome for Somebody': Age, the Body and Experience in the Music of Hank Williams." *Popular Music* 9.3 (1990): 259–74. Print.

Levinas, Emmanuel. *Totality and Infinity*. Trans. Alphonso Lingis. Pittsburgh: Duquesne University Press, 1969. Print.

Levy, Joe. "The Rolling Stone Interview with Bruce Springsteen." *Rolling Stone* 1 November 2007: 50–56. Print.

Loder, Kurt. "The *Rolling Stone* Interview: Bruce Springsteen." (6 December 1984). Rpt. in *Bruce Springsteen: The* Rolling Stone *Files*. New York: Hyperion, 1996: 151–65. Print.

Lord, Alfred S. *The Singer of Tales*. Cambridge, MA: Harvard University Press, 1960. Print.

Lorde, Audre. "Uses of the Erotic." *Sister Outsider: Essays and Speeches*. New York: Crossing, 1984. 53–59. Print.

Mackey-Kallis, Susan, and Ian McDermott. "Bruce Springsteen, Ronald Reagan and the American Dream." *Popular Music and Society* 16.4 (1992): 1–9. Print.

MacKinnon, Catharine A. "State of Emergency." *Women's Review of Books* 19.6 (March 2002): 7–8. Print.

Manual of Prayers. The Official Prayer Book of the Catholic Church. Baltimore and New York: John Murphy, 1916. Print.

Marcus, Greil. "Days between Stations: Nostalgia Isn't What It Used to Be (Beatles' 'Real Love' and Songs of the Kingston Trio)." *Interview* 26.6 (1996). Web. 14 February 2010.

Marsh, Dave. *Born to Run: The Bruce Springsteen Story*. New York: Doubleday, 1979. Print.

———. *Bruce Springsteen on Tour 1968–2005*. New York: Bloomsbury, 2006. Print.

———. *Bruce Springsteen: Two Hearts. The Definitive Biography, 1972–2003*. New York: Routledge, 2004. Print.

———. *Glory Days: Bruce Springsteen in the 1980s*. New York: Pantheon, 1987. Print.

Marshall, Lee. "Bob Dylan and the Academy." In *The Cambridge Companion to Bob Dylan*. Ed. Kevin J. H. Dettmar. Cambridge, UK: Cambridge University Press, 2009, 100–109. Print.

Masur, Louis P. *Runaway Dream: Born to Run and Bruce Springsteen's American Vision*. New York: Bloomsbury Press, 2009. Print.

May, Todd. *Gilles Deleuze: An Introduction*. Cambridge: Cambridge University Press, 2005. Print.

McCarthy, Kate. "Deliver Me from Nowhere: Bruce Springsteen and the Myth of the American Promised Land." *God in the Details: American Religion in Popular Culture.* Ed. Eric Mazur and Kate McCarthy. New York: Routledge, 2001, 23–45. Print.

Milton, John. *Paradise Lost.* Ed. Gordon Teskey. Norton Critical Ed. New York: Norton, 2005. Print.

Moore, Allan F. *Rock: The Primary Text—Developing a Musicology of Rock.* 2nd ed. Aldershot and Burlington, VT: Ashgate, 2001. Print.

Morrison, Toni. "The Dead of September 11." *Vanity Fair* 495 (November 2001): 48–49. Print.

Moss, Pamela. "Where Is the Promised Land? Class and Gender in Bruce Springsteen's Rock Lyrics," *Geografiska Annaler* 74.3 (1992): 167–87. Print.

Nabokov, Vladimir. Foreword. 1970. *Mary: A Novel,* by Nabokov. New York: Vintage, 1989. xiv. Print.

Nietzsche, Friederich. *Thus Spoke Zarathustra.* Trans. Walter Kaufmann. *The Portable Nietzsche.* New York: Viking Press, 1954. 115–439. Print.

Nussbaum, Martha C. *Upheavals of Thought: The Intelligence of Emotions.* Cambridge: Cambridge University Press, 2001. Print.

Obama, Barack. "Speech." *Kennedy Center Honors Bruce Springsteen.* 30 December 2009. *YouTube.* Web. 20 March 2010.

O'Connor, Flannery. *The Complete Stories.* New York: Farrar, 1971. Print.

———. *"A Good Man is Hard to Find": Women Writers: Texts and Contexts.* Ed. Frederick Asals. New Brunswick, NJ: Rutgers University Press, 1993. Print.

———. *The Habit of Being: Letters of Flannery O'Connor.* Ed. Sally Fitzgerald. New York: Farrar, 1979. Print.

———. *Mystery and Manners: Occasional Prose.* Eds. Sally Fitzgerald and Robert Fitzgerald. New York: Farrar, 1969. Print.

———. *Wise Blood.* 2nd ed. New York: Farrar, 1962. Print.

Ong, Walter J. *Orality and Literacy: The Technologizing of the Word.* London: Routledge, 1982. Print.

Palmer, Gareth. "Springsteen and Authentic Masculinity." *Sexing the Groove: Popular Music and Gender.* Ed. Sheila Whitely, New York: Routledge, 1997, 100–17. Print.

Pareles, Jon. "Bruce Almighty: The Boss Turns to God." *New York Times* 24 April 2005, late ed., sec. 2: 1+. Print.

———. "Bruce Springsteen." *New York Times* online, 13 March 2009. Web. 8 April 2010.

———. "The Rock Laureate." *New York Times,* 1 February 2009, "Arts and Leisure" sec., 26. Print.

Percy, Walker. "Diagnosing the Modern Malaise." *Signposts in a Strange Land.* Ed. Patrick Samway. New York: Farrar, Strauss, and Giroux, 1991. 204–21. Print.

———. *The Last Gentleman.* New York, Farrar, Strauss and Giroux, 1966. Print.

———. *The Message in the Bottle: How Queer Man Is, How Queer Language Is, and What One Has to Do with the Other.* New York: Picador USA, 2000. Print.

———. *The Moviegoer.* New York: Alfred A. Knopf, 1961. Print.

———. *The Second Coming.* New York: Farrar, Straus, and Giroux, 1980. Print.

———. *Signposts in a Strange Land.* Edited and with an introduction by Patrick Samway. New York: Picador USA, 2000. Print.

———. "Symbol as Hermeneutic in Existentialism." *The Message in the Bottle: How Queer Man Is, How Queer Language Is, and What One Has to Do with the Other.* 1975. New York: Farrar, Straus, and Giroux, 1980. 277–87. Print.

Percy, Will. "Rock and Read: Will Percy Interviews Bruce Springsteen." *DoubleTake* 4:2 (Spring 1998): 36–43. Print.

———. "Rock and Read: Will Percy Interviews Bruce Springsteen." In Sawyers. 305–20. Print.

———. "Will Percy Interviews Bruce Springsteen." *Writing Work: Writers on Working-Class Writing.* Eds. David Shevin, Janet Zandy, and Larry Smith. Huron: Bottom Dog P., 1999. 98–112. Print.

Pfeil, Fred. *White Guys: Studies in Postmodern Domination and Difference.* London and New York: Verso, 1995. Print.

Phillips, Christopher. "The Story So Far . . ." *Amazon.com.* Web. 11 January 2009.

Pirttijärvi, Johanna. "Storyteller: 25.02.88 Worcester, MA, Introduction to 'Born to Run.'" brucebase.org. Web. 20 February 2010.

Polito, Robert. "Shadow Play: B-C-D and Back." *Studio A: The Bob Dylan Reader.* Ed. Benjamin Heidin. New York: Norton, 2004. 244–51. Print.

Powers, Ann. "Album Review: Bruce Springsteen and The E Street Band's *Working on a Dream.*" *Los Angeles Times.* Web. 24 January 2009.

Prescott, Orville. "Books of the Times." Rev. of *A Good Man Is Hard to Find*, by Flannery O'Connor. *New York Times* 10 June 1955: 23. Print.

Reardon, Paul. "Leah the Unloved: Paul Reardon on Jacob's Other Wife." *New Directions. Trushare WebFiles No. 94.* Web. 20 February 2010.

Reed, T. V. *The Art of Protest: Culture and Activism from the Civil Rights Movement to the Streets of Seattle.* Minneapolis: University of Minnesota Press, 2005. Print.

Ridley, Aaron. *Music, Value, and the Passions.* Ithaca: Cornell University Press, 1995. Print.

Ritivoi, Andreea Deciu. "'Here and Now, There and Then': Nostalgic Identities and the Search for the Past." "Time, History, and Social Change." Conference of the Society for Philosophy in the Contemporary World. Estes Park, Colorado. 9 August 1999. Address.

Robinson, Douglas. *No Less a Man: Masculist Art in a Feminist Age.* Bowling Green: Bowling Green State University Popular Press, 1994. Print.

Romano, Carlin. "Review of *Shakespeare the Thinker* by A. D. Nuttall." Popmatters .com 16 May 2007. Web. 8 April 2010.

Rotundo, E. Anthony. *American Manhood: Transformations in Masculinity from the Revolution to the Modern Era.* New York: Basic Books, 1993. Print.

Samway, Patrick, S.J. *Walker Percy: A Life.* Chicago: Loyola Press, 1999. Print.

Santelli, Robert. *Greetings from E Street: The Story of Bruce Springsteen and the E Street Band.* San Francisco: Chronicle, 2006. Print.

Sartre, Jean-Paul. "Existentialism Is a Humanism." Trans. Philip Mairet. *Existentialism: From Dostoevsky to Sartre.* Ed. Walter Kaufmann. New York and London: New American Library. 280–378. Print.

Sawyers, June Skinner, ed. *Racing in the Street: The Bruce Springsteen Reader.* New York: Penguin, 2004. Print.

Schruers, Fred. "Bruce Springsteen and the Secret of the World: Fame grips a Jersey boy, but he gets out unscathed." *Rolling Stone.* 5 February 1981. Web. 21 March 2010.

Scott, A. O. "The Poet Laureate of 9/11: Apocalypse and Salvation on Springsteen's New Album." In Sawyers. 362–65. Print.

Sellnow, Deanna D., and Timothy L. Sellnow. "The Human Relationship from Idealism to Realism: An Analysis of the Music of Bruce Springsteen." *Popular Music and Society* 14.3 (1990): 71–88. Print.

"September 11 by the Numbers." *New York Magazine.* 15 September 2002. Web. 28 February 2009.

Shakespeare, William. *The Riverside Shakespeare.* Ed. G. Blakemore Evans. 2nd ed. Boston and New York: Houghton Mifflin, 1997. Print.

Sims, David S. "From Guthrie through Dylan to Springsteen: Losing the Working Touch." *Illusive Identity: The Blurring of Working-Class Consciousness in Modern Western Culture.* Ed. Thomas J. Edward Walker. Lanham: Lexington Books, 2002. 92–111. Print.

Smith, Greg. "Whitman, Springsteen, and the American Working Class." *Midwest Quarterly* 41:3 (Spring 2000): 302–20.

Smith, Kimberly K. "Mere Nostalgia: Notes on a Progressive Paratheory." *Rhetoric & Public Affairs* 3.4 (2000): 505–27. Print.

Smith, Larry David. *Bob Dylan, Bruce Springsteen, and American Song.* Westport, CT: Praeger, 2002. Print.

Smith, Martha Nell. "Sexual Mobilities in Bruce Springsteen: Performance as Commentary." *South Atlantic Quarterly* 90:4 (Fall 1991): 833–54. Print.

Spenser, Edmund. *The Faerie Queene* in *Edmund Spenser's Poetry.* Ed. Hugh Maclean and Anne Lake Prescott. 3rd Norton Critical Ed. New York: W.W. Norton, 1993. Print.

Springsteen, Bruce. *Born in the U.S.A.* Columbia Records, 1984. CD.

———. *Born to Run.* Columbia Records, 1975. CD.

———. *Brixton Nights.* [Bootleg recording]. Crystal Cat Records, 1996. CD.

———. "Bruce Springsteen, on a 'Magic' Campaign." National Public Radio. npr.org. 5 Mar. 2008. Web. 9 January 2010.

———. *Bruce Springsteen: VH1 Storytellers.* Sony, 2005. DVD.

———. *Bruce Springsteen.* www.brucespringsteen.net/news/index.html. Web.

———. "Bruce Springsteen Discusses His Music, New Album and Tour with E Street Band." Interview by Scott Pelley. *60 Minutes.* CBS News.com 7 October 2007. Web. 8 April 2010.

———. "Chords for Change." *New York Times* 5 Aug. 2004. Nytimes.com. Web. 13 April 2010.

———. *The Complete Video Anthology / 1978–2000.* Columbia Music Video, 2001. DVD.

———. *Concert.* [Bootleg recording]. St. Paul, Minnesota, 10 May 2005. DVD.

———. *Darkness on the Edge of Town.* Columbia Records, 1978. CD.

———. *Devils and Dust.* [Incl. "Bonus DVD," dir. Danny Clinch, and lyrics booklet]. Columbia Records, 2005. CD/DVD/Print.

———. *The Ghost of Tom Joad.* Columbia Records, 1995. CD.

———. *Girls in Their Summer Clothes.* Video. YouTube. Web. 15 January 2010.

———. *Greatest Hits.* Columbia Records, 1995. CD.

———. *Greetings from Asbury Park, N.J.* Columbia Records, 1973. CD.

———. *Human Touch.* Columbia Records, 1992. CD.

——. Interview by Ted Koppel. *Nightline*. ABC. 30 July 2002. Television.

——. *Into The River We Dive*. [Bootleg recording]. Godfather Records, 2009. CD.

——. *Lucky Town*. Columbia Records, 1992. CD.

——. *Magic*. Columbia Records, 2007. CD.

——. *My Lucky Day*. Video. YouTube. Web. 15 January 2010.

——. *Nebraska*. Columbia Records, 1982. CD.

——. *The Rising*. Columbia Records, 2002. CD.

——. *The Rising*. Video. YouTube. Web. 15 January 2010.

——. *The River*. Columbia Records, 1980. CD.

——. *Songs*. New York: Avon, 1998. Print.

——. *Songs*. New York: HarperEntertainment, 2003. Print.

——. *Tougher Than the Rest*. Video. YouTube. Web. 15 Jan. 2010.

——. *Tracks*. 4-discs and Liner notes. Columbia Records, 1998. CD/Print.

——. *Tunnel of Love*. Columbia Records, 1987. CD.

——. *The Wild, the Innocent & the E Street Shuffle*. Columbia Records, 1973. CD.

——. *Working on a Dream*. Columbia Records, 2009. CD.

——. *Working on a Dream*. Video. YouTube. Web. 15 January 2010.

Stamelman, Richard. "September 11: Between Memory and History." *Trauma at Home: After 9/11*. Ed. Judith Greenberg. Lincoln: University of Nebraska Press, 2003. 11–20. Print.

Storey, John. *Cultural Studies & the Study of Popular Culture: Theories and Methods*. Athens: University of Georgia Press, 1996. Print.

Stratton, Valerie N., and Annette H. Zalanowski. "Affective Impact of Music vs. Lyrics." *Empirical Studies of the Arts* 12.1 (1994): 173–84. Print.

——. "The Effects of Music and Cognition on Mood." *Psychology of Music* 19 (1991): 121–27. Print.

Strauss, Neil. "Springsteen Looks Back but Keeps Walking On." In Sawyers. 190–95. Print.

Symynkywicz, Jeffrey. *The Gospel According to Bruce Springsteen: Rock and Redemption, from Asbury Park to Magic*. Louisville: Westminster John Knox Press, 2008. Print.

Szatmary, David P. *Rockin' in Time: A Social History of Rock-and-Roll*. 2nd ed. Englewood Cliffs: Prentice-Hall, 1991. Print.

Tal, Kalí. *Worlds of Hurt: Reading the Literatures of Trauma*. New York: Cambridge University Press, 1996. Print.

Thérèse of Lisieux. *Autobiography of Saint Thérèse*. [*L'Histoire d'une Âme*.] Trans. Ronald Knox. New York: P. J. Kennedy & Sons, 1958. Print.

"Thunder." *Oxford English Dictionary*. Web. 13 February 2010.

Thunder Road. Dir. Arthur Ripley. Perf. Robert Mitchum. Distr. by United Artists, 1958. Film.

"TIVO Alert: Kennedy Center Honors Tonight." Backstreets.com. Web. 9 April 2010.

Tolson, Jay. *Pilgrim in the Ruins: A Life of Walker Percy*. New York: Simon & Schuster, 1992. Print.

"Track." *The Concise Oxford Dictionary of English Etymology*. Oxford University Press, 1996. *Oxford Reference Online*. Web. 11 January 2009.

"Track." *Online Etymology Dictionary*. Etymonline.com. Web. 11 January 2009.

Trumbower, Jeffrey. *Rescue for the Dead: The Posthumous Salvation of Non-Christians in Early Christianity*. Oxford: Oxford University Press, 2001. Print.

Tuan, Yi-Fu. "Place and Culture: Analeptic for Individuality and the World's Indifference." *Mapping American Culture*. Ed. Wayne Franklin and Michael Steiner. Iowa City: University of Iowa Press, 1992. 27–49. Print.

Tyrangiel, Josh. "Bruce Rising: An Intimate Look at How Springsteen Turned 9/11 into a Message of Hope." *Time* 160.6 (5 August 2002): 52–59. Print.

Vote for Change Rally. Philadelphia, PA. 4 October 2008. YouTube. Web. 21 March 2010.

Wenner, Jann S. "Bruce Springsteen: 'We've Been Misled': Springsteen Talks about His Conscience and the Nature of an Artist and His Audience. *Rolling Stone* 959 (14 October 2004): 73–76. Print.

West, Nancy Martha. *Kodak and the Lens of Nostalgia*. Charlottesville: University Press of Virginia, 2000. Print.

Whitman, Andy. "Nightmare on E Street." Pastemagazine.com. Web. 6 February 2009.

Wieder, Judy. "Bruce Springsteen: The Advocate Interview." *The Advocate* 704 (Apr. 1996): 46–52. In Sawyers. 211–20. Print.

Williams, William Carlos. *Paterson*. 1946. Ed. Christopher MacGowan. New York: New Directions, 1995. Print.

Wise Blood. Dir. John Huston. Perf. Brad Dourif, Ned Beatty, and Henry Dean Stanton. Criterion, 1979. Film.

Yamin, George Y., Jr. "The Theology of Bruce Springsteen." *Journal of Religious Studies* 16.1–2 (1990): 1–21. Print.

Zanes, R. J. Warren. "Too Much Mead?: Under the Influence (of Participant-Observation)." *Reading Rock and Roll: Authenticity, Appropriation, Aesthetics*. Ed. Kevin J. H. Dettmar and William Richey. New York: Columbia University Press, 1999. 37–71. Print.

General Index

fatherhood, 26, 35, 48, 69, 87–88, 101,
114, 136–37, 144–45, 217, 227,
231
Faulkner, William, 30
Federici, Danny, 50, 98
feminine spaces, 162–63
femininity, 165, 155, 160–62, 164, 166
feminism, 15, 151–52, 156, 162, 171
Fields, Peter, 16, 201, 286
Foley, John Miles, 186–87
Ford, John, 31, 35, 63, 237
foreign lands, 36, 65, 197
foreignness, 197
Foucault, Michel, 265
Frank, Robert, 103
Frears, Stephen, 226
"Free Bird" (Lynyrd Skynyrd), 126
freedom, 51, 90, 104–5, 127–28, 137,
158, 181–82, 186, 191–92, 194–95,
203, 230
Freehold, New Jersey, 35, 37, 47, 84,
103
Freeman, Mary E. Wilkins, 84
Frith, Simon, 10, 13, 223, 230, 233,
235, 237; *Performing Rites*, 10
Fugate, Caril, 33, 53, 57, 90
Fury, Frank, 7, 14, 15, 79, 286

garden, 163, 172, 207, 219, 221, 264
Garman, Bryan K., 2, 8, 112, 139, 141,
145, 147–48, 216–17, 227, 231,
240; *A Race of Singers: Whitman's
Working-Class Hero from Guthrie to
Springsteen*, 8, 216
gender, 15–16, 107, 132, 134, 151–55,
160–73, 231, 256
Genesis, the Book of, 181, 207, 220
geography, 13, 89, 104
The Ghost of Tom Joad (Springsteen), 2,
14, 23, 34, 59, 63, 71, 73, 190–1,
196–97, 211
Ginsberg, Merle, 235
Glory Days (Marsh), 11, 46, 68
God, 26, 29–30, 46, 48, 51, 69–73,
159, 170–71, 179–82, 194, 202,
204–7, 218–20
Golding, Arthur, 213

"A Good Man is Hard to Find"
(O'Connor), 56–57, 60–62, 84
Goodman, Fred, 12, 225, 227, 229,
236; *The Mansion on the Hill*, 12,
225
gospel, 46–61, 69, 207, 214, 220, 249
The Gospel According to Bruce Springsteen
(Symynkywicz), 13, 19, 71, 200n1
grace, 29, 46, 48–51, 56, 60, 65, 66–
67, 69, 69, 90, 211, 219, 260
graces: social, 156, 161, 218; the Graces
(personified), 211
The Grapes of Wrath (Steinbeck), 63,
196–97, 250
greed, 91, 199, 251–52
Greeley, Andrew, 30, 69–70, 218;
"The Catholic Imagination of Bruce
Springsteen," 69, 218
Greenberg, Judith, 249–51; "Wounded
New York," 249, 251
Greenblatt, Stephen, 206, 219; *Hamlet
in Purgatory*, 206
Greetings from Asbury Park, N.J.
(Springsteen), 2, 28, 30, 32, 80, 99,
107, 114, 164, 190–1, 202–4, 207,
234
grief, 148, 154, 244–46, 248–52, 254,
258
Gulf War, 221
Guterman, Jimmy, 1, 11, 140, 225,
228, 232–33, 237, 239; *Runaway
American Dream*, 1, 11
Guthrie, Woody, 8, 12, 32, 70, 111,
196, 216, 227

Hades, 213, 215. *See also* Hell
Hahn, Scott, 205–6; *Hail, Holy Queen*,
205, 207
Hail, Holy Queen (Hahn), 205, 207
Halbwachs, Maurice, 126
HaLevi, Yehudah, 177–78, 183
Hamlet (Shakespeare), 209
Hamlet in Purgatory (Greenblatt), 206
Hammond, John, 1, 228
Hampton, Howard, 86, 145
"happy songs," 190, 195–200n1
Harde, Roxanne, 17, 243, 286

Song Index

About the Editors and Contributors

Teresa V. Abbruzzese is a doctoral candidate in the Faculty of Environmental Studies at York University, Toronto, Canada. Her areas of academic interest include cultural studies, human geography, and social theory, with a particular research focus on how the intersections of power, identity, and difference shape marginality. Her current dissertation work examines Luna Park (the traveling amusement park) as a folkloric site of cultural expression and resistance through its current contested production in southern Italy.

Stephen Hazan Arnoff writes on music, religion, popular culture, and education for a wide variety of academic and popular publications, with work published in Hebrew, English, and Italian. He has been awarded the Rockower Jewish Press Award for Jewish Arts & Criticism (2006) and the New Voices Prize (2005). He is a doctoral candidate in Midrash at the Jewish Theological Seminary and serves as executive director of the 14th Street Y in New York City, home of LABA: The National Laboratory for New Jewish Culture.

Ann V. Bliss received her PhD from the University of California, Davis, in 2006. Her research focuses on twentieth- and twenty-first-century American literature and culture, particularly women's literature, and the intersection of literary and visual culture. She is currently a lecturer at the University of California, Merced.

Mike Cadó is currently a doctoral candidate in ethnomusicology at York University, Toronto, Canada, where his work focuses on jazz in Canada. His current dissertation research examines the role of the Canadian Broadcasting Corporation (CBC) in shaping Canadian identity through specific music programming. He teaches courses in theory, composition, and performance at York, and is also active as a composer/arranger and guitarist.

Peter J. Fields finished his PhD in 1994 at the University of Denver where he met his wife, Jacqueline. He is the author of *Craft and Anticraft in Chaucer's Canterbury Tales* (2001) and the editor of the medieval journal *In Geardagum*. He teaches early English literature at Midwestern State University in Wichita Falls, Texas.

Frank P. Fury is a lecturer in English at Monmouth University in West Long Branch, New Jersey. His primary fields of study are nineteenth- and twentieth-century American fiction and the short story. He is especially interested in the interconnections of literature and cultural phenomena such as sport and music.

Roxanne Harde is an associate professor of English and a McCalla University Professor at the University of Alberta, Augustana Faculty. She studies American literature and culture, and teaches courses in literary theory and American literature. She currently has two papers on Steve Earle in press, and her work has appeared in several journals, including *Christianity and Literature, Legacy, Studies in Puritan American Spirituality, Critique, Feminist Theology,* and *Mosaic,* and several edited collections.

Michael Kobre is the Dana Professor of English at Queens University of Charlotte, North Carolina, where he also serves as on-campus director of the Queens Low-Residency MFA Program in Creative Writing. His fiction and critical writing have appeared in *TriQuarterly, Tin House, West Branch, Critique,* and other journals. He is the author of *Walker Percy's Voices* (2000).

June Skinner Sawyers has written extensively about music and popular culture. Born in Glasgow, Scotland, she is the author or editor of twenty-one books, including *Ten Songs That Changed the World* (2009); *Read the Beatles: Classic and New Writings on the Beatles, Their Legacy, and Why They Still Matter* (2006); *Tougher Than the Rest: 100 Best Bruce Springsteen Songs* (2006); *Racing in the Street: The Bruce Springsteen Reader* (2001); *Celtic Music: A Complete Guide* (2006); and the forthcoming *Bob Dylan's New York.* She is an adjunct lecturer at the Newberry Library in Chicago. Sawyers has presented twice at the Glory Days Symposium held by Penn State.

John J. Sheinbaum is an associate professor of musicology at the University of Denver's Lamont School of Music. He holds a PhD from Cornell University, and has contributed essays on popular music topics in the journal *Cur-*

rent Musicology and in the collections *Progressive Rock Reconsidered* (2001) and *Rock Over the Edge: Transformations in Popular Music Culture* (2002).

Irwin Streight is an associate professor in the Department of English at the Royal Military College of Canada, in Kingston, Ontario. He is coeditor with R. Neil Scott (Middle State University, Tennessee) of two major reference works on American author Flannery O'Connor: *Flannery O'Connor: An Annotated Reference Guide to Criticism* (2002), which won a *Choice* "Outstanding Academic Title" award; and *Flannery O'Connor: The Contemporary Reviews* (2009), volume 16 in Cambridge's American Critical Archives series.

Kenneth Womack is professor of English and associate dean for academic affairs at Penn State University's Altoona College. He serves as editor of *Interdisciplinary Literary Studies: A Journal of Criticism and Theory* and as coeditor (with William Baker) of Oxford University Press's *Year's Work in English Studies*. He is the author or editor of nearly twenty books, including *Long and Winding Roads: The Evolving Artistry of the Beatles* (2007) and the *Cambridge Companion to the Beatles* (2009).

Liza Zitelli is a doctoral candidate in English at the Fordham University Graduate School of Arts and Sciences. Her interests include nineteenth-, twentieth-, and twenty-first-century American literature and culture, with a specialization in gender studies and cognitive disability studies. She presented her work on gender and Bruce Springsteen at the Glory Days Symposium hosted by Penn State in 2005.

CPSIA information can be obtained at www.ICGtesting.com
Printed in the USA
268704BV00001B/6/P